AHH, FREEDOM...

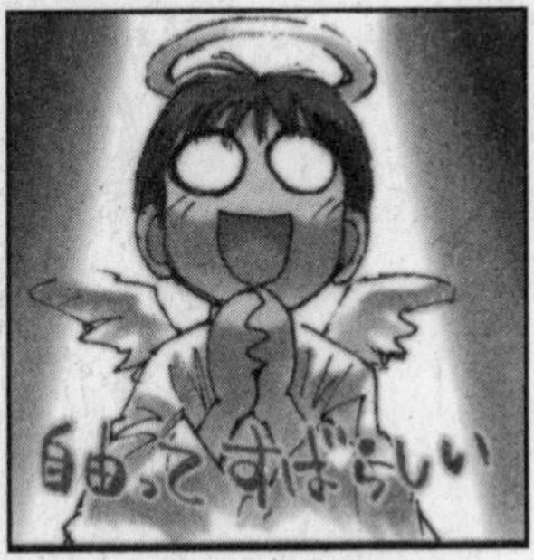
自由ってすばらしい

叶 恭弘

For all of my male readers, I'm sorry if the cover makes this book difficult to buy. For all of my female readers, I'm sorry for all the below-the-belt humor. For this series, I tried a lot of different things by trial and error. In one way it was fun, and in another way a lot of the stories were difficult to write. It was interesting to see how different people can read the same story and get completely different things out of it. I started to [illegible] manga can be.

[illegible]no, 2003

Yasuhiro Kano made his manga debut in 1992 with *Black City*, which won *Weekly Shonen Jump*'s Hop★Step Award for new artists. From 1993 to 2001, he illustrated Mugen's serialized novels *Midnight Magic* in *Jump Novel* magazine, and also produced a manga adaptation. *Pretty Face* appeared in *Weekly Shonen Jump* from 2002 to 2003. Kano's newest series, *M x O*, began running in *Weekly Shonen Jump* in 2006.

PRETTY FACE
VOL. 5

The SHONEN JUMP ADVANCED Manga Edition

STORY AND ART BY
YASUHIRO KANO

Translation & English Adaptation/Anita Sengupta
Touch-up Art & Lettering/Eric Erbes
Design/Hidemi Dunn
Editor/Jason Thompson

Editor in Chief, Books/Alvin Lu
Editor in Chief, Magazines/Marc Weidenbaum
VP of Publishing Licensing/Rika Inouye
VP of Sales/Gonzalo Ferreyra
Sr. VP of Marketing/Liza Coppola
Publisher/Hyoe Narita

PRETTY FACE © 2002 by Yasuhiro Kano. All rights reserved. First published in Japan in 2002 by SHUEISHA Inc., Tokyo. English translation rights arranged by SHUEISHA Inc. The stories, characters and incidents mentioned in this publication are entirely fictional.

Printed in the U.S.A.

Published by VIZ Media, LLC
P.O. Box 77010
San Francisco, CA 94107

SHONEN JUMP ADVANCED Manga Edition
10 9 8 7 6 5 4 3 2 1
First printing, April 2008

www.viz.com

www.shonenjump.com

Pretty Face

Vol. 5

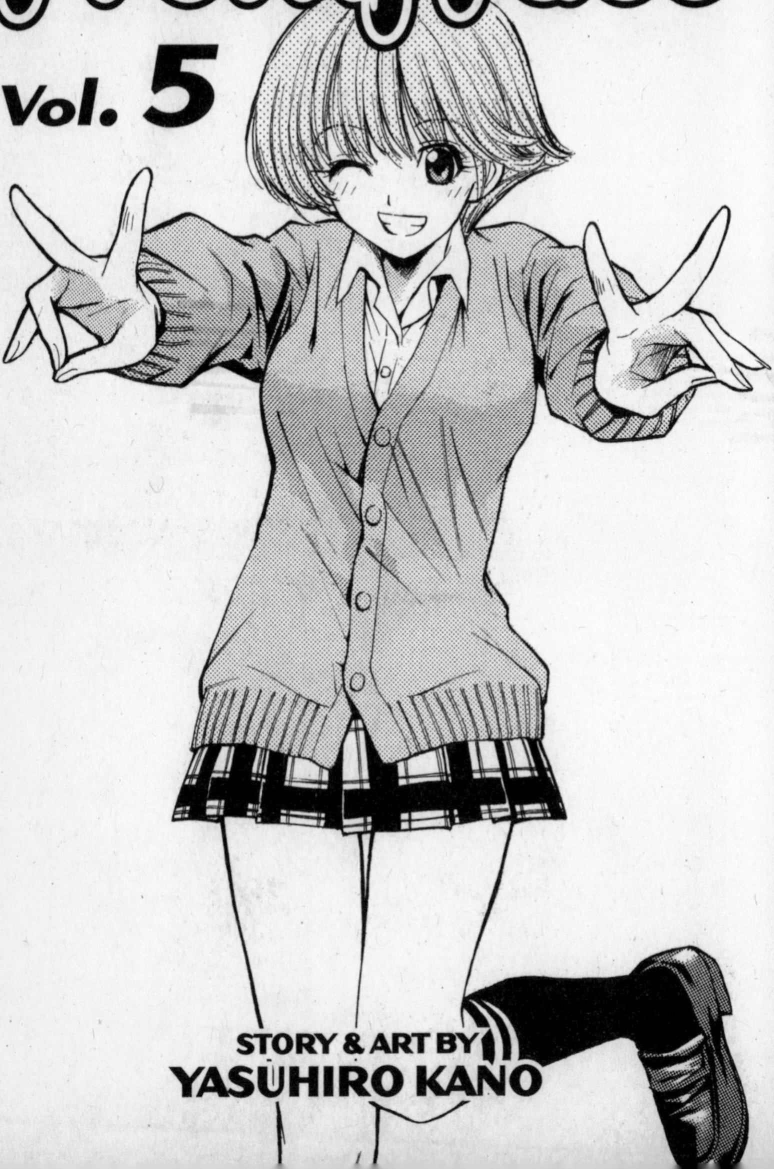

STORY & ART BY
YASUHIRO KANO

CHARACTERS

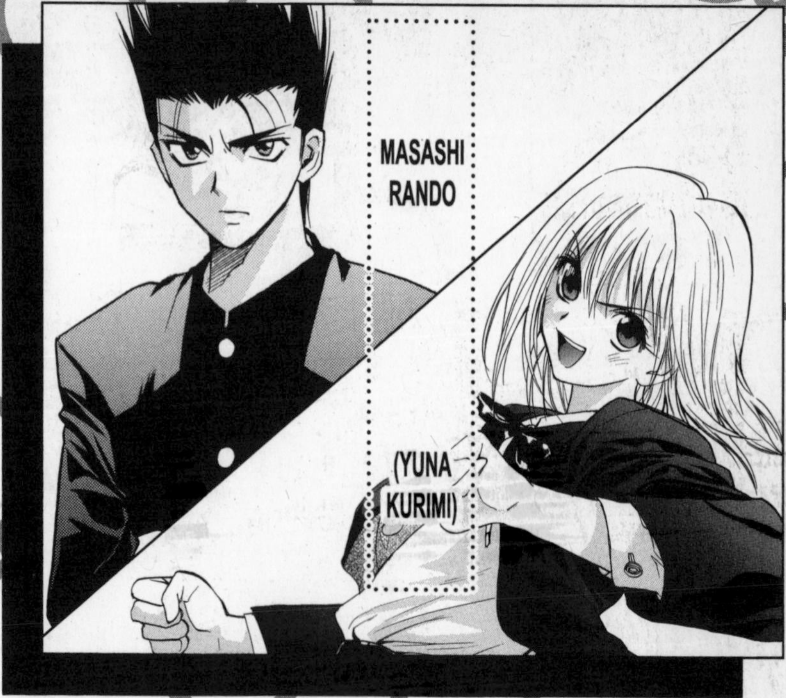
MASASHI RANDO
(YUNA KURIMI)

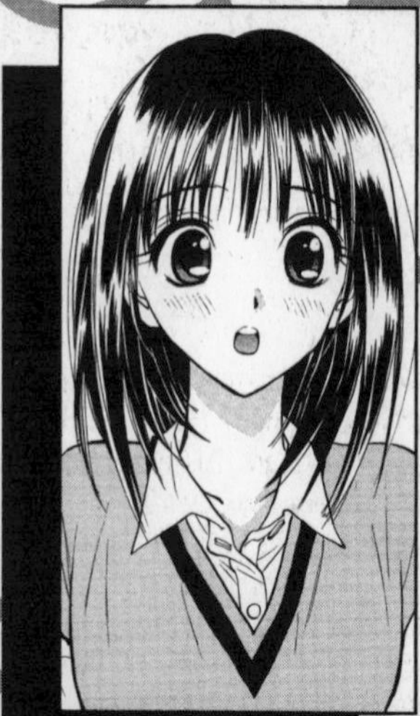

RINA KURIMI

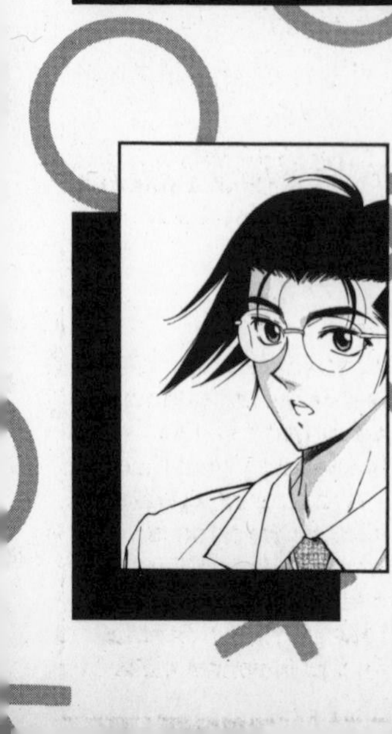

DR. MANABE

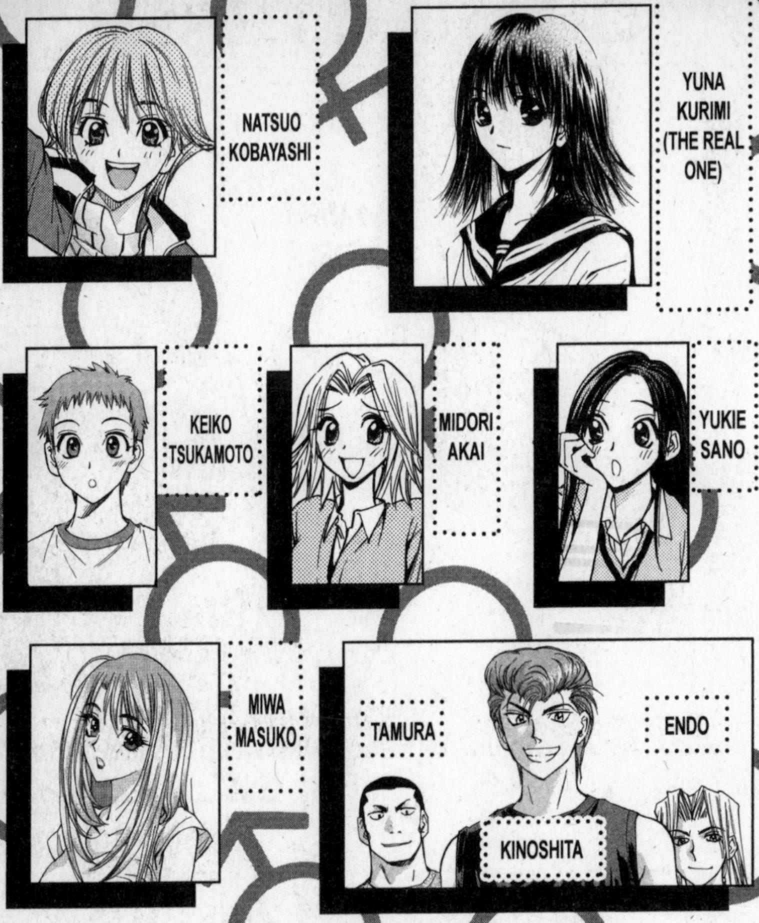
YUNA KURIMI (THE REAL ONE)
NATSUO KOBAYASHI
YUKIE SANO
MIDORI AKAI
KEIKO TSUKAMOTO
ENDO
TAMURA
KINOSHITA
MIWA MASUKO

STORY

On the way home from a karate tournament, teenage badass Masashi Rando is caught in a horrible bus accident. When he wakes up from his coma a year later, his disfigured face has been reconstructed into the image of *Rina Kurimi, the girl he has a crush on!* Not knowing what Rando originally looked like, the mad plastic surgeon Dr. Manabe used a photo in Rando's wallet as the model for his resconstruction. Abandoned by his friends and parents, Rando is mistaken for Rina's long-lost twin sister and adopted into her family. But when Rando's old karate student Natsuo transfers into school, she quickly becomes suspicious of "Yuna." Then, at a critical moment, Rando's fake breasts fall off in front of the entire class...!

PRETTY FACE
Vol. 5
CONTENTS

Chapter 37: Give it up, Natsuo!

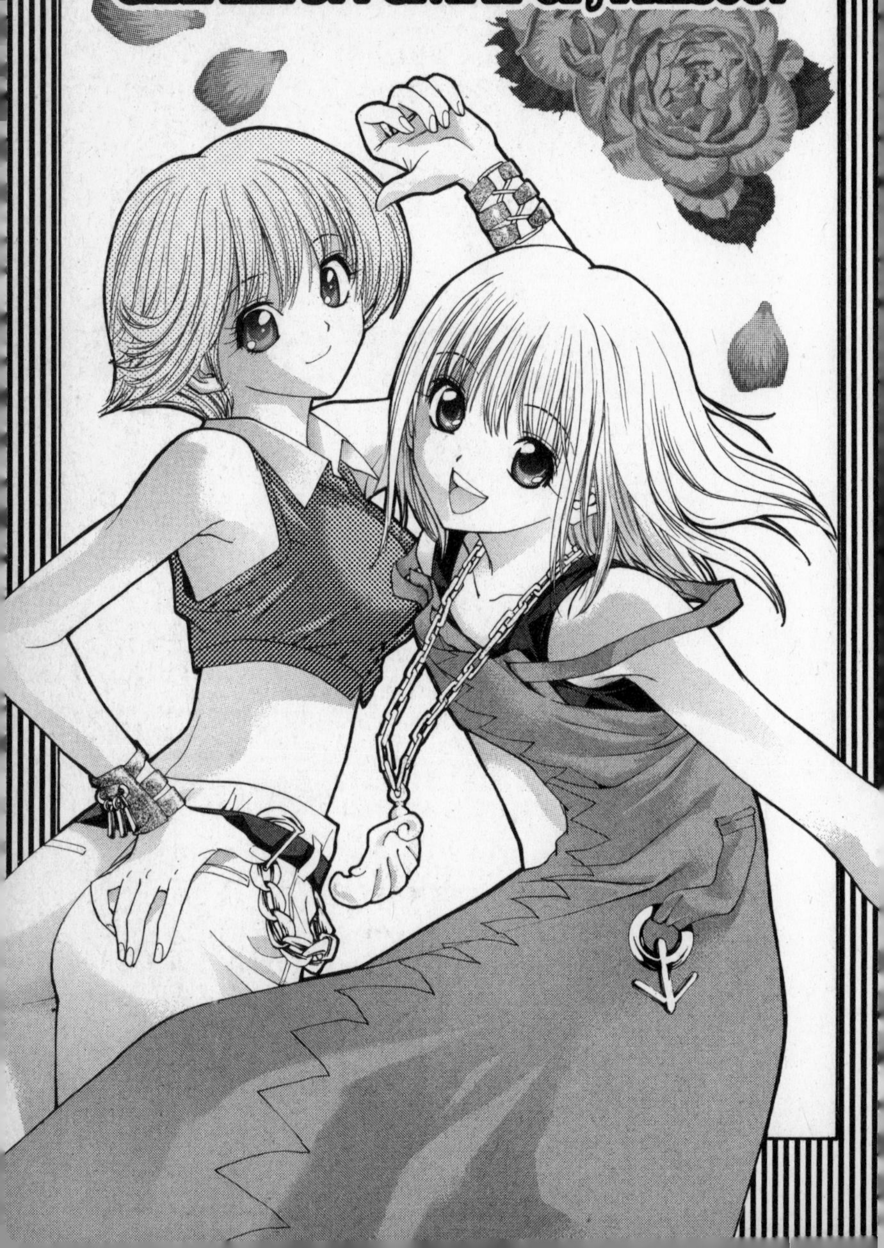

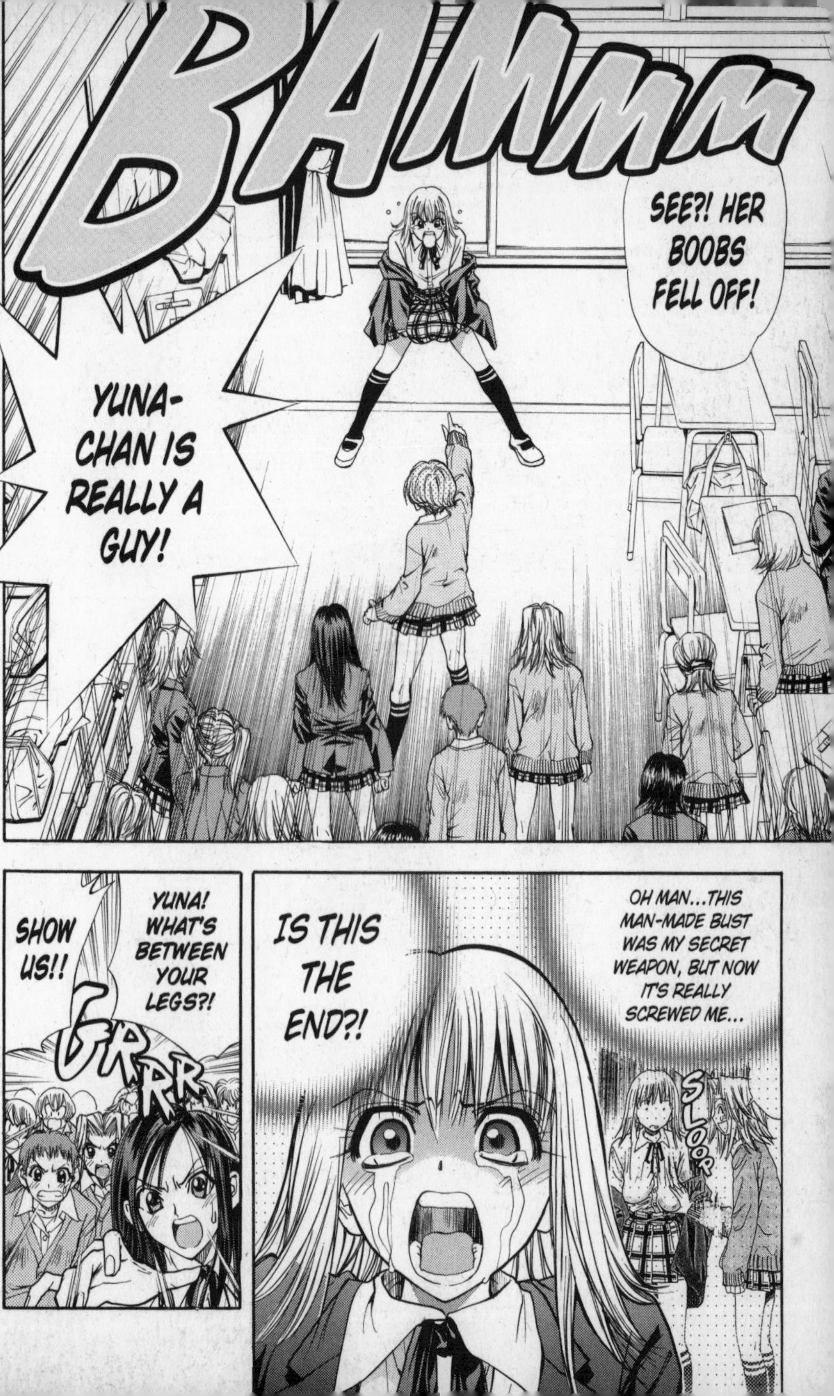
BAMMM
SEE?! HER BOOBS FELL OFF!
YUNA-CHAN IS REALLY A GUY!
OH MAN...THIS MAN-MADE BUST WAS MY SECRET WEAPON, BUT NOW IT'S REALLY SCREWED ME...
IS THIS THE END?!
SLOOOP
YUNA! WHAT'S BETWEEN YOUR LEGS?!
SHOW US!!
GRRR

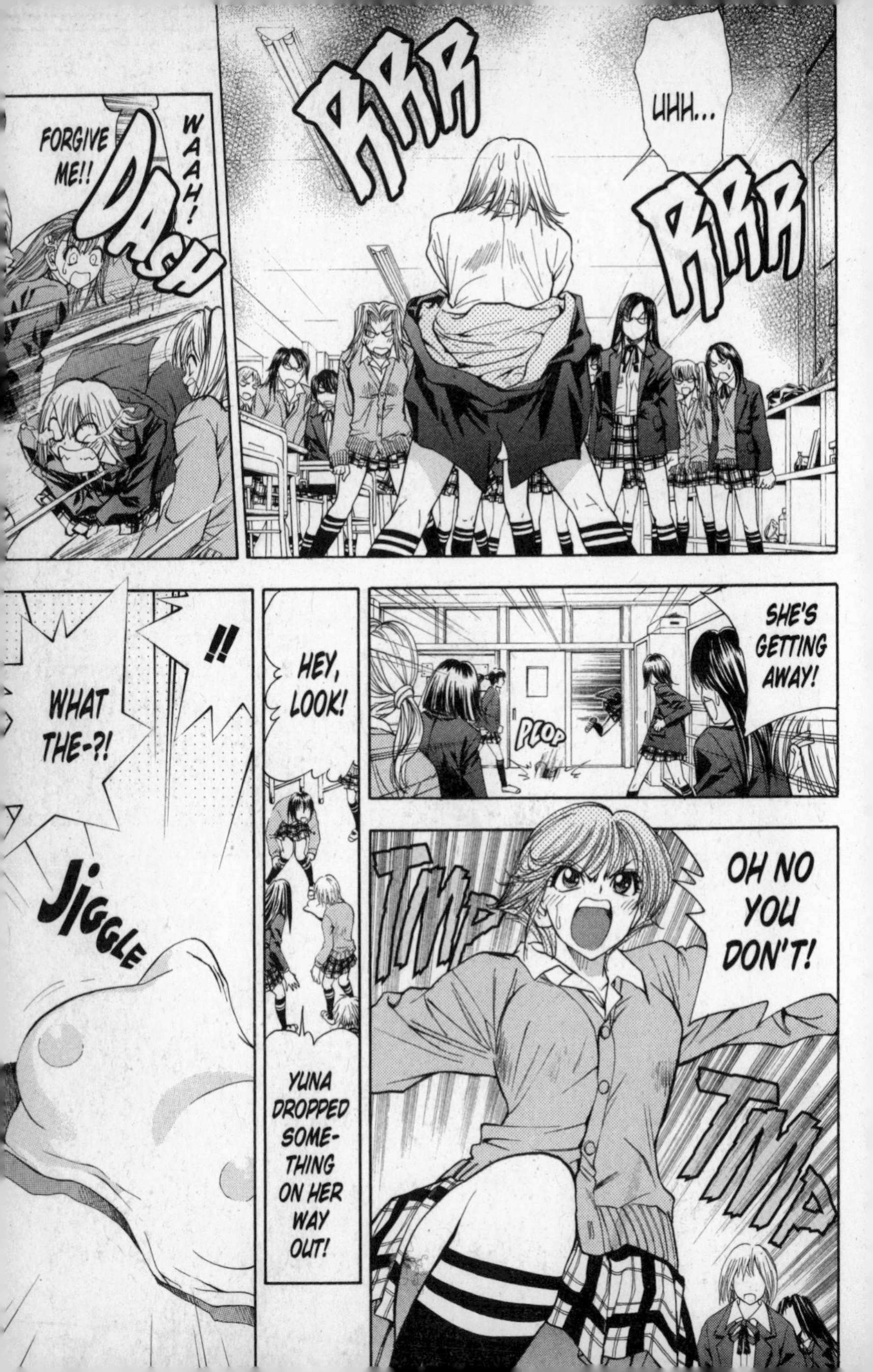
UHH...
RRR
RRR
WAAAH!
FORGIVE ME!!
DASH
SHE'S GETTING AWAY!
PLOP
OH NO YOU DON'T!
TMP
TMP
HEY, LOOK!
YUNA DROPPED SOME-THING ON HER WAY OUT!
!!
WHAT THE-?!
JIGGLE

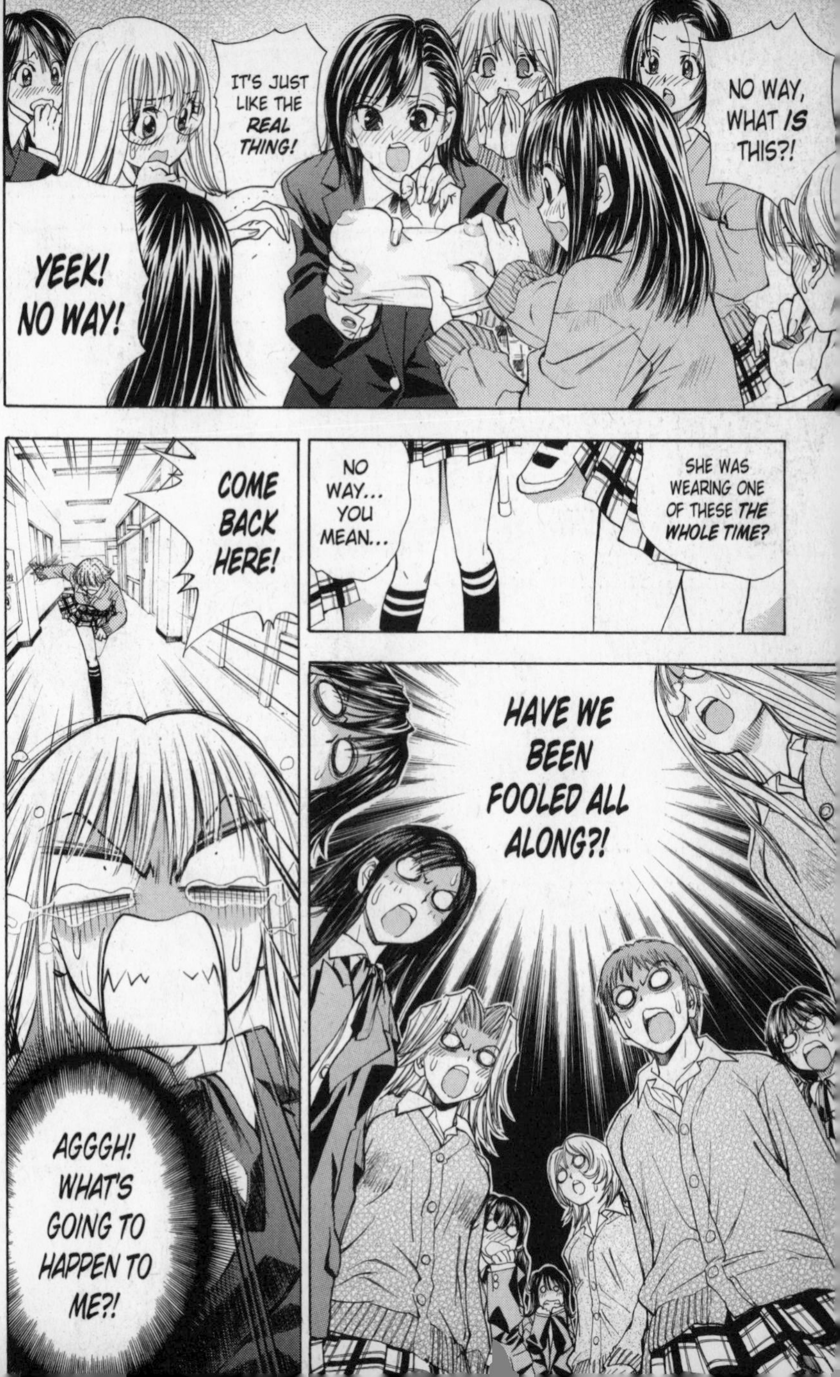
NO WAY, WHAT IS THIS?!
IT'S JUST LIKE THE REAL THING!
YEEK! NO WAY!
SHE WAS WEARING ONE OF THESE THE WHOLE TIME?
NO WAY... YOU MEAN...
HAVE WE BEEN FOOLED ALL ALONG?!
COME BACK HERE!
AGGGH! WHAT'S GOING TO HAPPEN TO ME?!

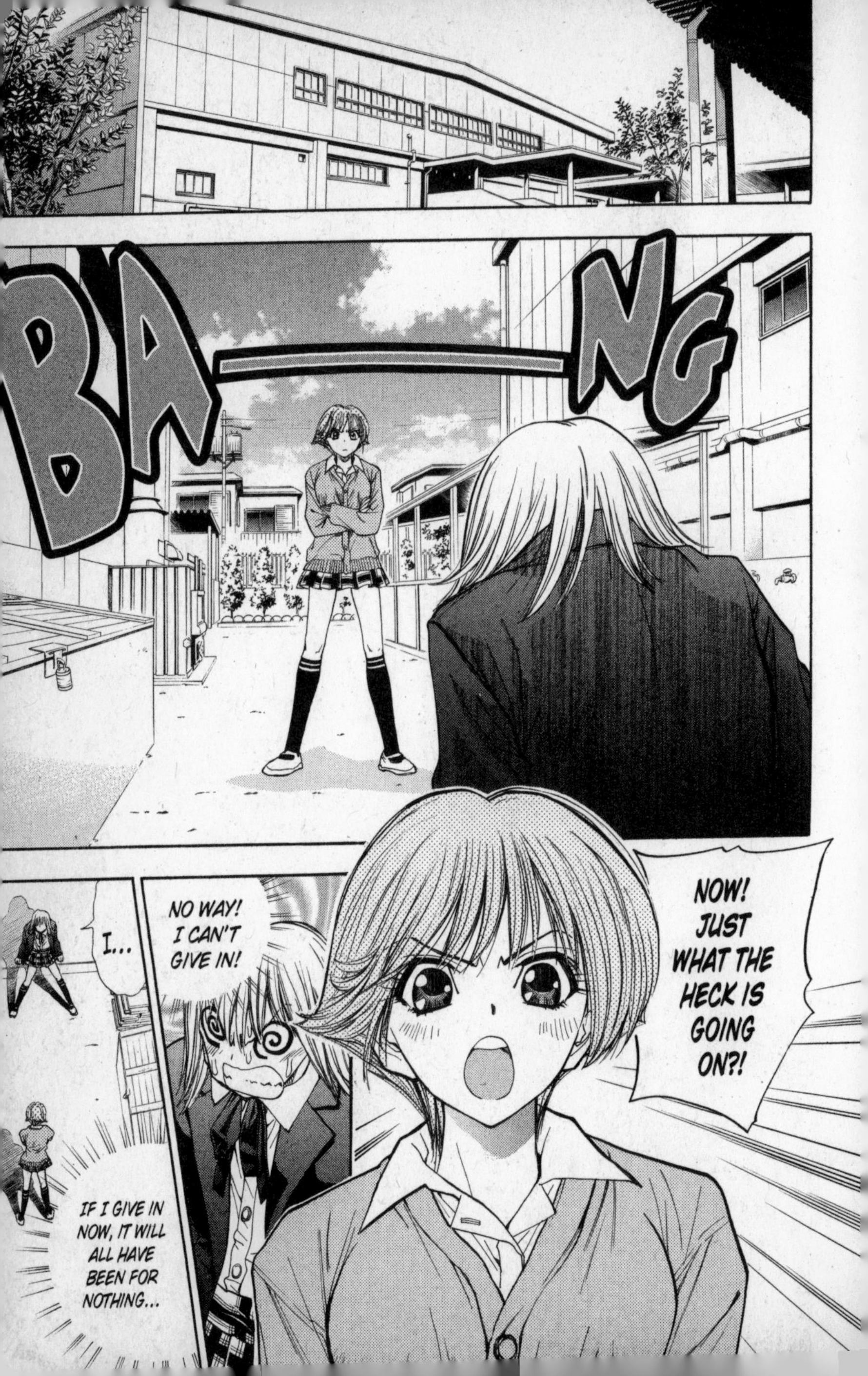
BANG
NOW! JUST WHAT THE HECK IS GOING ON?!
NO WAY! I CAN'T GIVE IN!
I...
IF I GIVE IN NOW, IT WILL ALL HAVE BEEN FOR NOTHING...

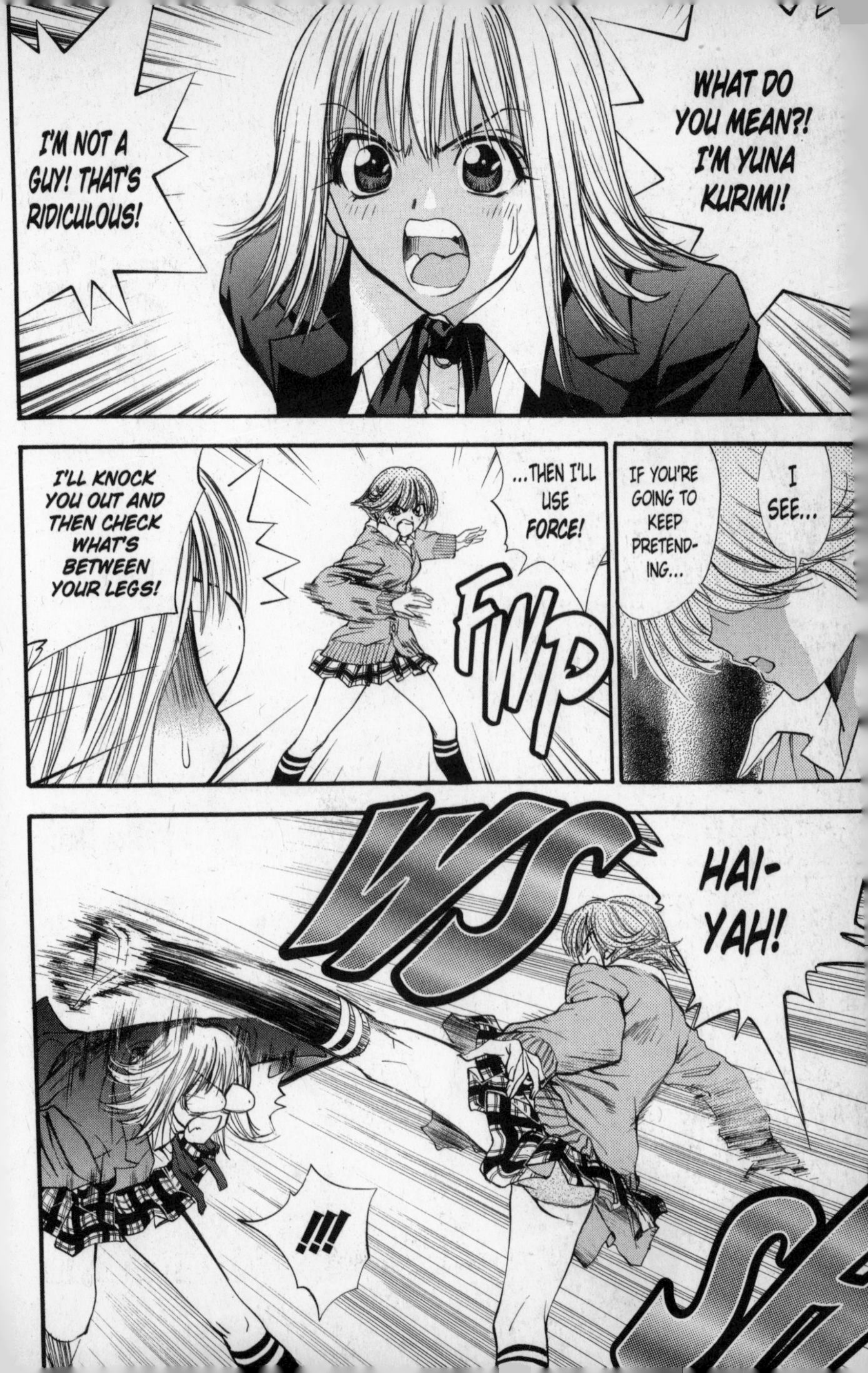
WHAT DO YOU MEAN?! I'M YUNA KURIMI!
I'M NOT A GUY! THAT'S RIDICULOUS!
I SEE...
IF YOU'RE GOING TO KEEP PRETEND-ING...
...THEN I'LL USE FORCE!
FWP
I'LL KNOCK YOU OUT AND THEN CHECK WHAT'S BETWEEN YOUR LEGS!
HAI-YAH!
WS
!!!

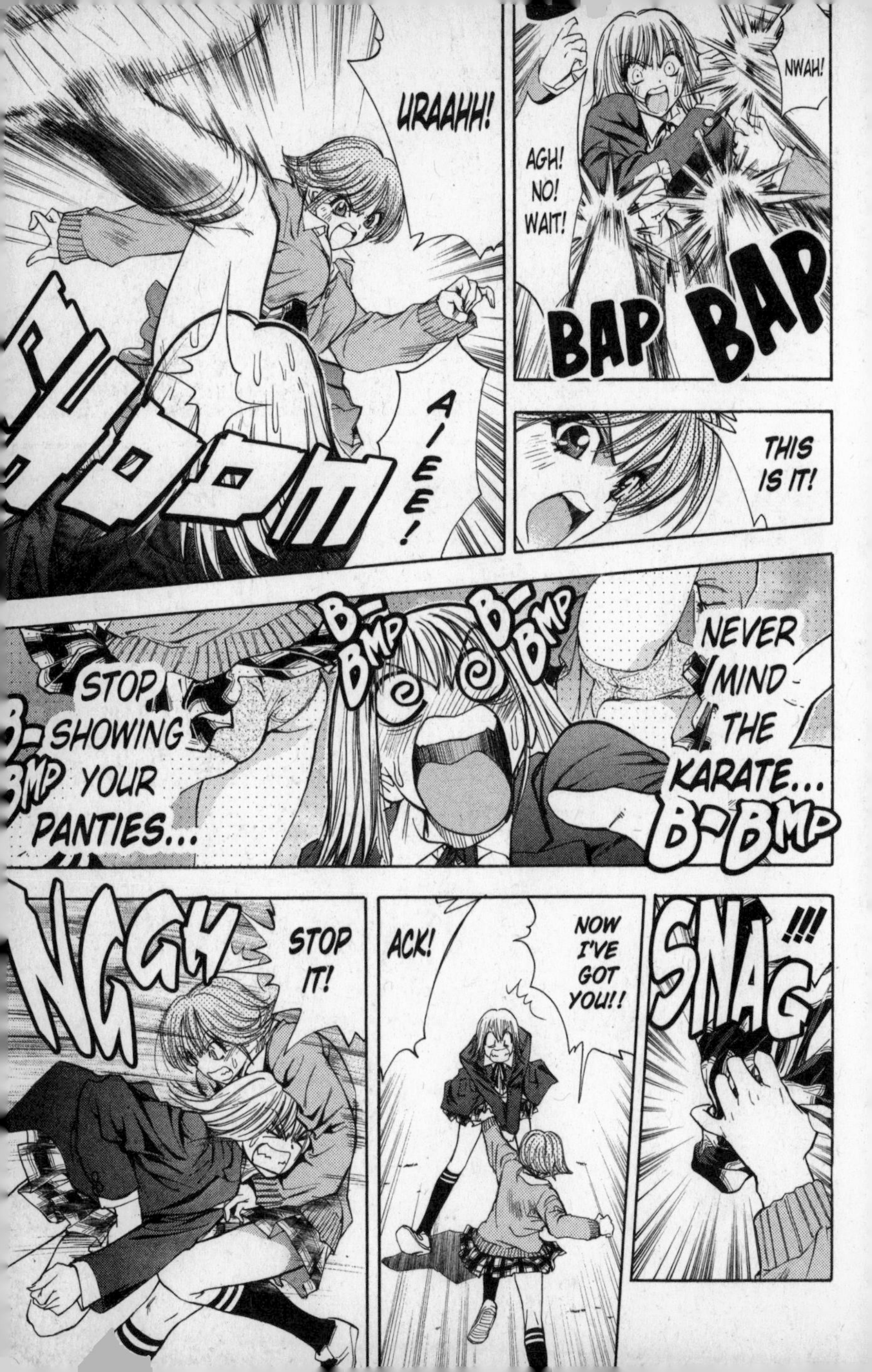
NWAH!
AGH! NO! WAIT!
BAP BAP
THIS IS IT!
URAAHH!
AIEEE!
NEVER MIND THE KARATE...
B-BMP
B-BMP
B-BMP
STOP SHOWING YOUR PANTIES...
B-BMP
SNAG!!!
NOW I'VE GOT YOU!!
ACK!
STOP IT!
NGGH

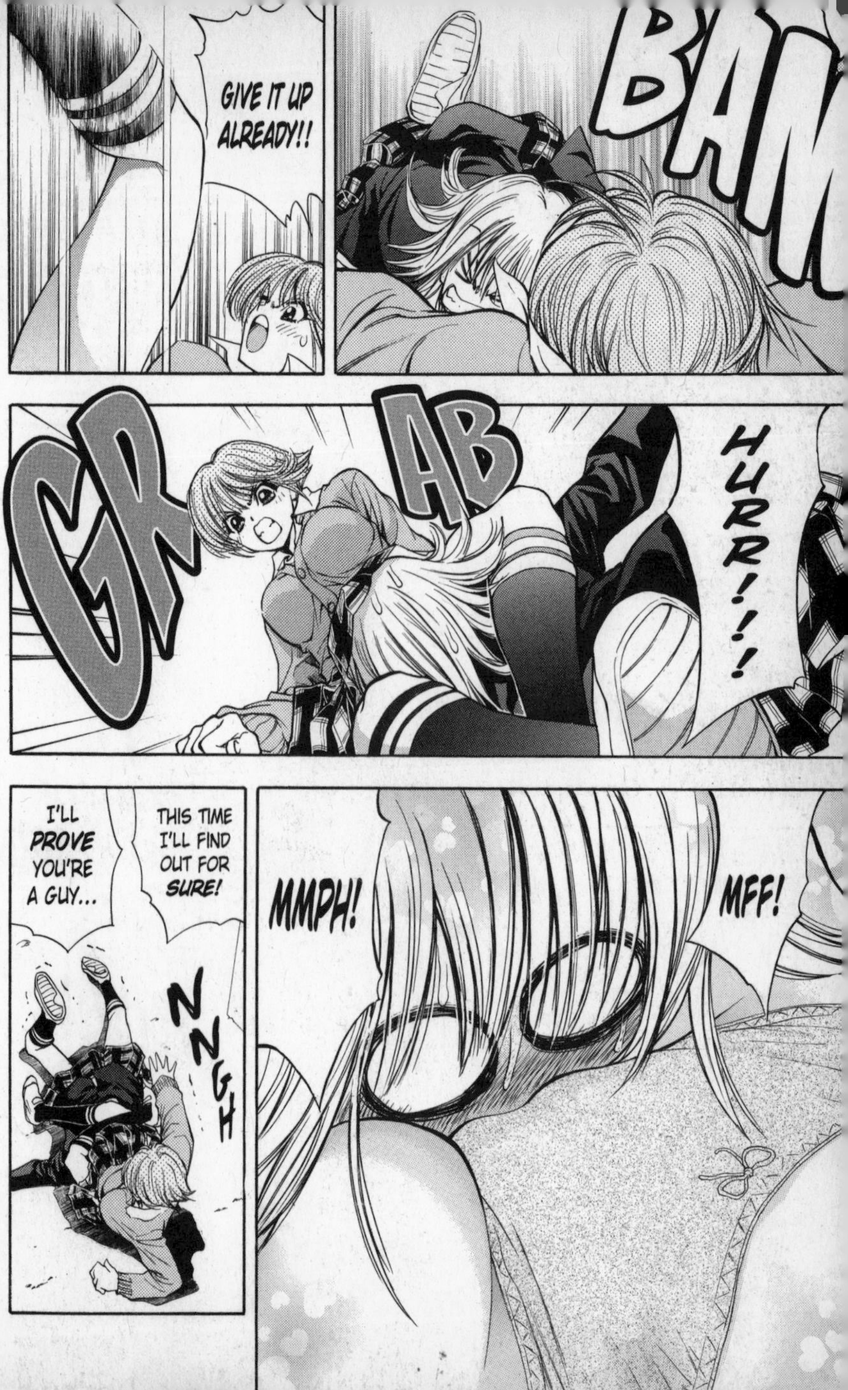
BAM
GIVE IT UP ALREADY!!
HURR!!!
GRAB
MFF!
MMPH!
THIS TIME I'LL FIND OUT FOR SURE!
I'LL PROVE YOU'RE A GUY...
NNGH

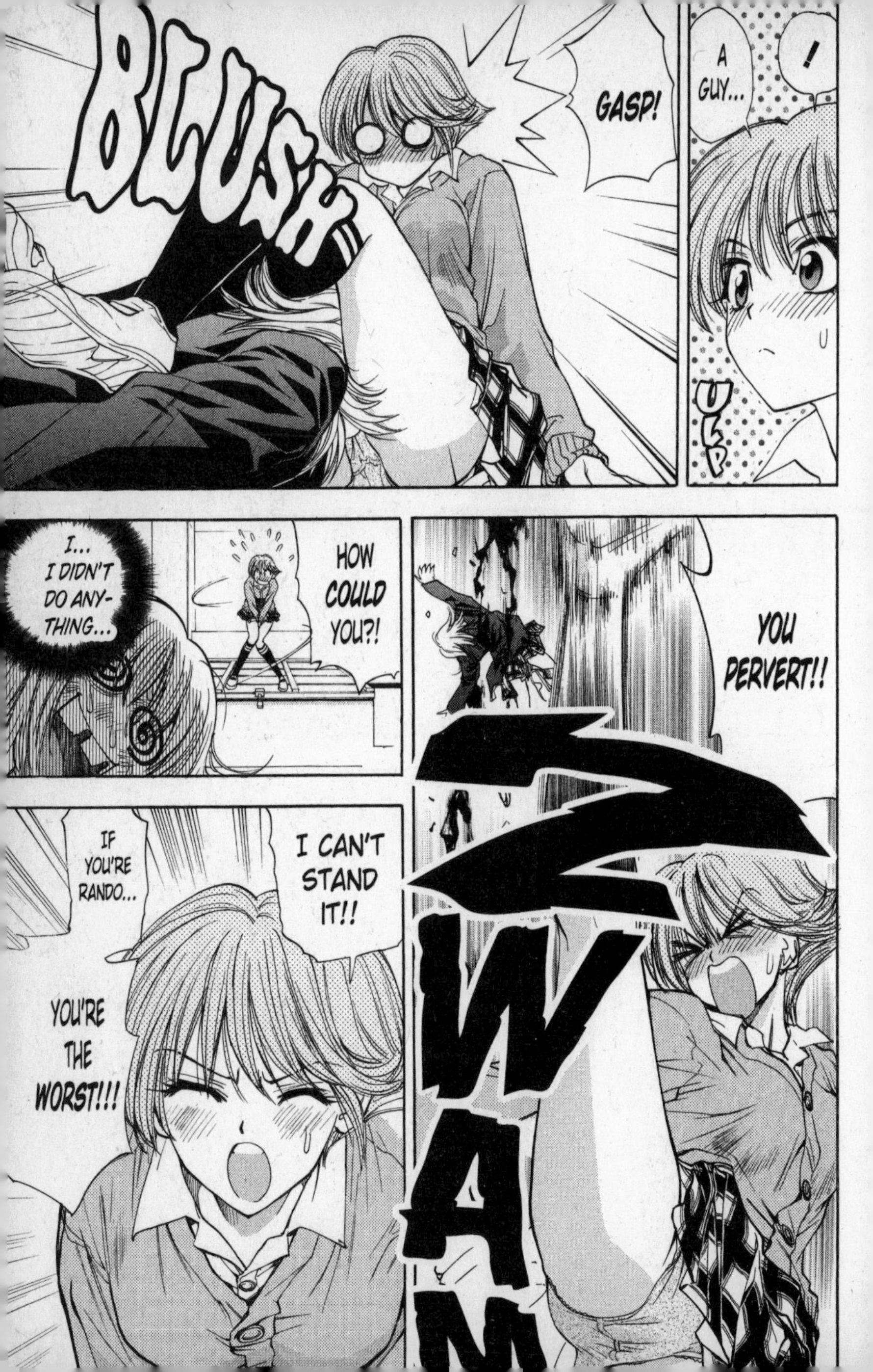
!
A GUY...
ULP
GASP!
BLUSH
YOU PERVERT!!
WAM
HOW COULD YOU?!
I... I DIDN'T DO ANY-THING...
I CAN'T STAND IT!!
IF YOU'RE RANDO...
YOU'RE THE WORST!!!

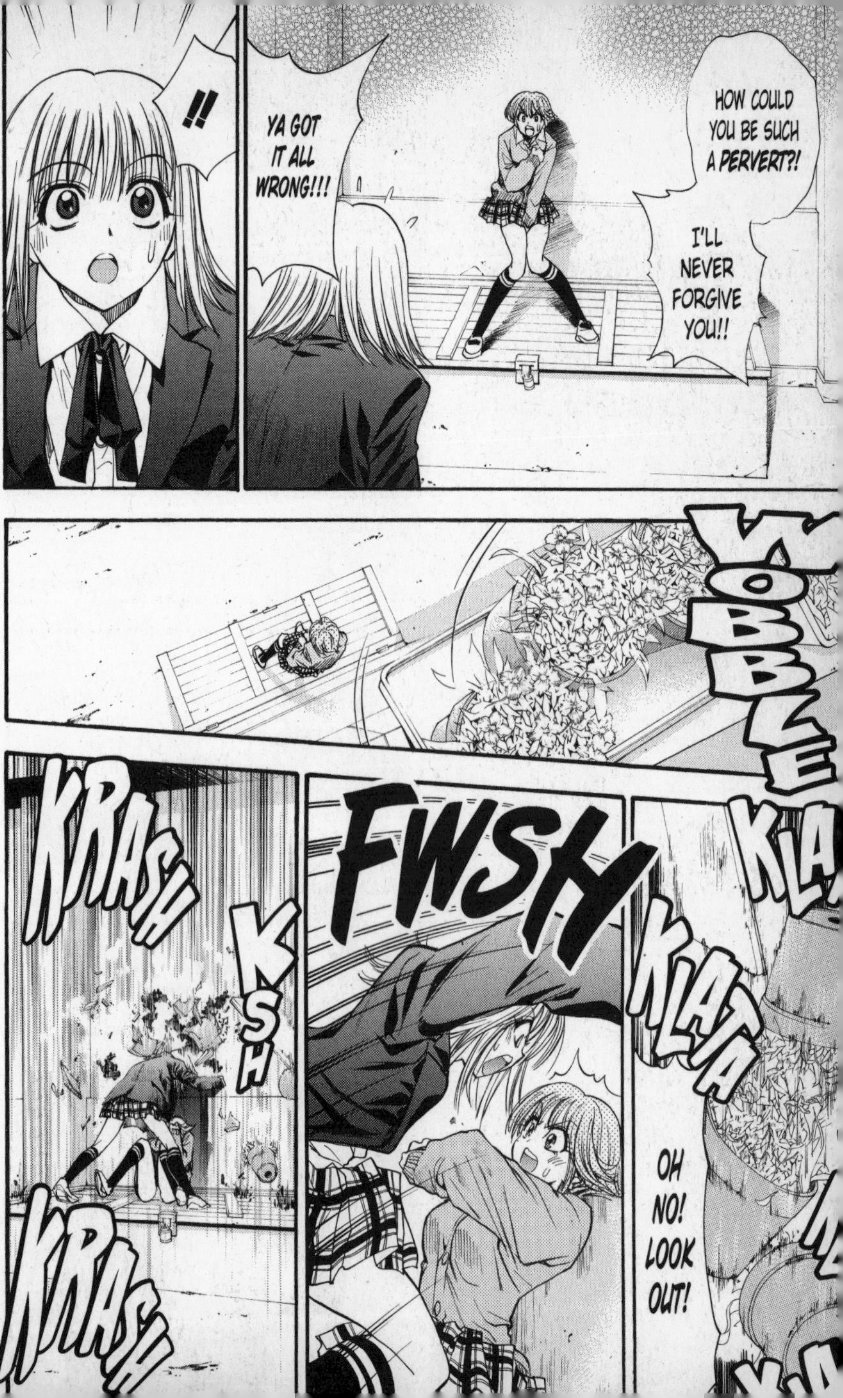
HOW COULD YOU BE SUCH A PERVERT?!
I'LL NEVER FORGIVE YOU!!
YA GOT IT ALL WRONG!!!
!!
WOBBLE
KLA
KLATA
OH NO! LOOK OUT!
FWSH
KSH
KRASH
KRASH

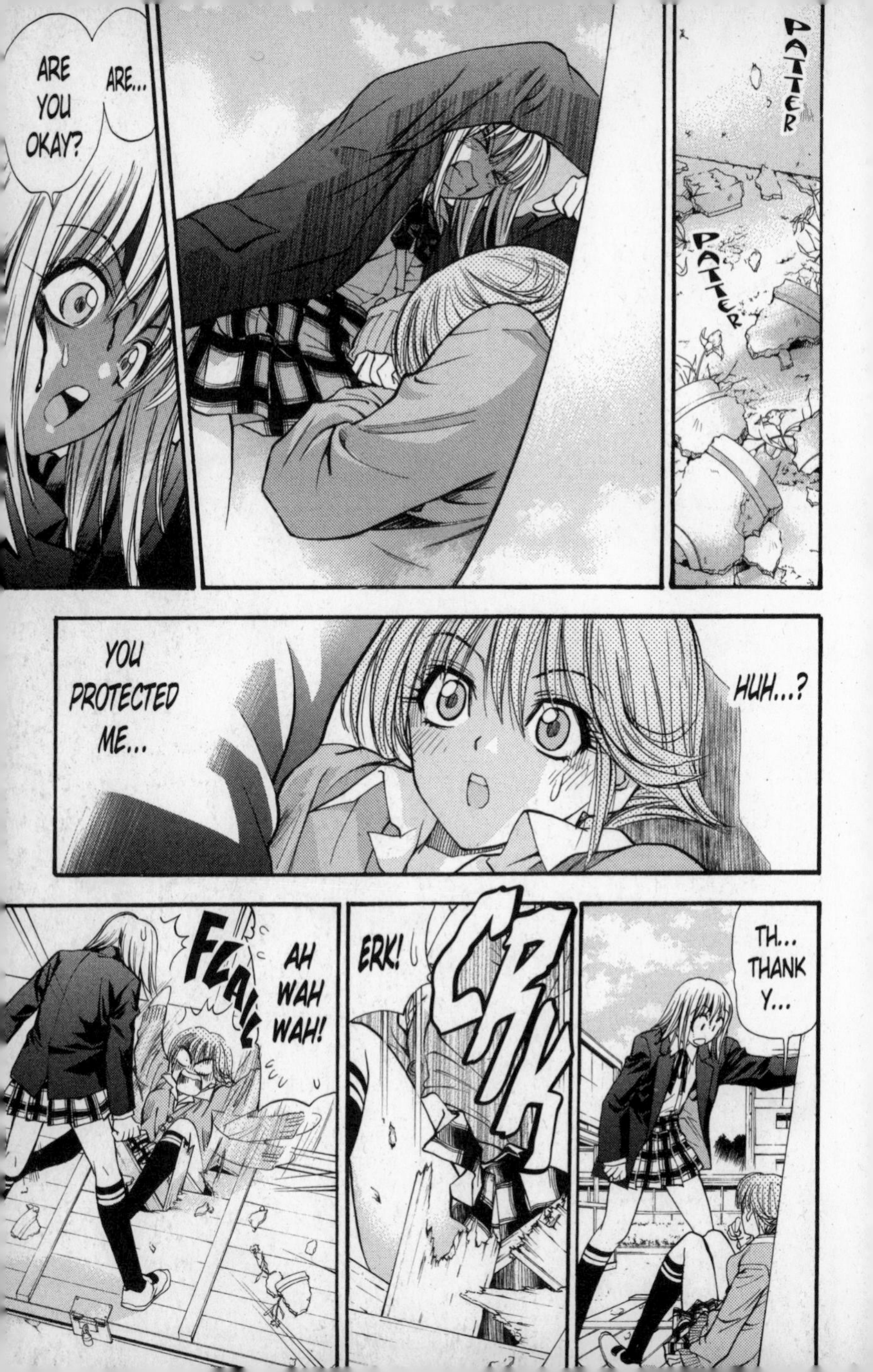
PATTER
PATTER
ARE... ARE YOU OKAY?
HUH...?
YOU PROTECTED ME...
TH... THANK Y...
CRK
ERK!
AH WAH WAH!
FLAIL

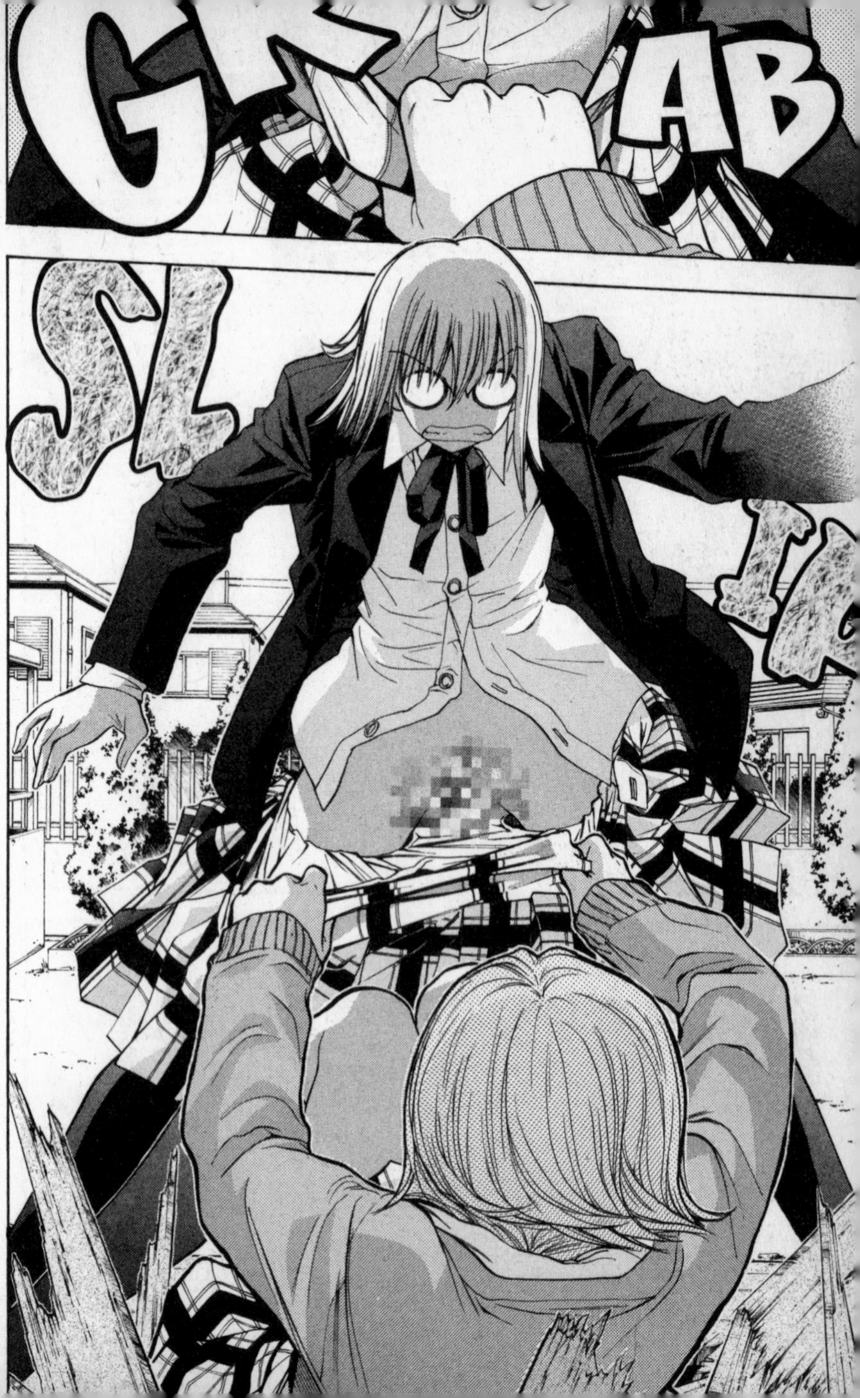
G AB
SL

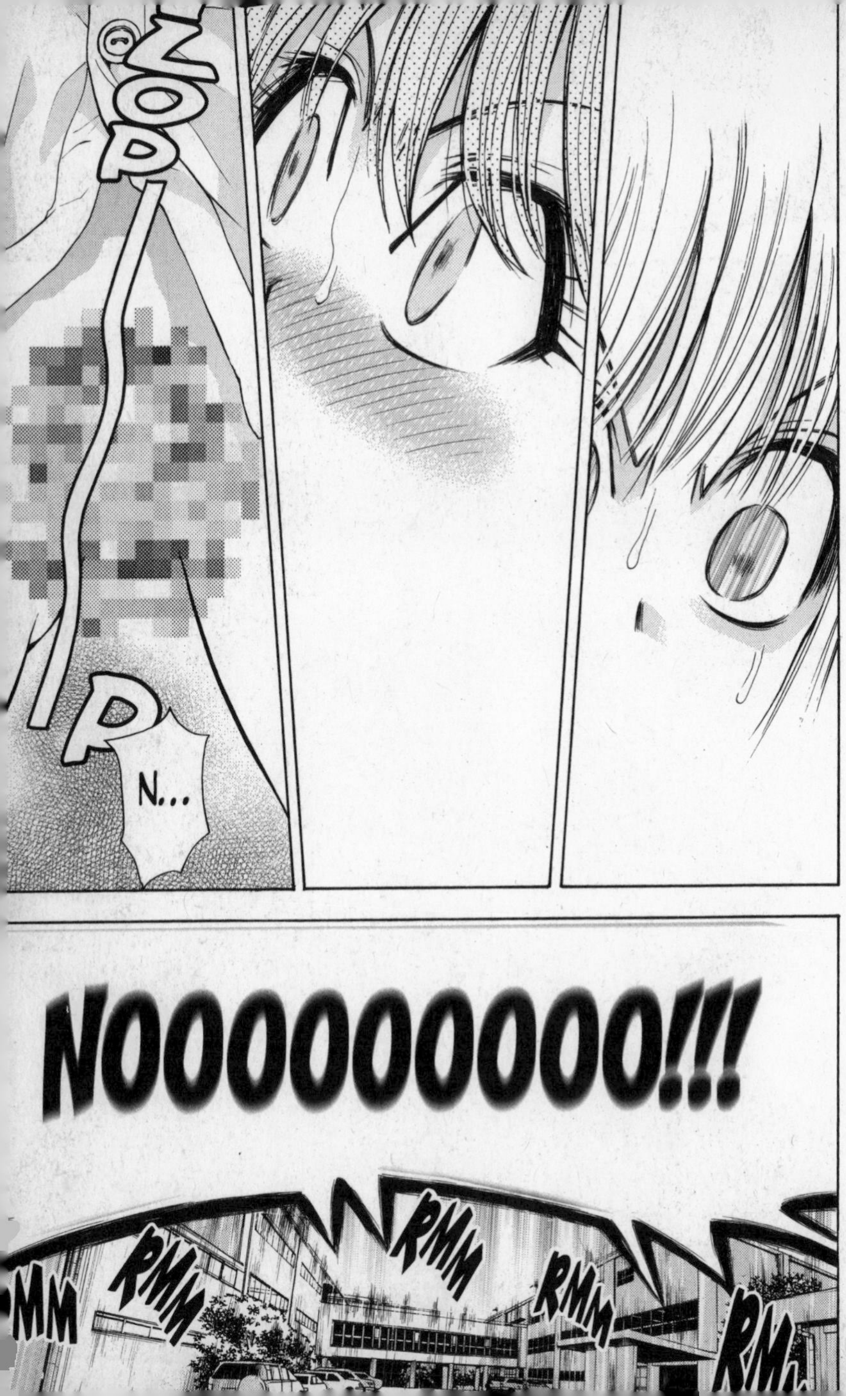
N...
NOOOOOOOOO!!!
RMM
RMM
RMM
RMM

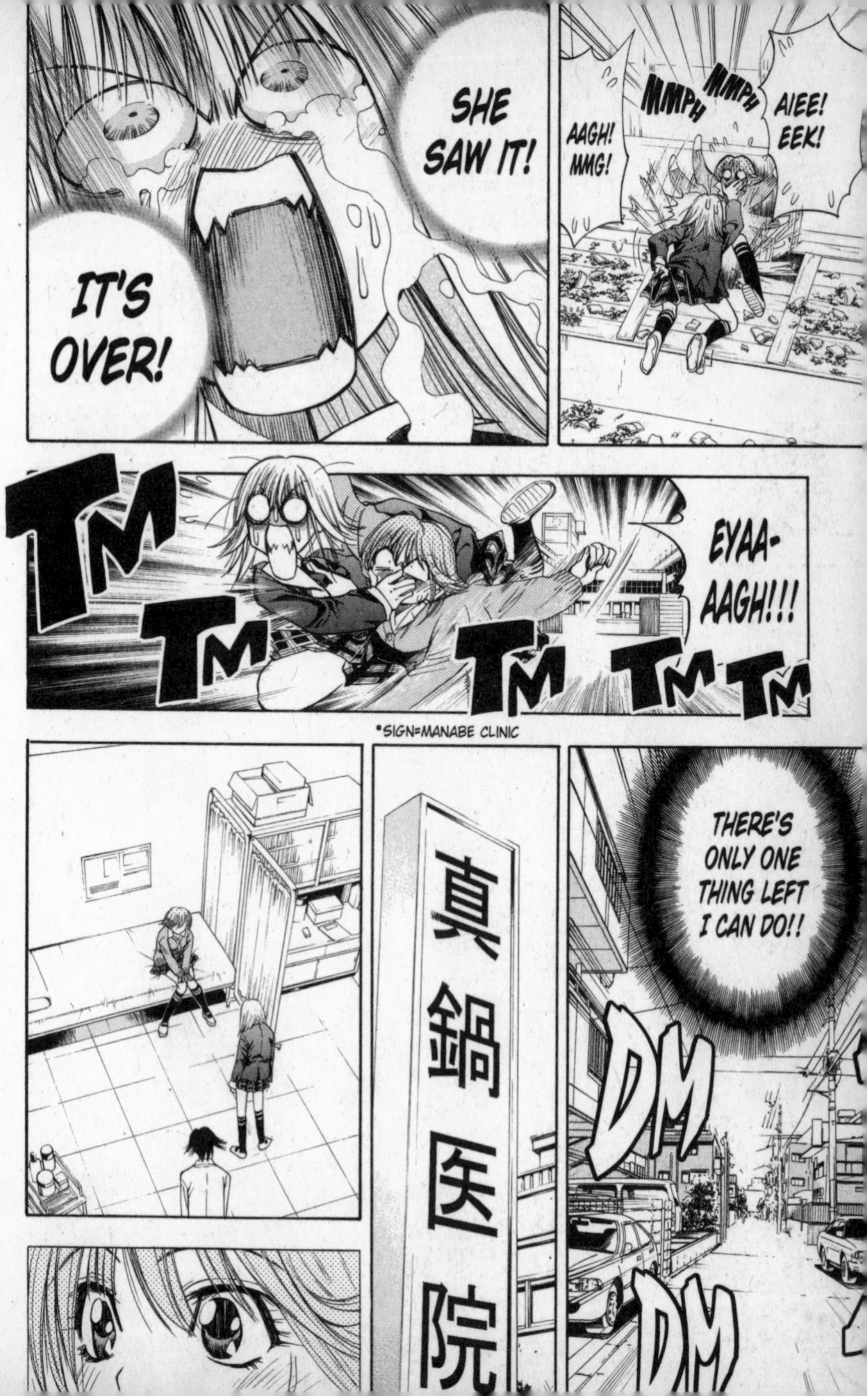
AIEE! EEK!
MMPH MMPH
AAGH! MMG!
SHE SAW IT!
IT'S OVER!
EYAA-AAGH!!!
TM TM TM TM TM
*SIGN=MANABE CLINIC
THERE'S ONLY ONE THING LEFT I CAN DO!!
DM DM
真鍋医院

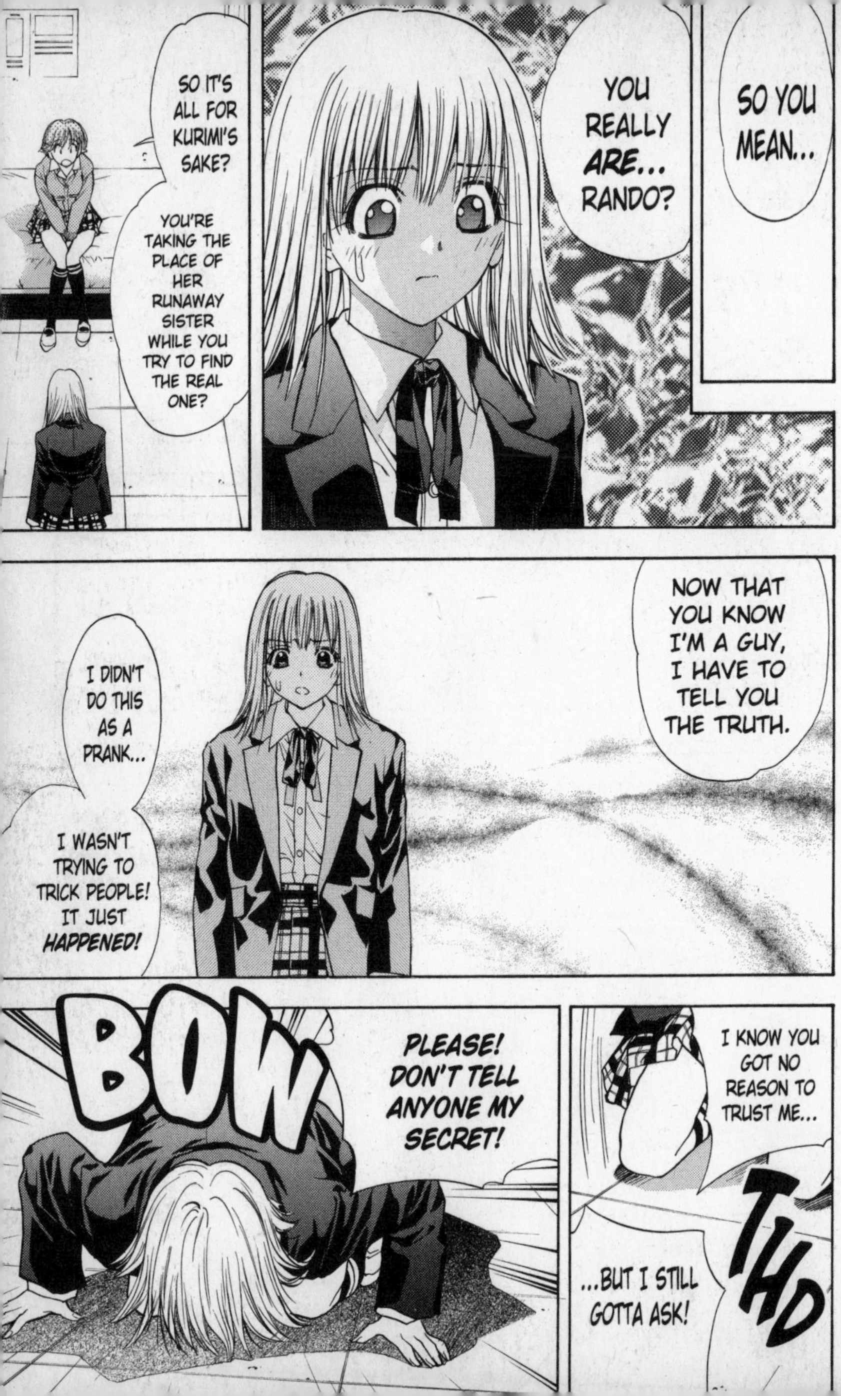
SO YOU MEAN...
YOU REALLY ARE... RANDO?
SO IT'S ALL FOR KURIMI'S SAKE?
YOU'RE TAKING THE PLACE OF HER RUNAWAY SISTER WHILE YOU TRY TO FIND THE REAL ONE?
NOW THAT YOU KNOW I'M A GUY, I HAVE TO TELL YOU THE TRUTH.
I DIDN'T DO THIS AS A PRANK...
I WASN'T TRYING TO TRICK PEOPLE! IT JUST HAPPENED!
I KNOW YOU GOT NO REASON TO TRUST ME...
THD
...BUT I STILL GOTTA ASK!
BOW
PLEASE! DON'T TELL ANYONE MY SECRET!

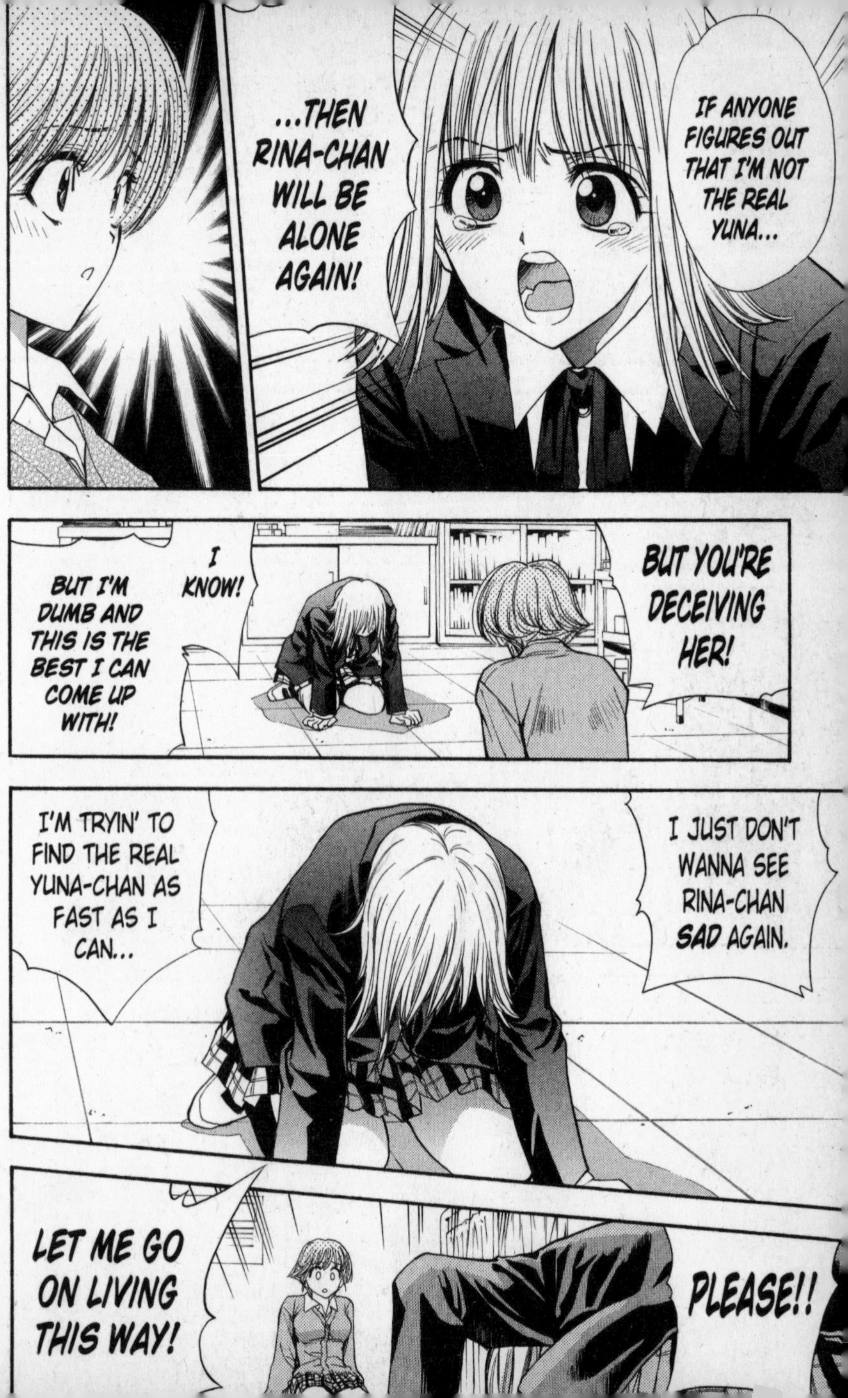

IF ANYONE FIGURES OUT THAT I'M NOT THE REAL YUNA...
...THEN RINA-CHAN WILL BE ALONE AGAIN!
BUT YOU'RE DECEIVING HER!
I KNOW!
BUT I'M DUMB AND THIS IS THE BEST I CAN COME UP WITH!
I JUST DON'T WANNA SEE RINA-CHAN SAD AGAIN.
I'M TRYIN' TO FIND THE REAL YUNA-CHAN AS FAST AS I CAN...
PLEASE!!
LET ME GO ON LIVING THIS WAY!

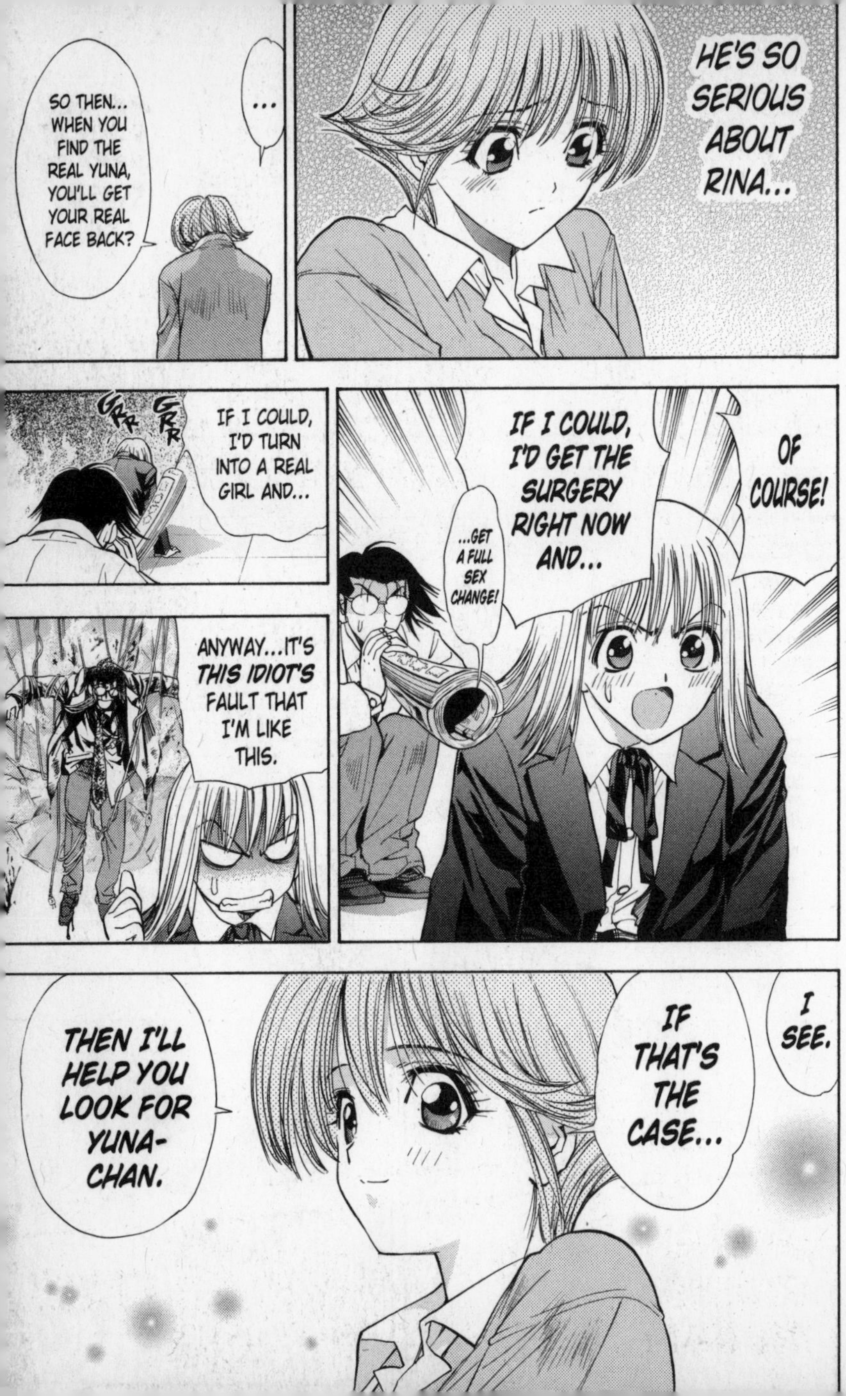
HE'S SO SERIOUS ABOUT RINA...
...
SO THEN... WHEN YOU FIND THE REAL YUNA, YOU'LL GET YOUR REAL FACE BACK?
OF COURSE!
IF I COULD, I'D GET THE SURGERY RIGHT NOW AND...
...GET A FULL SEX CHANGE!
GRRR GRRR
IF I COULD, I'D TURN INTO A REAL GIRL AND...
ANYWAY...IT'S THIS IDIOT'S FAULT THAT I'M LIKE THIS.
I SEE.
IF THAT'S THE CASE...
THEN I'LL HELP YOU LOOK FOR YUNA-CHAN.

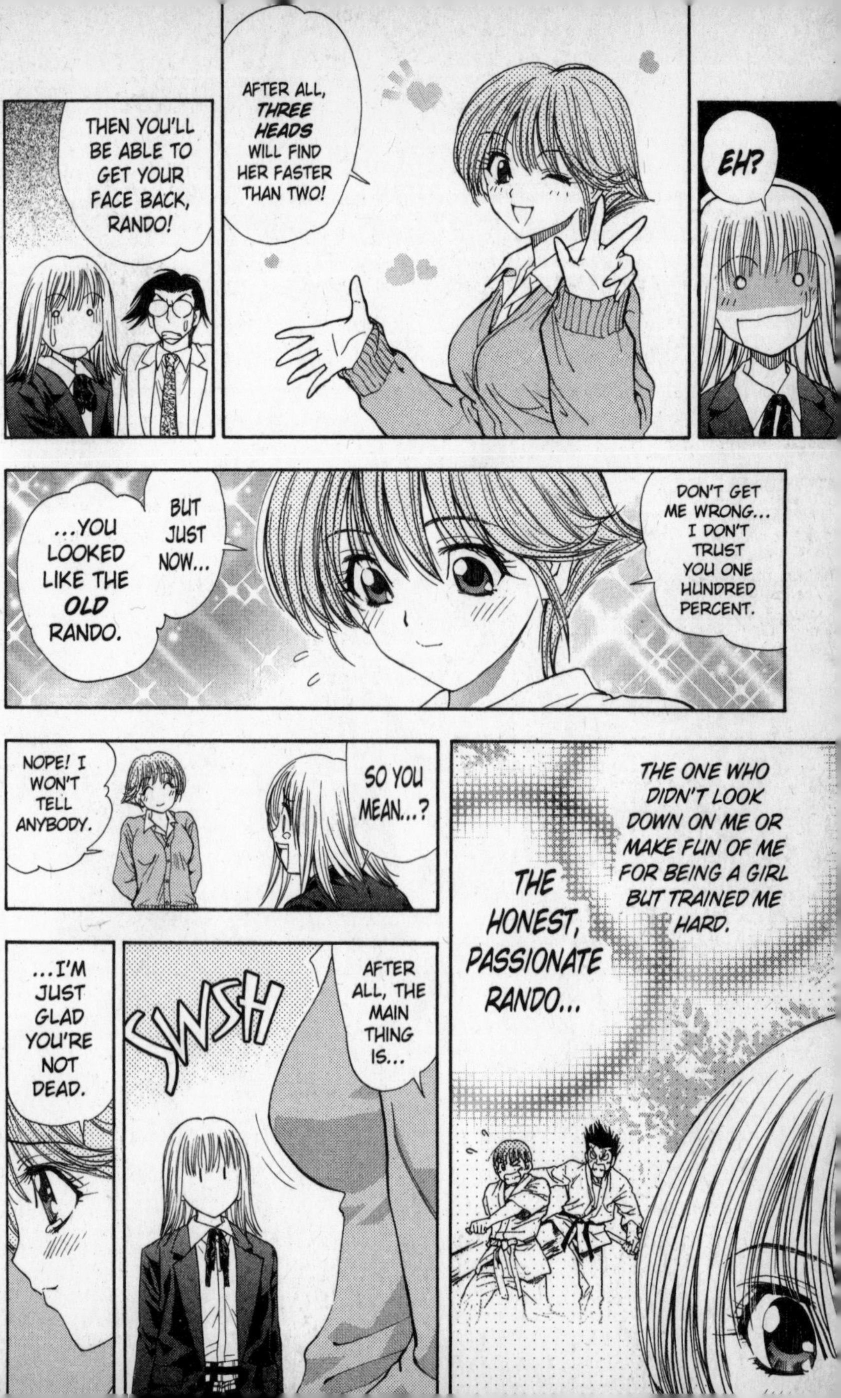
EH?
AFTER ALL, THREE HEADS WILL FIND HER FASTER THAN TWO!
THEN YOU'LL BE ABLE TO GET YOUR FACE BACK, RANDO!
DON'T GET ME WRONG... I DON'T TRUST YOU ONE HUNDRED PERCENT.
BUT JUST NOW...
...YOU LOOKED LIKE THE OLD RANDO.
THE ONE WHO DIDN'T LOOK DOWN ON ME OR MAKE FUN OF ME FOR BEING A GIRL BUT TRAINED ME HARD.
THE HONEST, PASSIONATE RANDO...
SO YOU MEAN...?
NOPE! I WON'T TELL ANYBODY.
AFTER ALL, THE MAIN THING IS...
SWSH
...I'M JUST GLAD YOU'RE NOT DEAD.

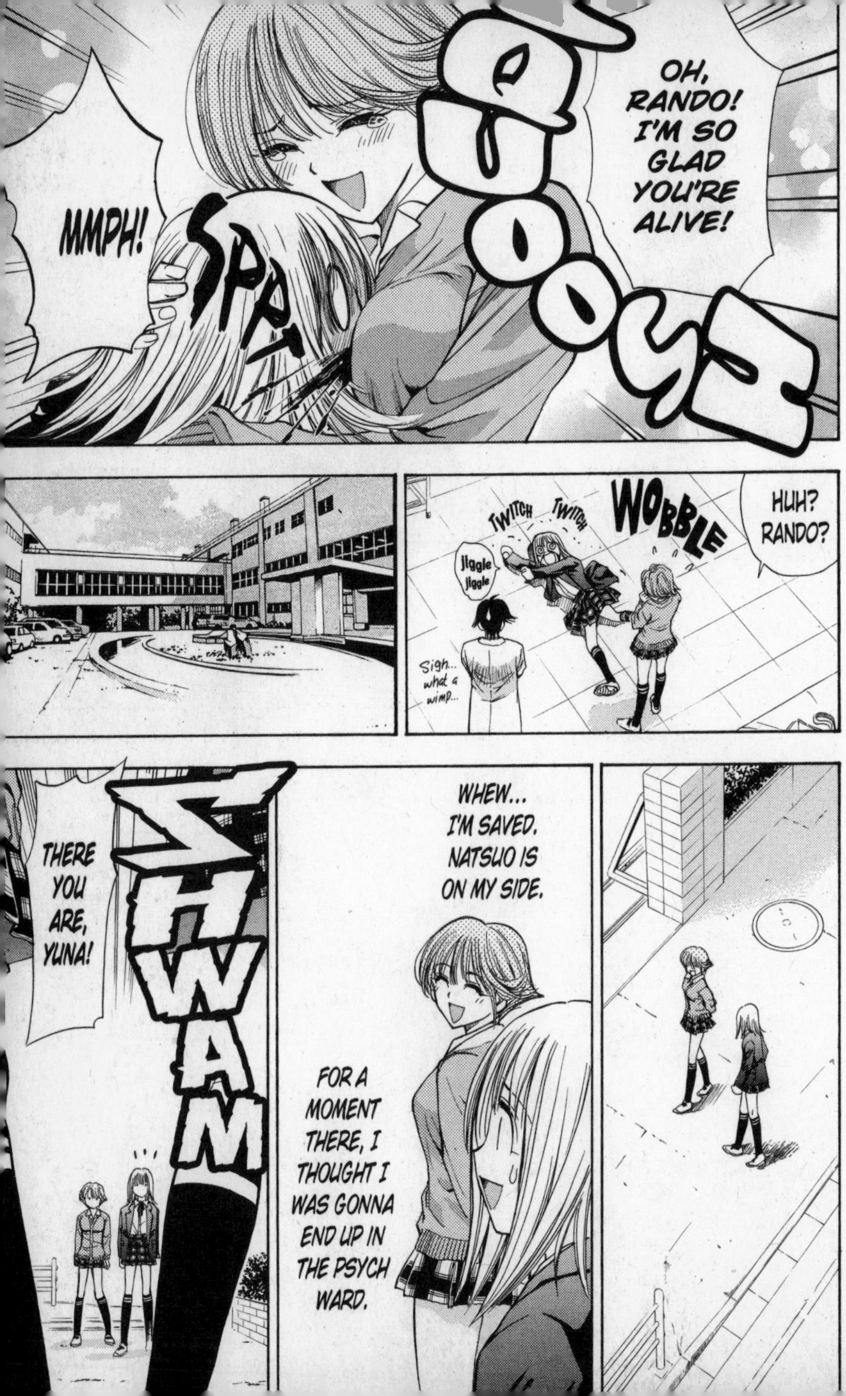
OH, RANDO! I'M SO GLAD YOU'RE ALIVE!
MMPH!
HUH? RANDO?
WOBBLE
TWITCH TWITCH
jiggle jiggle
Sigh... what a wimp...
WHEW... I'M SAVED. NATSUO IS ON MY SIDE.
FOR A MOMENT THERE, I THOUGHT I WAS GONNA END UP IN THE PSYCH WARD.
THERE YOU ARE, YUNA!
SHWAM

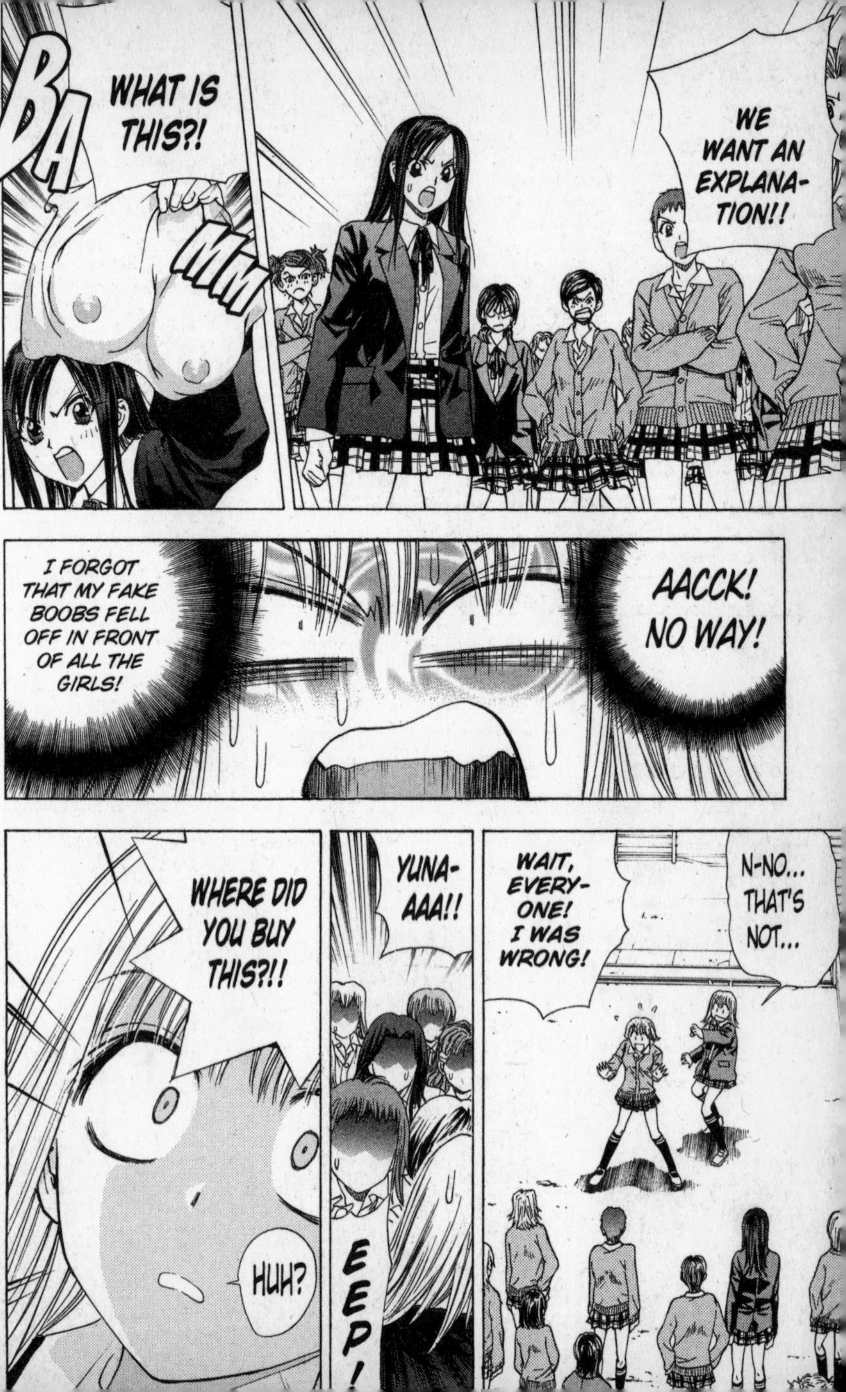
WE WANT AN EXPLANA-TION!!
WHAT IS THIS?!
BA
MM
AACCK! NO WAY!
I FORGOT THAT MY FAKE BOOBS FELL OFF IN FRONT OF ALL THE GIRLS!
N-NO... THAT'S NOT...
WAIT, EVERY-ONE! I WAS WRONG!
YUNA-AAA!!
EEP!
WHERE DID YOU BUY THIS?!!
HUH?

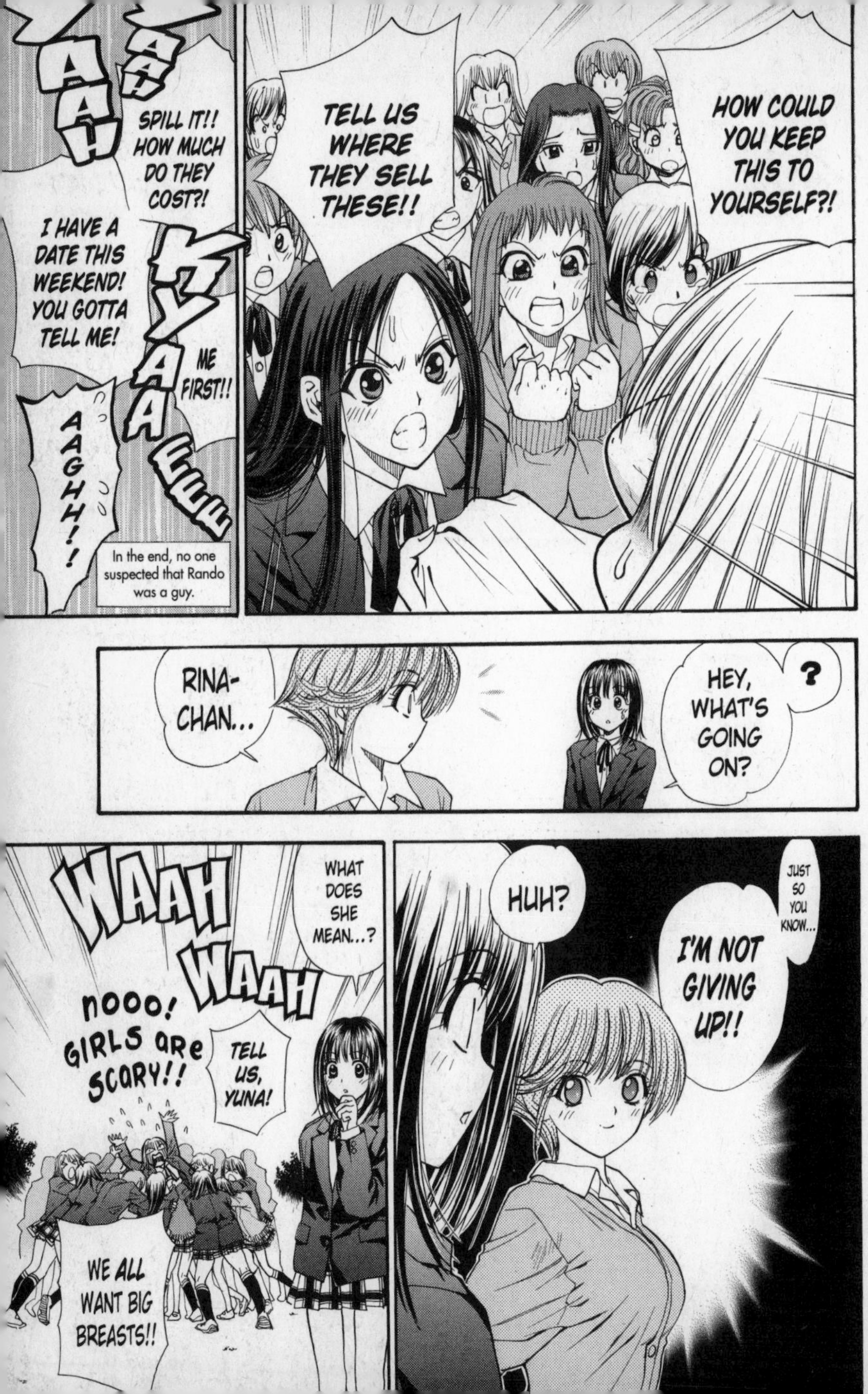
HOW COULD YOU KEEP THIS TO YOURSELF?!
TELL US WHERE THEY SELL THESE!!
AAAH
AAH
SPILL IT!! HOW MUCH DO THEY COST?!
KYAAAEEE
I HAVE A DATE THIS WEEKEND! YOU GOTTA TELL ME!
ME FIRST!!
AAGHH!!
In the end, no one suspected that Rando was a guy.
?
HEY, WHAT'S GOING ON?
RINA-CHAN...
JUST SO YOU KNOW...
I'M NOT GIVING UP!!
HUH?
WHAT DOES SHE MEAN...?
WAAH
WAAH
TELL US, YUNA!
nooo! GIRLS are SCARY!!
WE ALL WANT BIG BREASTS!!

BONUS: REJECTED STORIES (part 1)

DOES THIS MEAN...
UM...
COULD IT BE...
WE'RE TWINS?
OR SOMETHING...
YES! YES! DO YOU REMEMBER, BIG SIS?!
GRAB
I GOT IT RIGHT?!
IS THIS OKAY?
YUNA'S ROOM
SO THIS MEANS WHAT? I'VE BECOME YUNA KURIMI?
RINA'S OLDER TWIN SISTER?
THEN, FROM NOW ON, I'LL SPEND EVERY DAY TOGETHER IN THE SAME HOUSE WITH RINA-CHAN?
BASH
NOOO! THAT'S INSANE! I CAN'T DO THAT!
SHAKE
SHAKE
20
mirror
THE MORE I LOOK, THE MORE I SEE... I HAVE THE EXACT SAME FACE AS RINA-CHAN.
BUT...
BECAUSE I WAS ASLEEP FOR A YEAR, MY LEGS HAVE LOST A LOT OF MUSCLE DEFINITION. THEY'RE SO SLENDER...
SHAAA—AA
I DON'T HAVE BREASTS...
BUT I LOOK LIKE A GIRL FROM ANY ANGLE.
I DON'T THINK I'D BE FOUND OUT THAT EASILY...
mirror
MAYBE I SHOULD JUST PASS AS HER BIG SISTER...
AND LIVE WITH RINA HERE...
SIS? CAN I COME IN?
KNOCK
KNOCK
URK
YEEP! I DIDN'T MEAN IT!!!
CLICK
21

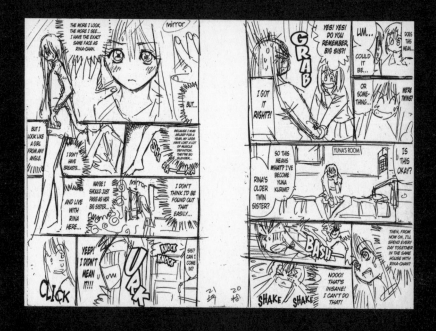

THIS ISN'T A REJECTED STORY, BUT IT IS AN IMPORTANT MEMENTO—THE STORYBOARDS (WHAT THEY CALL *NAME* IN JAPANESE MANGA TERMS) FOR THE FIRST ISSUE.

IT'S ALMOST EXACTLY THE SAME AS THE PUBLISHED VERSION, BUT SEVERAL PLOT POINTS WERE DIFFERENT. YUNA (RANDO)'S HAIR WAS LONGER, AND INSTEAD OF RUNNING AWAY, THE REAL YUNA HAD BEEN KIDNAPPED WHEN SHE WAS YOUNG AND HER WHEREABOUTS WERE UNKNOWN. STILL, THIS IS WHERE IT ALL BEGAN, SO THESE PAGES HAVE A LOT OF MEANING FOR ME.

Chapter 38: Poke, Prod, Panic

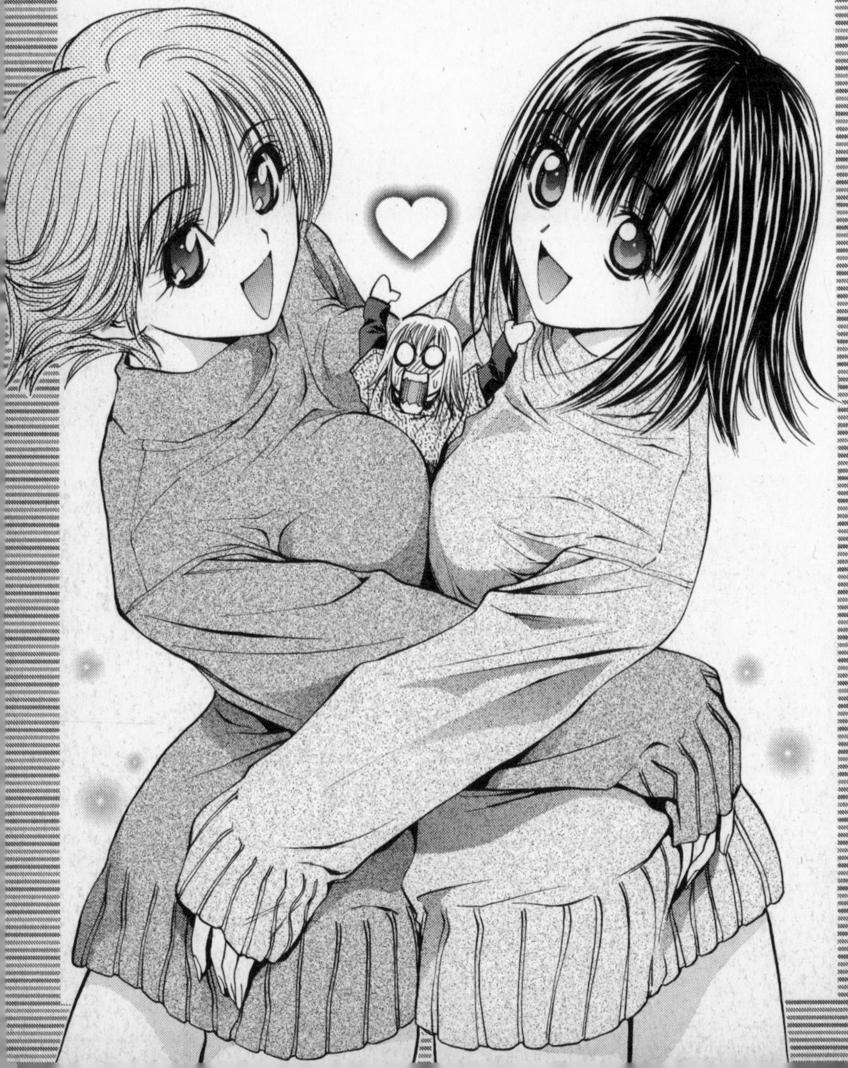

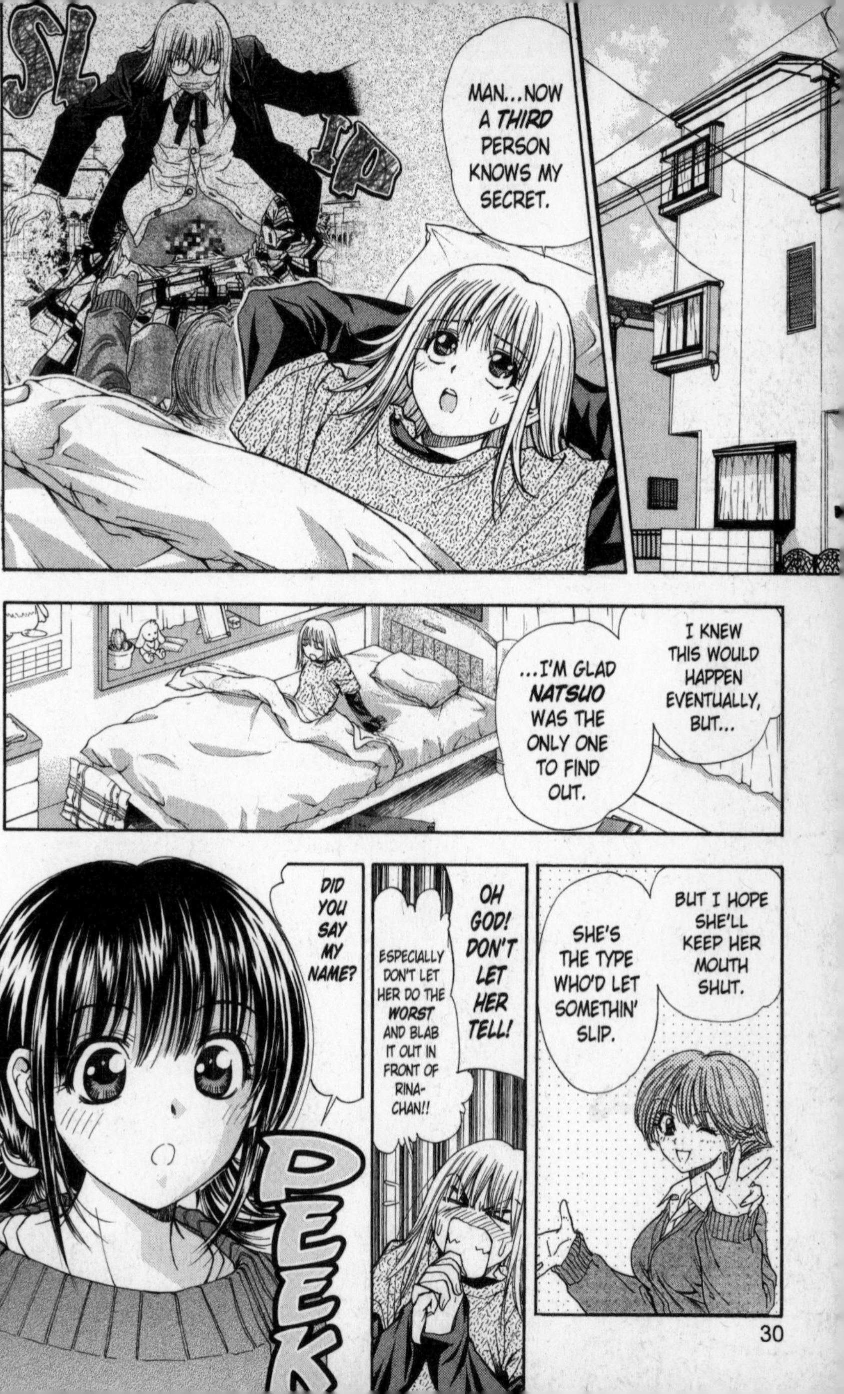
MAN...NOW A THIRD PERSON KNOWS MY SECRET.
SLIP
I KNEW THIS WOULD HAPPEN EVENTUALLY, BUT...
...I'M GLAD NATSUO WAS THE ONLY ONE TO FIND OUT.
BUT I HOPE SHE'LL KEEP HER MOUTH SHUT.
SHE'S THE TYPE WHO'D LET SOMETHIN' SLIP.
OH GOD! DON'T LET HER TELL!
ESPECIALLY DON'T LET HER DO THE WORST AND BLAB IT OUT IN FRONT OF RINA-CHAN!!
DID YOU SAY MY NAME?
PEEK

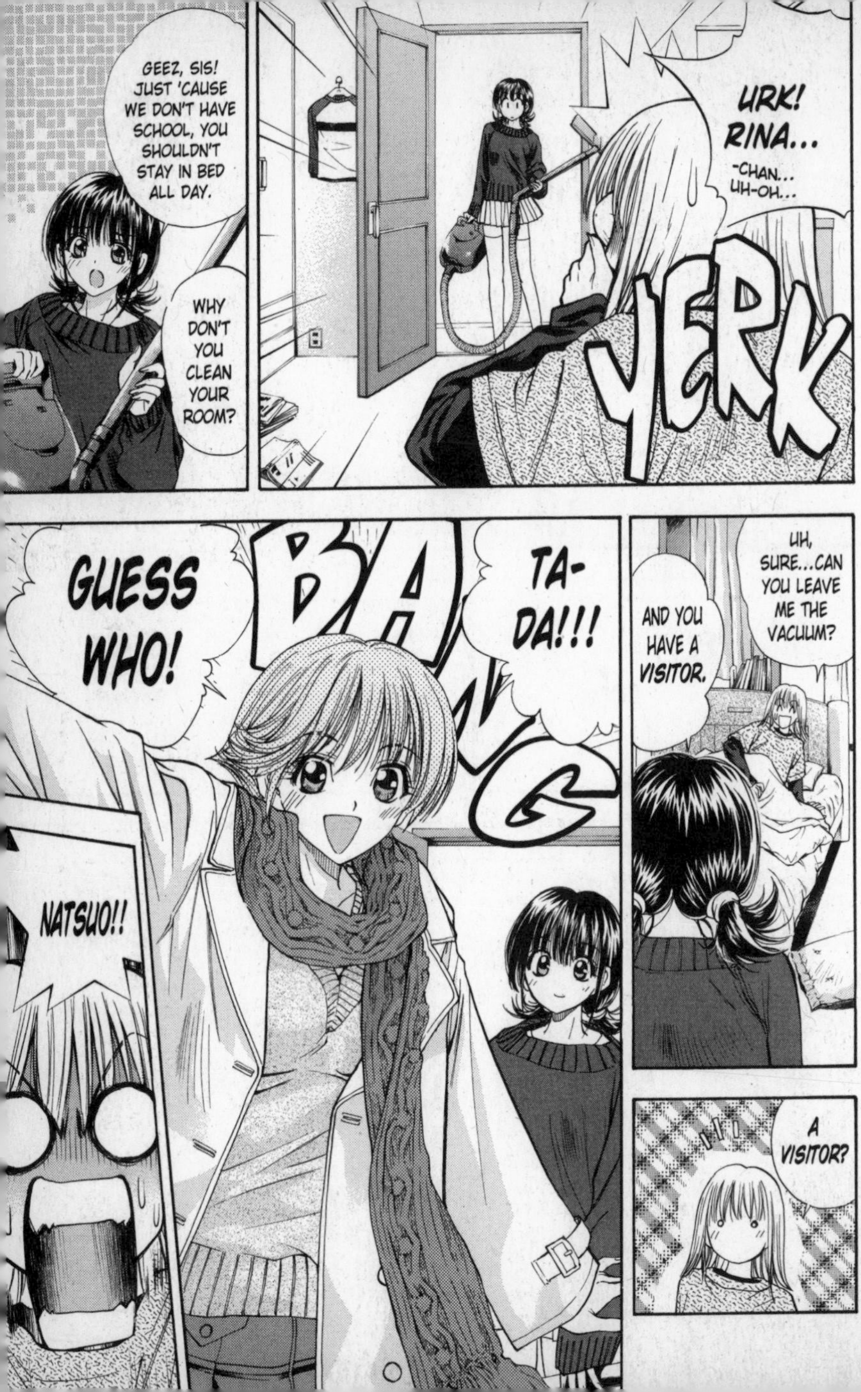
URK! RINA... -CHAN... UH-OH...
YERK
GEEZ, SIS! JUST 'CAUSE WE DON'T HAVE SCHOOL, YOU SHOULDN'T STAY IN BED ALL DAY.
WHY DON'T YOU CLEAN YOUR ROOM?
UH, SURE...CAN YOU LEAVE ME THE VACUUM?
AND YOU HAVE A VISITOR.
A VISITOR?
TA-DA!!!
BANG
GUESS WHO!
NATSUO!!

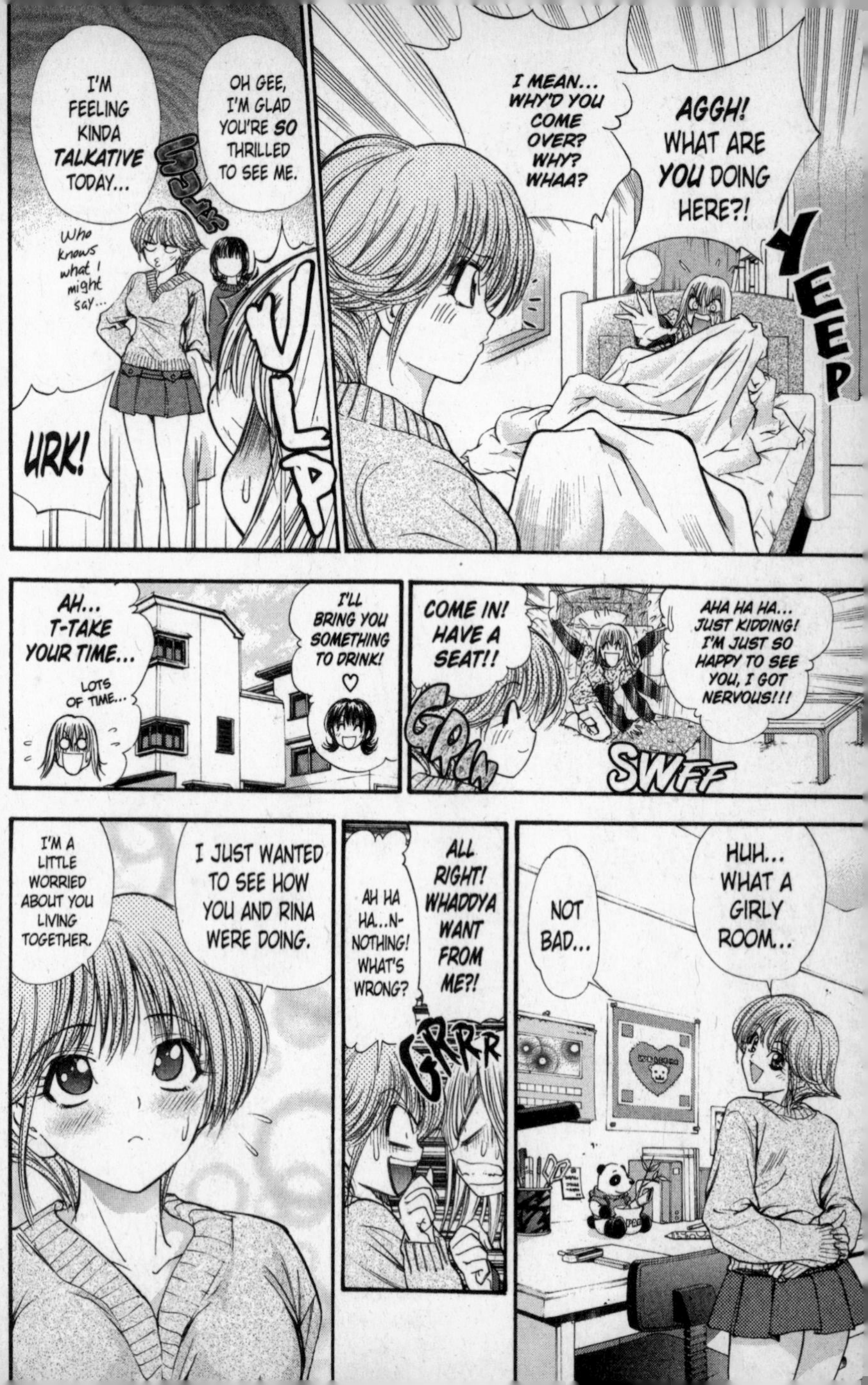
AGGH! WHAT ARE YOU DOING HERE?!
YEEP
I MEAN... WHY'D YOU COME OVER? WHY? WHAA?
OH GEE, I'M GLAD YOU'RE SO THRILLED TO SEE ME.
I'M FEELING KINDA TALKATIVE TODAY...
SULK
Who knows what I might say...
ULP
URK!
AHA HA HA... JUST KIDDING! I'M JUST SO HAPPY TO SEE YOU, I GOT NERVOUS!!!
COME IN! HAVE A SEAT!!
SWFF
I'LL BRING YOU SOMETHING TO DRINK! ♡
AH... T-TAKE YOUR TIME...
LOTS OF TIME...
HUH... WHAT A GIRLY ROOM...
NOT BAD...
ALL RIGHT! WHADDYA WANT FROM ME?!
AH HA HA...N-NOTHING! WHAT'S WRONG?
GRRR
I JUST WANTED TO SEE HOW YOU AND RINA WERE DOING.
I'M A LITTLE WORRIED ABOUT YOU LIVING TOGETHER.

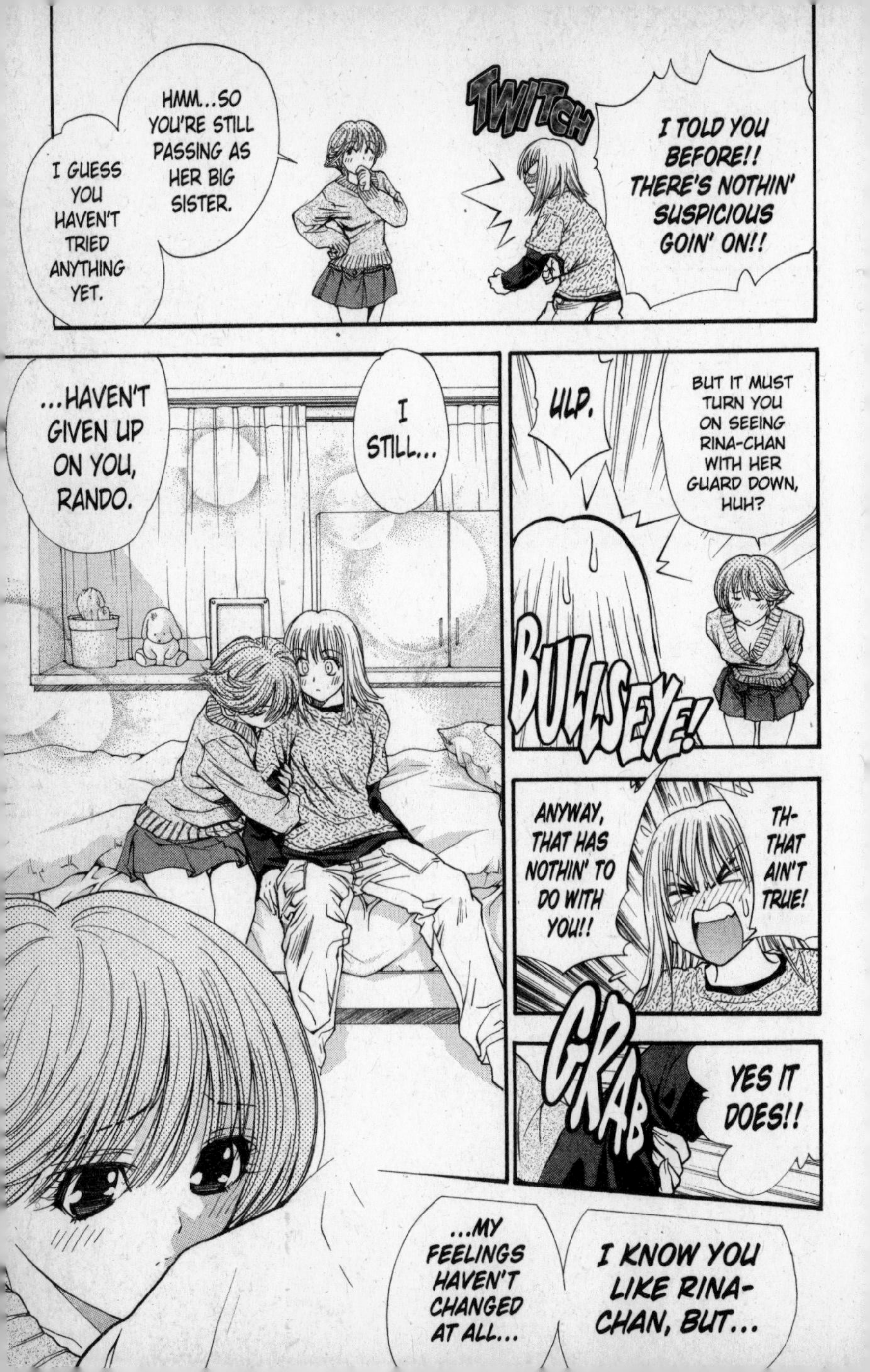
HMM...SO YOU'RE STILL PASSING AS HER BIG SISTER.
I GUESS YOU HAVEN'T TRIED ANYTHING YET.
TWITCH
I TOLD YOU BEFORE!! THERE'S NOTHIN' SUSPICIOUS GOIN' ON!!
BUT IT MUST TURN YOU ON SEEING RINA-CHAN WITH HER GUARD DOWN, HUH?
ULP.
BULLSEYE!
TH-THAT AIN'T TRUE!
ANYWAY, THAT HAS NOTHIN' TO DO WITH YOU!!
YES IT DOES!!
GRAB
I STILL...
...HAVEN'T GIVEN UP ON YOU, RANDO.
I KNOW YOU LIKE RINA-CHAN, BUT...
...MY FEELINGS HAVEN'T CHANGED AT ALL...

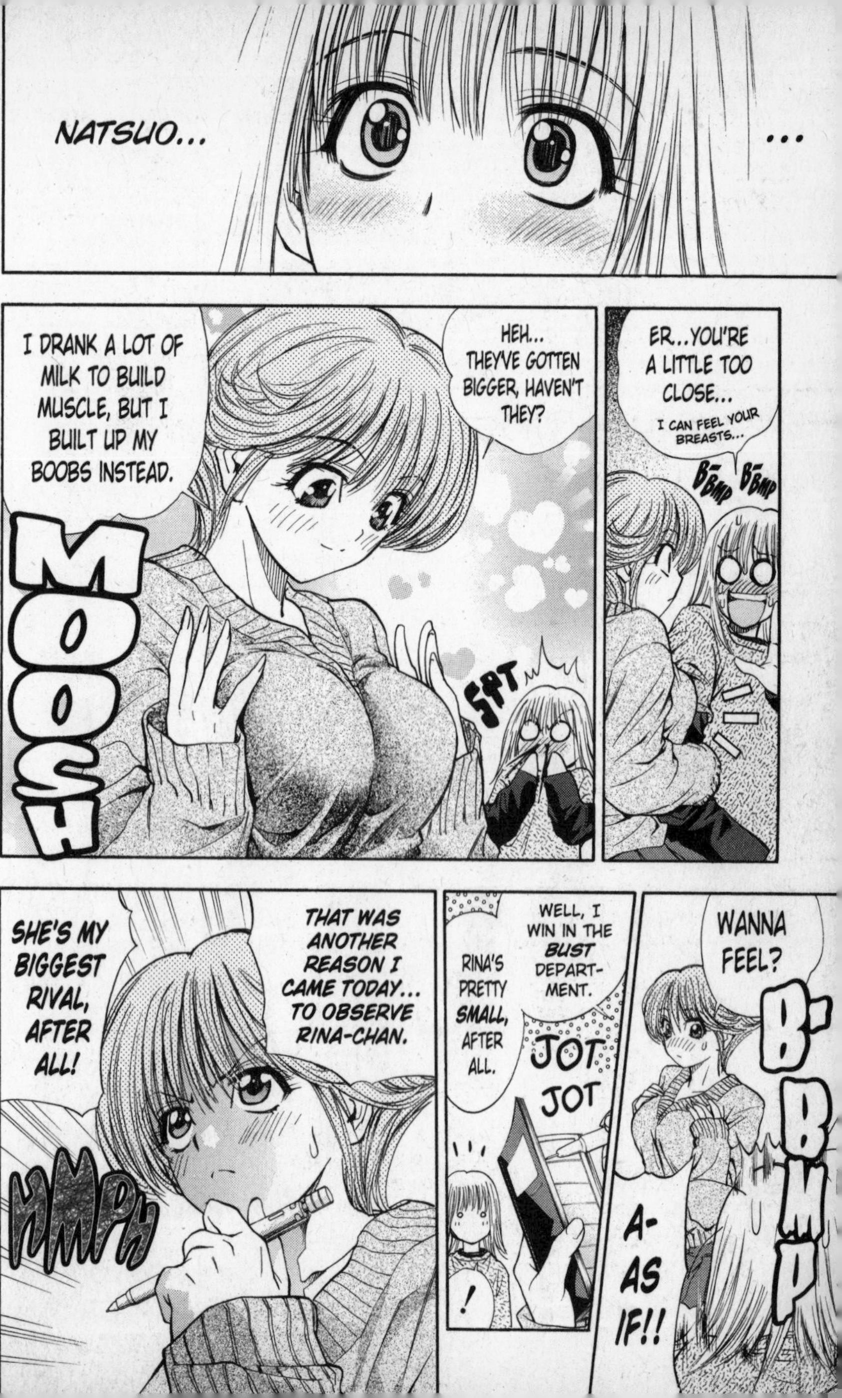
...
NATSUO...
ER...YOU'RE A LITTLE TOO CLOSE...
I CAN FEEL YOUR BREASTS...
B-BMP
B-BMP
HEH... THEY'VE GOTTEN BIGGER, HAVEN'T THEY?
I DRANK A LOT OF MILK TO BUILD MUSCLE, BUT I BUILT UP MY BOOBS INSTEAD.
MOOSH
SPT
WANNA FEEL?
B-BMP
A-AS IF!!
WELL, I WIN IN THE *BUST* DEPARTMENT.
RINA'S PRETTY SMALL, AFTER ALL.
JOT
JOT
!
THAT WAS ANOTHER REASON I CAME TODAY... TO OBSERVE RINA-CHAN.
SHE'S MY BIGGEST RIVAL, AFTER ALL!
HMPH

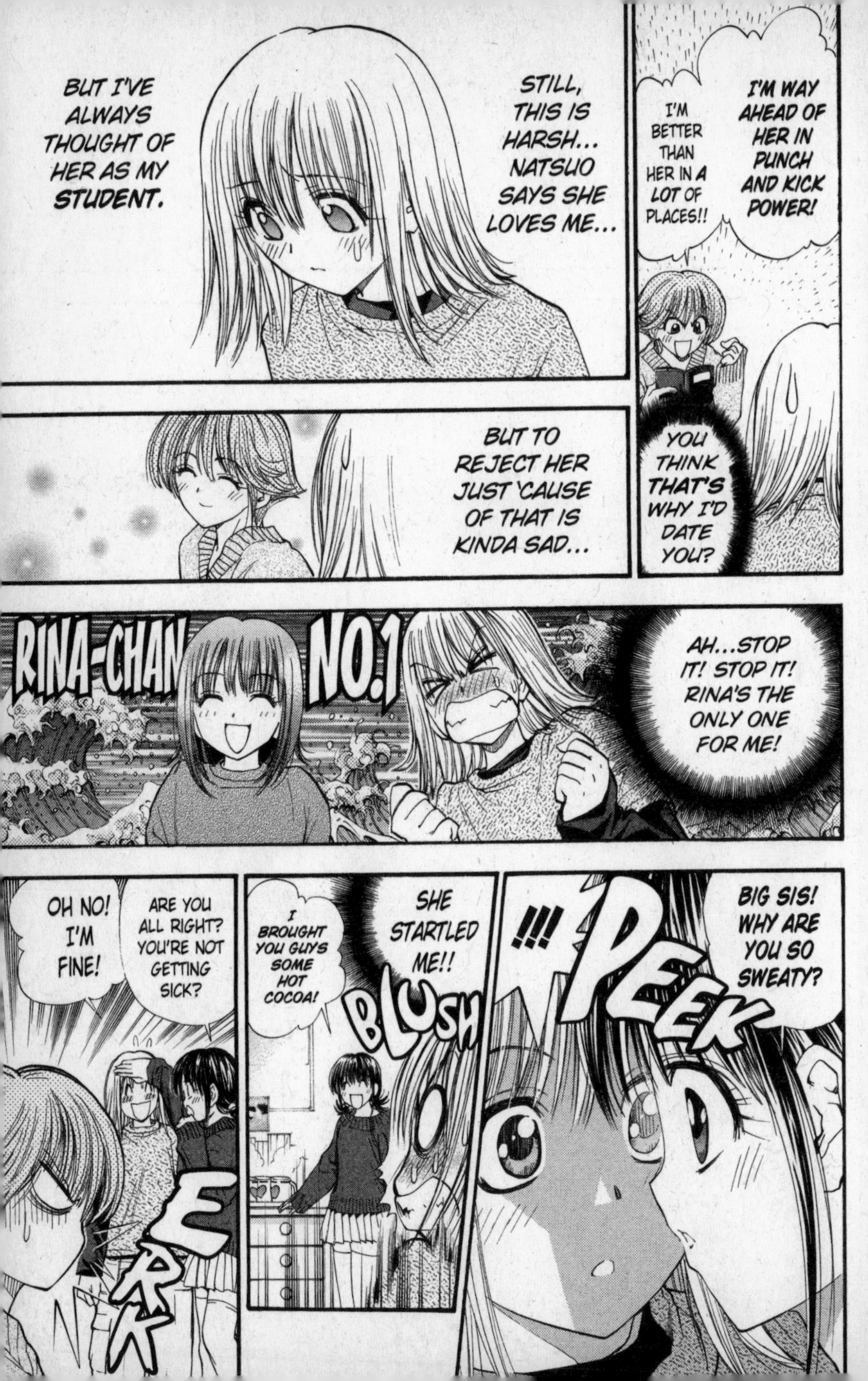
I'M WAY AHEAD OF HER IN PUNCH AND KICK POWER!
I'M BETTER THAN HER IN A LOT OF PLACES!!
YOU THINK THAT'S WHY I'D DATE YOU?
STILL, THIS IS HARSH... NATSUO SAYS SHE LOVES ME...
BUT I'VE ALWAYS THOUGHT OF HER AS MY STUDENT.
BUT TO REJECT HER JUST 'CAUSE OF THAT IS KINDA SAD...
AH...STOP IT! STOP IT! RINA'S THE ONLY ONE FOR ME!
RINA-CHAN NO.1
BIG SIS! WHY ARE YOU SO SWEATY?
PEEK
!!!
SHE STARTLED ME!!
BLUSH
I BROUGHT YOU GUYS SOME HOT COCOA!
ARE YOU ALL RIGHT? YOU'RE NOT GETTING SICK?
OH NO! I'M FINE!
ERRK

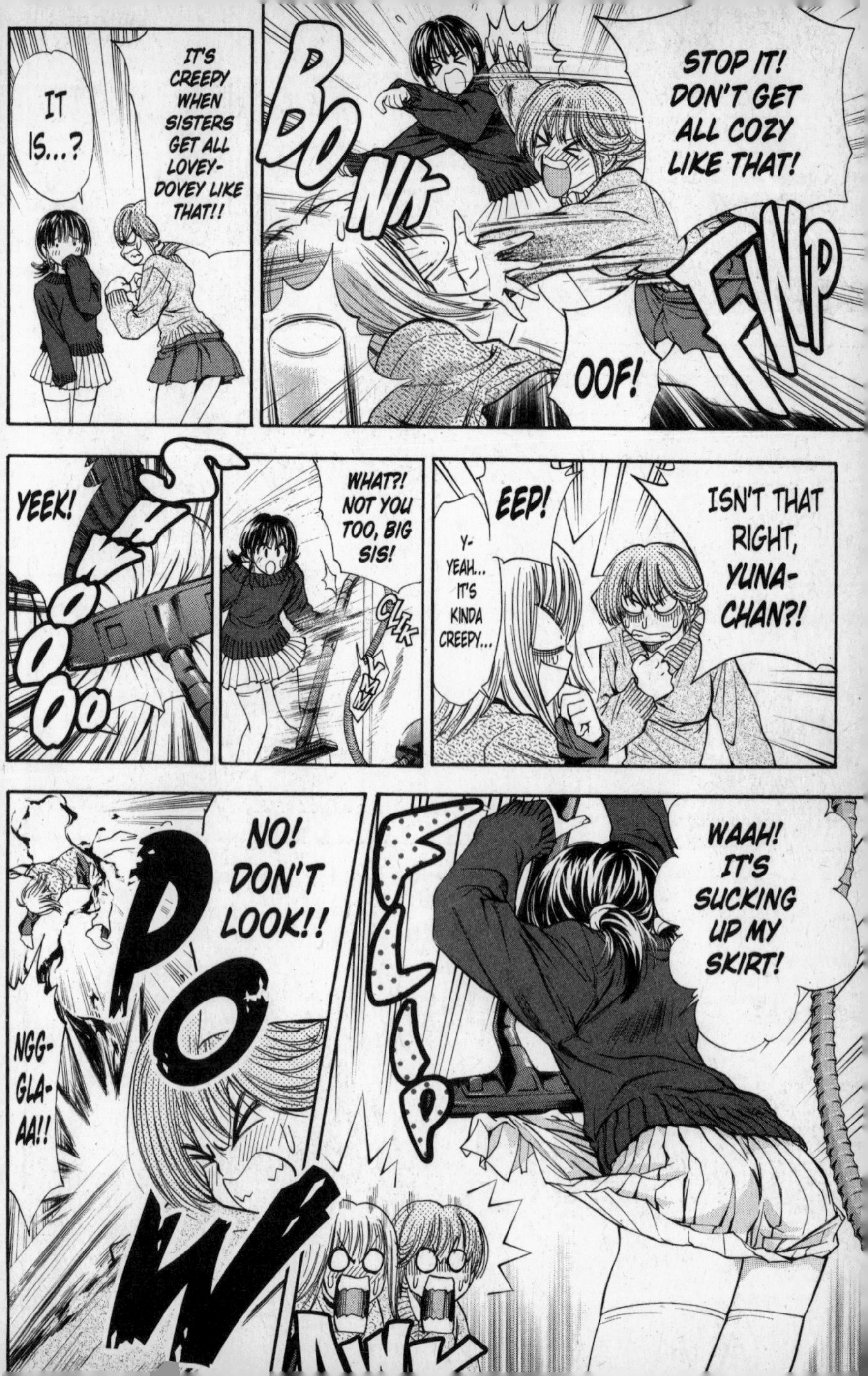
STOP IT! DON'T GET ALL COZY LIKE THAT!
BONK
FWIP
OOF!
IT'S CREEPY WHEN SISTERS GET ALL LOVEY-DOVEY LIKE THAT!!
IT IS...?
ISN'T THAT RIGHT, YUNA-CHAN?!
EEP!
Y-YEAH... IT'S KINDA CREEPY...
WHAT?! NOT YOU TOO, BIG SIS!
CLIK
YEEK!
WAAH! IT'S SUCKING UP MY SKIRT!
NO! DON'T LOOK!!
POW
NGG-GLA-AA!!

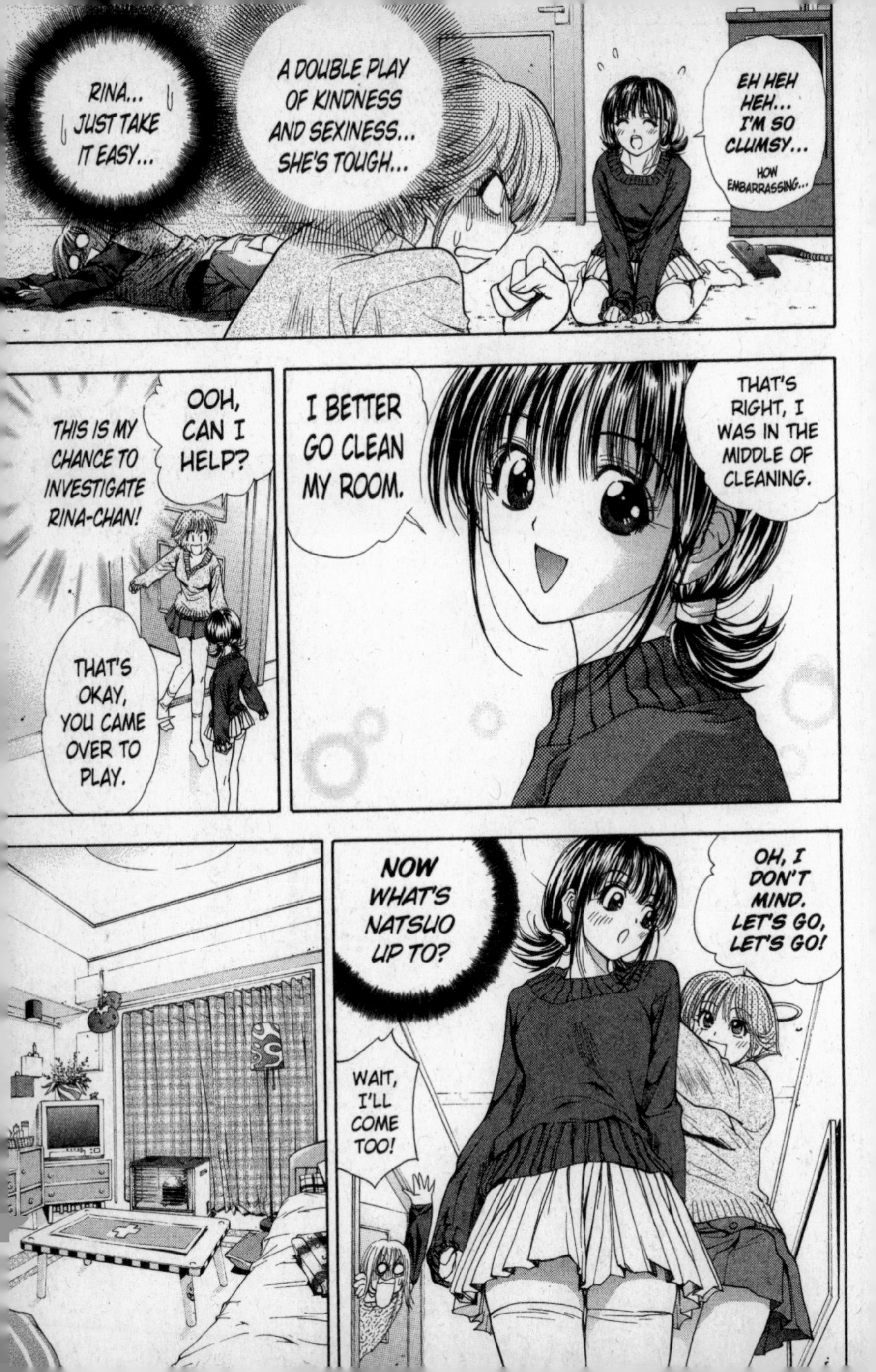
EH HEH HEH... I'M SO CLUMSY...
HOW EMBARRASSING...
A DOUBLE PLAY OF KINDNESS AND SEXINESS... SHE'S TOUGH...
RINA... JUST TAKE IT EASY...
THAT'S RIGHT, I WAS IN THE MIDDLE OF CLEANING.
I BETTER GO CLEAN MY ROOM.
OOH, CAN I HELP?
THIS IS MY CHANCE TO INVESTIGATE RINA-CHAN!
THAT'S OKAY, YOU CAME OVER TO PLAY.
OH, I DON'T MIND. LET'S GO, LET'S GO!
NOW WHAT'S NATSUO UP TO?
WAIT, I'LL COME TOO!

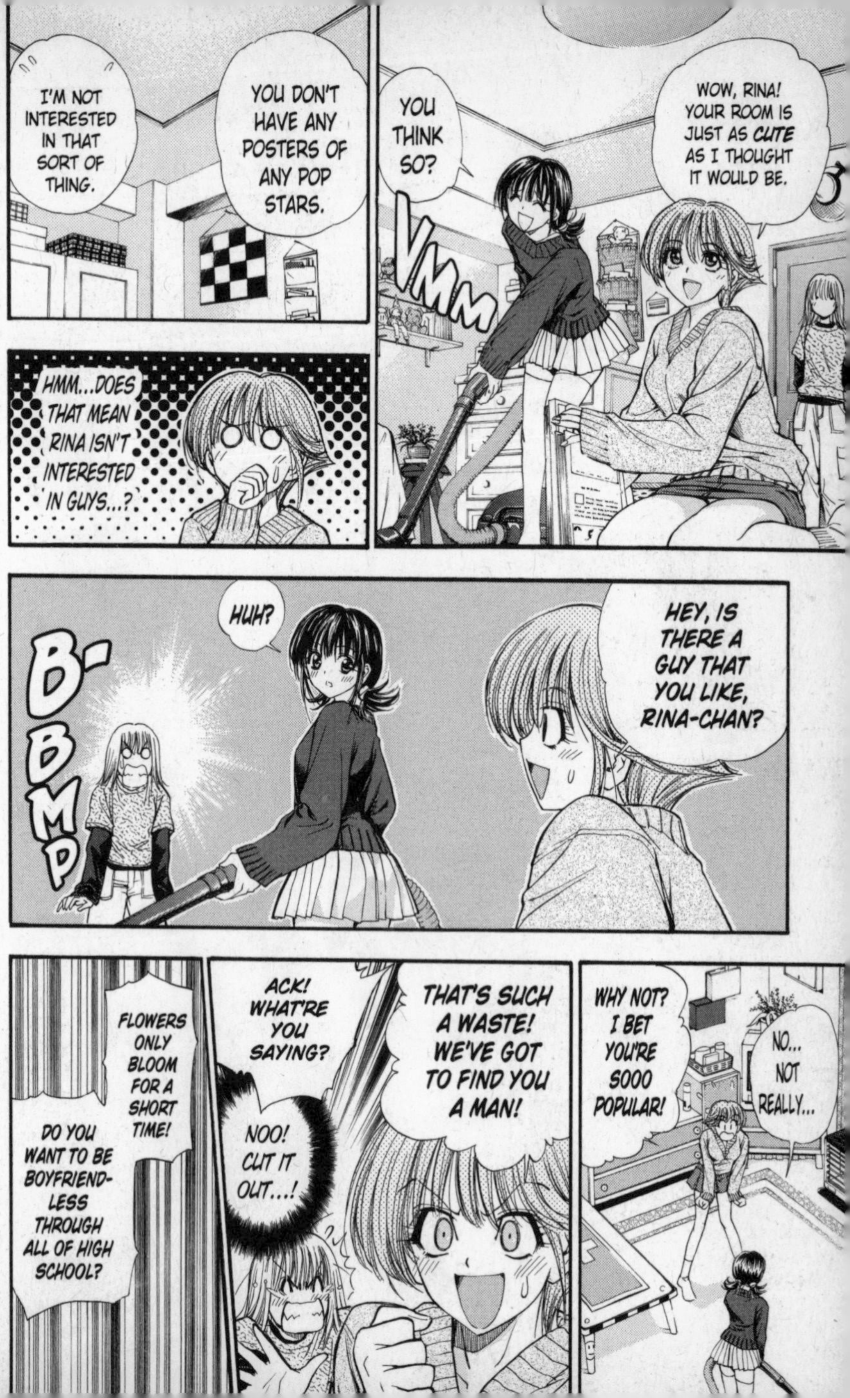
WOW, RINA! YOUR ROOM IS JUST AS CUTE AS I THOUGHT IT WOULD BE.
YOU THINK SO?
VMM
YOU DON'T HAVE ANY POSTERS OF ANY POP STARS.
I'M NOT INTERESTED IN THAT SORT OF THING.
HMM...DOES THAT MEAN RINA ISN'T INTERESTED IN GUYS...?
HEY, IS THERE A GUY THAT YOU LIKE, RINA-CHAN?
HUH?
B-BMP
WHY NOT? I BET YOU'RE SOOO POPULAR!
NO... NOT REALLY...
THAT'S SUCH A WASTE! WE'VE GOT TO FIND YOU A MAN!
ACK! WHAT'RE YOU SAYING?
NOO! CUT IT OUT...!
FLOWERS ONLY BLOOM FOR A SHORT TIME!
DO YOU WANT TO BE BOYFRIEND-LESS THROUGH ALL OF HIGH SCHOOL?

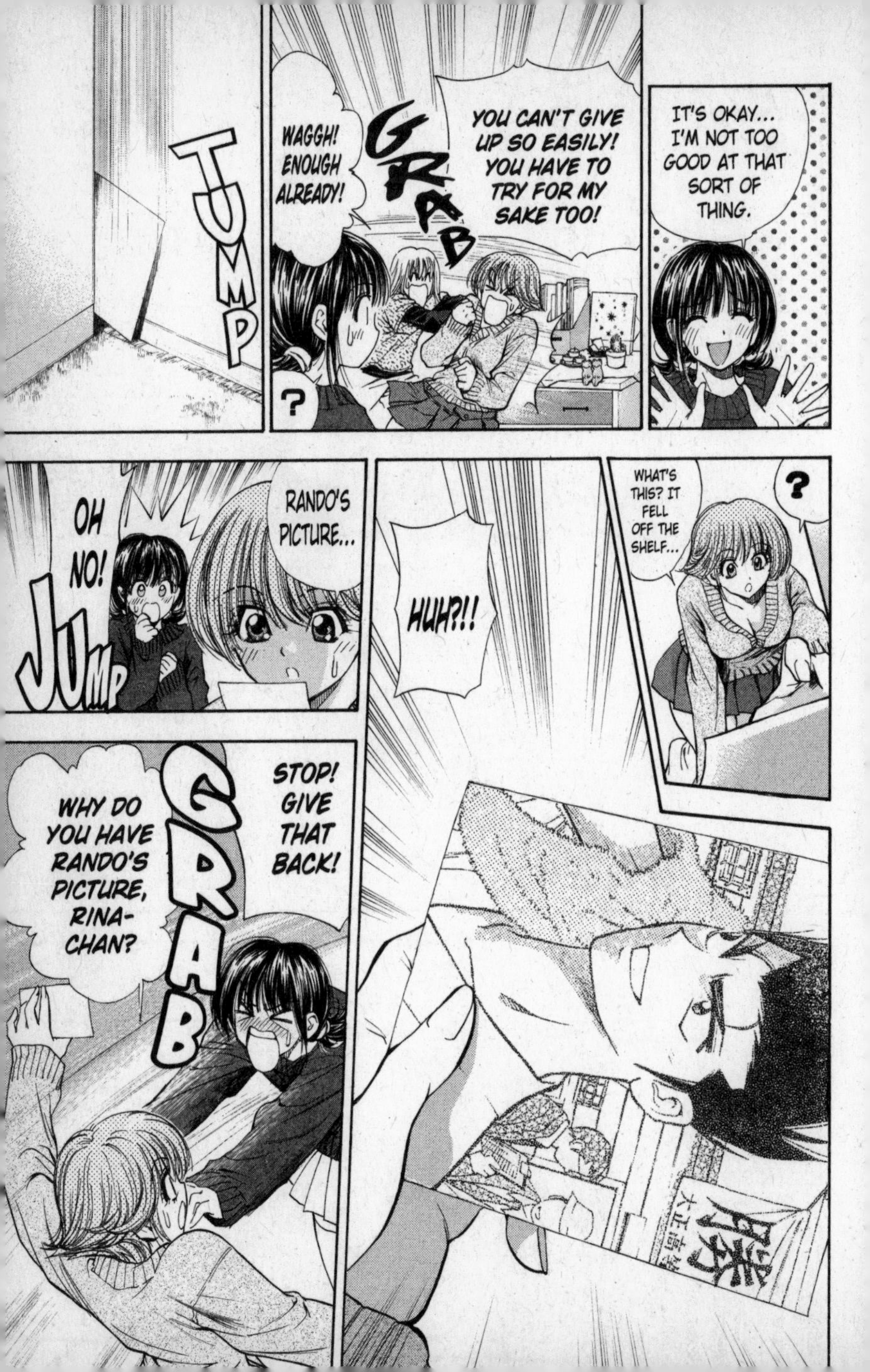
IT'S OKAY... I'M NOT TOO GOOD AT THAT SORT OF THING.
YOU CAN'T GIVE UP SO EASILY! YOU HAVE TO TRY FOR MY SAKE TOO!
GRAB
WAGGH! ENOUGH ALREADY!
?
JUMP
?
WHAT'S THIS? IT FELL OFF THE SHELF...
HUH?!!
RANDO'S PICTURE...
OH NO!
JUMP
STOP! GIVE THAT BACK!
GRAB
WHY DO YOU HAVE RANDO'S PICTURE, RINA-CHAN?

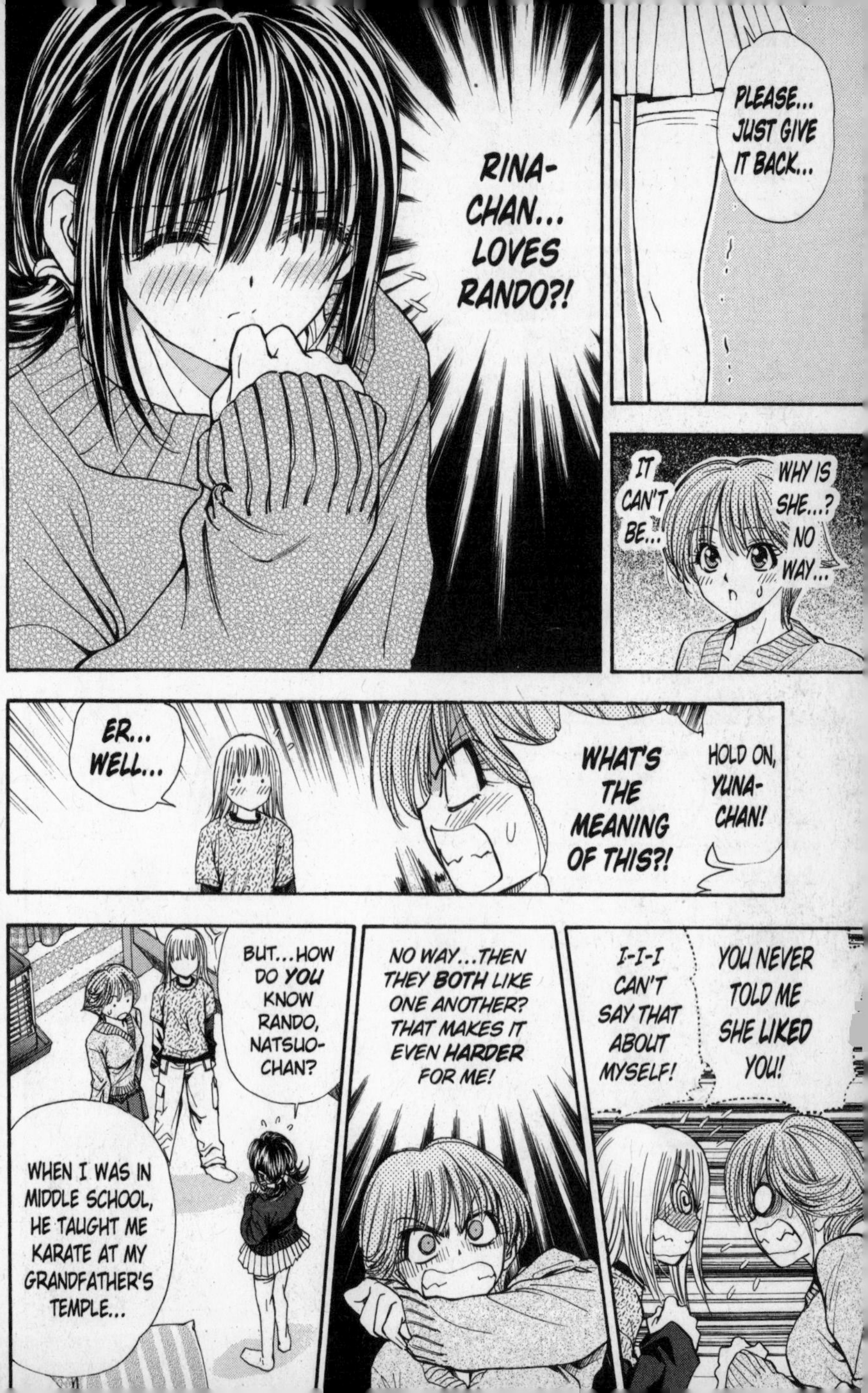
PLEASE... JUST GIVE IT BACK...
WHY IS SHE...? NO WAY...
IT CAN'T BE...
RINA-CHAN... LOVES RANDO?!
HOLD ON, YUNA-CHAN!
WHAT'S THE MEANING OF THIS?!
ER... WELL...
YOU NEVER TOLD ME SHE LIKED YOU!
I-I-I CAN'T SAY THAT ABOUT MYSELF!
NO WAY...THEN THEY BOTH LIKE ONE ANOTHER? THAT MAKES IT EVEN HARDER FOR ME!
BUT...HOW DO YOU KNOW RANDO, NATSUO-CHAN?
WHEN I WAS IN MIDDLE SCHOOL, HE TAUGHT ME KARATE AT MY GRANDFATHER'S TEMPLE...

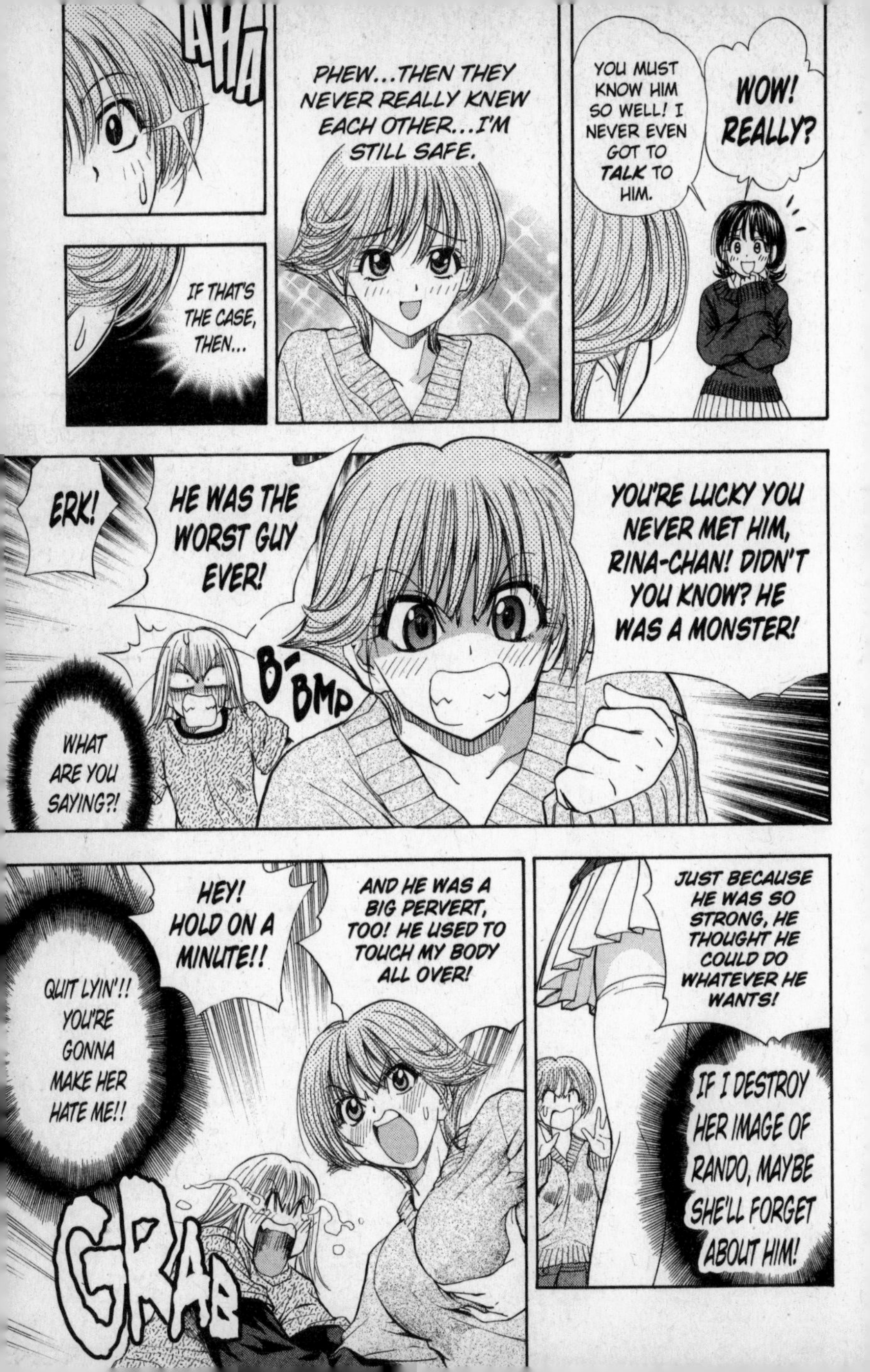
WOW! REALLY?
YOU MUST KNOW HIM SO WELL! I NEVER EVEN GOT TO TALK TO HIM.
PHEW...THEN THEY NEVER REALLY KNEW EACH OTHER...I'M STILL SAFE.
AHA
IF THAT'S THE CASE, THEN...
YOU'RE LUCKY YOU NEVER MET HIM, RINA-CHAN! DIDN'T YOU KNOW? HE WAS A MONSTER!
HE WAS THE WORST GUY EVER!
ERK!
B-BMP
WHAT ARE YOU SAYING?!
JUST BECAUSE HE WAS SO STRONG, HE THOUGHT HE COULD DO WHATEVER HE WANTS!
IF I DESTROY HER IMAGE OF RANDO, MAYBE SHE'LL FORGET ABOUT HIM!
AND HE WAS A BIG PERVERT, TOO! HE USED TO TOUCH MY BODY ALL OVER!
HEY! HOLD ON A MINUTE!!
QUIT LYIN'!! YOU'RE GONNA MAKE HER HATE ME!!
GRAB

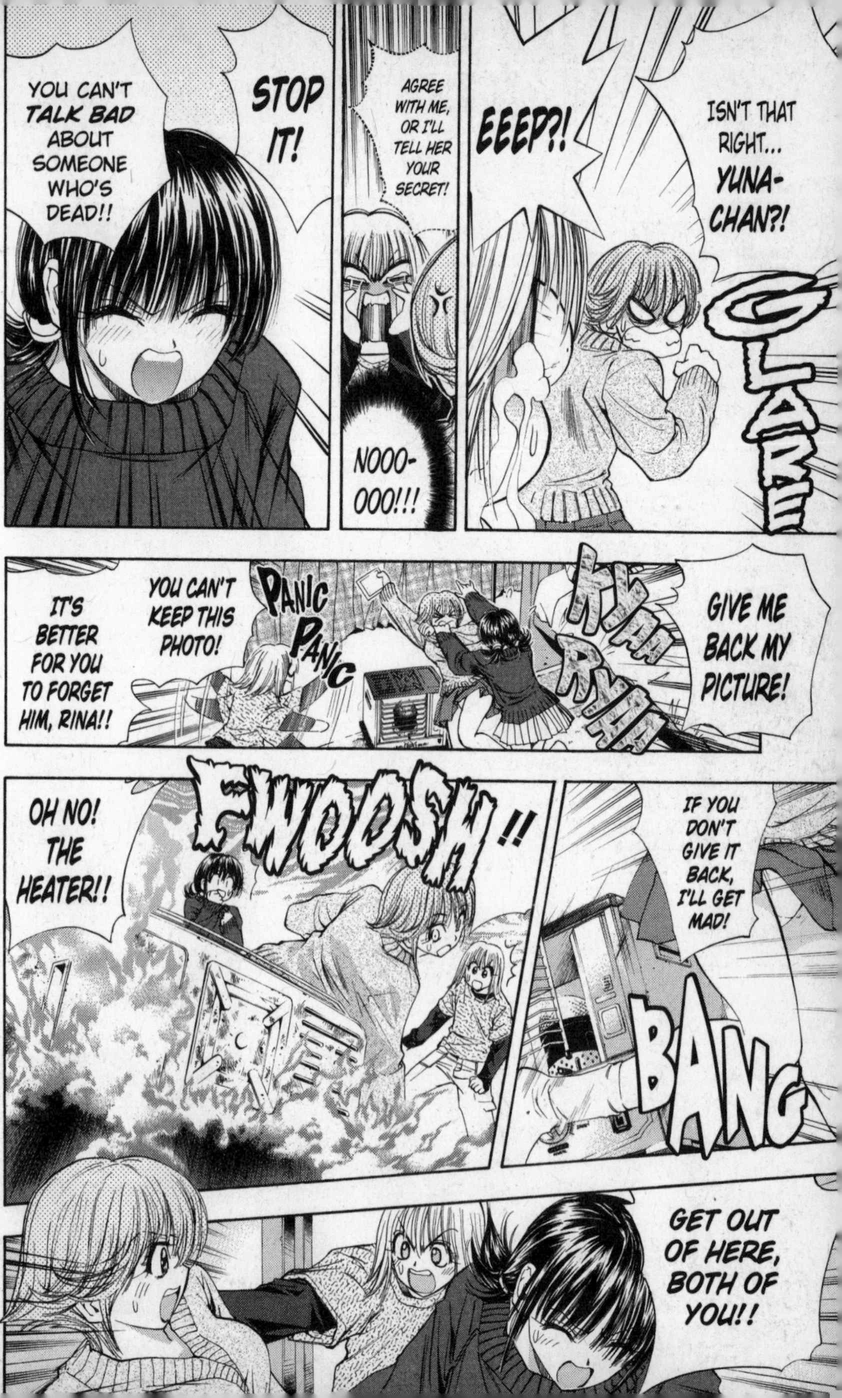
ISN'T THAT RIGHT... YUNA-CHAN?!
EEEP?!
GLARE
AGREE WITH ME, OR I'LL TELL HER YOUR SECRET!
NOOO-OOO!!!
STOP IT!
YOU CAN'T TALK BAD ABOUT SOMEONE WHO'S DEAD!!
GIVE ME BACK MY PICTURE!
PANIC PANIC
YOU CAN'T KEEP THIS PHOTO!
IT'S BETTER FOR YOU TO FORGET HIM, RINA!!
IF YOU DON'T GIVE IT BACK, I'LL GET MAD!
BANG
FWOOSH!!
OH NO! THE HEATER!!
GET OUT OF HERE, BOTH OF YOU!!

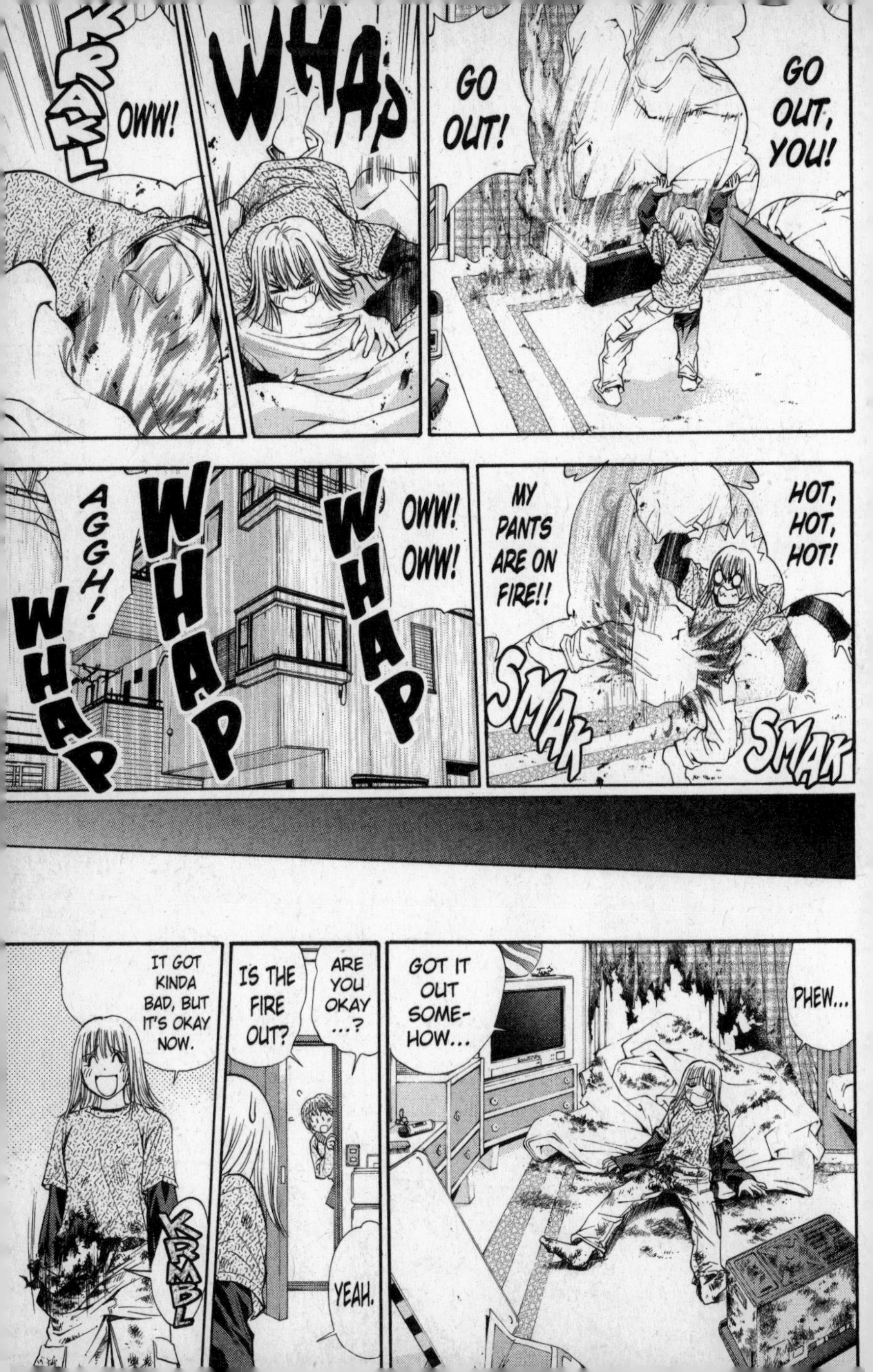
GO OUT, YOU!
GO OUT!
WHAP
KRAKL
OWW!
HOT, HOT, HOT!
MY PANTS ARE ON FIRE!!
SMAK
SMAK
OWW! OWW!
WHAP
WHAP
AGGH!
WHAP
PHEW...
GOT IT OUT SOME-HOW...
ARE YOU OKAY ...?
IS THE FIRE OUT?
YEAH.
IT GOT KINDA BAD, BUT IT'S OKAY NOW.
KRMBL

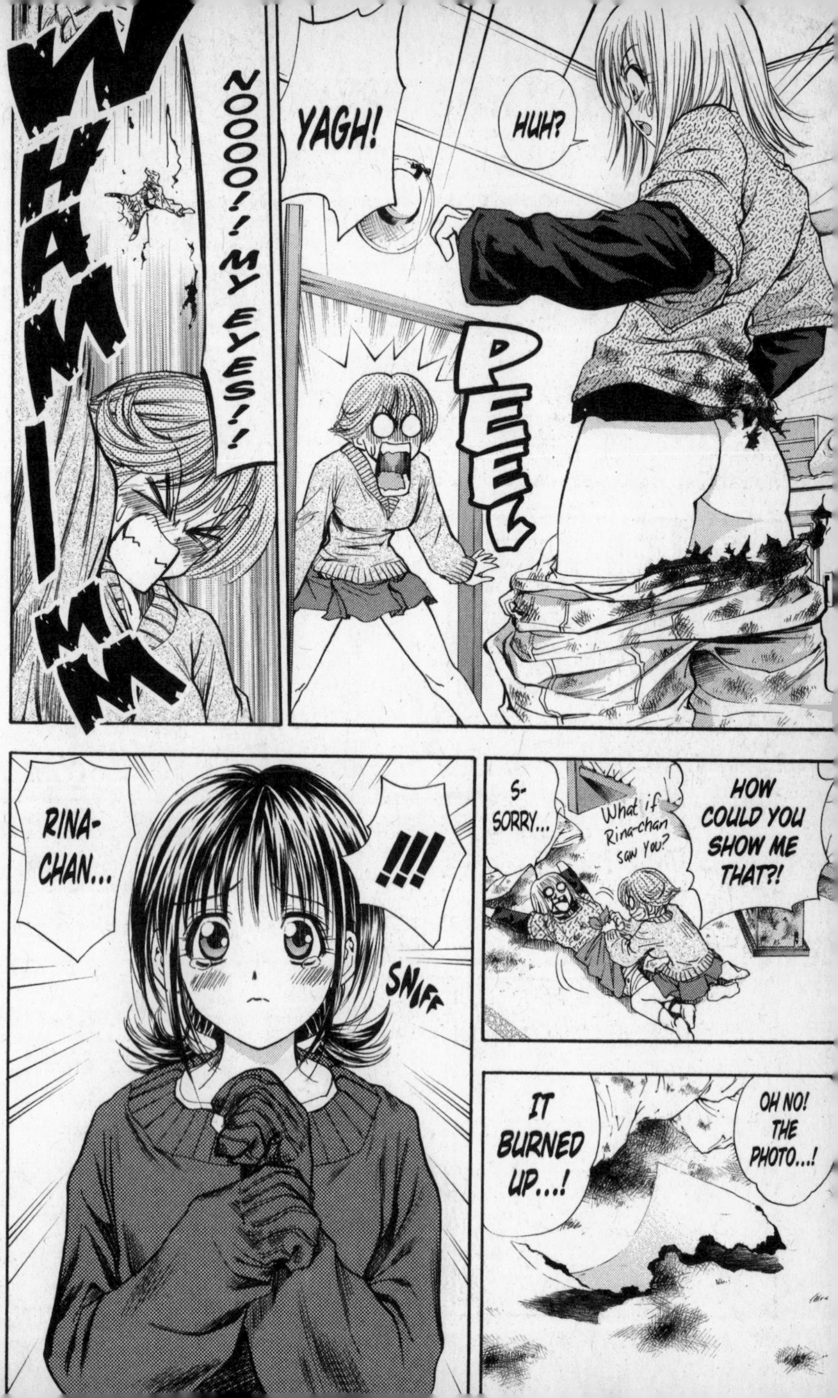
HUH?
YAGH!
PEEL
NOOOOO!! MY EYES!!
WHAMMM
HOW COULD YOU SHOW ME THAT?!
What if Rina-chan saw you?
S-SORRY...
OH NO! THE PHOTO...!
IT BURNED UP...!
!!!
SNIFF
RINA-CHAN...

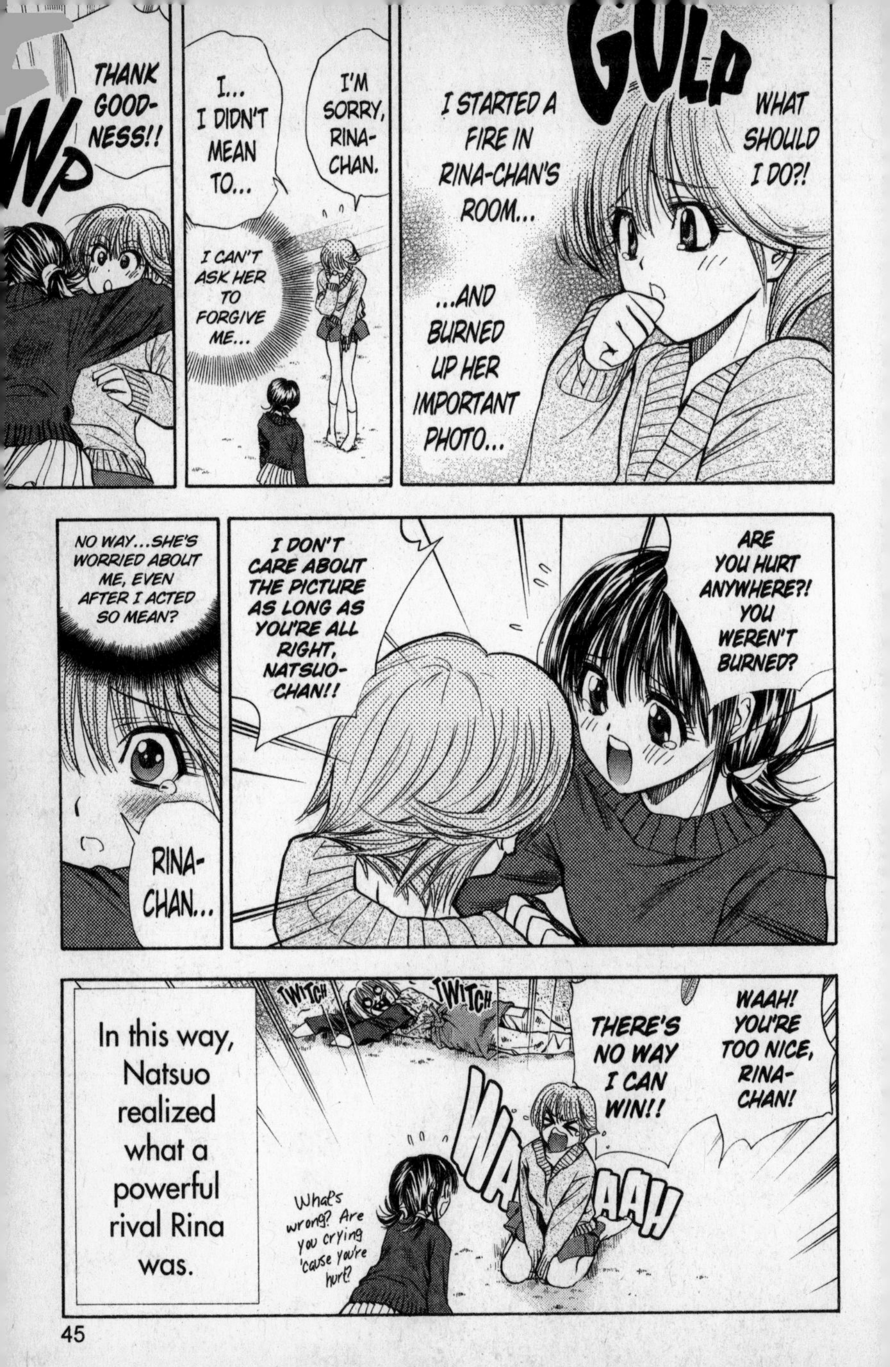
GULP
WHAT SHOULD I DO?!
I STARTED A FIRE IN RINA-CHAN'S ROOM...
...AND BURNED UP HER IMPORTANT PHOTO...
I'M SORRY, RINA-CHAN.
I... I DIDN'T MEAN TO...
I CAN'T ASK HER TO FORGIVE ME...
THANK GOOD-NESS!!
ARE YOU HURT ANYWHERE?! YOU WEREN'T BURNED?
I DON'T CARE ABOUT THE PICTURE AS LONG AS YOU'RE ALL RIGHT, NATSUO-CHAN!!
NO WAY...SHE'S WORRIED ABOUT ME, EVEN AFTER I ACTED SO MEAN?
RINA-CHAN...
WAAH! YOU'RE TOO NICE, RINA-CHAN!
THERE'S NO WAY I CAN WIN!!
TWITCH
TWITCH
WAAAAH
What's wrong? Are you crying 'cause you're hurt?
In this way, Natsuo realized what a powerful rival Rina was.

BONUS: REJECTED STORIES (part 2)

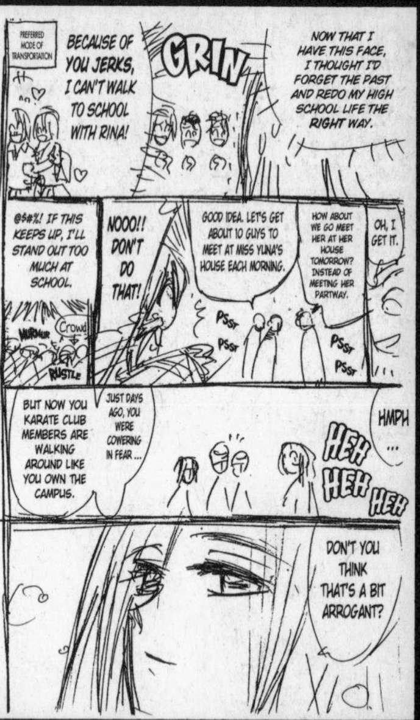
NOW THAT I HAVE THIS FACE, I THOUGHT I'D FORGET THE PAST AND REDO MY HIGH SCHOOL LIFE THE RIGHT WAY.
GRIN
BECAUSE OF YOU JERKS, I CAN'T WALK TO SCHOOL WITH RINA!
PREFERRED MODE OF TRANSPORTATION
OH, I GET IT.
HOW ABOUT WE GO MEET HER AT HER HOUSE TOMORROW? INSTEAD OF MEETING HER PARTWAY.
GOOD IDEA. LET'S GET ABOUT 10 GUYS TO MEET AT MISS YUNA'S HOUSE EACH MORNING.
PSST
PSST
PSST
PSST
NOOO!! DON'T DO THAT!
@$#%! IF THIS KEEPS UP, I'LL STAND OUT TOO MUCH AT SCHOOL.
MURMUR
Crowd
RUSTLE
HMPH...
HEH HEH HEH
JUST DAYS AGO, YOU WERE COWERING IN FEAR...
BUT NOW YOU KARATE CLUB MEMBERS ARE WALKING AROUND LIKE YOU OWN THE CAMPUS.
DON'T YOU THINK THAT'S A BIT ARROGANT?

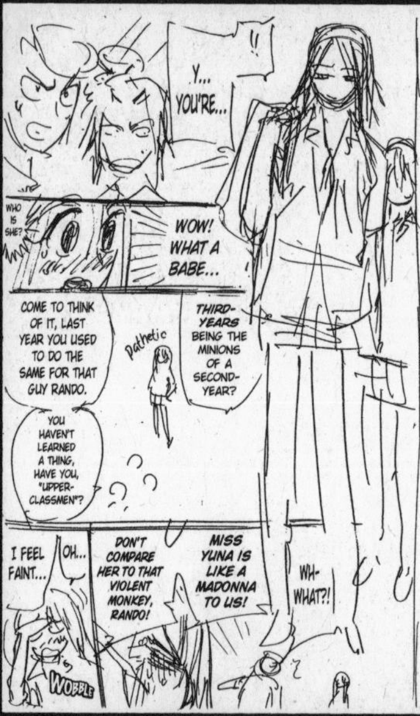
!!
Y... YOU'RE...
WOW! WHAT A BABE...
WHO IS SHE?
THIRD-YEARS BEING THE MINIONS OF A SECOND-YEAR?
Pathetic
COME TO THINK OF IT, LAST YEAR YOU USED TO DO THE SAME FOR THAT GUY RANDO.
YOU HAVEN'T LEARNED A THING, HAVE YOU, "UPPER-CLASSMEN"?
WH-WHAT?!
MISS YUNA IS LIKE A MADONNA TO US!
DON'T COMPARE HER TO THAT VIOLENT MONKEY, RANDO!
OH...
I FEEL FAINT...
WOBBLE

THIS WAS A CANCELED STORY FROM THE BEGINNING OF THE SERIES. IT'S A STORY ABOUT THE YOUNGER SISTER OF THE JUDO CLUB CAPTAIN, YAMAKAMI. HER NAME WAS AI YAMAKAMI AND SHE WAS THE CAPTAIN OF THE GIRL'S JUDO CLUB. AS THE STORY WENT, AFTER THIS SHE DRAGGED RANDO TO THE CLUB TO GET REVENGE FOR HER BROTHER, BUT I COULDN'T QUITE PULL IT TOGETHER SO IT WAS REJECTED. ALSO, AT THIS POINT KEIKO WAS IN THE JUDO CLUB. MY CONCEPT FOR AI WAS THAT SHE WOULD BE A GIRL WHO USED TO LIKE THE MALE RANDO, SO IN A WAY SHE BECAME THE ORIGINAL FOR NATSUO.

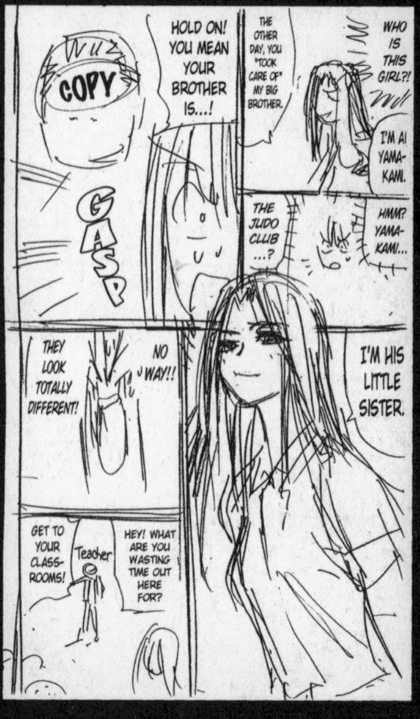
WHO IS THIS GIRL?!
I'M AI YAMA-KAMI.
THE OTHER DAY, YOU "TOOK CARE OF" MY BIG BROTHER.
HOLD ON! YOU MEAN YOUR BROTHER IS...!
COPY
HMM? YAMA-KAMI...
THE JUDO CLUB...?
GASP
I'M HIS LITTLE SISTER.
NO WAY!!
THEY LOOK TOTALLY DIFFERENT!
HEY! WHAT ARE YOU WASTING TIME OUT HERE FOR?
Teacher
GET TO YOUR CLASS-ROOMS!

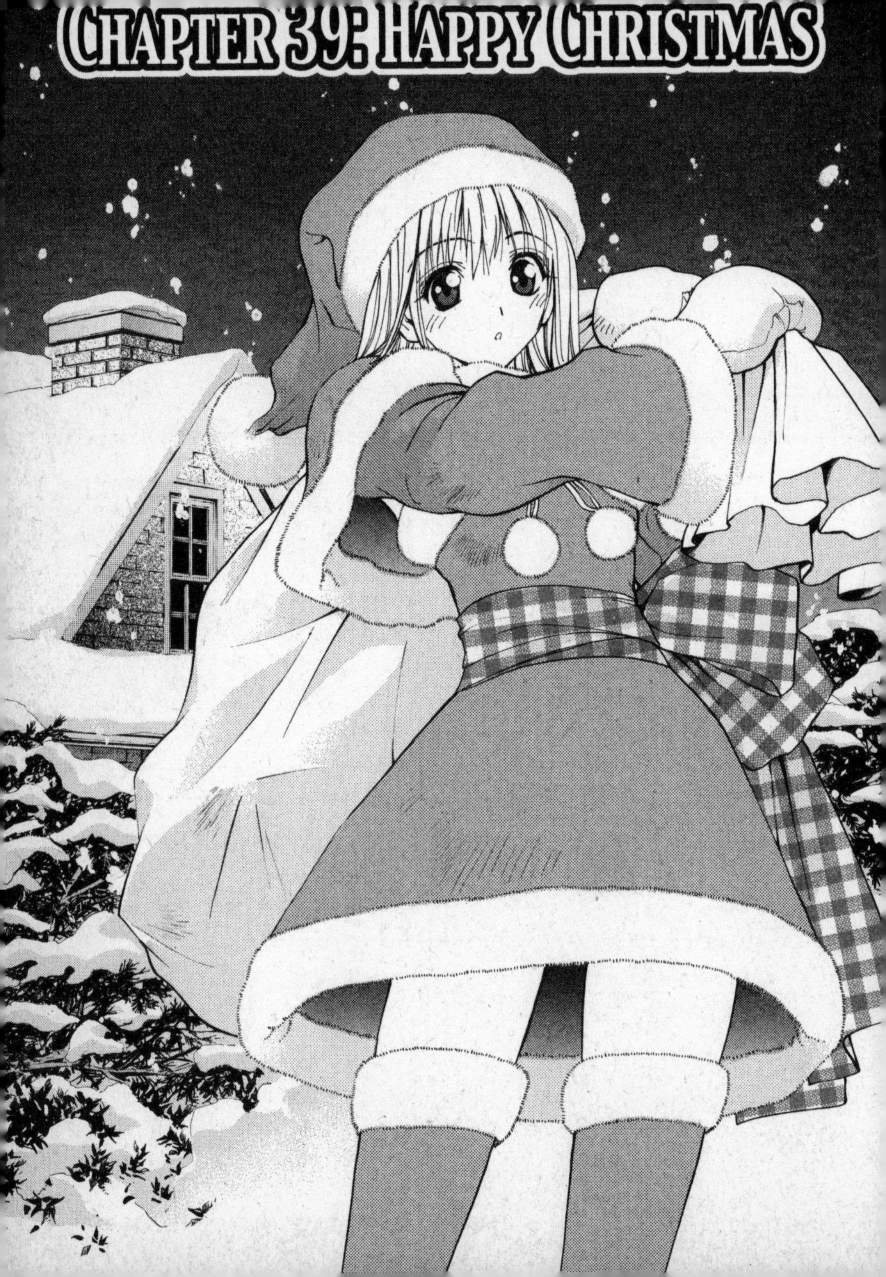
CHAPTER 39: HAPPY CHRISTMAS

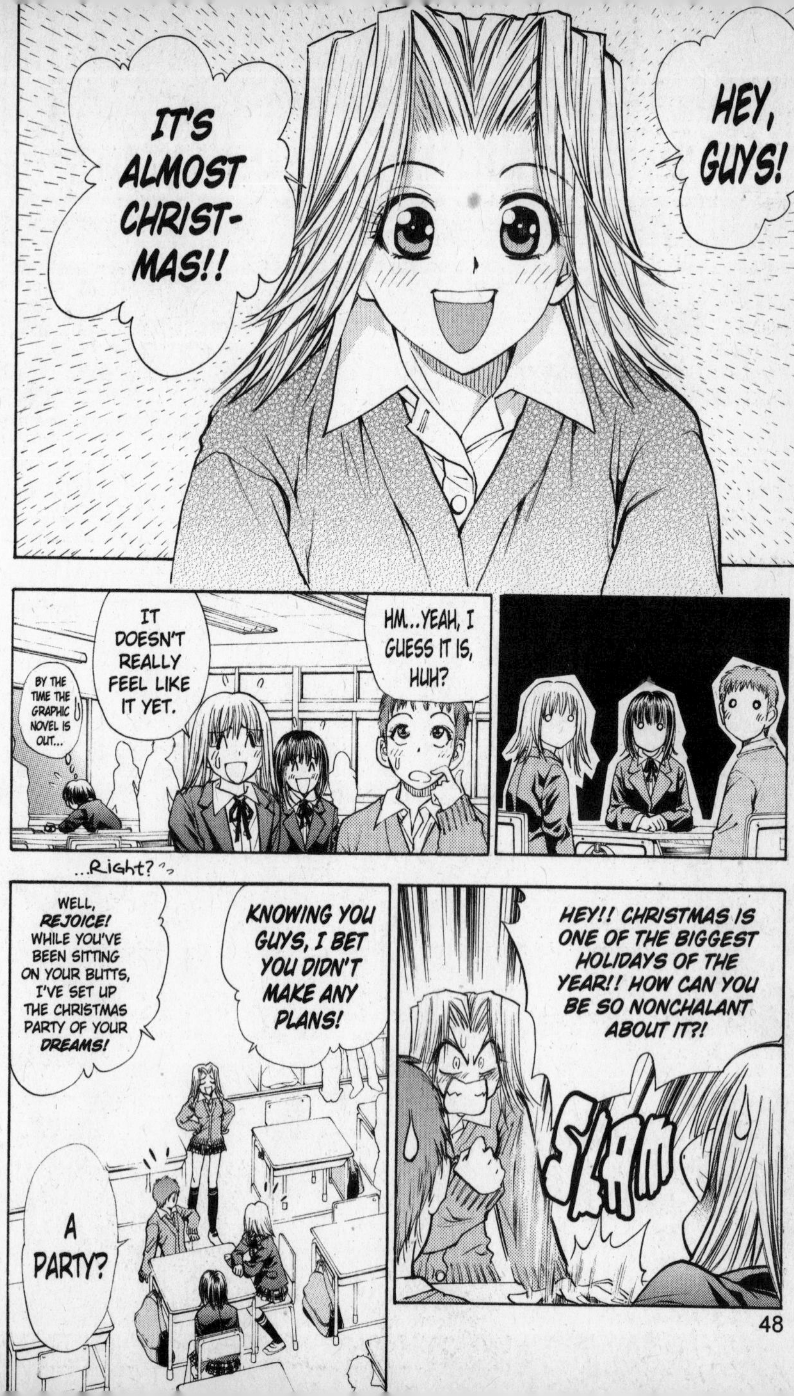
HEY, GUYS!
IT'S ALMOST CHRISTMAS!!
HM...YEAH, I GUESS IT IS, HUH?
IT DOESN'T REALLY FEEL LIKE IT YET.
BY THE TIME THE GRAPHIC NOVEL IS OUT...
...Right?
HEY!! CHRISTMAS IS ONE OF THE BIGGEST HOLIDAYS OF THE YEAR!! HOW CAN YOU BE SO NONCHALANT ABOUT IT?!
SLAM
KNOWING YOU GUYS, I BET YOU DIDN'T MAKE ANY PLANS!
WELL, REJOICE! WHILE YOU'VE BEEN SITTING ON YOUR BUTTS, I'VE SET UP THE CHRISTMAS PARTY OF YOUR DREAMS!
A PARTY?

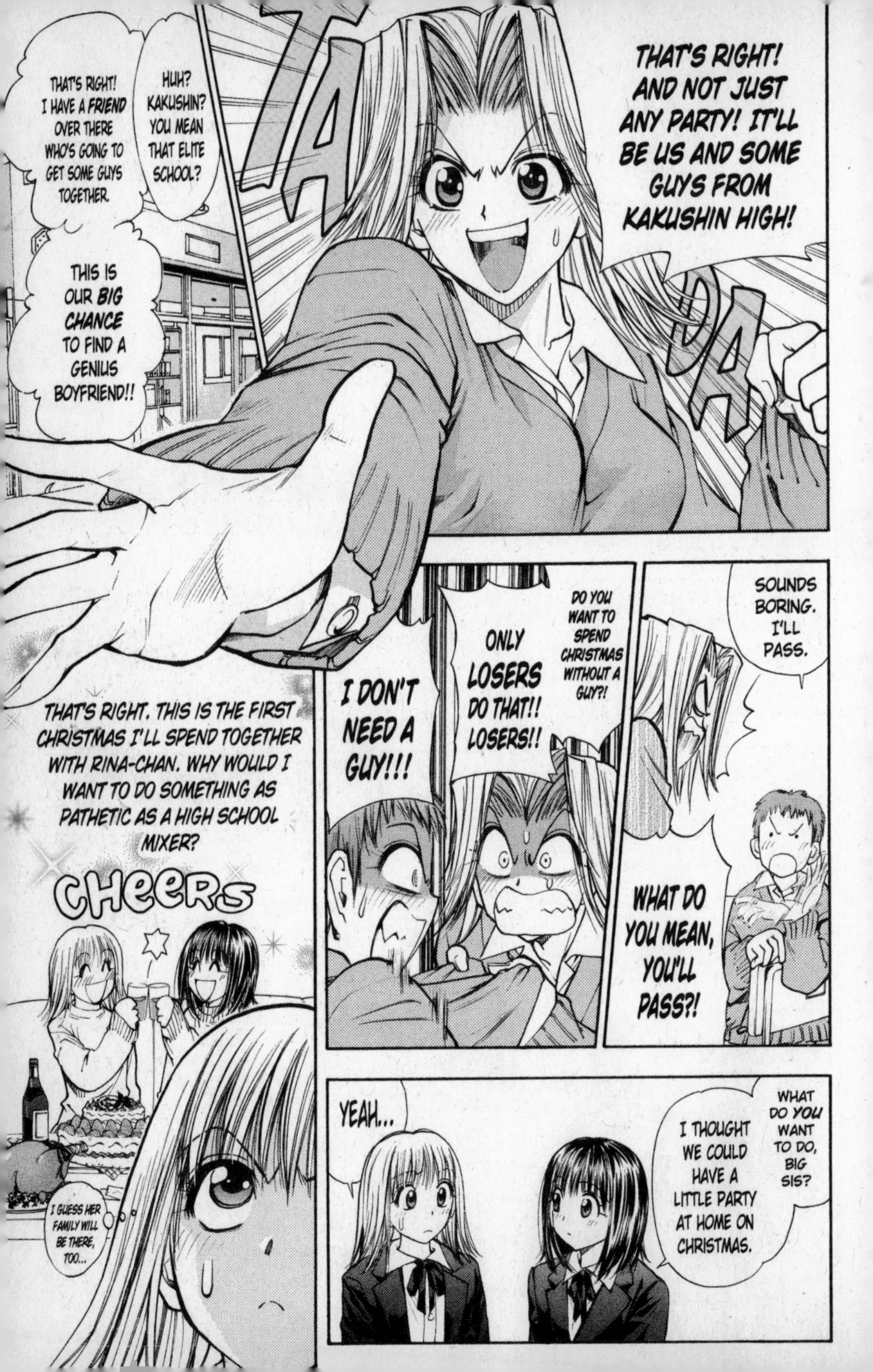
TA
THAT'S RIGHT! AND NOT JUST ANY PARTY! IT'LL BE US AND SOME GUYS FROM KAKUSHIN HIGH!
DA
HUH? KAKUSHIN? YOU MEAN THAT ELITE SCHOOL?
THAT'S RIGHT! I HAVE A FRIEND OVER THERE WHO'S GOING TO GET SOME GUYS TOGETHER.
THIS IS OUR BIG CHANCE TO FIND A GENIUS BOYFRIEND!!
SOUNDS BORING. I'LL PASS.
WHAT DO YOU MEAN, YOU'LL PASS?!
DO YOU WANT TO SPEND CHRISTMAS WITHOUT A GUY?!
ONLY LOSERS DO THAT!! LOSERS!!
I DON'T NEED A GUY!!!
WHAT DO YOU WANT TO DO, BIG SIS?
I THOUGHT WE COULD HAVE A LITTLE PARTY AT HOME ON CHRISTMAS.
YEAH...
THAT'S RIGHT. THIS IS THE FIRST CHRISTMAS I'LL SPEND TOGETHER WITH RINA-CHAN. WHY WOULD I WANT TO DO SOMETHING AS PATHETIC AS A HIGH SCHOOL MIXER?
CHEERS
I GUESS HER FAMILY WILL BE THERE, TOO...

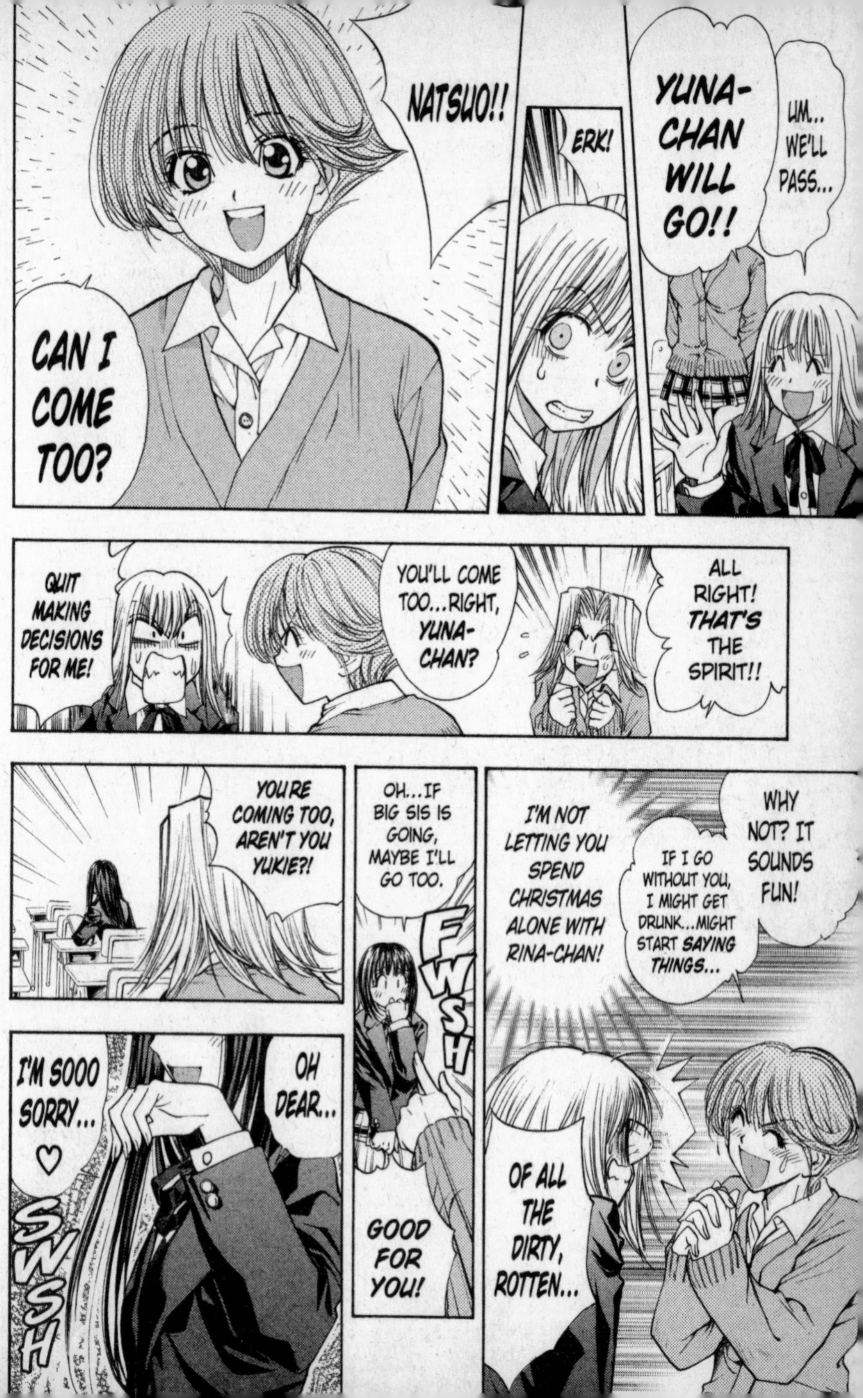
YUNA-CHAN WILL GO!!
UM... WE'LL PASS...
ERK!
NATSUO!!
CAN I COME TOO?
ALL RIGHT! THAT'S THE SPIRIT!!
YOU'LL COME TOO...RIGHT, YUNA-CHAN?
QUIT MAKING DECISIONS FOR ME!
WHY NOT? IT SOUNDS FUN!
IF I GO WITHOUT YOU, I MIGHT GET DRUNK...MIGHT START SAYING THINGS...
I'M NOT LETTING YOU SPEND CHRISTMAS ALONE WITH RINA-CHAN!
OF ALL THE DIRTY, ROTTEN...
OH...IF BIG SIS IS GOING, MAYBE I'LL GO TOO.
FWSH
GOOD FOR YOU!
YOU'RE COMING TOO, AREN'T YOU YUKIE?!
OH DEAR...
I'M SOOO SORRY... ♡
SWSH

YOU THINK JUST 'CAUSE YOU'VE GOT A BOYFRIEND, YOU CAN FORGET ABOUT YOUR FRIENDS?!

HEY! WHAT'S WITH THAT ATTITUDE?!

I HOPE YOU HAVE A LOT OF FUN. ♡

I ALREADY HAVE PLANS WITH MY BOYFRIEND.

SULK

PING

OH, I DON'T MEAN IT *THAT* WAY.

YUKIE	STATUS
The only one in the group with a boyfriend.	

WHO'S A DOG?! YOU'VE NEVER MET HIM!

GRAAH

DON'T REGRET IT WHEN WE'RE GOING OUT WITH DROP DEAD GORGEOUS GUYS!!

HUH! SO WHY DON'T YOU JUST LIVE IT UP WITH YOUR DOG OF A BOYFRIEND!

GRAAH

GRAAH

...we all got together on Christmas Eve.

And so...

@#%$! WHAT DO YOU MEAN BY THAT?!!

GRAAH

WHAT ABOUT ALL THE GUYS YOU MACK ON JUST TO MAKE IT LOOK LIKE YOU HAVE A BOYFRIEND?!!

A CHRISTMAS PARTY... THAT COULD BE FUN.

I GUESS...

She's gonna make me go, isn't she...?

GRAAH

I don't like the sound of this.

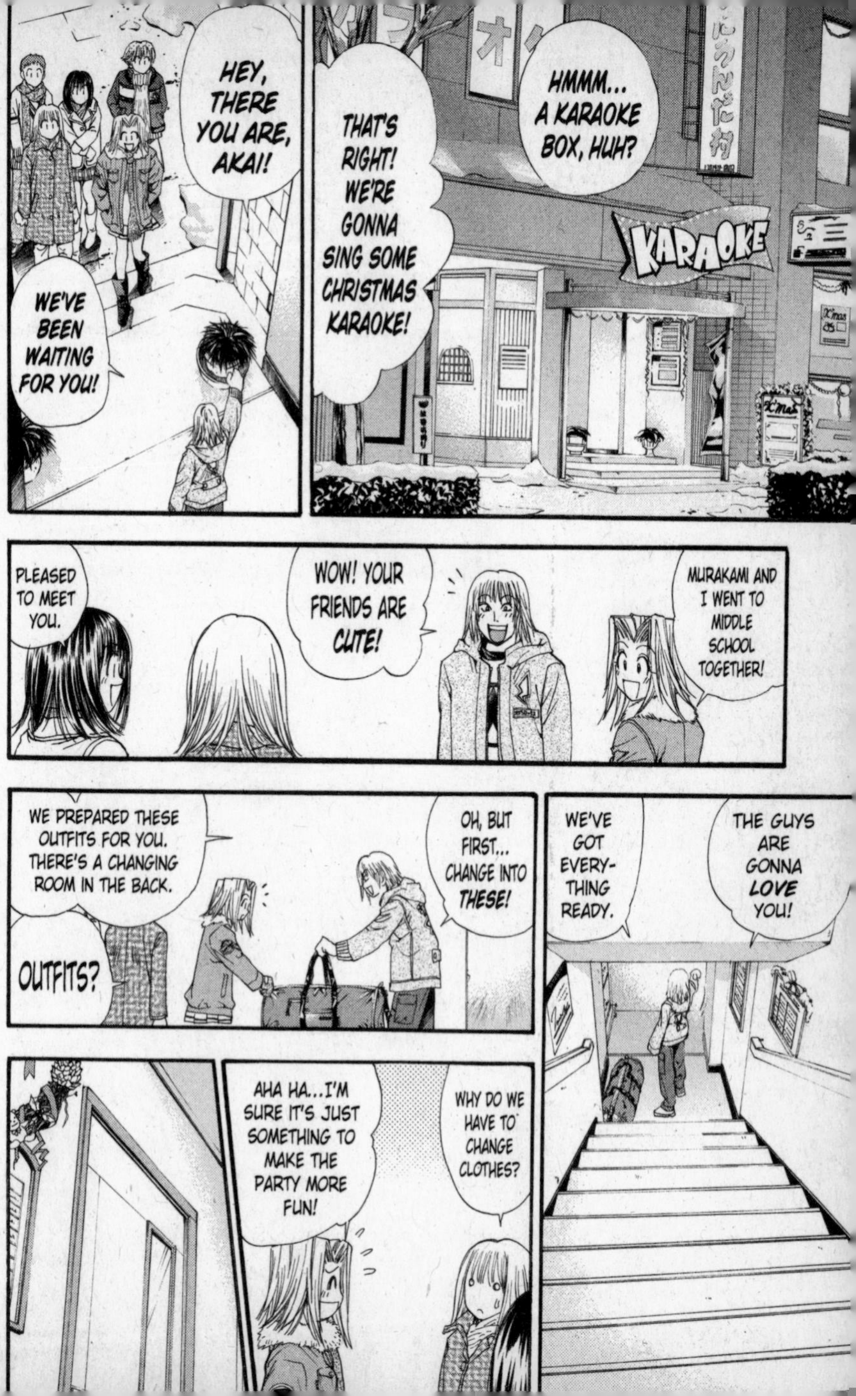
HMMM... A KARAOKE BOX, HUH?
THAT'S RIGHT! WE'RE GONNA SING SOME CHRISTMAS KARAOKE!
KARAOKE
HEY, THERE YOU ARE, AKAI!
WE'VE BEEN WAITING FOR YOU!
MURAKAMI AND I WENT TO MIDDLE SCHOOL TOGETHER!
WOW! YOUR FRIENDS ARE CUTE!
PLEASED TO MEET YOU.
THE GUYS ARE GONNA LOVE YOU!
WE'VE GOT EVERYTHING READY.
OH, BUT FIRST... CHANGE INTO THESE!
WE PREPARED THESE OUTFITS FOR YOU. THERE'S A CHANGING ROOM IN THE BACK.
OUTFITS?
WHY DO WE HAVE TO CHANGE CLOTHES?
AHA HA...I'M SURE IT'S JUST SOMETHING TO MAKE THE PARTY MORE FUN!

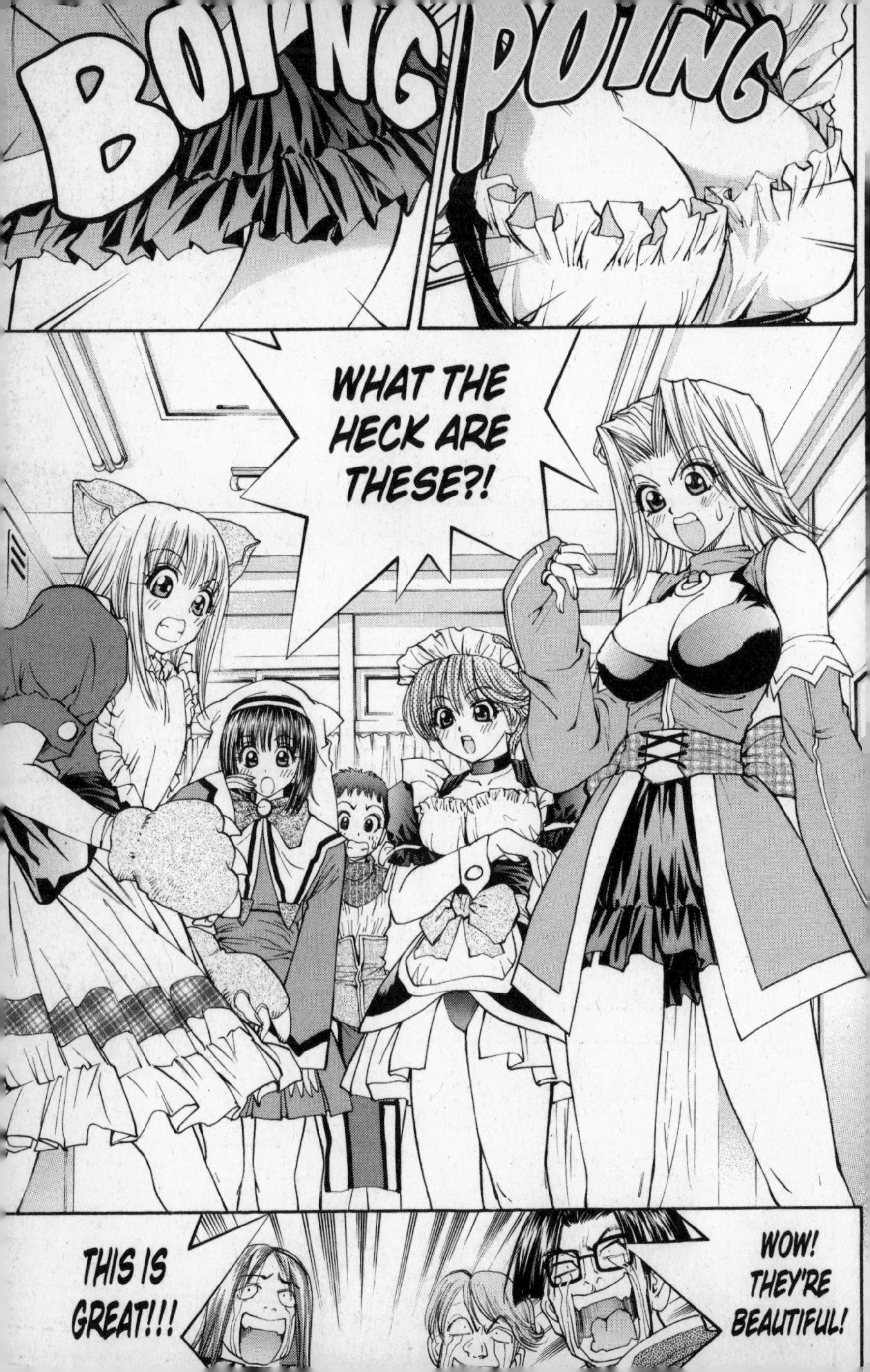
POING
BOING
WHAT THE HECK ARE THESE?!
WOW! THEY'RE BEAUTIFUL!
THIS IS GREAT!!!

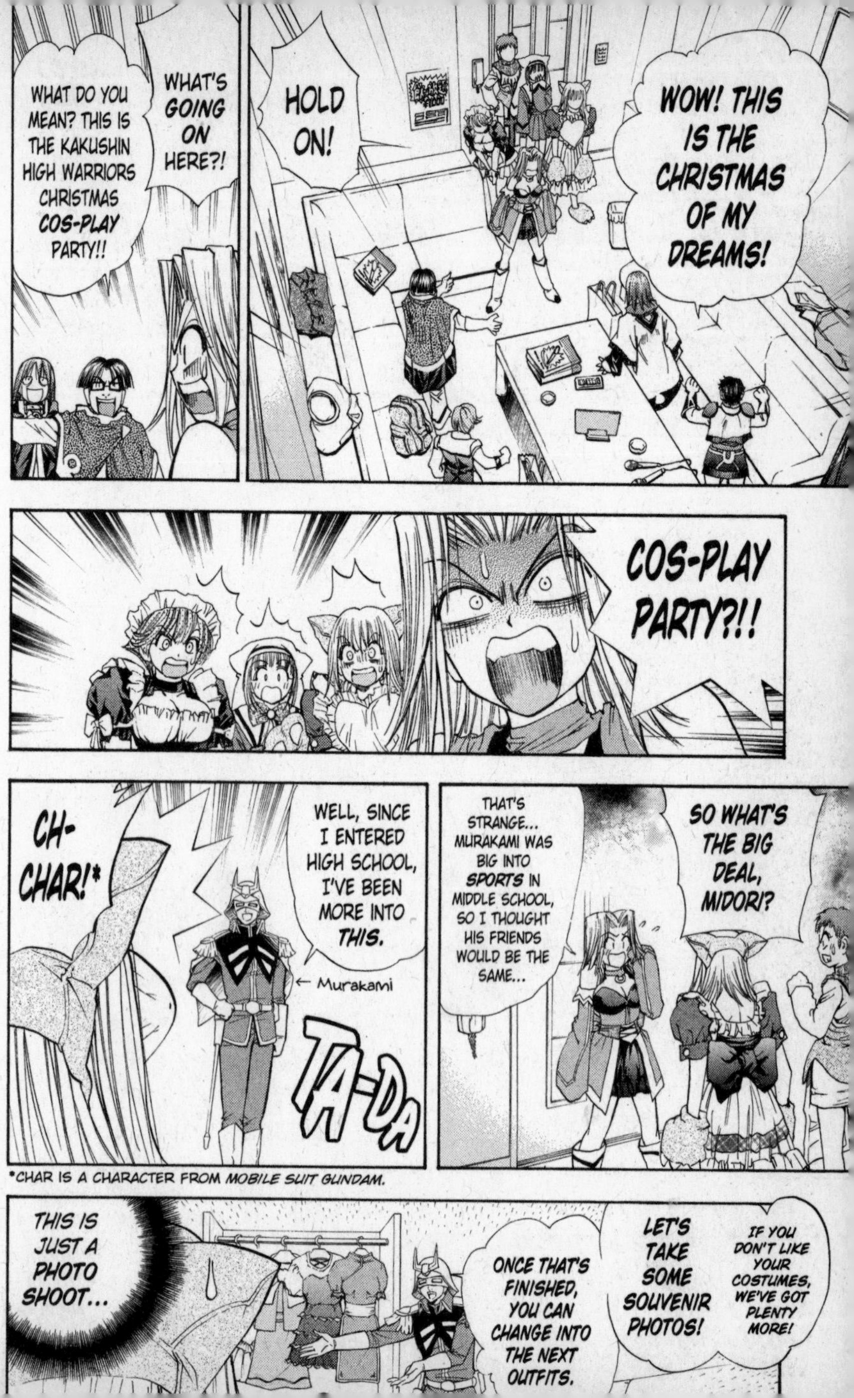
WOW! THIS IS THE CHRISTMAS OF MY DREAMS!
HOLD ON!
WHAT'S GOING ON HERE?!
WHAT DO YOU MEAN? THIS IS THE KAKUSHIN HIGH WARRIORS CHRISTMAS COS-PLAY PARTY!!
COS-PLAY PARTY?!!
SO WHAT'S THE BIG DEAL, MIDORI?
THAT'S STRANGE... MURAKAMI WAS BIG INTO SPORTS IN MIDDLE SCHOOL, SO I THOUGHT HIS FRIENDS WOULD BE THE SAME...
WELL, SINCE I ENTERED HIGH SCHOOL, I'VE BEEN MORE INTO THIS.
CH-CHAR!*
← Murakami
TA-DA
IF YOU DON'T LIKE YOUR COSTUMES, WE'VE GOT PLENTY MORE!
LET'S TAKE SOME SOUVENIR PHOTOS!
ONCE THAT'S FINISHED, YOU CAN CHANGE INTO THE NEXT OUTFITS.
THIS IS JUST A PHOTO SHOOT...

*CHAR IS A CHARACTER FROM *MOBILE SUIT GUNDAM*.

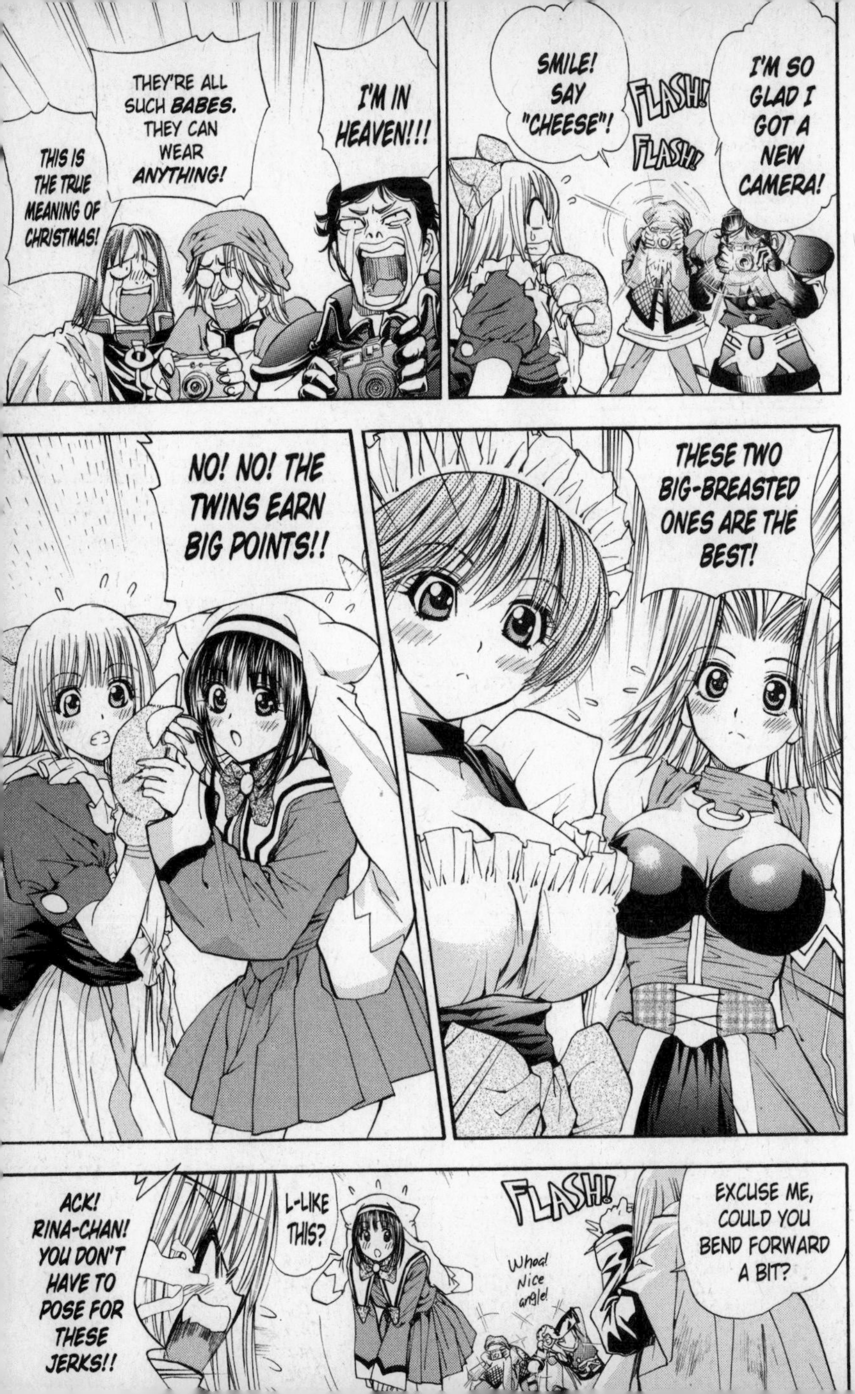
I'M SO GLAD I GOT A NEW CAMERA!
FLASH!
FLASH!
SMILE! SAY "CHEESE"!
I'M IN HEAVEN!!!
THEY'RE ALL SUCH BABES. THEY CAN WEAR ANYTHING!
THIS IS THE TRUE MEANING OF CHRISTMAS!
THESE TWO BIG-BREASTED ONES ARE THE BEST!
NO! NO! THE TWINS EARN BIG POINTS!!
EXCUSE ME, COULD YOU BEND FORWARD A BIT?
FLASH!
Whoa! Nice angle!
L-LIKE THIS?
ACK! RINA-CHAN! YOU DON'T HAVE TO POSE FOR THESE JERKS!!

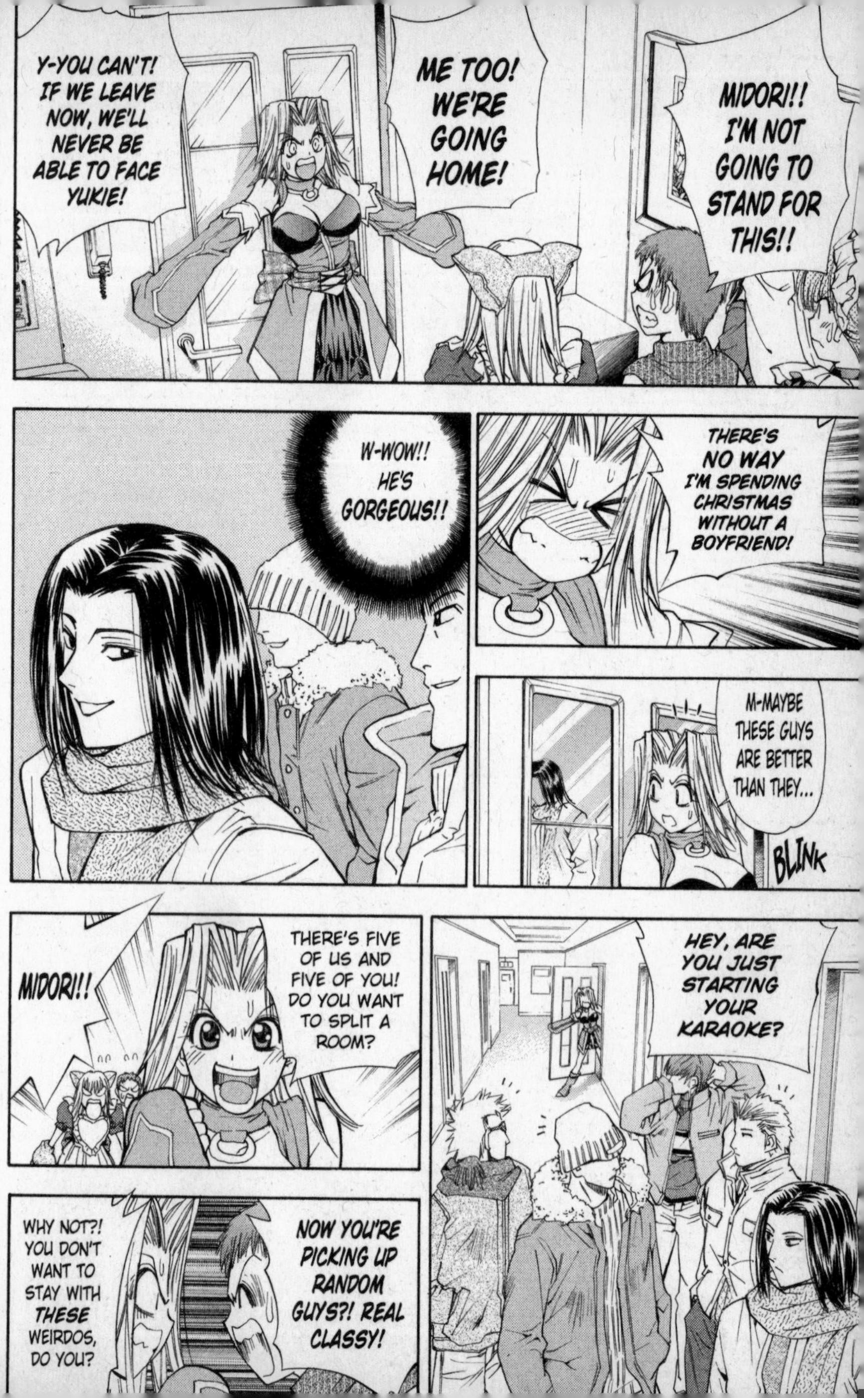
MIDORI!! I'M NOT GOING TO STAND FOR THIS!!
ME TOO! WE'RE GOING HOME!
Y-YOU CAN'T! IF WE LEAVE NOW, WE'LL NEVER BE ABLE TO FACE YUKIE!
THERE'S NO WAY I'M SPENDING CHRISTMAS WITHOUT A BOYFRIEND!
M-MAYBE THESE GUYS ARE BETTER THAN THEY...
BLINK
W-WOW!! HE'S GORGEOUS!!
HEY, ARE YOU JUST STARTING YOUR KARAOKE?
THERE'S FIVE OF US AND FIVE OF YOU! DO YOU WANT TO SPLIT A ROOM?
MIDORI!!
NOW YOU'RE PICKING UP RANDOM GUYS?! REAL CLASSY!
WHY NOT?! YOU DON'T WANT TO STAY WITH THESE WEIRDOS, DO YOU?

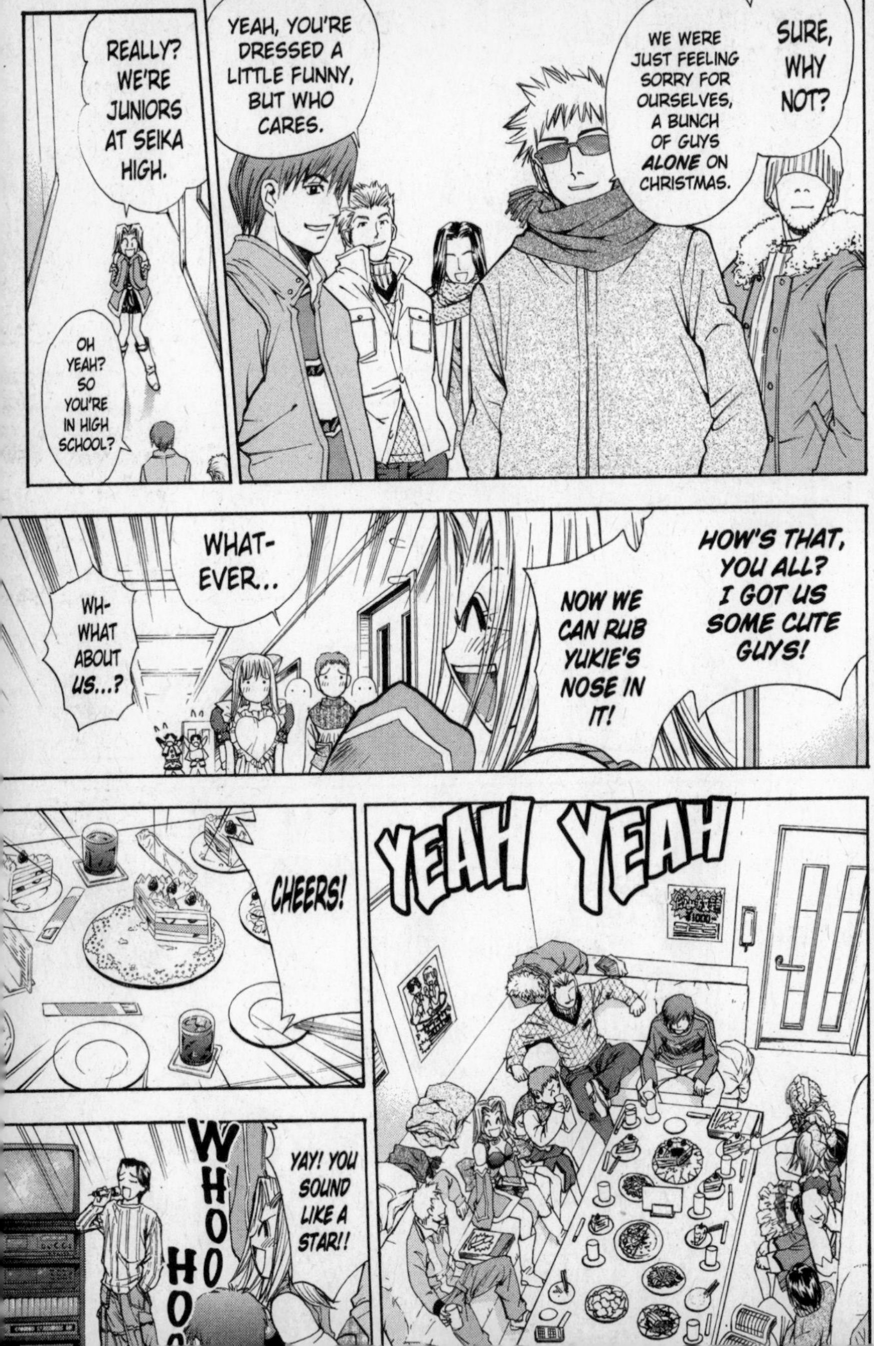
SURE, WHY NOT?
WE WERE JUST FEELING SORRY FOR OURSELVES, A BUNCH OF GUYS *ALONE* ON CHRISTMAS.
YEAH, YOU'RE DRESSED A LITTLE FUNNY, BUT WHO CARES.
REALLY? WE'RE JUNIORS AT SEIKA HIGH.
OH YEAH? SO YOU'RE IN HIGH SCHOOL?
HOW'S THAT, YOU ALL? I GOT US SOME CUTE GUYS!
NOW WE CAN RUB YUKIE'S NOSE IN IT!
WHAT-EVER...
WH-WHAT ABOUT US...?
YEAH YEAH
CHEERS!
YAY! YOU SOUND LIKE A STAR!!
WHOO
HOO

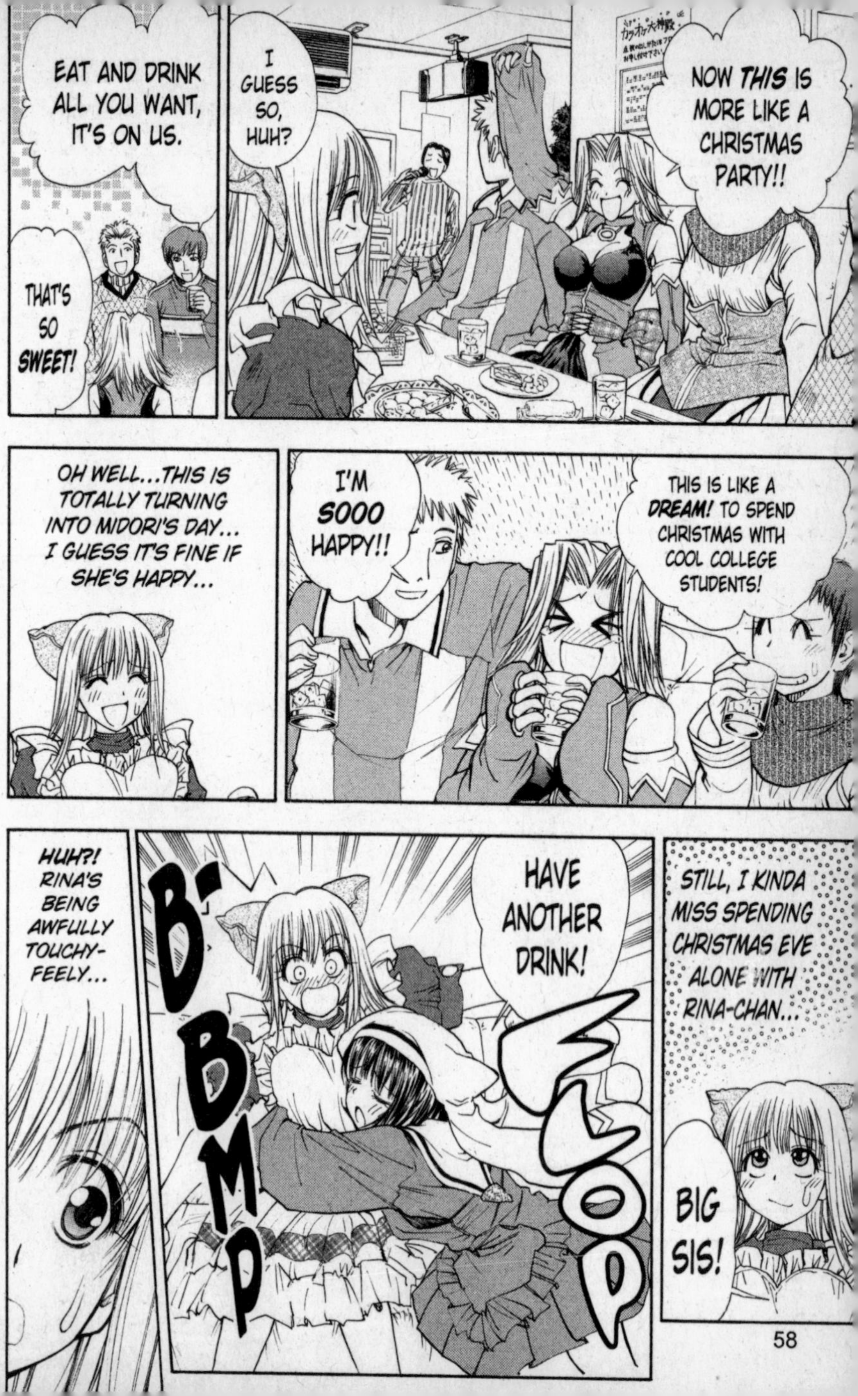
NOW THIS IS MORE LIKE A CHRISTMAS PARTY!!
I GUESS SO, HUH?
EAT AND DRINK ALL YOU WANT, IT'S ON US.
THAT'S SO SWEET!
THIS IS LIKE A DREAM! TO SPEND CHRISTMAS WITH COOL COLLEGE STUDENTS!
I'M SOOO HAPPY!!
OH WELL...THIS IS TOTALLY TURNING INTO MIDORI'S DAY... I GUESS IT'S FINE IF SHE'S HAPPY...
STILL, I KINDA MISS SPENDING CHRISTMAS EVE ALONE WITH RINA-CHAN...
BIG SIS!
HAVE ANOTHER DRINK!
B-BMP
HUH?! RINA'S BEING AWFULLY TOUCHY-FEELY...

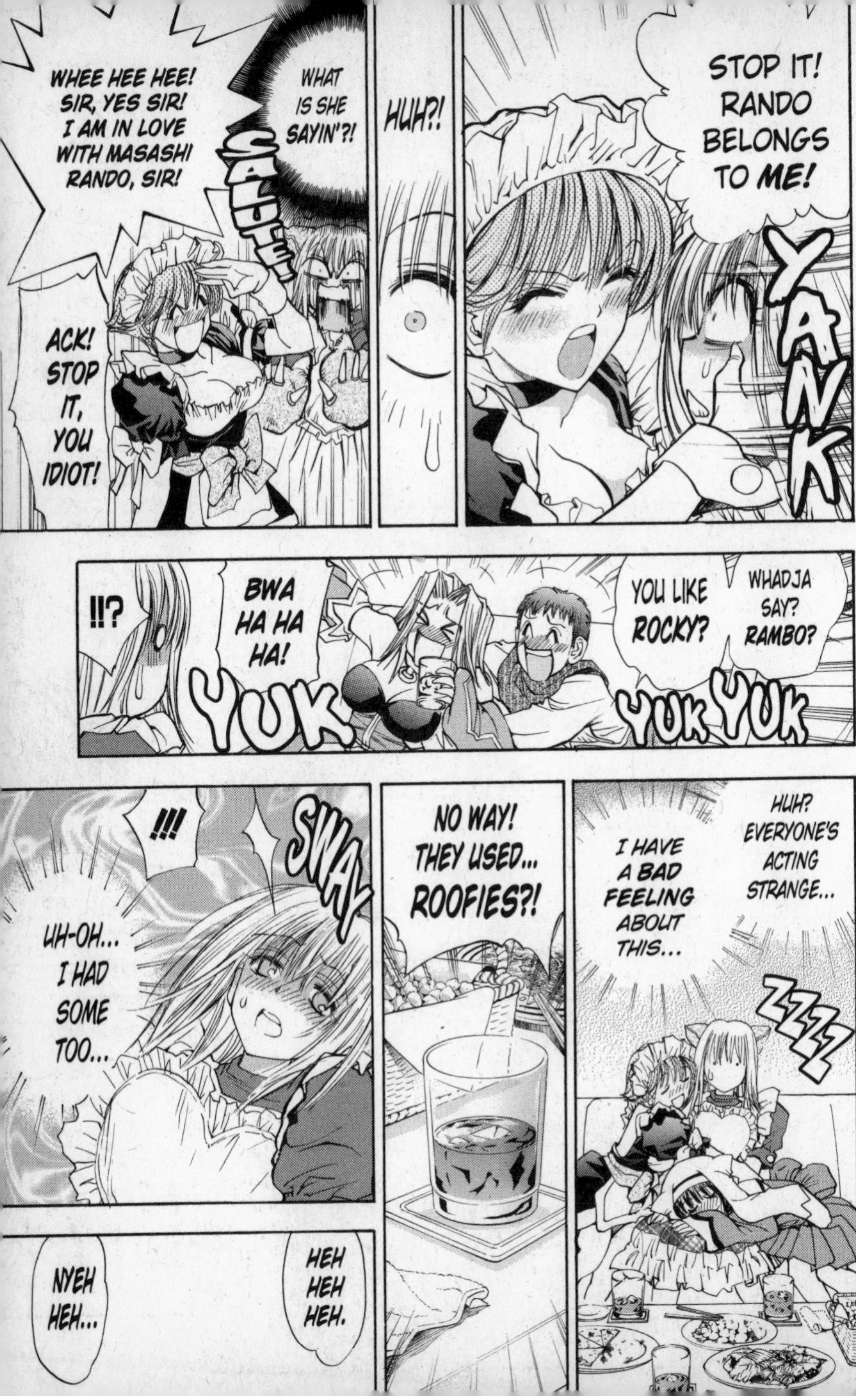
STOP IT! RANDO BELONGS TO ME!
YANK
HUH?!
WHAT IS SHE SAYIN'?!
WHEE HEE HEE! SIR, YES SIR! I AM IN LOVE WITH MASASHI RANDO, SIR!
SALUTE
ACK! STOP IT, YOU IDIOT!
WHADJA SAY? RAMBO?
YOU LIKE ROCKY?
YUK YUK
BWA HA HA HA!
YUK
!!?
HUH? EVERYONE'S ACTING STRANGE...
I HAVE A BAD FEELING ABOUT THIS...
ZZZZ
NO WAY! THEY USED... ROOFIES?!
SWAY
!!!
UH-OH... I HAD SOME TOO...
HEH HEH HEH.
NYEH HEH...

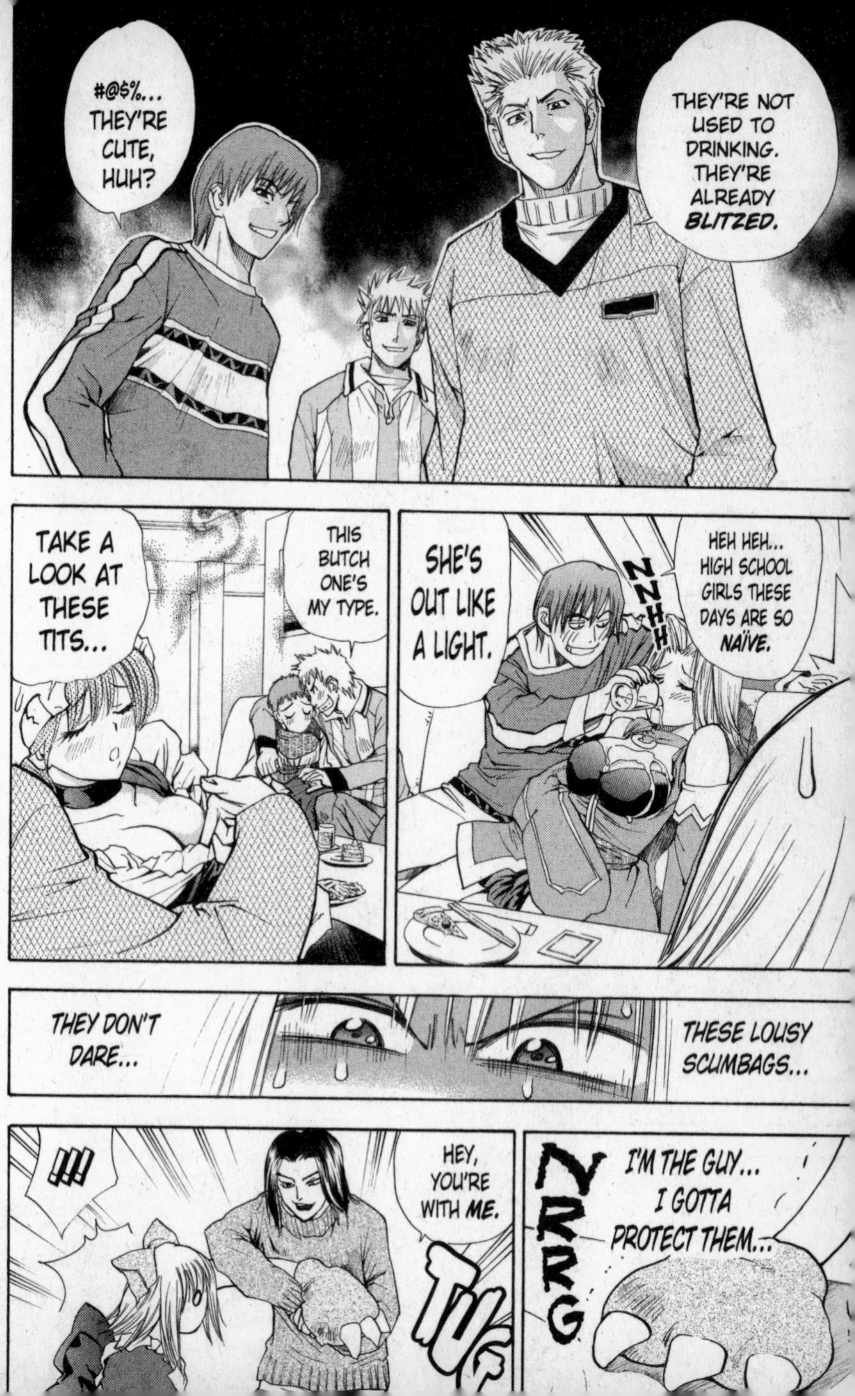
THEY'RE NOT USED TO DRINKING. THEY'RE ALREADY BLITZED.
#@$%... THEY'RE CUTE, HUH?
HEH HEH... HIGH SCHOOL GIRLS THESE DAYS ARE SO NAÏVE.
NNHH
SHE'S OUT LIKE A LIGHT.
THIS BUTCH ONE'S MY TYPE.
TAKE A LOOK AT THESE TITS...
THESE LOUSY SCUMBAGS...
THEY DON'T DARE...
I'M THE GUY... I GOTTA PROTECT THEM...
NRRG
HEY, YOU'RE WITH ME.
!!!
TU

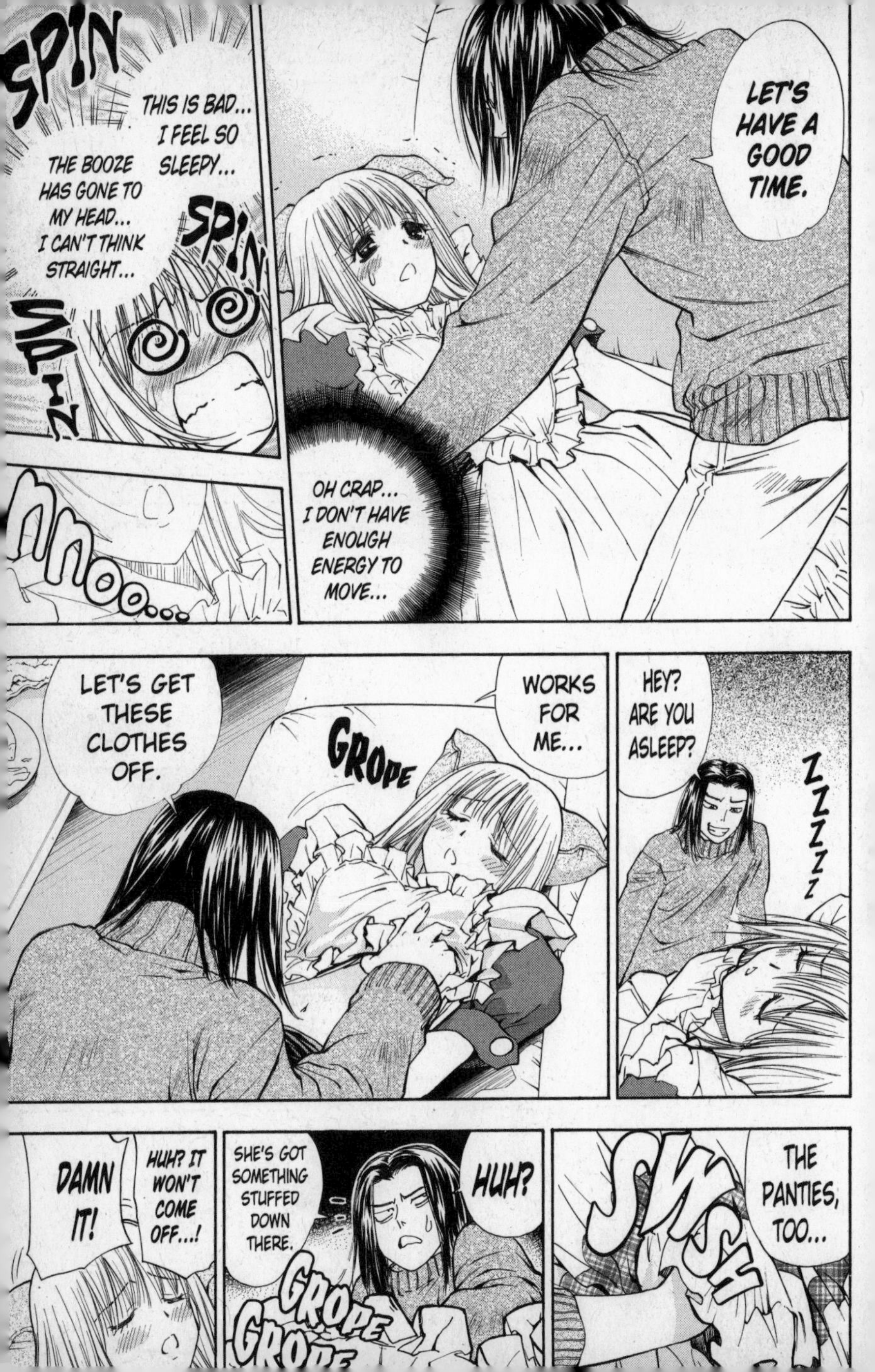

LET'S HAVE A GOOD TIME.
OH CRAP... I DON'T HAVE ENOUGH ENERGY TO MOVE...
SPIN
THIS IS BAD... I FEEL SO SLEEPY...
THE BOOZE HAS GONE TO MY HEAD... I CAN'T THINK STRAIGHT...
SPIN
SPIN
MNOOO...
HEY? ARE YOU ASLEEP?
ZZZZZ
WORKS FOR ME...
GROPE
LET'S GET THESE CLOTHES OFF.
THE PANTIES, TOO...
SWSH
HUH?
SHE'S GOT SOMETHING STUFFED DOWN THERE.
GROPE GROPE
HUH? IT WON'T COME OFF...!
DAMN IT!

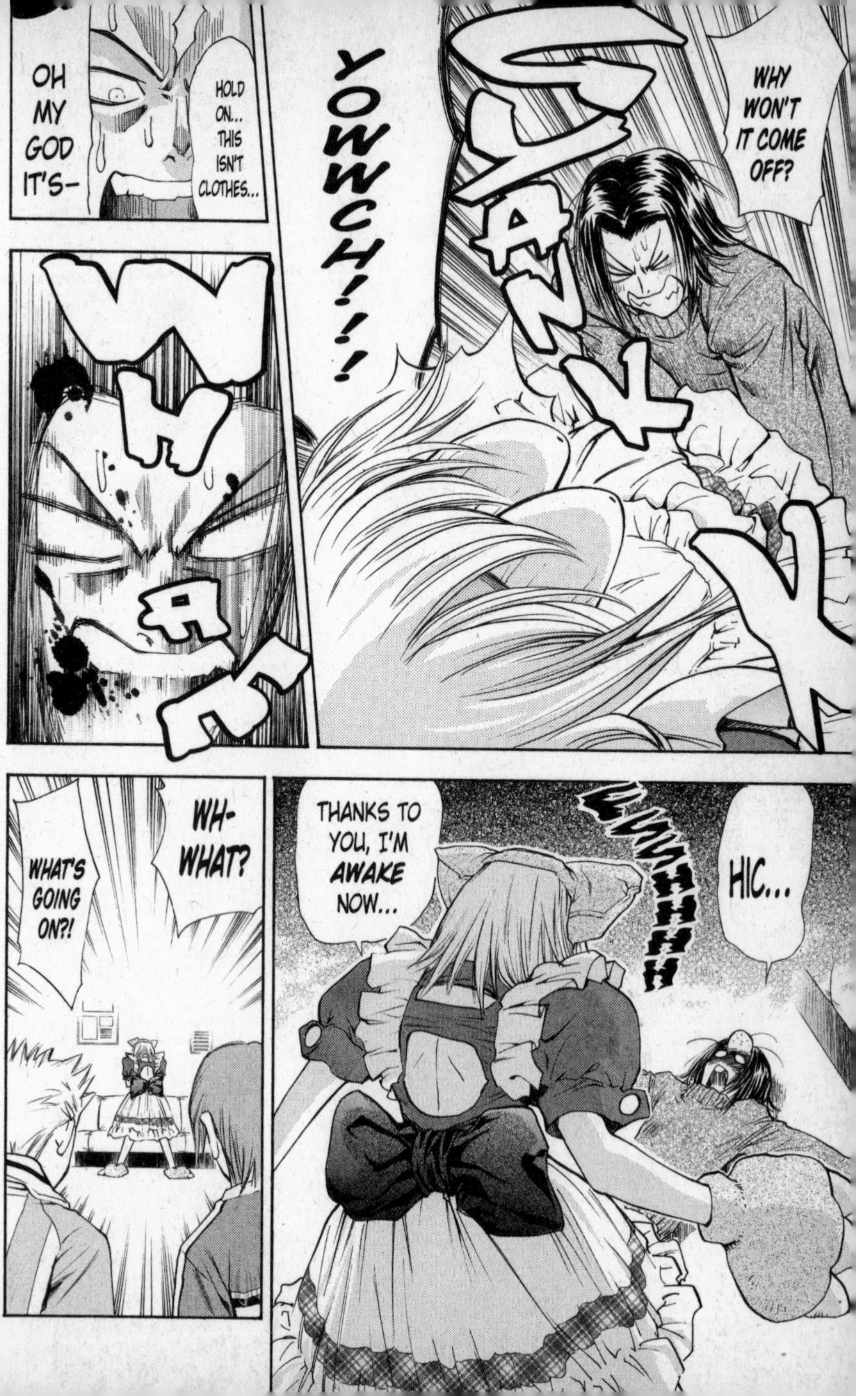
WHY WON'T IT COME OFF?
YANK
YOWWCH!!!
HOLD ON... THIS ISN'T CLOTHES...
OH MY GOD IT'S-
WHAK
HIC...
THANKS TO YOU, I'M AWAKE NOW...
WH- WHAT?
WHAT'S GOING ON?!

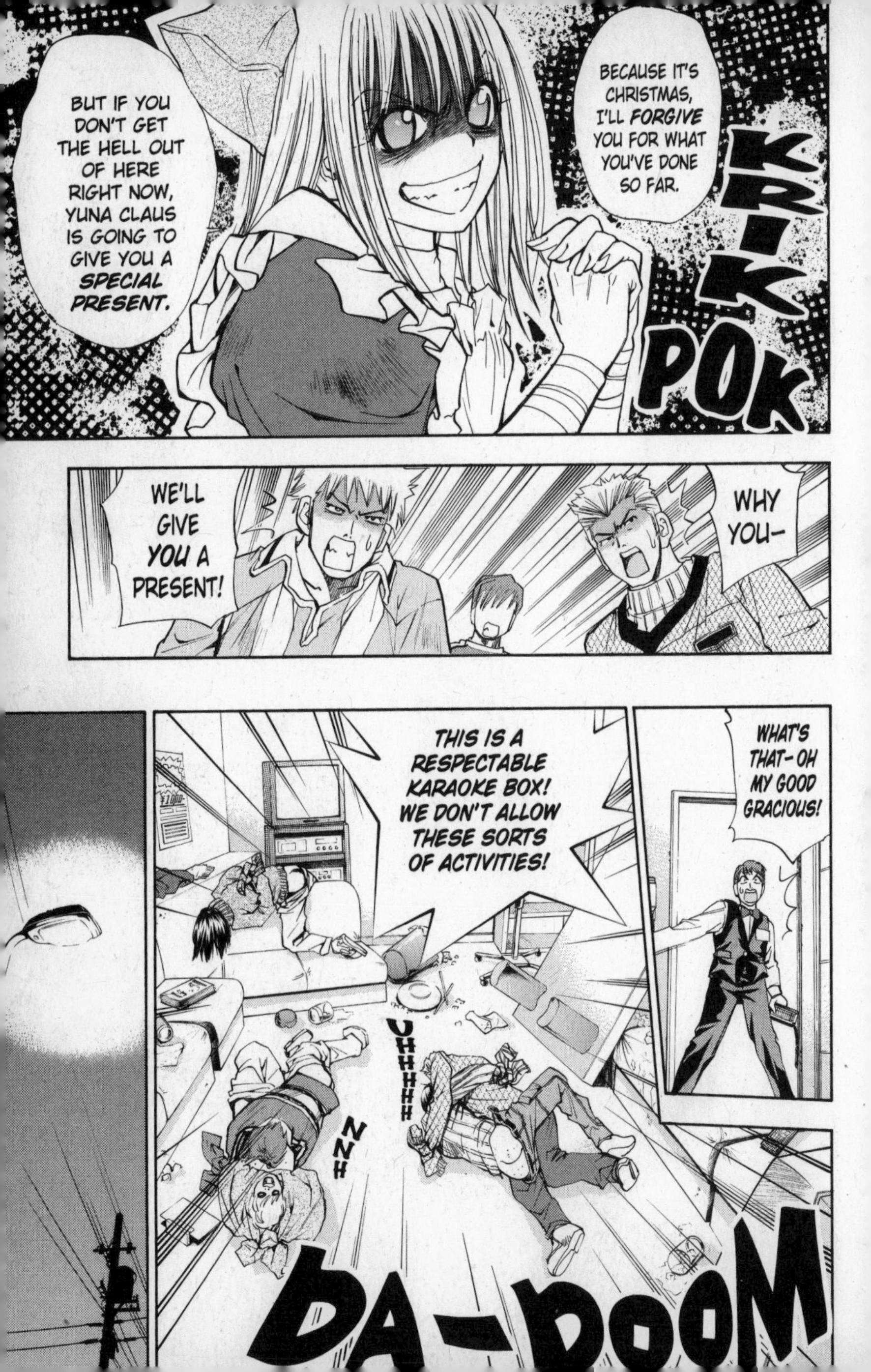
BECAUSE IT'S CHRISTMAS, I'LL *FORGIVE* YOU FOR WHAT YOU'VE DONE SO FAR.
KRIK
POK
BUT IF YOU DON'T GET THE HELL OUT OF HERE RIGHT NOW, YUNA CLAUS IS GOING TO GIVE YOU A *SPECIAL PRESENT.*
WHY YOU-
WE'LL GIVE *YOU* A PRESENT!
WHAT'S THAT-OH MY GOOD GRACIOUS!
THIS IS A RESPECTABLE KARAOKE BOX! WE DON'T ALLOW THESE SORTS OF ACTIVITIES!
UHHHHHH
NNH
DA-DOOM

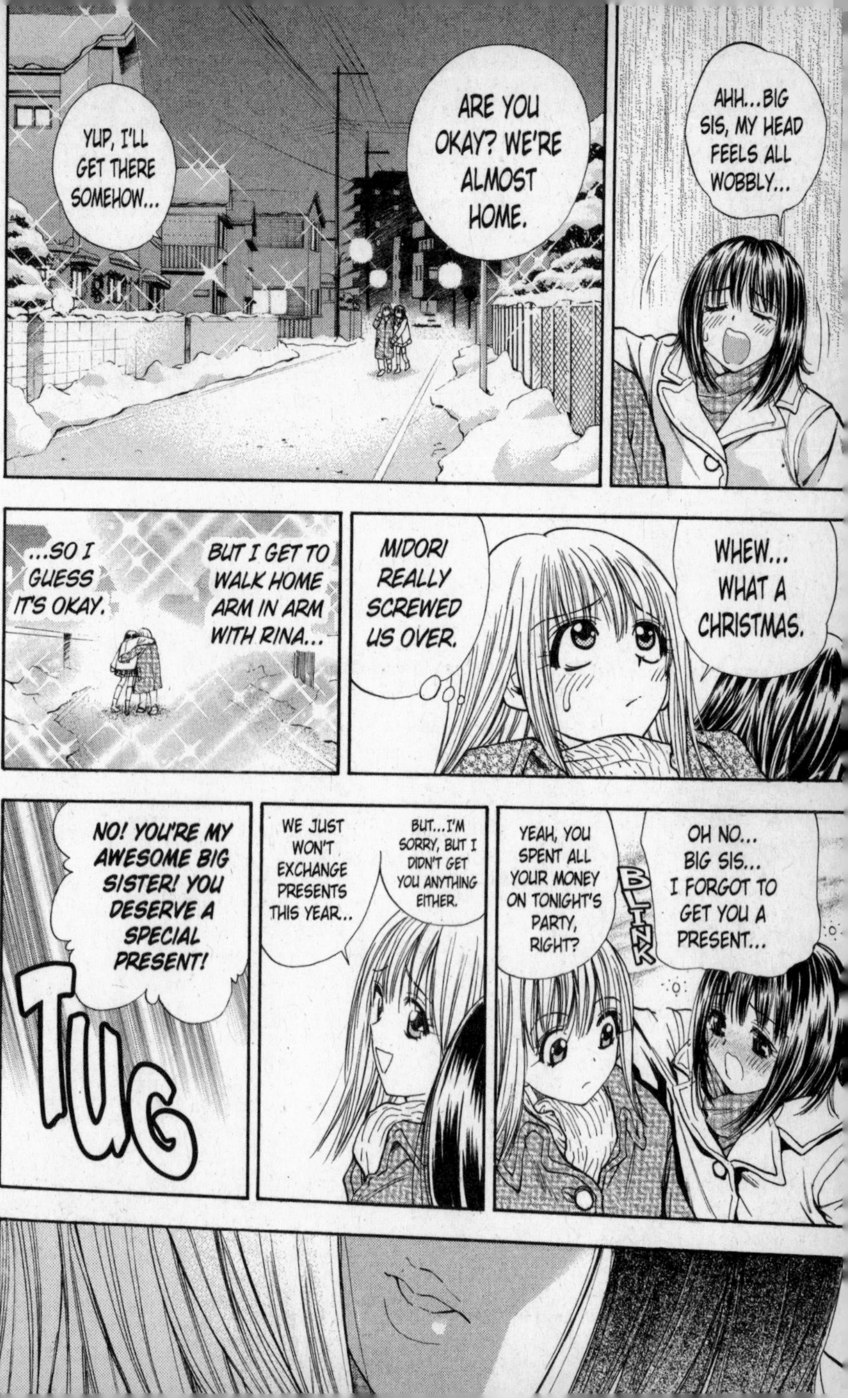
AHH...BIG SIS, MY HEAD FEELS ALL WOBBLY...
ARE YOU OKAY? WE'RE ALMOST HOME.
YUP, I'LL GET THERE SOMEHOW...
WHEW... WHAT A CHRISTMAS.
MIDORI REALLY SCREWED US OVER.
BUT I GET TO WALK HOME ARM IN ARM WITH RINA...
...SO I GUESS IT'S OKAY.
OH NO... BIG SIS... I FORGOT TO GET YOU A PRESENT...
BLINK
YEAH, YOU SPENT ALL YOUR MONEY ON TONIGHT'S PARTY, RIGHT?
BUT...I'M SORRY, BUT I DIDN'T GET YOU ANYTHING EITHER.
WE JUST WON'T EXCHANGE PRESENTS THIS YEAR...
NO! YOU'RE MY AWESOME BIG SISTER! YOU DESERVE A SPECIAL PRESENT!
TUG

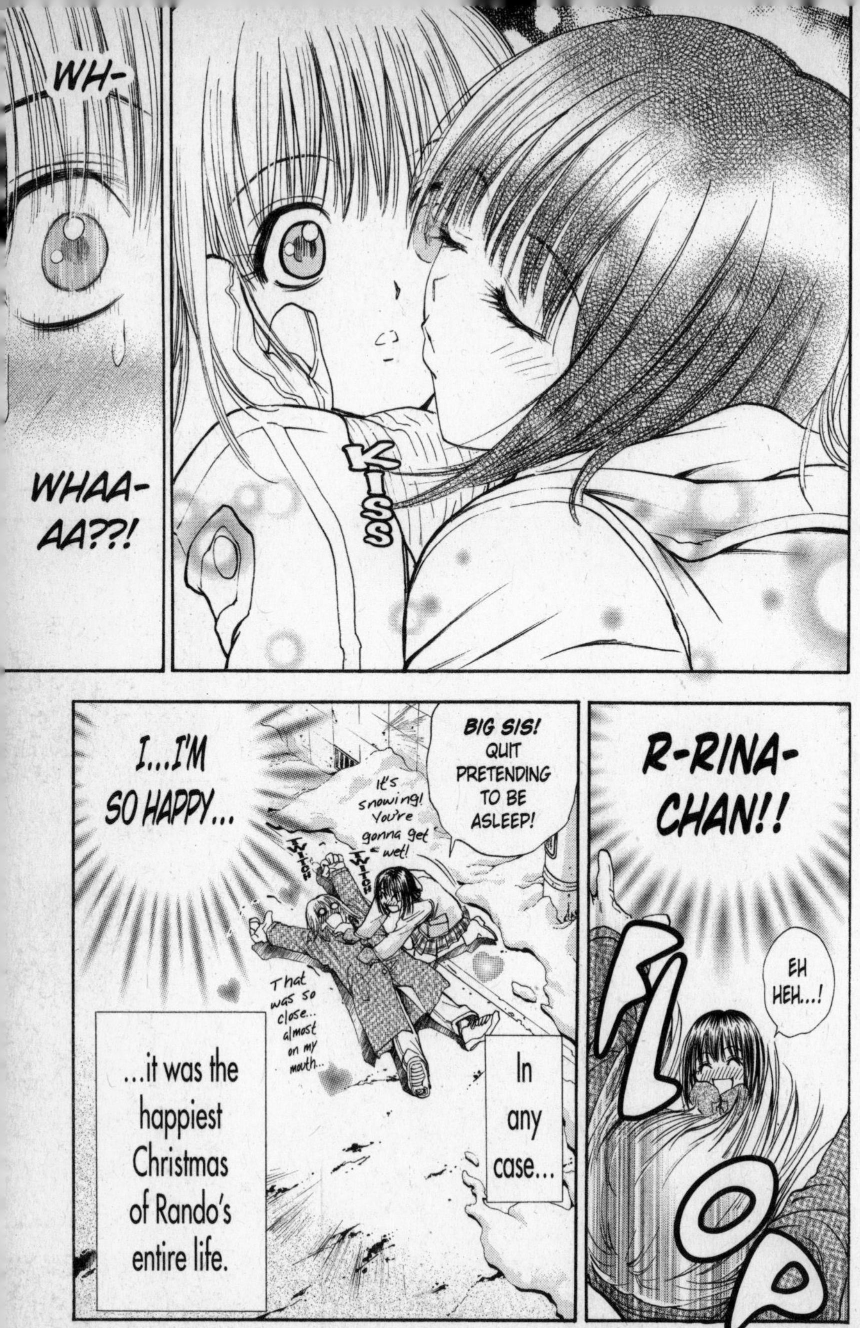
KISS
WH-
WHAA-AA??!
R-RINA-CHAN!!
EH HEH...!
FLOP
BIG SIS! QUIT PRETENDING TO BE ASLEEP!
I...I'M SO HAPPY...
It's snowing! You're gonna get wet!
TWITCH
TWITCH
That was so close... almost on my mouth...
In any case...
...it was the happiest Christmas of Rando's entire life.

BONUS: REJECTED STORIES (part 3)

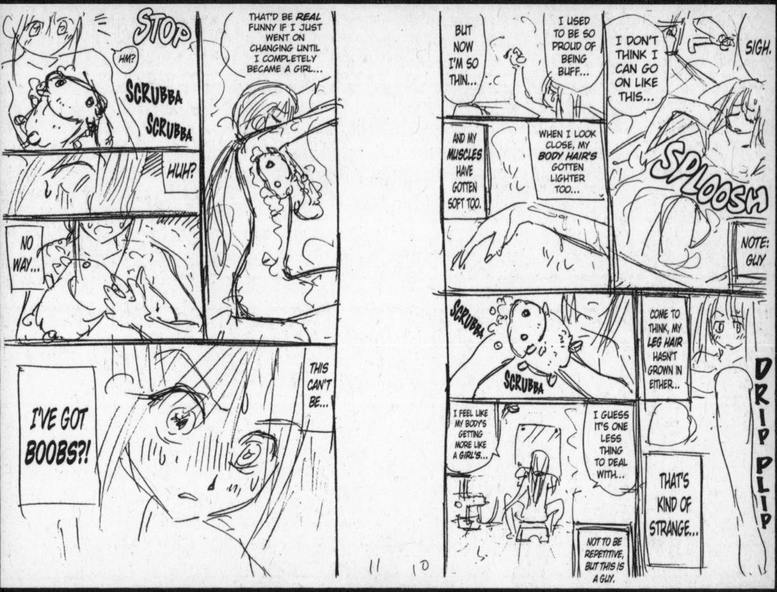
SIGH.
I DON'T THINK I CAN GO ON LIKE THIS...
SPLOOSH
NOTE: GUY
I USED TO BE SO PROUD OF BEING BUFF...
BUT NOW I'M SO THIN...
WHEN I LOOK CLOSE, MY BODY HAIR'S GOTTEN LIGHTER TOO...
AND MY MUSCLES HAVE GOTTEN SOFT TOO.
DRIP PLIP
COME TO THINK, MY LEG HAIR HASN'T GROWN IN EITHER...
SCRUBBA
SCRUBBA
THAT'S KIND OF STRANGE...
I GUESS IT'S ONE LESS THING TO DEAL WITH...
I FEEL LIKE MY BODY'S GETTING MORE LIKE A GIRL'S...
NOT TO BE REPETITIVE, BUT THIS IS A GUY.
10
THAT'D BE REAL FUNNY IF I JUST WENT ON CHANGING UNTIL I COMPLETELY BECAME A GIRL...
STOP
HM?
SCRUBBA
SCRUBBA
HUH?
NO WAY...
THIS CAN'T BE...
I'VE GOT BOOBS?!
11

THIS WAS GOING TO BE THE THIRD STORY. RIGHT AFTER HE WAKES UP, RANDO STARTS HAVING DOUBTS ABOUT HIS BODY. WHAT'S MORE, HIS BREASTS START GROWING SO HE'S ***REALLY*** FREAKED OUT. BUT IN THE END, I THOUGHT IT BETTER IF THE THIRD CHAPTER WAS ABOUT HIS RELATIONSHIP WITH RINA, SO IT GOT DROPPED. I PUT IT ON THE SHELF, THINKING THAT I MIGHT USE IT SOMETIME. IT ENDED UP THAT THE CHANGES WERE DUE TO MANABE'S MEDDLING AND THE FACT THAT HE HIT HIS CHEST TO MAKE IT SWELL. NOW THAT I THINK ABOUT IT, THIS STORY MAKES YOU THINK OF HORMONE SHOTS AND TAKES YOUR THOUGHTS IN A DANGEROUS DIRECTION, SO IT'S PROBABLY BETTER THAT IT WAS REJECTED.

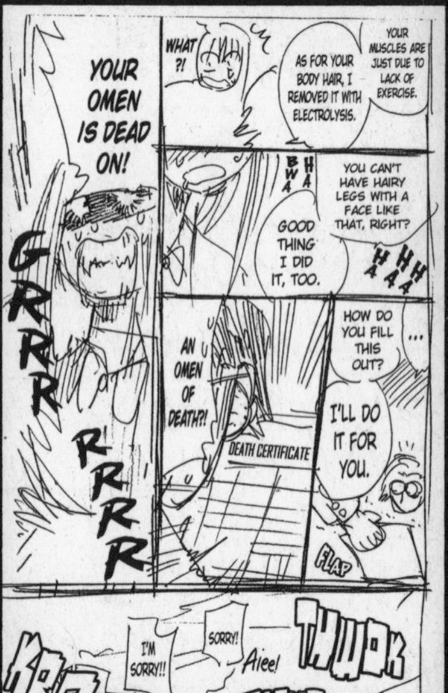
YOUR MUSCLES ARE JUST DUE TO LACK OF EXERCISE.
AS FOR YOUR BODY HAIR, I REMOVED IT WITH ELECTROLYSIS.
WHAT?!
YOU CAN'T HAVE HAIRY LEGS WITH A FACE LIKE THAT, RIGHT?
BWAHA
GOOD THING I DID IT, TOO.
HAHAHA
...
HOW DO YOU FILL THIS OUT?
I'LL DO IT FOR YOU.
FLAP
AN OMEN OF DEATH?!
DEATH CERTIFICATE
YOUR OMEN IS DEAD ON!
GRRRRRRR
THWOK
THUD
Aiee!
SORRY!
I'M SORRY!!
KRAK

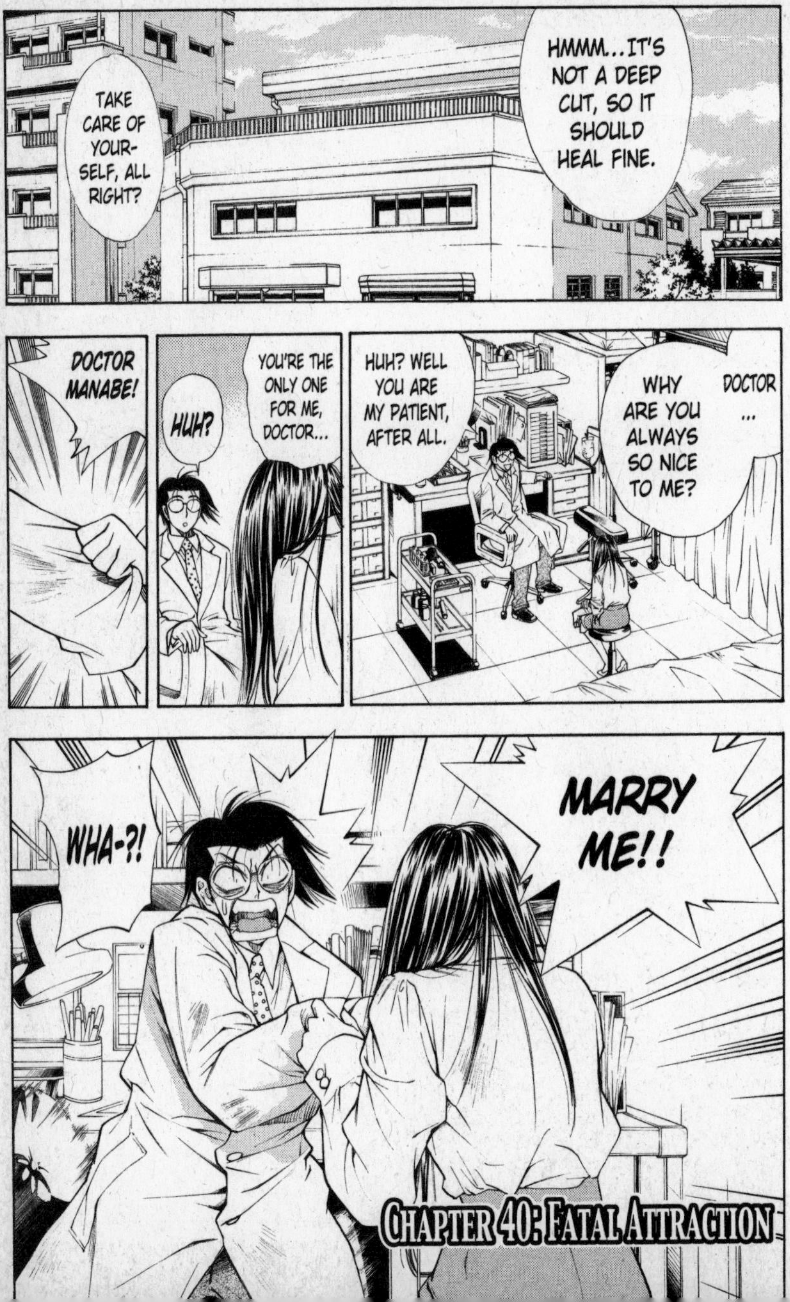
HMMM...IT'S NOT A DEEP CUT, SO IT SHOULD HEAL FINE.
TAKE CARE OF YOUR-SELF, ALL RIGHT?
DOCTOR ...
WHY ARE YOU ALWAYS SO NICE TO ME?
HUH? WELL YOU ARE MY PATIENT, AFTER ALL.
YOU'RE THE ONLY ONE FOR ME, DOCTOR...
HUH?
DOCTOR MANABE!
MARRY ME!!
WHA-?!
CHAPTER 40: FATAL ATTRACTION

Chapter 40: Fatal Attraction

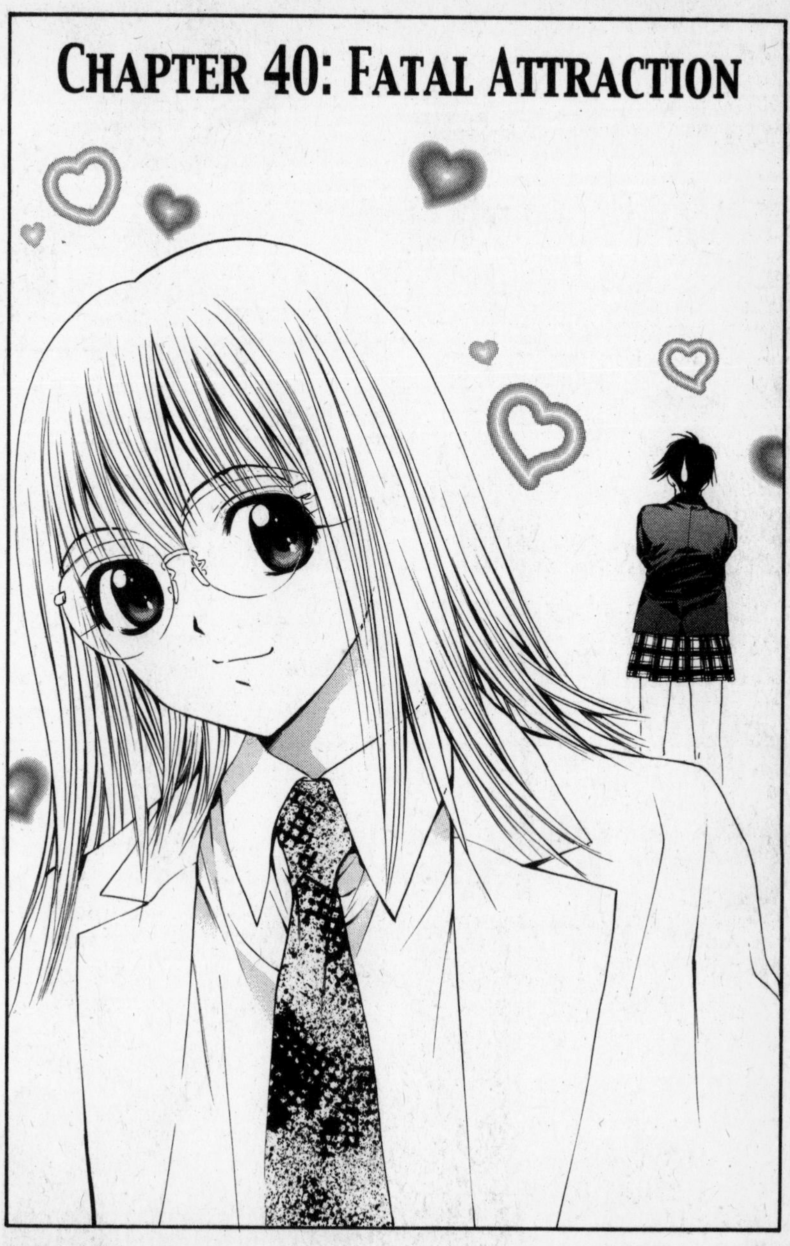

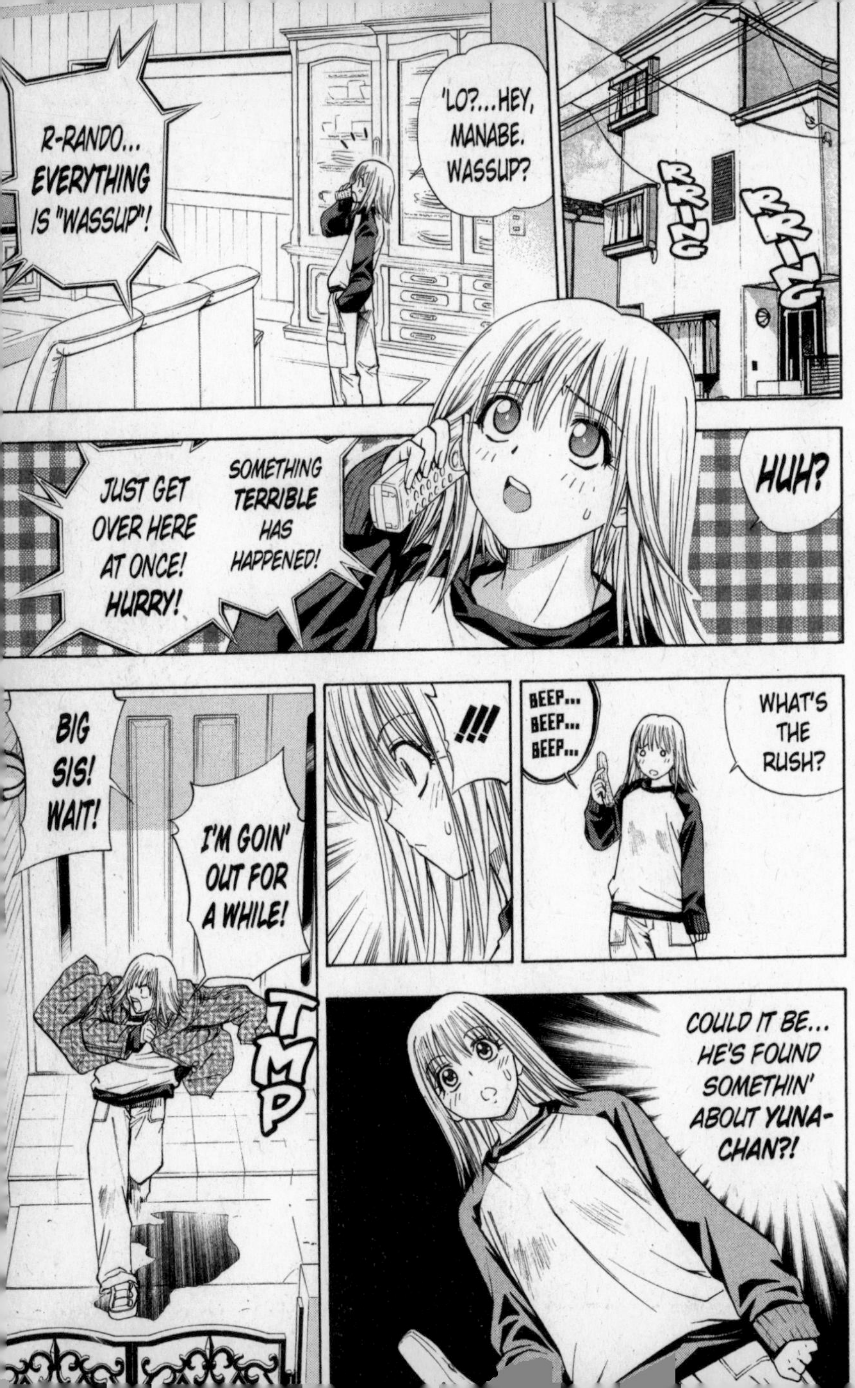
RRING
RRING
'LO?...HEY, MANABE. WASSUP?
R-RANDO... EVERYTHING IS "WASSUP"!
HUH?
SOMETHING TERRIBLE HAS HAPPENED!
JUST GET OVER HERE AT ONCE! HURRY!
WHAT'S THE RUSH?
BEEP... BEEP... BEEP...
!!!
COULD IT BE... HE'S FOUND SOMETHIN' ABOUT YUNA-CHAN?!
I'M GOIN' OUT FOR A WHILE!
TMP
BIG SIS! WAIT!

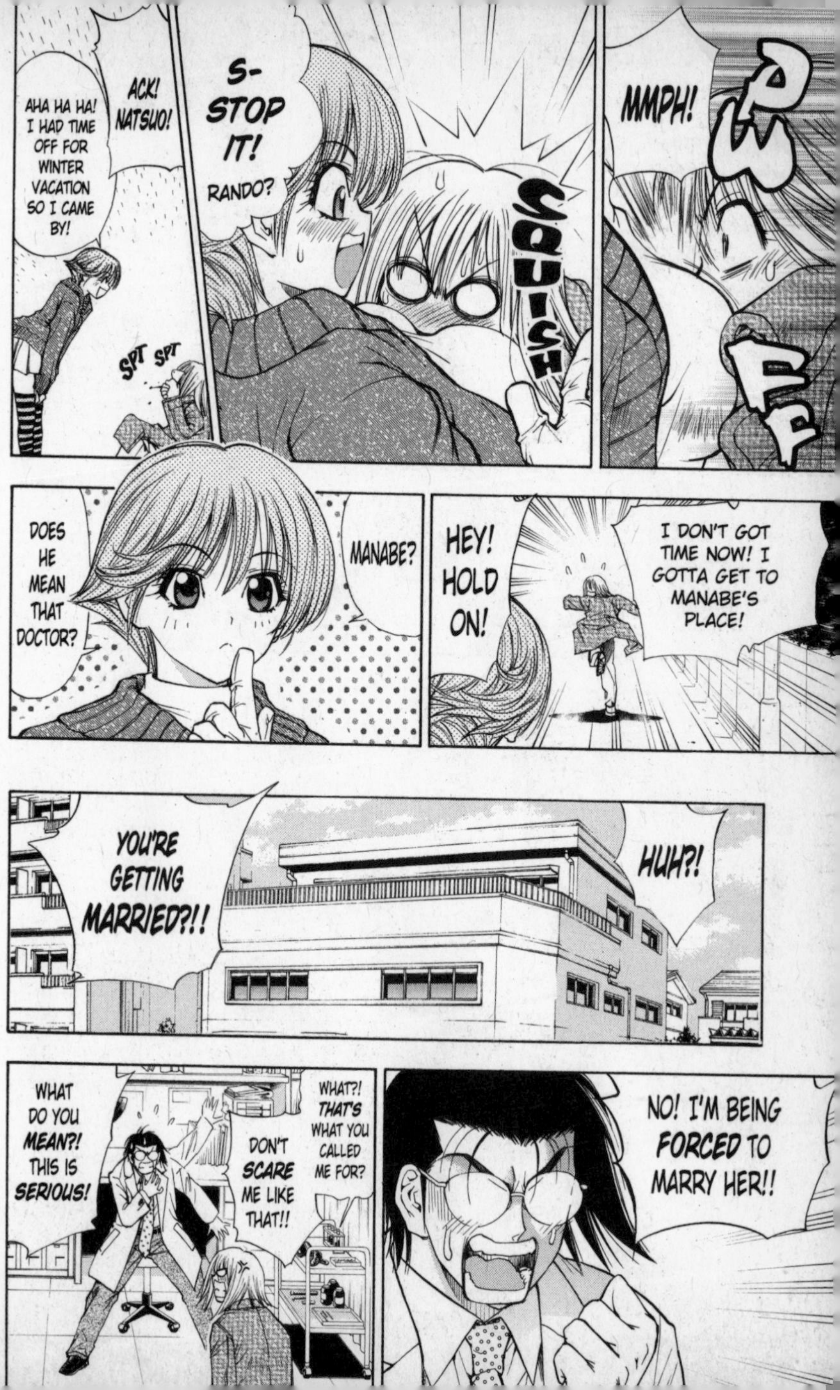
MMPH!
PUFF
S- STOP IT!
RANDO?
SQUISH
ACK! NATSUO!
AHA HA HA! I HAD TIME OFF FOR WINTER VACATION SO I CAME BY!
SPT SPT
I DON'T GOT TIME NOW! I GOTTA GET TO MANABE'S PLACE!
HEY! HOLD ON!
MANABE?
DOES HE MEAN THAT DOCTOR?
HUH?!
YOU'RE GETTING MARRIED?!!
NO! I'M BEING FORCED TO MARRY HER!!
WHAT?! THAT'S WHAT YOU CALLED ME FOR?
DON'T SCARE ME LIKE THAT!!
WHAT DO YOU MEAN?! THIS IS SERIOUS!

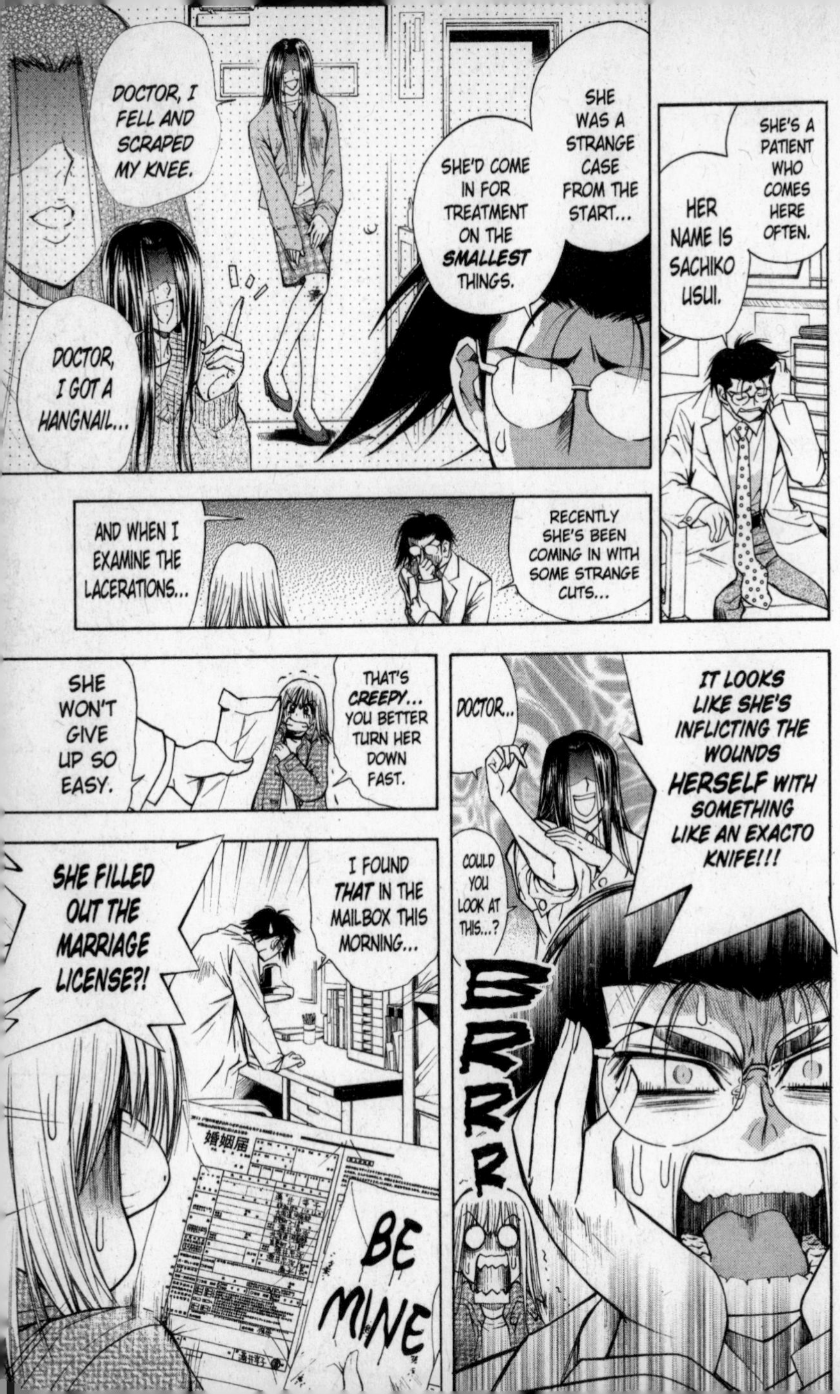
SHE'S A PATIENT WHO COMES HERE OFTEN.
HER NAME IS SACHIKO USUI.
SHE WAS A STRANGE CASE FROM THE START...
SHE'D COME IN FOR TREATMENT ON THE SMALLEST THINGS.
DOCTOR, I FELL AND SCRAPED MY KNEE.
DOCTOR, I GOT A HANGNAIL...
RECENTLY SHE'S BEEN COMING IN WITH SOME STRANGE CUTS...
AND WHEN I EXAMINE THE LACERATIONS...
IT LOOKS LIKE SHE'S INFLICTING THE WOUNDS HERSELF WITH SOMETHING LIKE AN EXACTO KNIFE!!!
DOCTOR...
COULD YOU LOOK AT THIS...?
BRRR
THAT'S CREEPY... YOU BETTER TURN HER DOWN FAST.
SHE WON'T GIVE UP SO EASY.
I FOUND THAT IN THE MAILBOX THIS MORNING...
SHE FILLED OUT THE MARRIAGE LICENSE?!
婚姻届
BE MINE

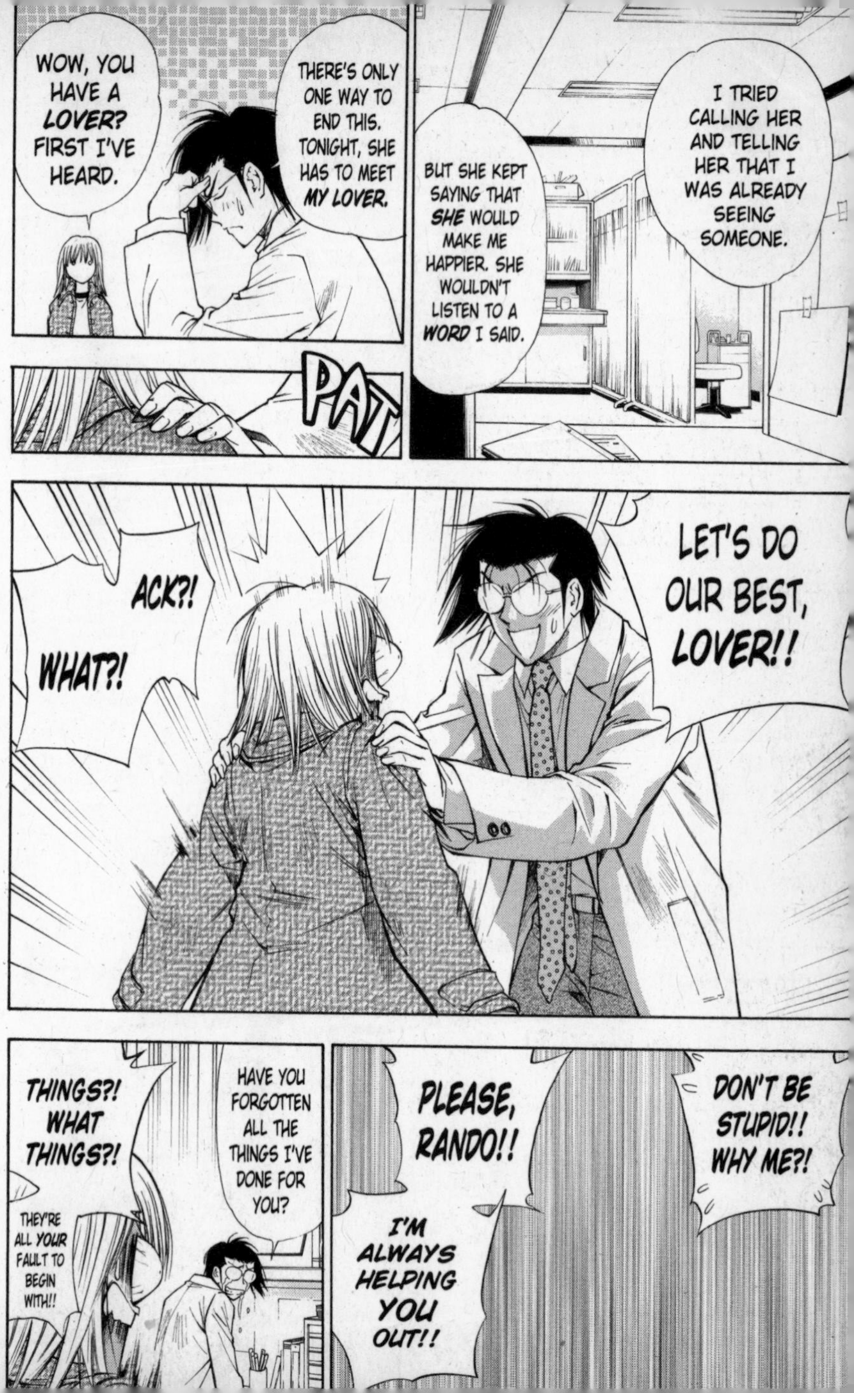
I TRIED CALLING HER AND TELLING HER THAT I WAS ALREADY SEEING SOMEONE.
BUT SHE KEPT SAYING THAT SHE WOULD MAKE ME HAPPIER. SHE WOULDN'T LISTEN TO A WORD I SAID.
THERE'S ONLY ONE WAY TO END THIS. TONIGHT, SHE HAS TO MEET MY LOVER.
WOW, YOU HAVE A LOVER? FIRST I'VE HEARD.
PAT
LET'S DO OUR BEST, LOVER!!
ACK?!
WHAT?!
DON'T BE STUPID!! WHY ME?!
PLEASE, RANDO!!
I'M ALWAYS HELPING YOU OUT!!
HAVE YOU FORGOTTEN ALL THE THINGS I'VE DONE FOR YOU?
THINGS?! WHAT THINGS?!
THEY'RE ALL YOUR FAULT TO BEGIN WITH!!

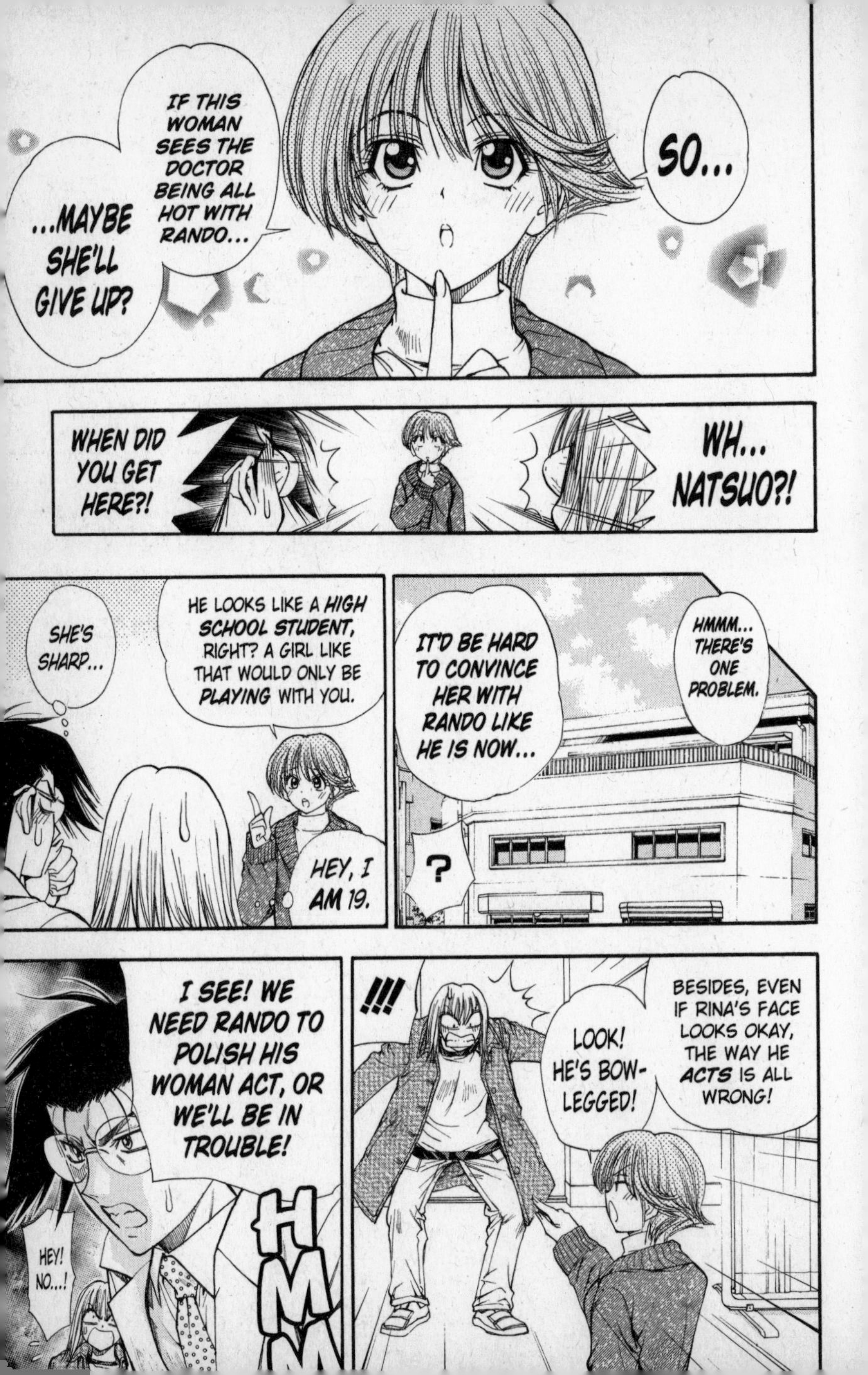
SO...
IF THIS WOMAN SEES THE DOCTOR BEING ALL HOT WITH RANDO...
...MAYBE SHE'LL GIVE UP?
WH... NATSUO?!
WHEN DID YOU GET HERE?!
HMMM... THERE'S ONE PROBLEM.
IT'D BE HARD TO CONVINCE HER WITH RANDO LIKE HE IS NOW...
?
HE LOOKS LIKE A HIGH SCHOOL STUDENT, RIGHT? A GIRL LIKE THAT WOULD ONLY BE PLAYING WITH YOU.
SHE'S SHARP...
HEY, I AM 19.
BESIDES, EVEN IF RINA'S FACE LOOKS OKAY, THE WAY HE ACTS IS ALL WRONG!
LOOK! HE'S BOW-LEGGED!
!!!
I SEE! WE NEED RANDO TO POLISH HIS WOMAN ACT, OR WE'LL BE IN TROUBLE!
HMM
HEY! NO...!

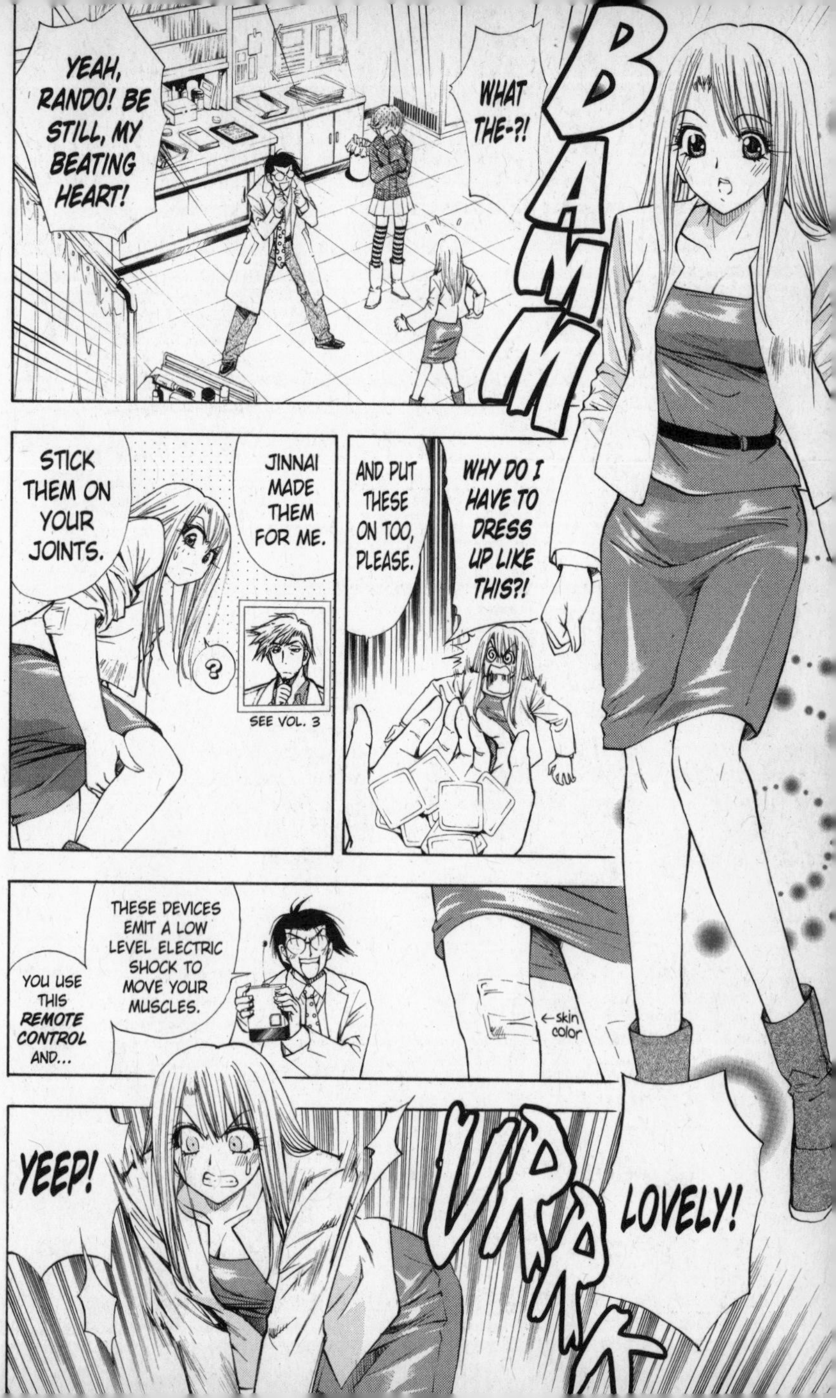
BAMM
WHAT THE-?!
YEAH, RANDO! BE STILL, MY BEATING HEART!
WHY DO I HAVE TO DRESS UP LIKE THIS?!
AND PUT THESE ON TOO, PLEASE.
JINNAI MADE THEM FOR ME.
STICK THEM ON YOUR JOINTS.
?
SEE VOL. 3
←skin color
THESE DEVICES EMIT A LOW LEVEL ELECTRIC SHOCK TO MOVE YOUR MUSCLES.
YOU USE THIS REMOTE CONTROL AND...
LOVELY!
VRRK
YEEP!

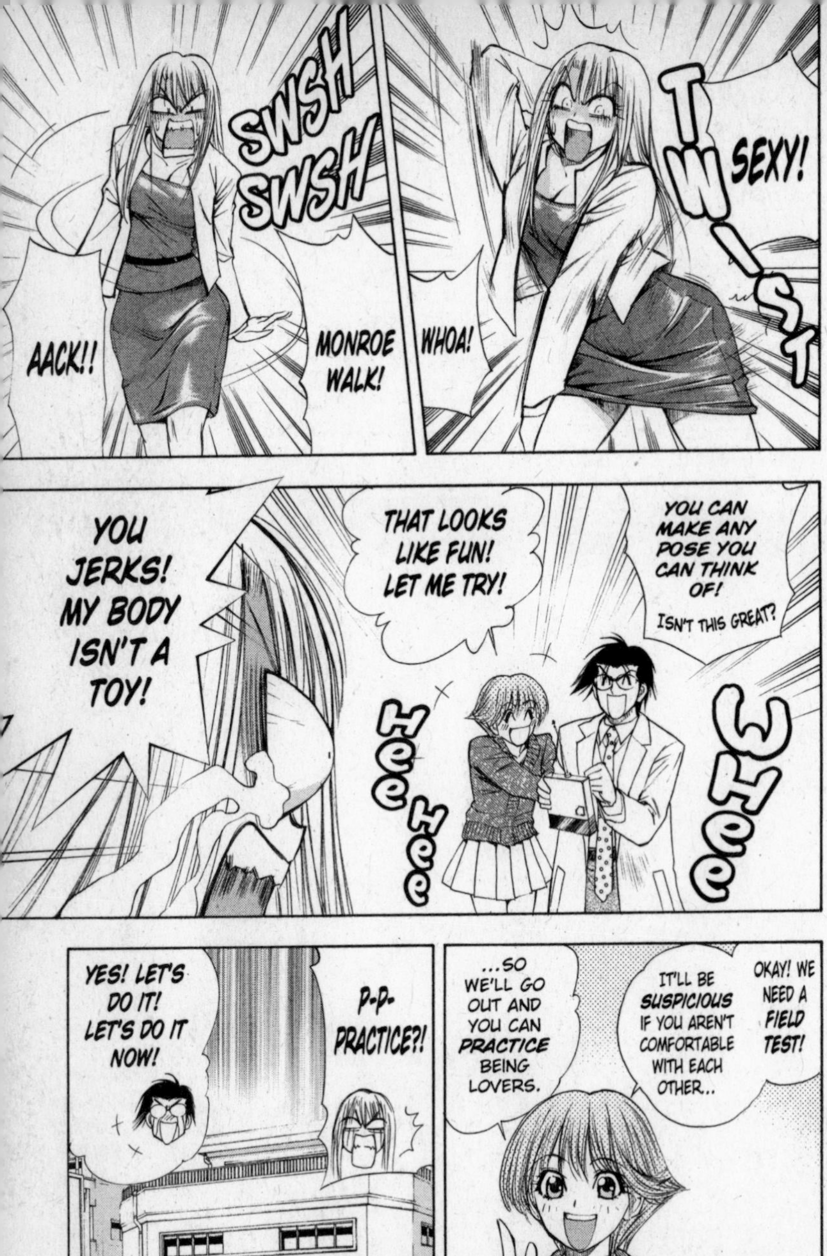
SEXY!
TWIST
WHOA!
MONROE WALK!
SWSH SWSH
AACK!!
YOU CAN MAKE ANY POSE YOU CAN THINK OF!
ISN'T THIS GREAT?
WHEE
THAT LOOKS LIKE FUN! LET ME TRY!
HEE HEE
YOU JERKS! MY BODY ISN'T A TOY!
OKAY! WE NEED A FIELD TEST!
IT'LL BE SUSPICIOUS IF YOU AREN'T COMFORTABLE WITH EACH OTHER...
...SO WE'LL GO OUT AND YOU CAN PRACTICE BEING LOVERS.
P-P-PRACTICE?!
YES! LET'S DO IT! LET'S DO IT NOW!

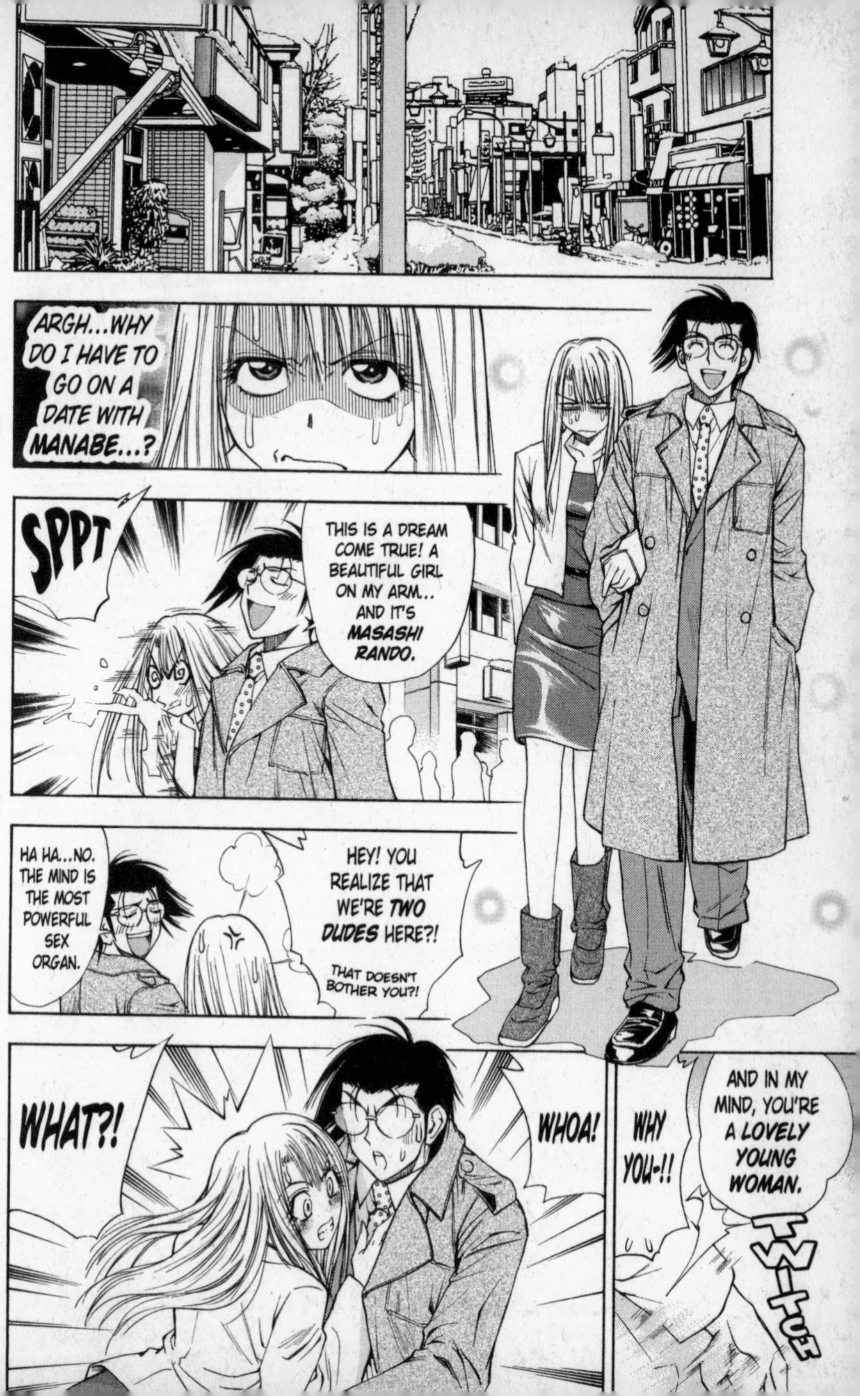
ARGH...WHY DO I HAVE TO GO ON A DATE WITH MANABE...?
THIS IS A DREAM COME TRUE! A BEAUTIFUL GIRL ON MY ARM.. AND IT'S MASASHI RANDO.
SPPT
HEY! YOU REALIZE THAT WE'RE TWO DUDES HERE?!
THAT DOESN'T BOTHER YOU?!
HA HA...NO. THE MIND IS THE MOST POWERFUL SEX ORGAN.
AND IN MY MIND, YOU'RE A LOVELY YOUNG WOMAN.
WHY YOU-!!
TWITCH
WHOA!
WHAT?!

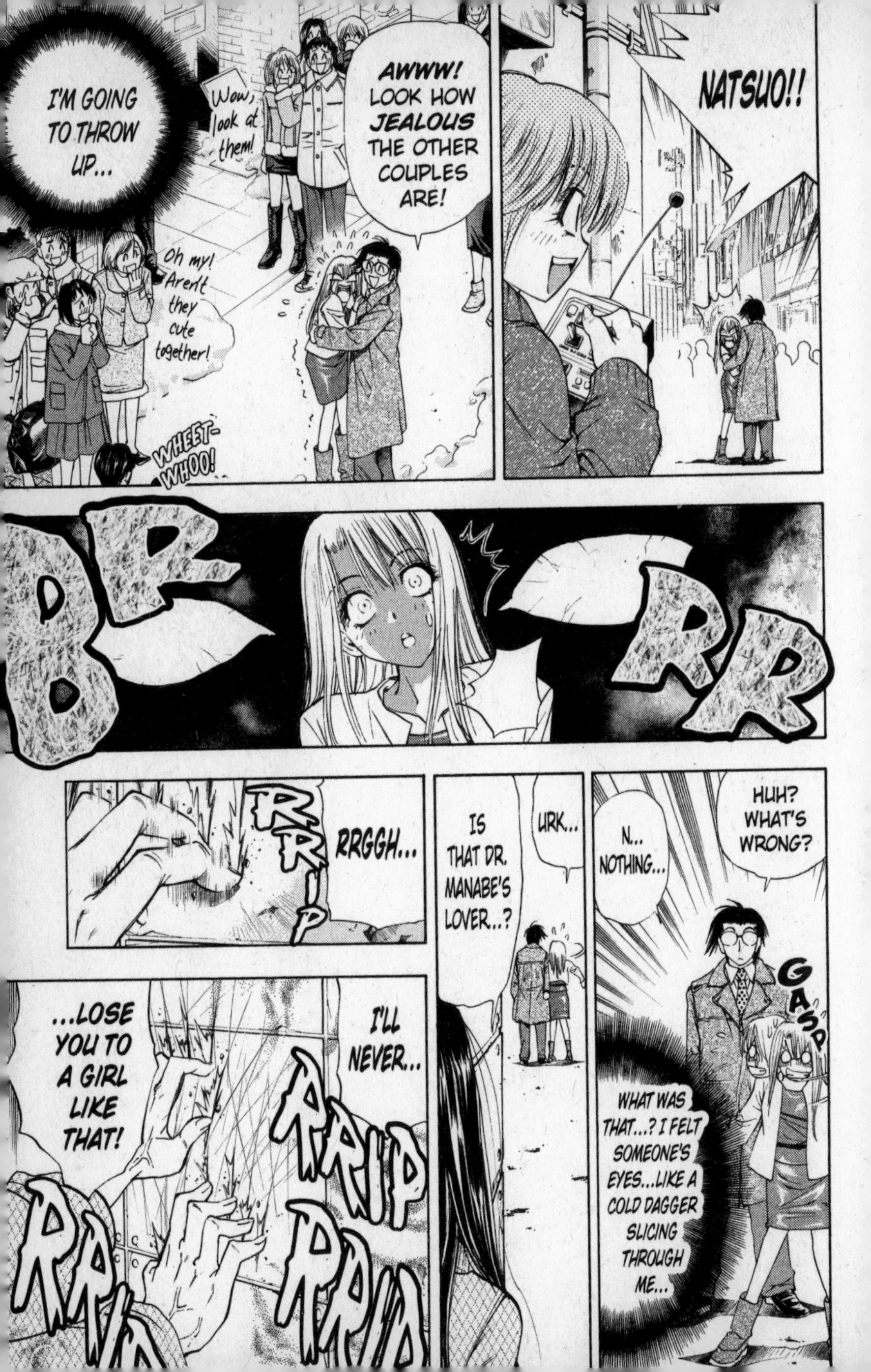
NATSUO!!
AWWW! LOOK HOW JEALOUS THE OTHER COUPLES ARE!
Wow, look at them!
I'M GOING TO THROW UP...
Oh my! Aren't they cute together!
WHEET-WHOO!
BRRRR
HUH? WHAT'S WRONG?
N... NOTHING...
GASP
WHAT WAS THAT...? I FELT SOMEONE'S EYES...LIKE A COLD DAGGER SLICING THROUGH ME...
URK...
IS THAT DR. MANABE'S LOVER...?
RRGGH...
RRIP
I'LL NEVER...
...LOSE YOU TO A GIRL LIKE THAT!
RRIP
RRIP

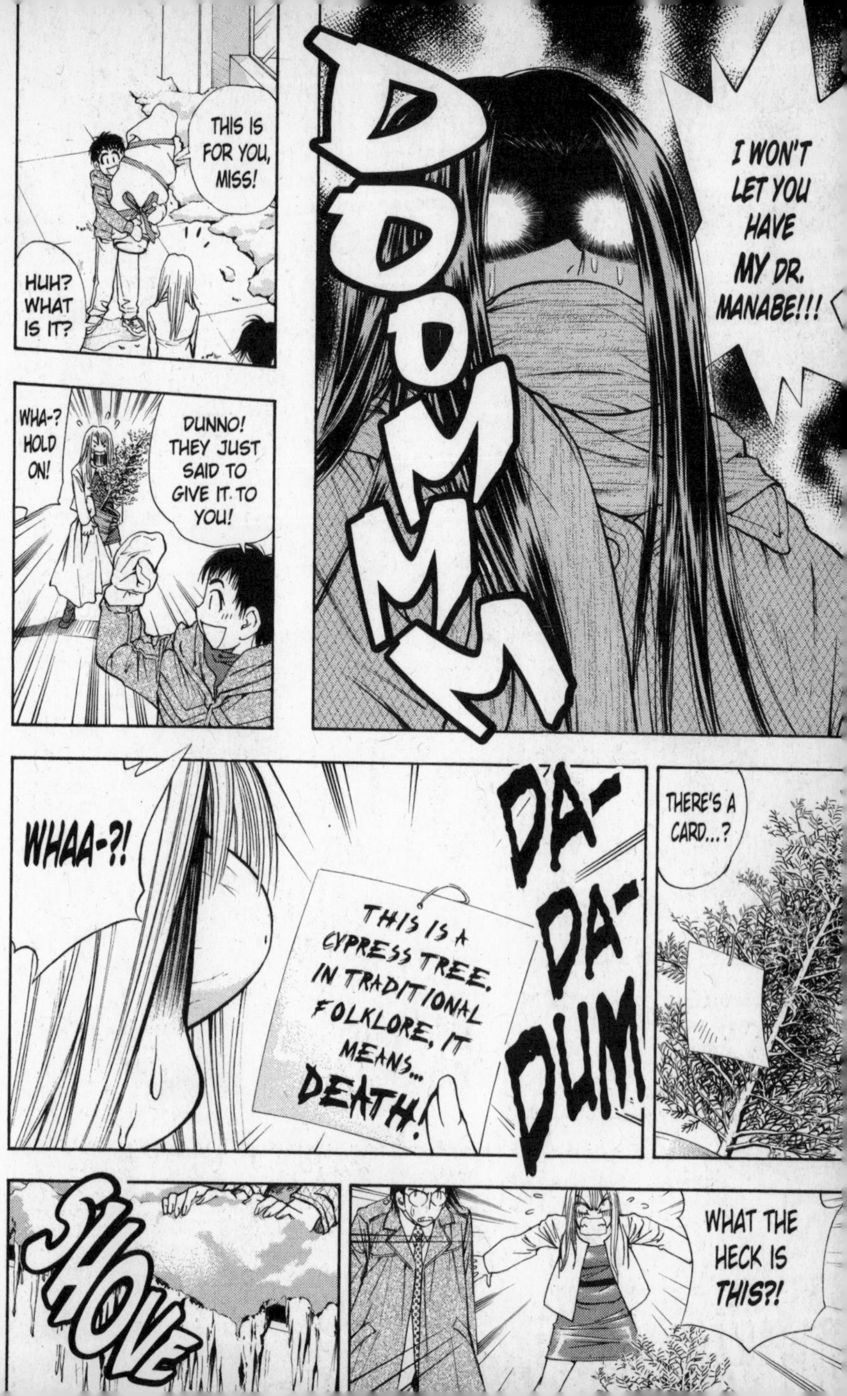
DOOMMMM
I WON'T LET YOU HAVE MY DR. MANABE!!!
THIS IS FOR YOU, MISS!
HUH? WHAT IS IT?
DUNNO! THEY JUST SAID TO GIVE IT TO YOU!
WHA-? HOLD ON!
THERE'S A CARD...?
DA-DA-DUM
THIS IS A CYPRESS TREE. IN TRADITIONAL FOLKLORE, IT MEANS... DEATH!
WHAA-?!
WHAT THE HECK IS THIS?!
SHOVE

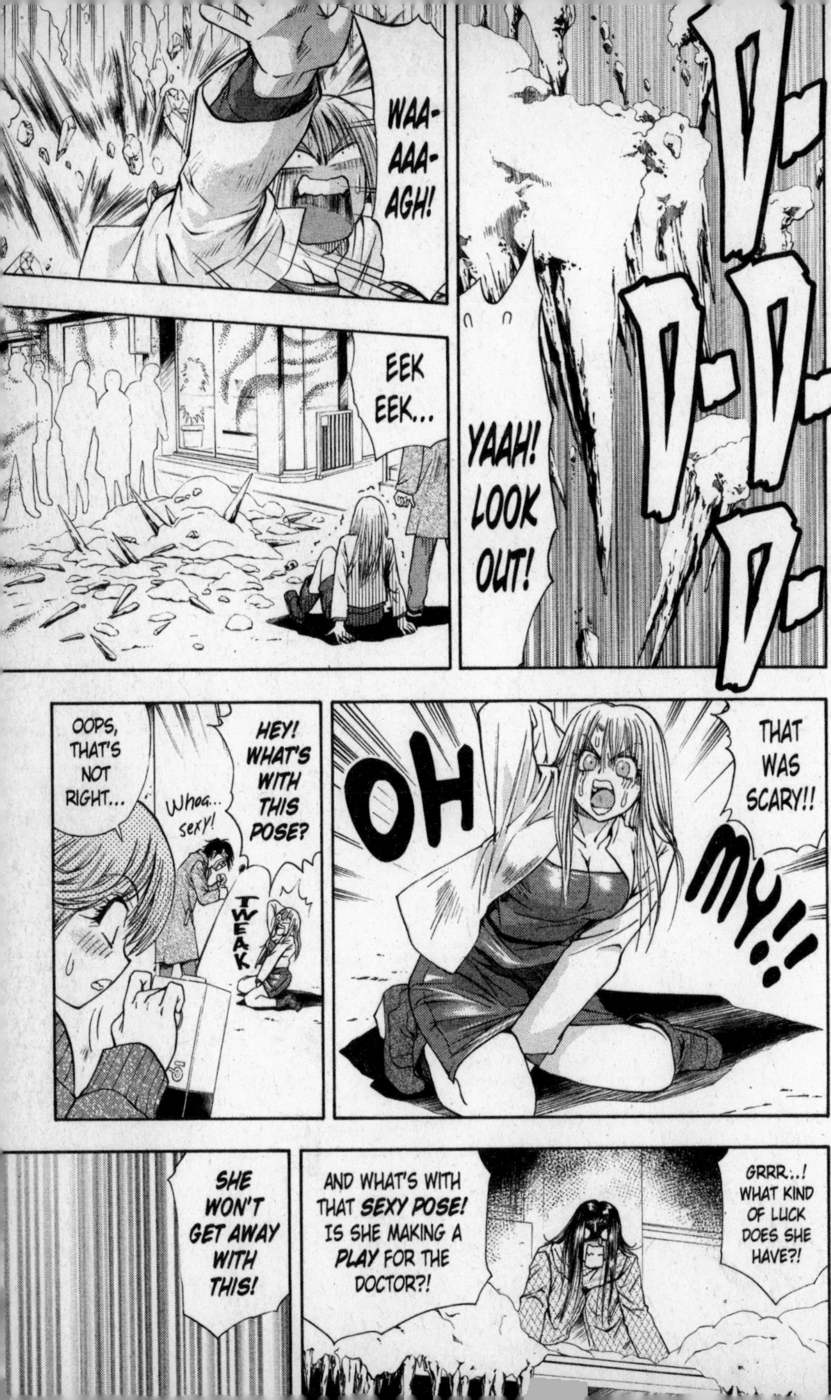
D-D-D-D-
YAAH! LOOK OUT!
WAA-AAA-AGH!
EEK EEK...
THAT WAS SCARY!!
OH MY!!
HEY! WHAT'S WITH THIS POSE?
TWEAK
Whoa... sexy!
OOPS, THAT'S NOT RIGHT...
GRRR..! WHAT KIND OF LUCK DOES SHE HAVE?!
AND WHAT'S WITH THAT SEXY POSE! IS SHE MAKING A PLAY FOR THE DOCTOR?!
SHE WON'T GET AWAY WITH THIS!

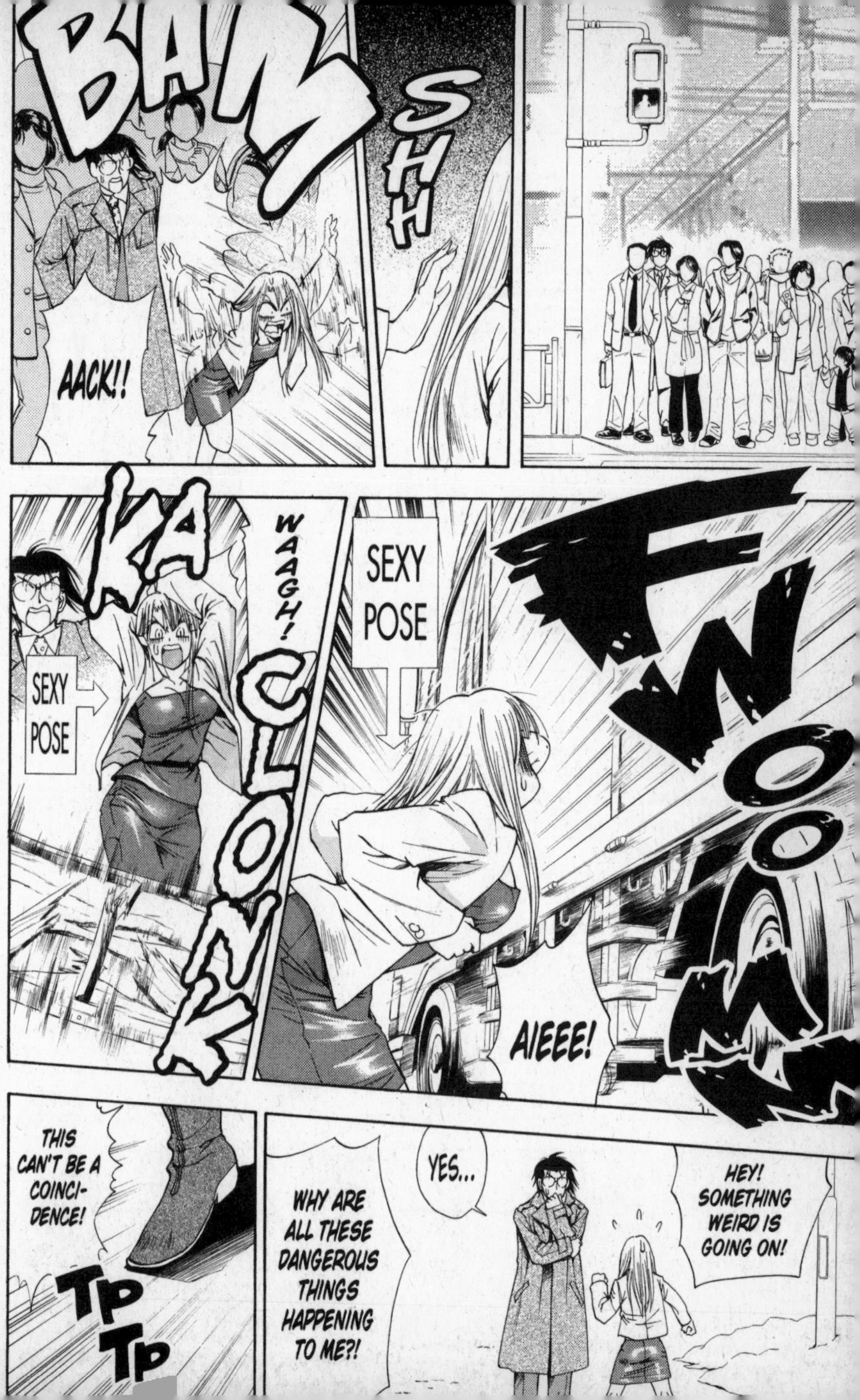
SHH
BAM
AACK!!
SEXY POSE
FWOOOM
AIEEE!
K'A
WAAGH!
SEXY POSE
CLONK
HEY! SOMETHING WEIRD IS GOING ON!
YES...
WHY ARE ALL THESE DANGEROUS THINGS HAPPENING TO ME?!
THIS CAN'T BE A COINCI-DENCE!
TP TP

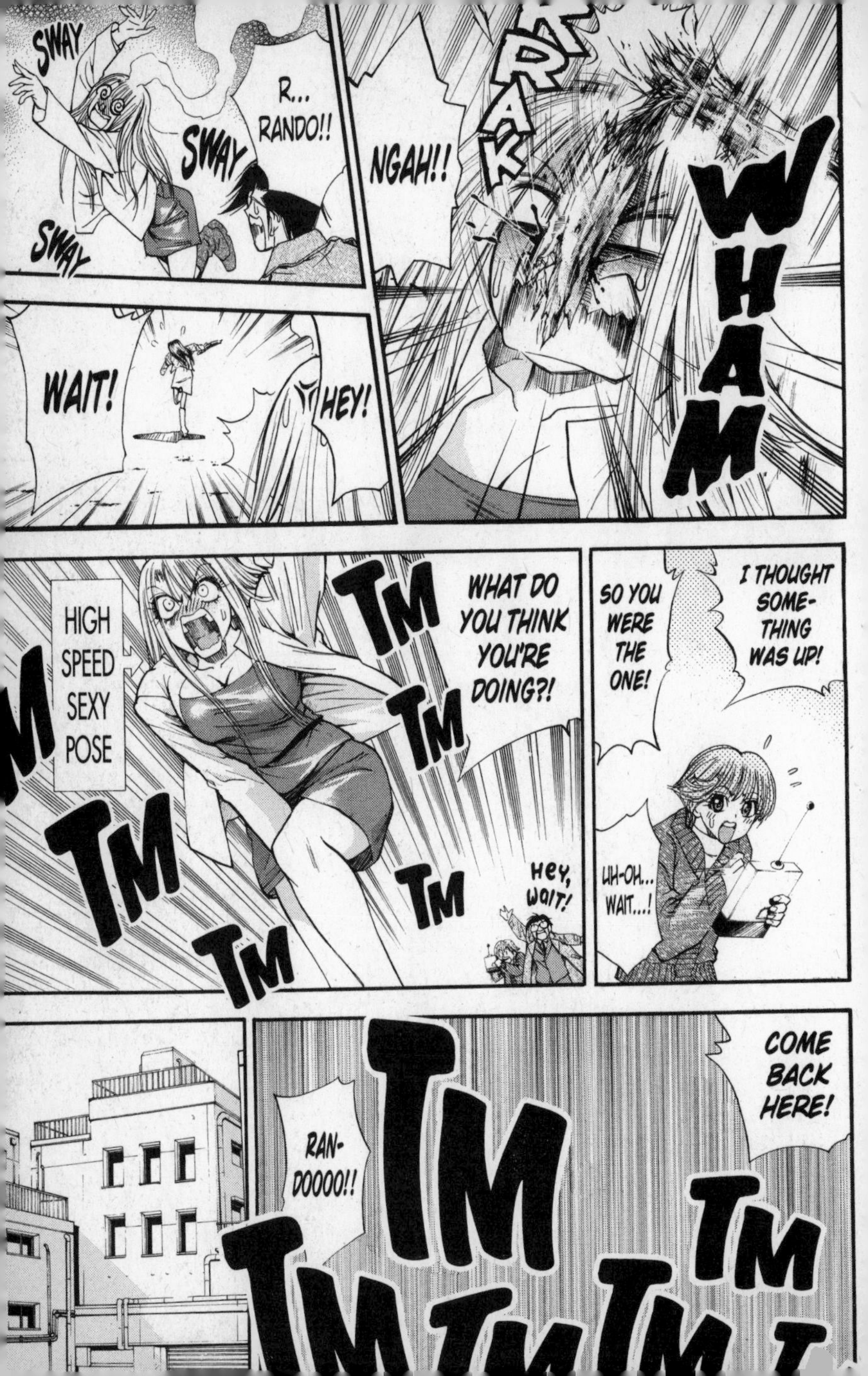
RAK
WHAM
NGAH!!
R... RANDO!!
SWAY
SWAY
SWAY
HEY!
WAIT!
I THOUGHT SOME-THING WAS UP!
SO YOU WERE THE ONE!
UH-OH... WAIT...!
WHAT DO YOU THINK YOU'RE DOING?!
TM TM TM TM TM
HIGH SPEED SEXY POSE
Hey, wait!
COME BACK HERE!
RAN-DOOOO!!
TM TM

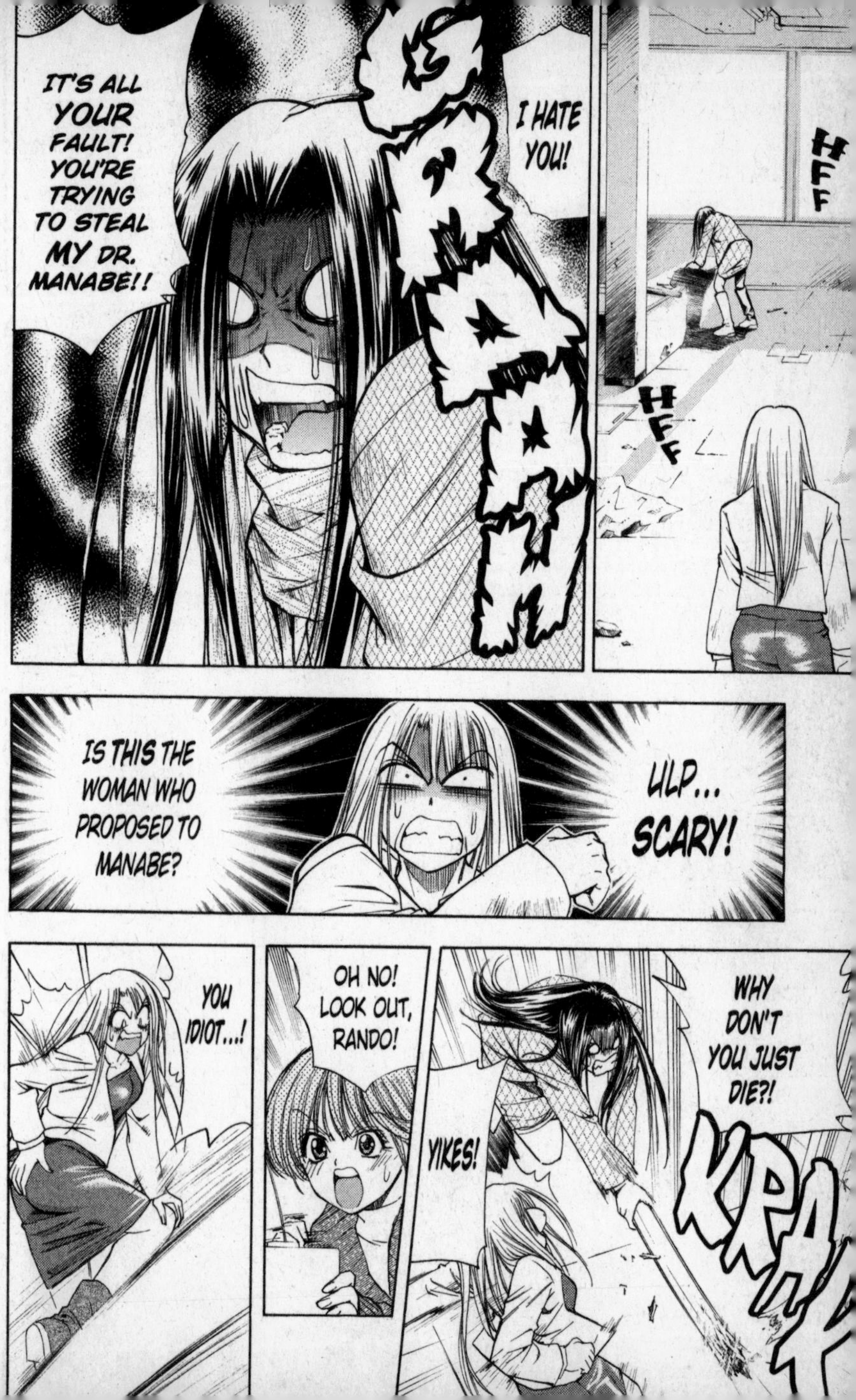
HFF
HFF
I HATE YOU!
IT'S ALL YOUR FAULT! YOU'RE TRYING TO STEAL MY DR. MANABE!!
ULP... SCARY!
IS THIS THE WOMAN WHO PROPOSED TO MANABE?
WHY DON'T YOU JUST DIE?!
YIKES!
OH NO! LOOK OUT, RANDO!
YOU IDIOT...!

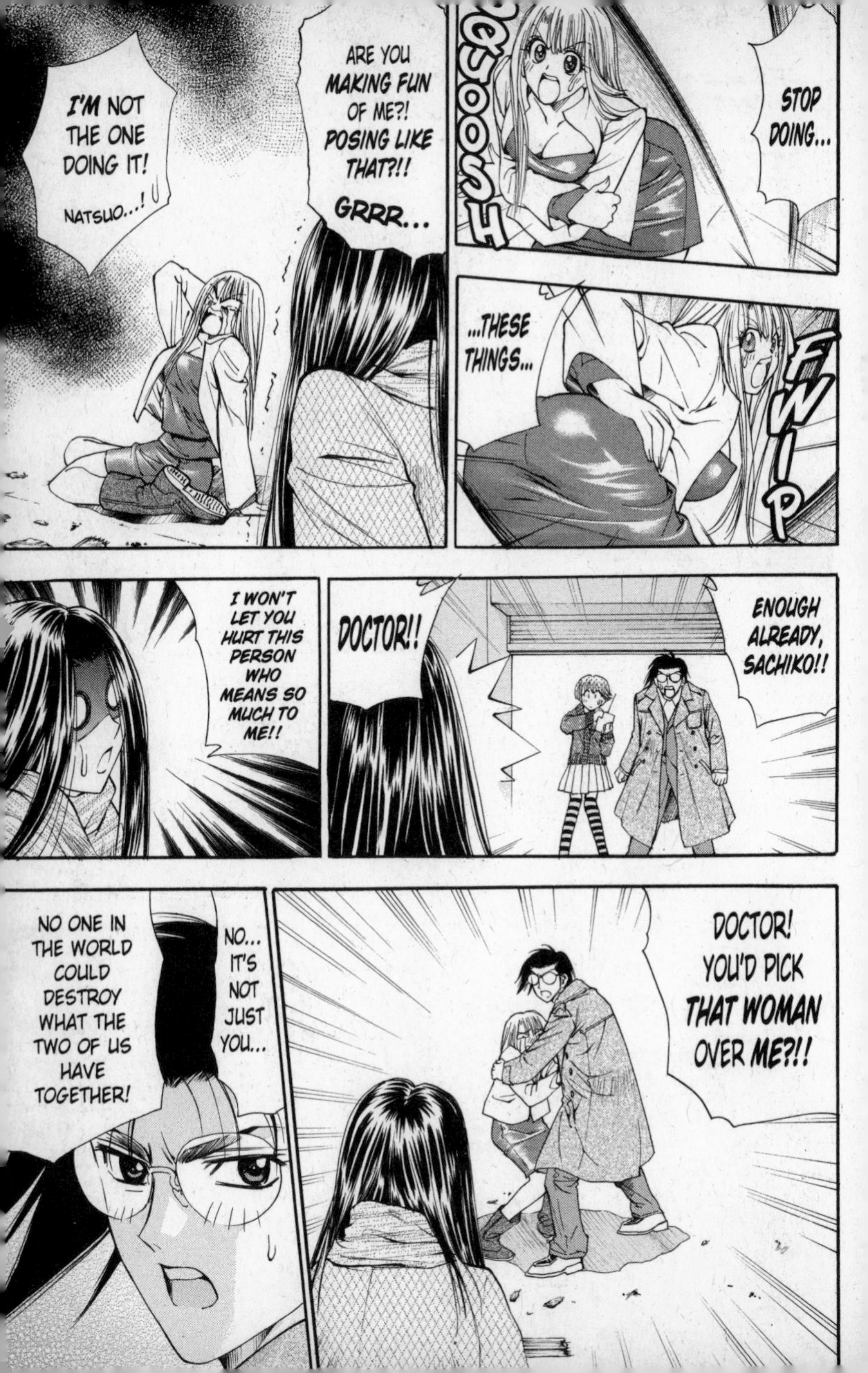
STOP DOING...
SWOOSH
...THESE THINGS...
FWIP
ARE YOU MAKING FUN OF ME?! POSING LIKE THAT?!!
GRRR...
I'M NOT THE ONE DOING IT!
NATSUO...!
ENOUGH ALREADY, SACHIKO!!
DOCTOR!!
I WON'T LET YOU HURT THIS PERSON WHO MEANS SO MUCH TO ME!!
DOCTOR! YOU'D PICK THAT WOMAN OVER ME?!!
NO... IT'S NOT JUST YOU...
NO ONE IN THE WORLD COULD DESTROY WHAT THE TWO OF US HAVE TOGETHER!

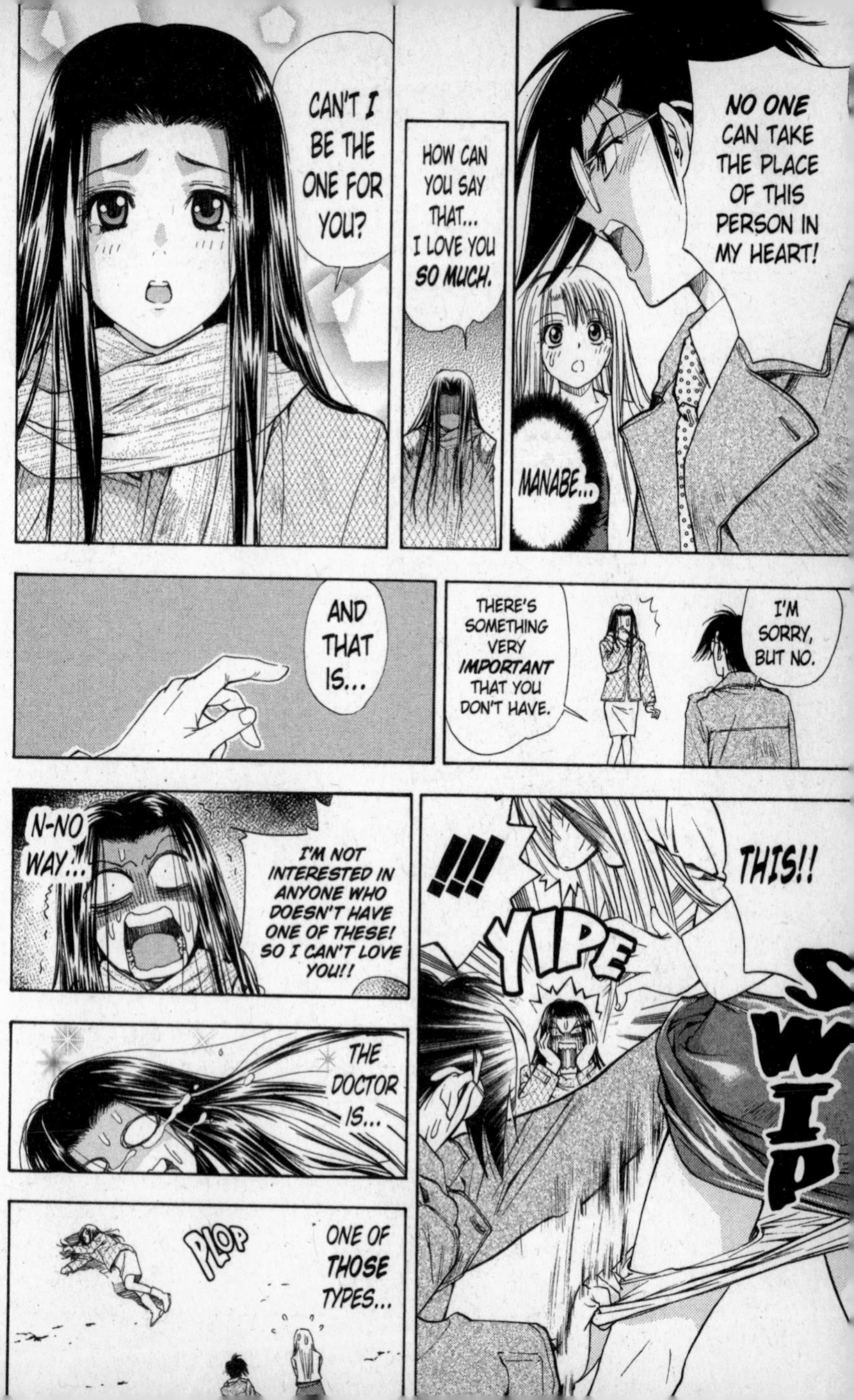
NO ONE CAN TAKE THE PLACE OF THIS PERSON IN MY HEART!
MANABE...
HOW CAN YOU SAY THAT... I LOVE YOU SO MUCH.
CAN'T I BE THE ONE FOR YOU?
I'M SORRY, BUT NO.
THERE'S SOMETHING VERY IMPORTANT THAT YOU DON'T HAVE.
AND THAT IS...
THIS!!
!!!
YIPE
SWIP
N-NO WAY...
I'M NOT INTERESTED IN ANYONE WHO DOESN'T HAVE ONE OF THESE! SO I CAN'T LOVE YOU!!
THE DOCTOR IS...
PLOP
ONE OF THOSE TYPES...

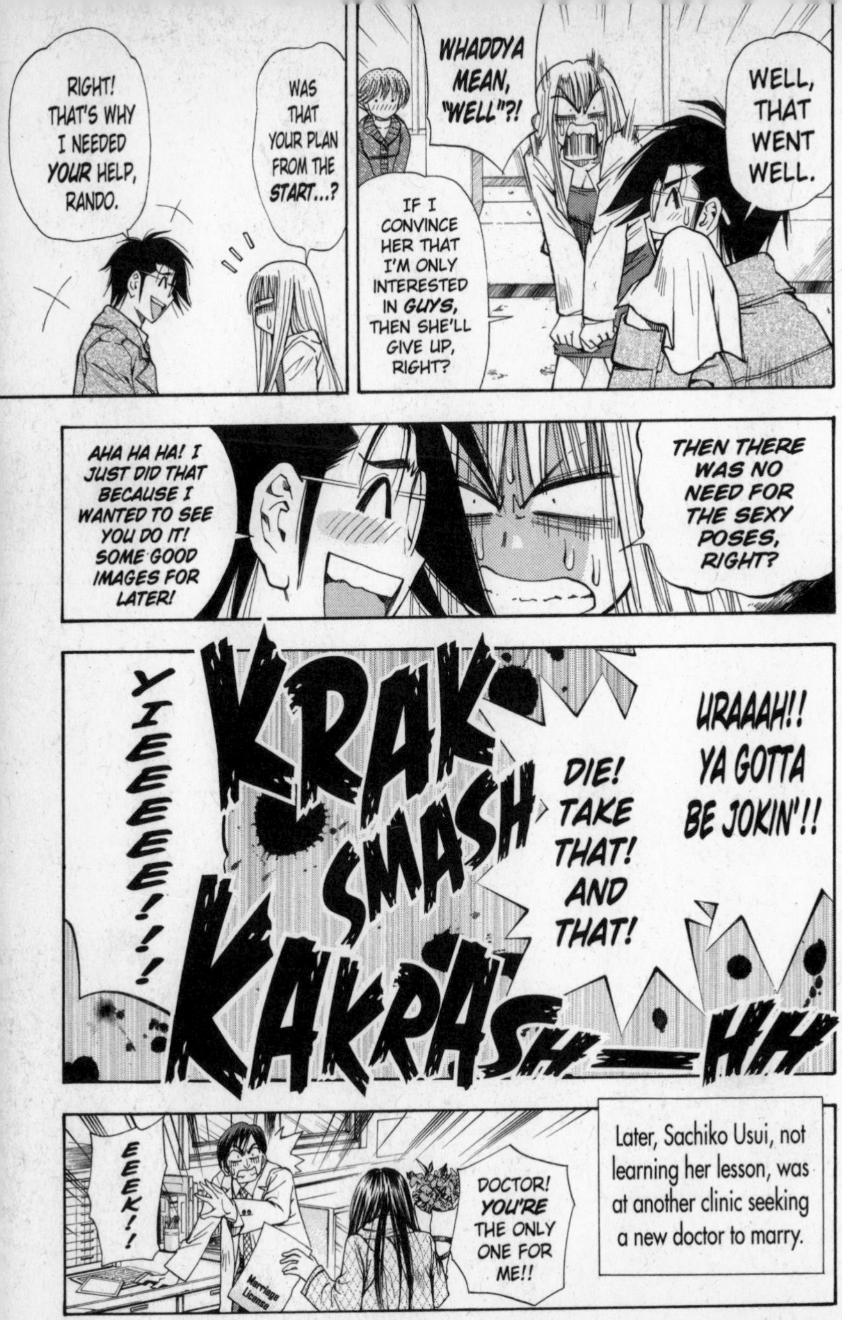
WELL, THAT WENT WELL.
WHADDYA MEAN, "WELL"?!
IF I CONVINCE HER THAT I'M ONLY INTERESTED IN GUYS, THEN SHE'LL GIVE UP, RIGHT?
WAS THAT YOUR PLAN FROM THE START...?
RIGHT! THAT'S WHY I NEEDED YOUR HELP, RANDO.
THEN THERE WAS NO NEED FOR THE SEXY POSES, RIGHT?
AHA HA HA! I JUST DID THAT BECAUSE I WANTED TO SEE YOU DO IT! SOME GOOD IMAGES FOR LATER!
URAAAH!! YA GOTTA BE JOKIN'!!
DIE! TAKE THAT! AND THAT!
KRAK SMASH KAKRASH—HH
YIEEEEEE!!!
Later, Sachiko Usui, not learning her lesson, was at another clinic seeking a new doctor to marry.
DOCTOR! YOU'RE THE ONLY ONE FOR ME!!
Marriage License
EEEK!!

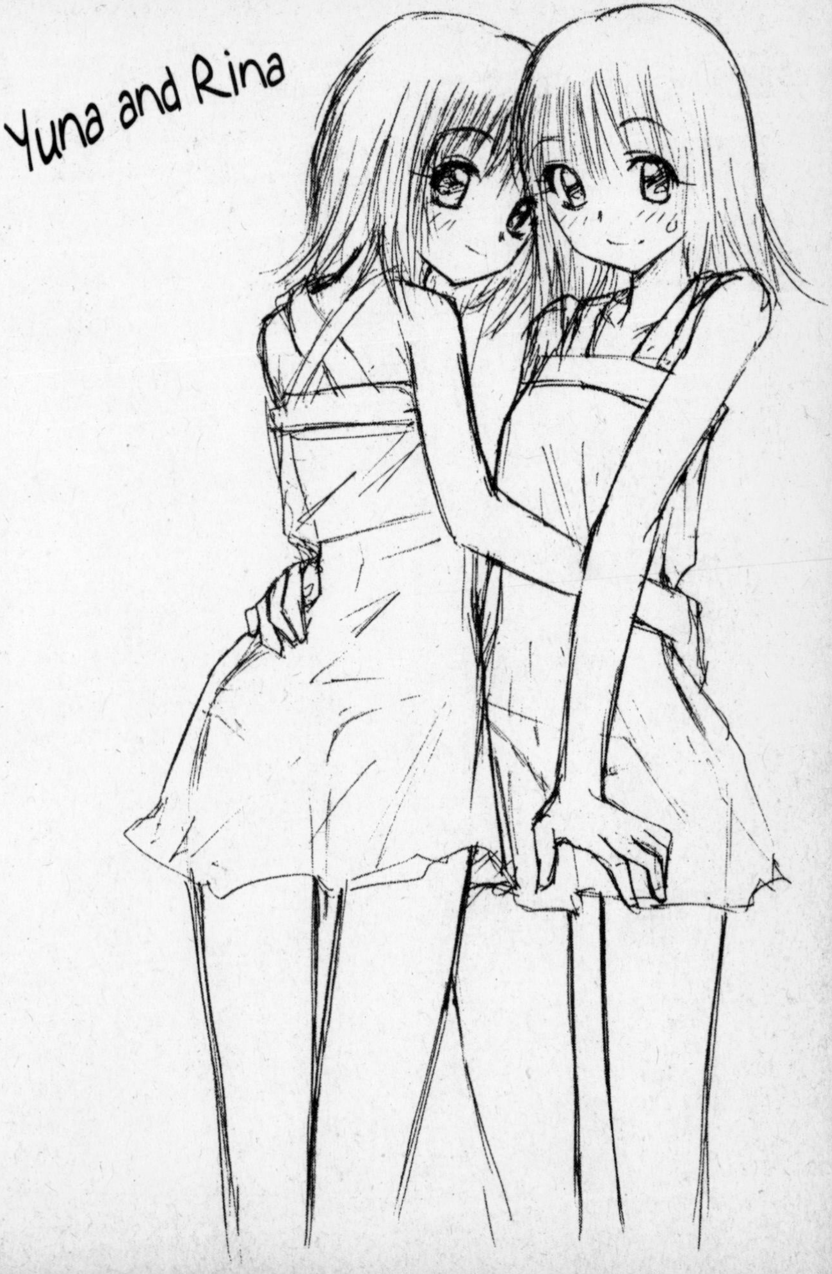
Yuna and Rina

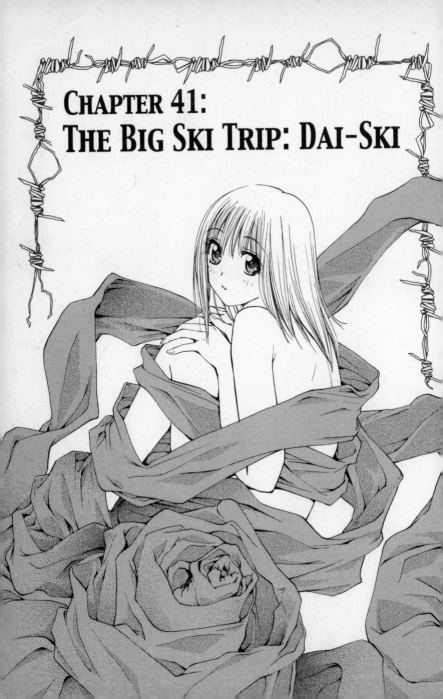

Chapter 41:
The Big Ski Trip: Dai-Ski

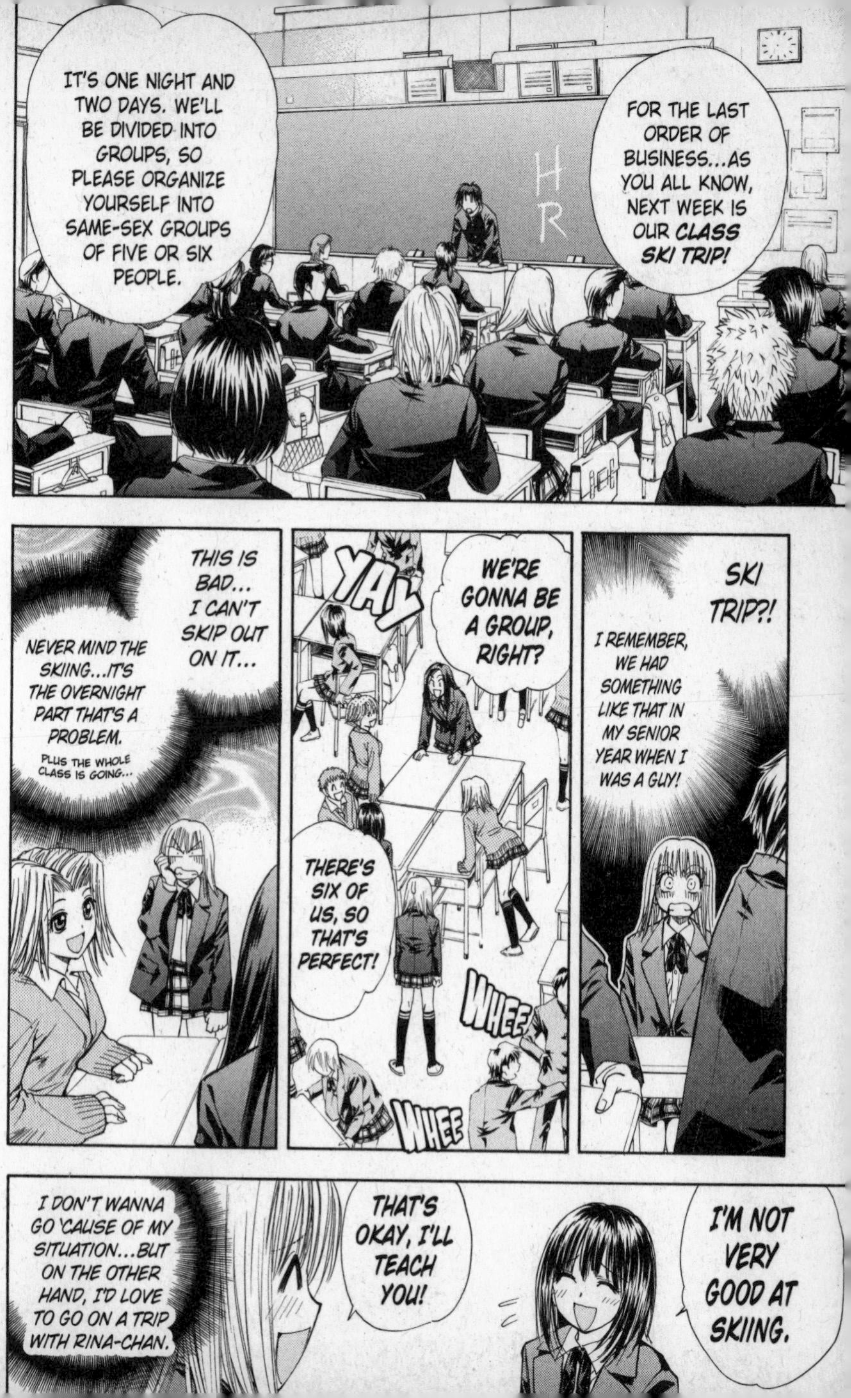
FOR THE LAST ORDER OF BUSINESS...AS YOU ALL KNOW, NEXT WEEK IS OUR CLASS SKI TRIP!
IT'S ONE NIGHT AND TWO DAYS. WE'LL BE DIVIDED INTO GROUPS, SO PLEASE ORGANIZE YOURSELF INTO SAME-SEX GROUPS OF FIVE OR SIX PEOPLE.
HR
SKI TRIP?!
I REMEMBER, WE HAD SOMETHING LIKE THAT IN MY SENIOR YEAR WHEN I WAS A GUY!
YAY
WE'RE GONNA BE A GROUP, RIGHT?
THERE'S SIX OF US, SO THAT'S PERFECT!
WHEE
WHEE
THIS IS BAD... I CAN'T SKIP OUT ON IT...
NEVER MIND THE SKIING...IT'S THE OVERNIGHT PART THAT'S A PROBLEM.
PLUS THE WHOLE CLASS IS GOING...
I'M NOT VERY GOOD AT SKIING.
THAT'S OKAY, I'LL TEACH YOU!
I DON'T WANNA GO 'CAUSE OF MY SITUATION...BUT ON THE OTHER HAND, I'D LOVE TO GO ON A TRIP WITH RINA-CHAN.

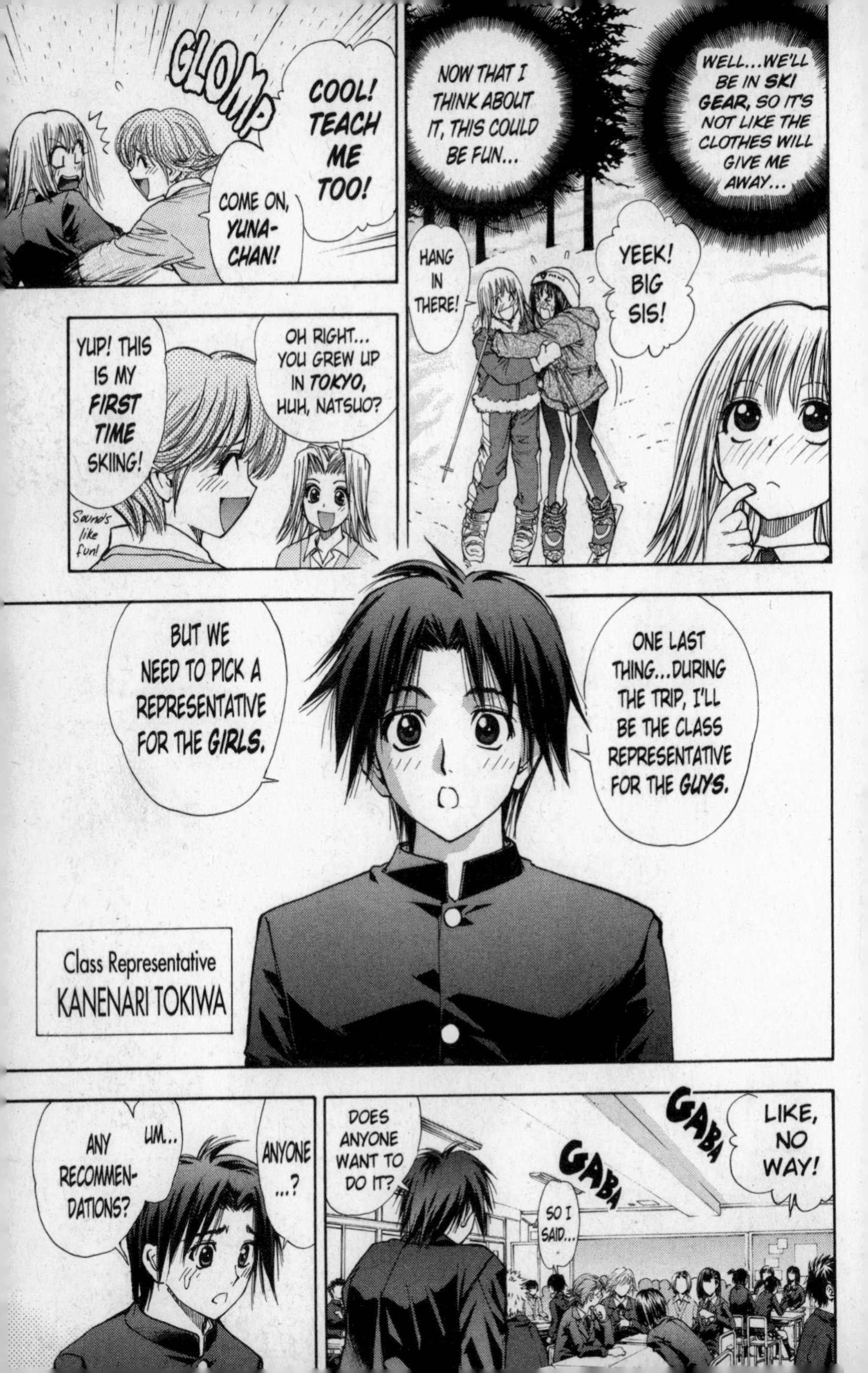
WELL...WE'LL BE IN SKI GEAR, SO IT'S NOT LIKE THE CLOTHES WILL GIVE ME AWAY...
NOW THAT I THINK ABOUT IT, THIS COULD BE FUN...
YEEK! BIG SIS!
HANG IN THERE!
GLOMP
COOL! TEACH ME TOO!
COME ON, YUNA-CHAN!
OH RIGHT... YOU GREW UP IN TOKYO, HUH, NATSUO?
YUP! THIS IS MY FIRST TIME SKIING!
Sounds like fun!
ONE LAST THING...DURING THE TRIP, I'LL BE THE CLASS REPRESENTATIVE FOR THE GUYS.
BUT WE NEED TO PICK A REPRESENTATIVE FOR THE GIRLS.
Class Representative
KANENARI TOKIWA
LIKE, NO WAY!
GABA
GABA
SO I SAID...
DOES ANYONE WANT TO DO IT?
ANYONE ...?
UM...
ANY RECOMMEN-DATIONS?

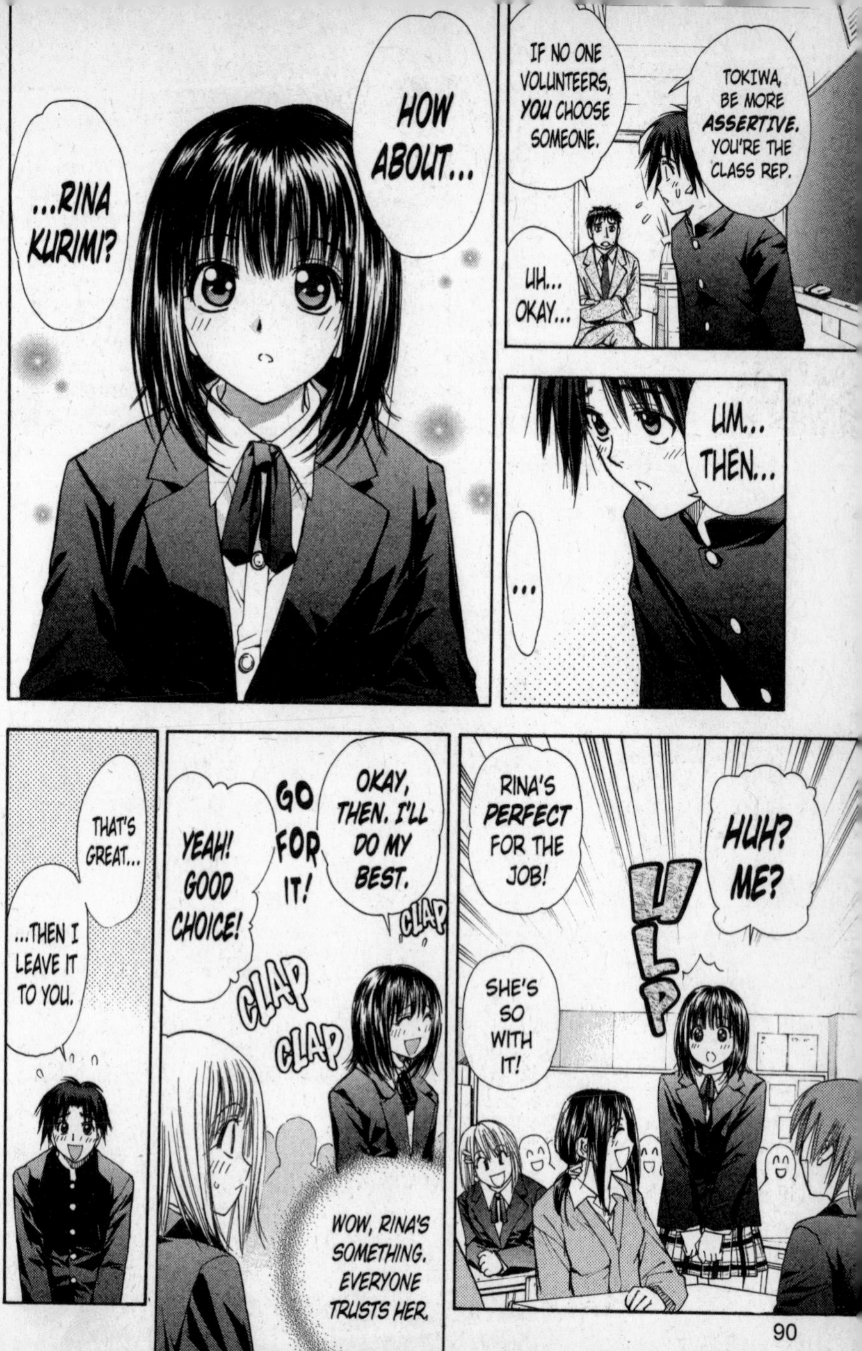
TOKIWA, BE MORE ASSERTIVE. YOU'RE THE CLASS REP.
IF NO ONE VOLUNTEERS, YOU CHOOSE SOMEONE.
UH... OKAY...
UM... THEN...
...
HOW ABOUT...
...RINA KURIMI?
HUH? ME?
ULP
RINA'S PERFECT FOR THE JOB!
SHE'S SO WITH IT!
OKAY, THEN. I'LL DO MY BEST.
CLAP
GO FOR IT!
YEAH! GOOD CHOICE!
CLAP
CLAP
WOW, RINA'S SOMETHING. EVERYONE TRUSTS HER.
THAT'S GREAT...
...THEN I LEAVE IT TO YOU.

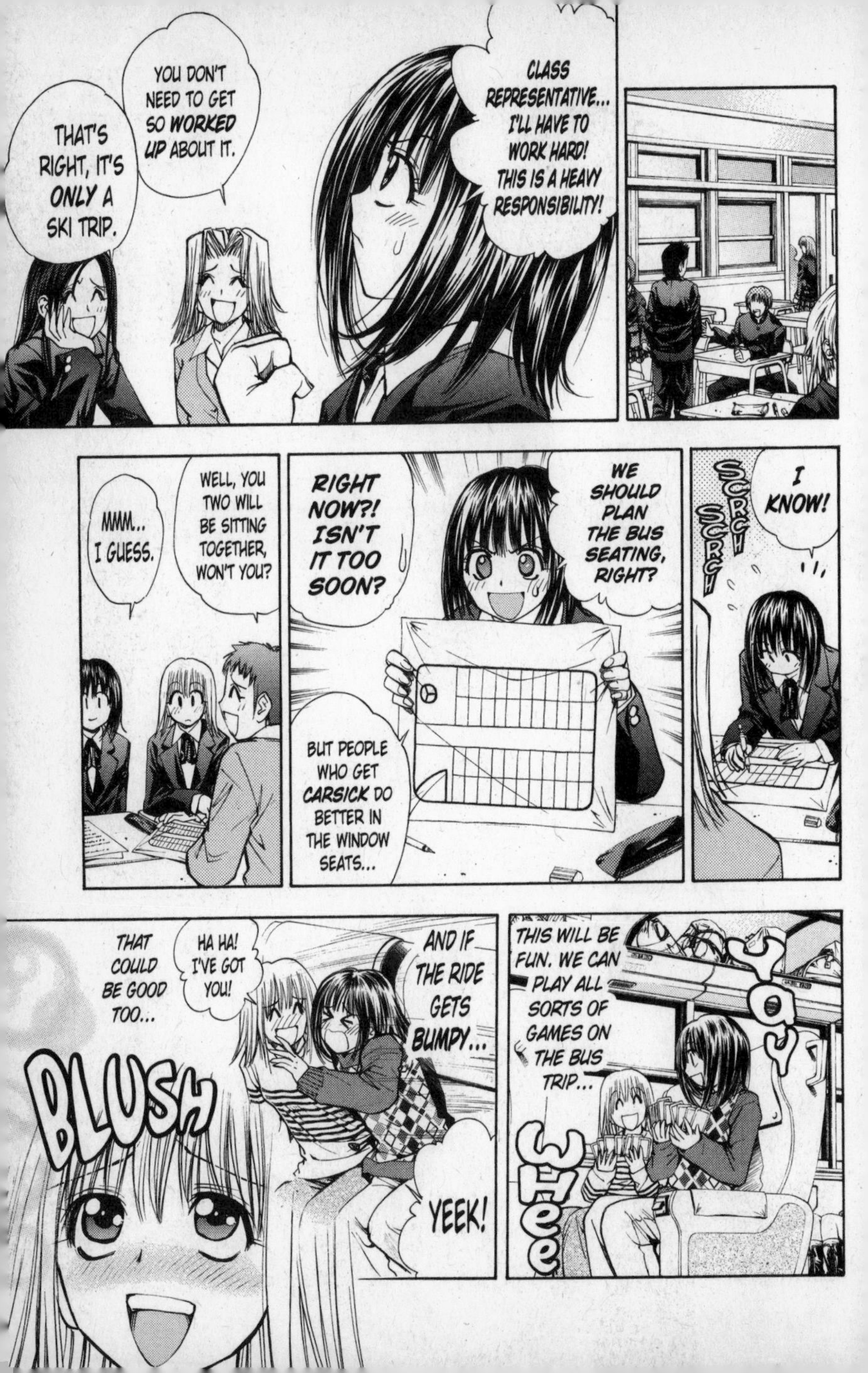
CLASS REPRESENTATIVE... I'LL HAVE TO WORK HARD! THIS IS A HEAVY RESPONSIBILITY!
YOU DON'T NEED TO GET SO WORKED UP ABOUT IT.
THAT'S RIGHT, IT'S ONLY A SKI TRIP.
SCRCH SCRCH
I KNOW!
WE SHOULD PLAN THE BUS SEATING, RIGHT?
RIGHT NOW?! ISN'T IT TOO SOON?
BUT PEOPLE WHO GET CARSICK DO BETTER IN THE WINDOW SEATS...
WELL, YOU TWO WILL BE SITTING TOGETHER, WON'T YOU?
MMM... I GUESS.
Yay
THIS WILL BE FUN. WE CAN PLAY ALL SORTS OF GAMES ON THE BUS TRIP...
Whee
AND IF THE RIDE GETS BUMPY...
HA HA! I'VE GOT YOU!
YEEK!
THAT COULD BE GOOD TOO...
BLUSH

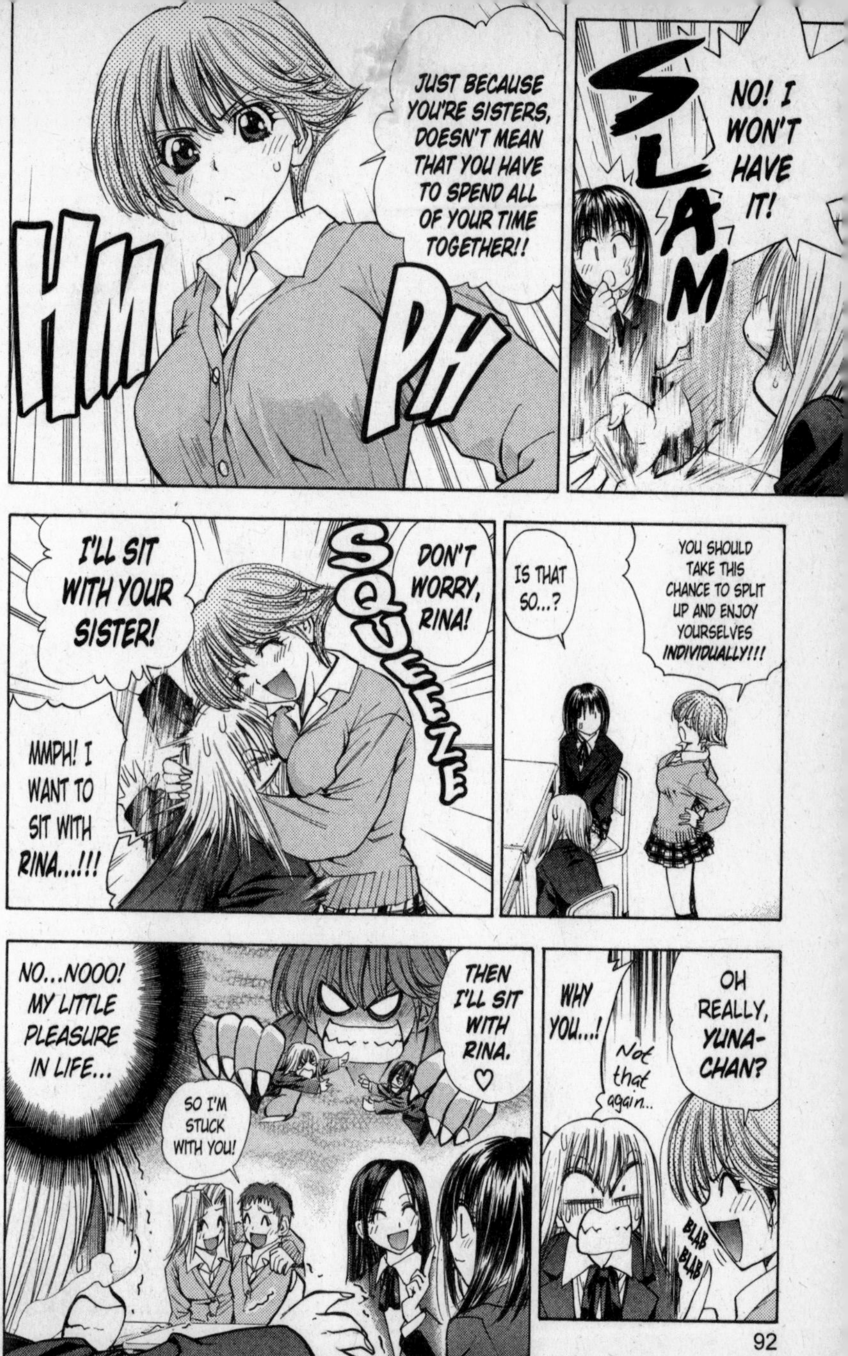
SLAM
NO! I WON'T HAVE IT!
JUST BECAUSE YOU'RE SISTERS, DOESN'T MEAN THAT YOU HAVE TO SPEND ALL OF YOUR TIME TOGETHER!!
HMPH
YOU SHOULD TAKE THIS CHANCE TO SPLIT UP AND ENJOY YOURSELVES INDIVIDUALLY!!!
IS THAT SO...?
DON'T WORRY, RINA!
SQUEEZE
I'LL SIT WITH YOUR SISTER!
MMPH! I WANT TO SIT WITH RINA...!!!
OH REALLY, YUNA-CHAN?
Not that again...
WHY YOU...!
BLAB BLAB
THEN I'LL SIT WITH RINA. ♡
NO...NOOO! MY LITTLE PLEASURE IN LIFE...
SO I'M STUCK WITH YOU!

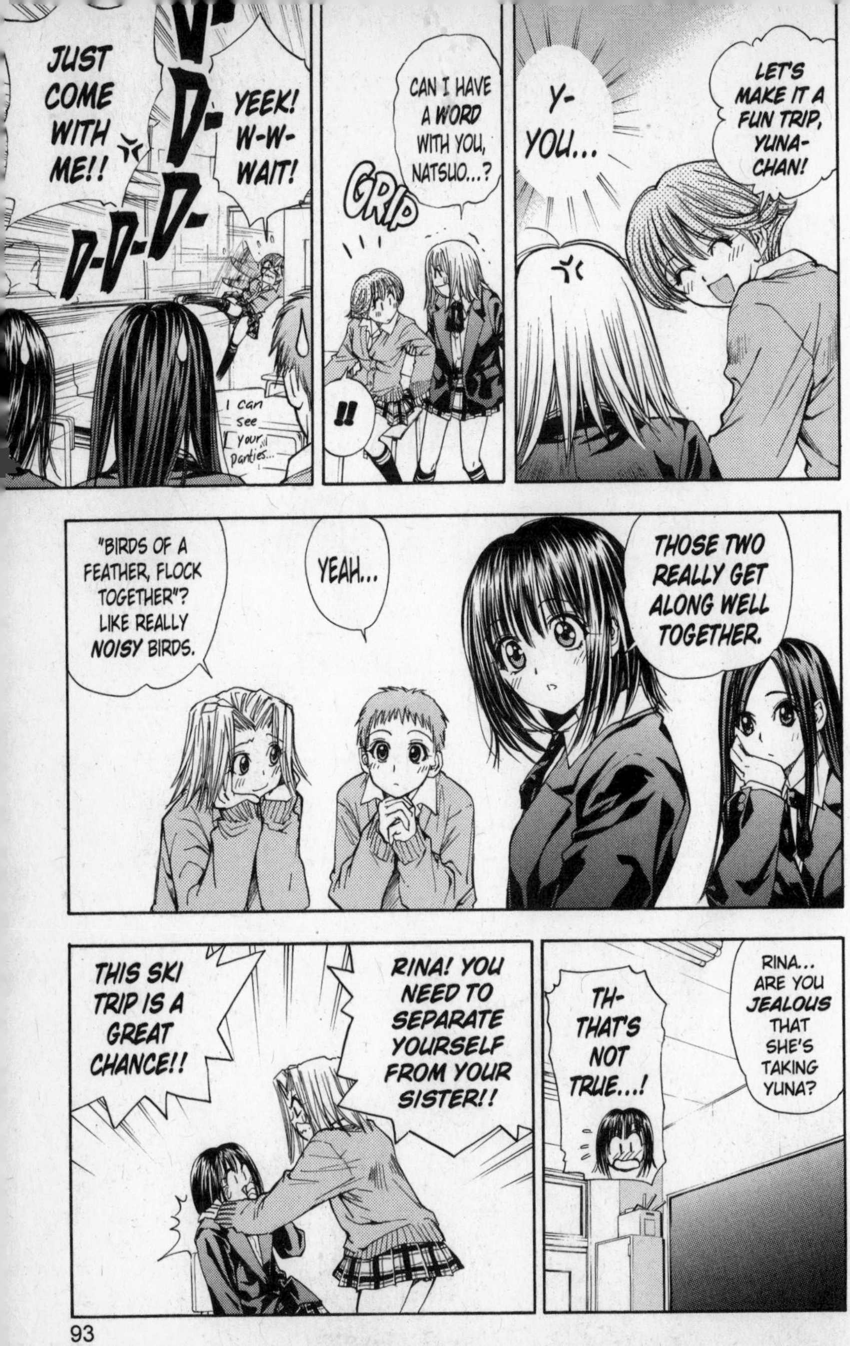
LET'S MAKE IT A FUN TRIP, YUNA-CHAN!
Y-YOU...
CAN I HAVE A WORD WITH YOU, NATSUO...?
GRIP
!!
YEEK! W-W-WAIT!
JUST COME WITH ME!!
D-D-D-D-D-D-
I can see your panties...
THOSE TWO REALLY GET ALONG WELL TOGETHER.
YEAH...
"BIRDS OF A FEATHER, FLOCK TOGETHER"? LIKE REALLY NOISY BIRDS.
RINA... ARE YOU JEALOUS THAT SHE'S TAKING YUNA?
TH-THAT'S NOT TRUE...!
RINA! YOU NEED TO SEPARATE YOURSELF FROM YOUR SISTER!!
THIS SKI TRIP IS A GREAT CHANCE!!

I'M SORRY, BUT COULD YOU STAY AFTER SCHOOL FOR A BIT? IT'S ABOUT THE SKI TRIP.

TOKIWA...

WE'RE NOT ALL LIKE YOU...

CLONK

IT'S EASY TO HOOK UP AT AN EVENT LIKE THIS! THINK OF IT...ALONE IN A CABIN IN THE WOODS!

THIS IS YOUR BIG CHANCE TO GET A GUY!

UM... EXCUSE ME, KURIMI...

What was that for?!

WAAH

OWIE!

Y'KNOW, YOU'RE GETTIN' A BIT PUSHY THESE DAYS.

WHAT'S THE BIG DEAL, YUNA-CHAN?

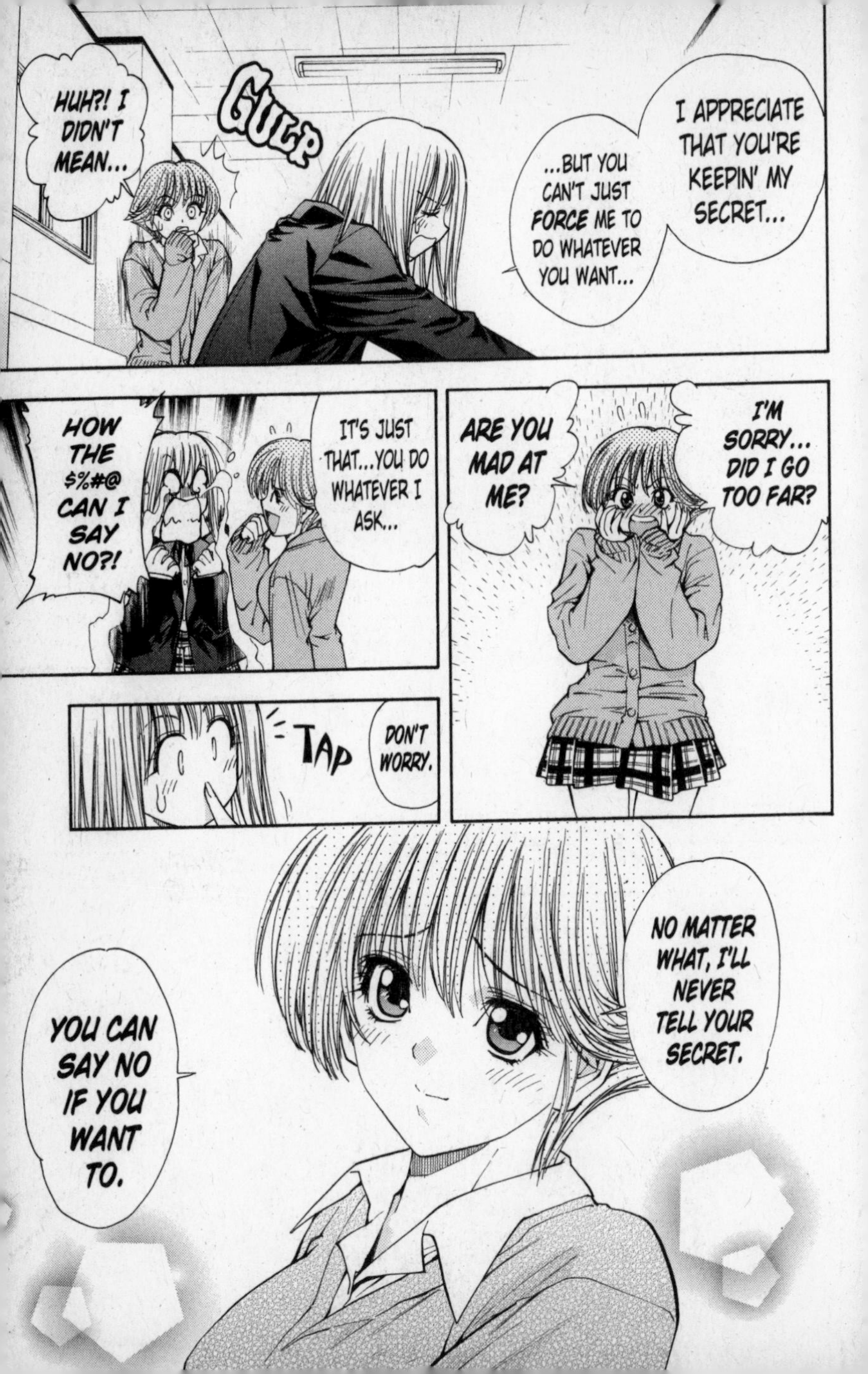
I APPRECIATE THAT YOU'RE KEEPIN' MY SECRET...
...BUT YOU CAN'T JUST FORCE ME TO DO WHATEVER YOU WANT...
GULP
HUH?! I DIDN'T MEAN...
I'M SORRY... DID I GO TOO FAR?
ARE YOU MAD AT ME?
IT'S JUST THAT...YOU DO WHATEVER I ASK...
HOW THE $%#@ CAN I SAY NO?!
DON'T WORRY.
TAP
NO MATTER WHAT, I'LL NEVER TELL YOUR SECRET.
YOU CAN SAY NO IF YOU WANT TO.

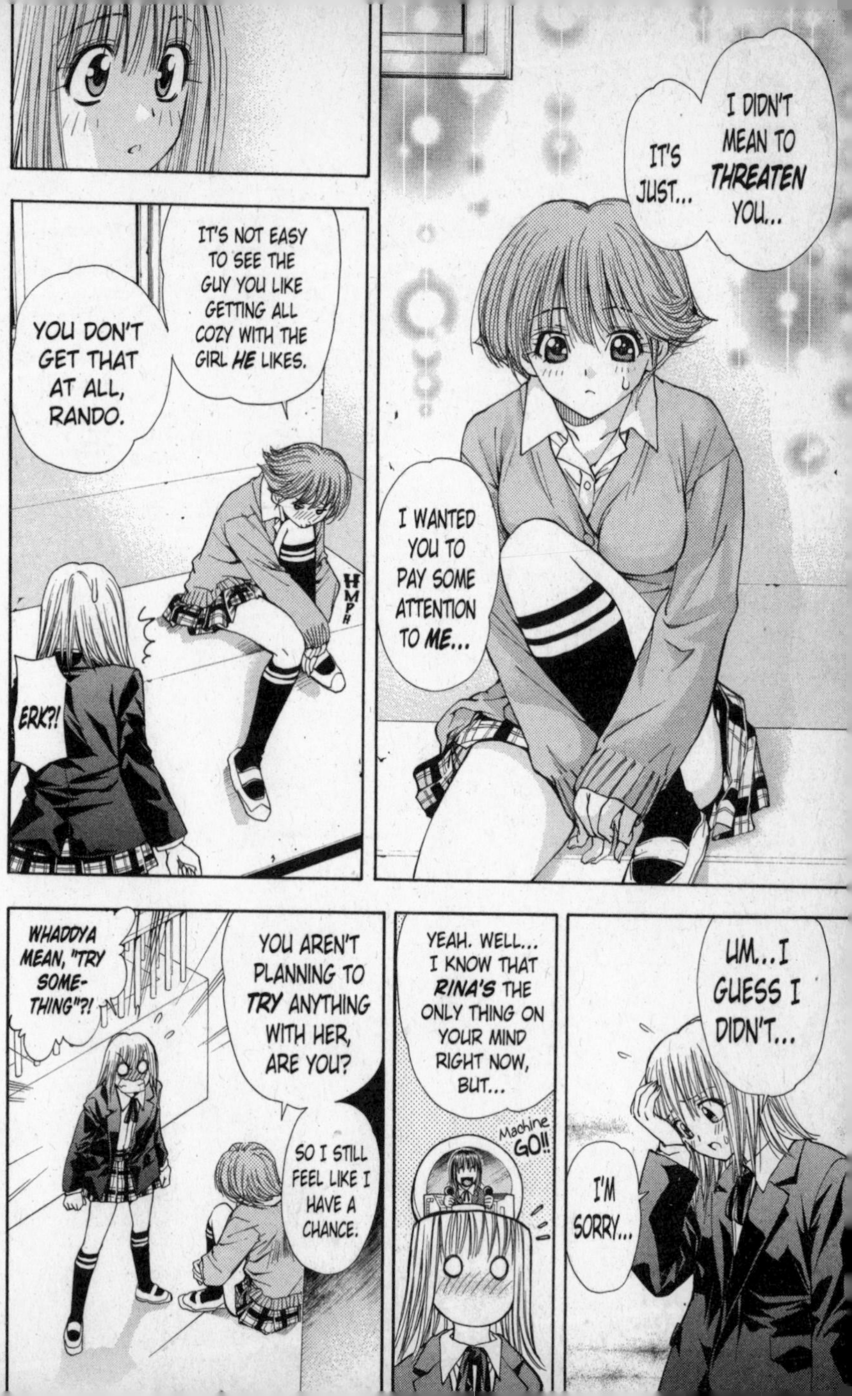
I DIDN'T MEAN TO **THREATEN** YOU...
IT'S JUST...
I WANTED YOU TO PAY SOME ATTENTION TO **ME**...
IT'S NOT EASY TO SEE THE GUY YOU LIKE GETTING ALL COZY WITH THE GIRL **HE** LIKES.
YOU DON'T GET THAT AT ALL, RANDO.
HMPH
ERK?!
UM...I GUESS I DIDN'T...
I'M SORRY...
YEAH. WELL... I KNOW THAT **RINA'S** THE ONLY THING ON YOUR MIND RIGHT NOW, BUT...
Machine GO!!
YOU AREN'T PLANNING TO **TRY** ANYTHING WITH HER, ARE YOU?
WHADDYA MEAN, "TRY SOME-THING"?!
SO I STILL FEEL LIKE I HAVE A CHANCE.

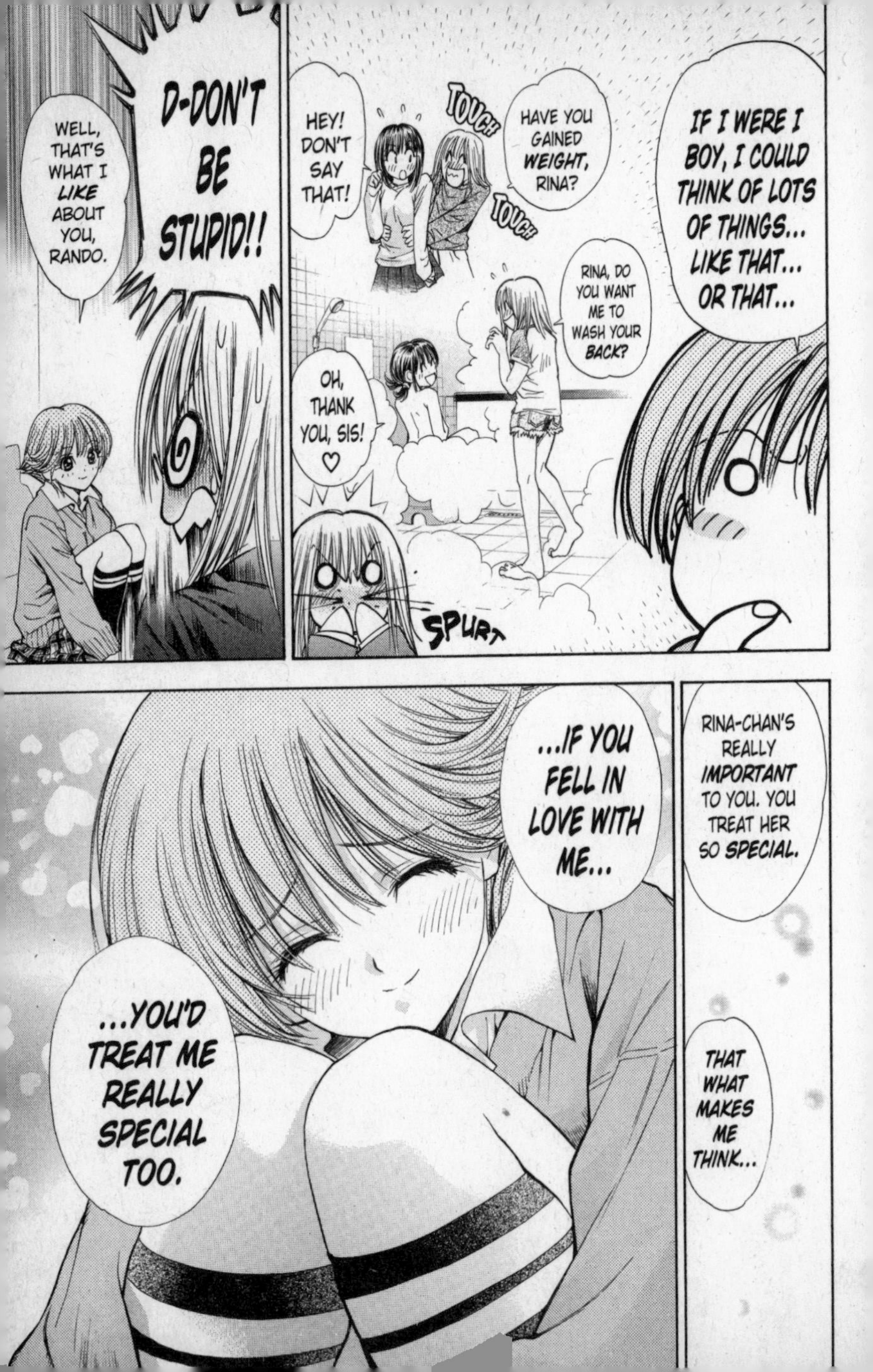
IF I WERE I BOY, I COULD THINK OF LOTS OF THINGS... LIKE THAT... OR THAT...
TOUCH
HAVE YOU GAINED WEIGHT, RINA?
TOUCH
HEY! DON'T SAY THAT!
RINA, DO YOU WANT ME TO WASH YOUR BACK?
OH, THANK YOU, SIS! ♡
SPURT
D-DON'T BE STUPID!!
WELL, THAT'S WHAT I LIKE ABOUT YOU, RANDO.
RINA-CHAN'S REALLY IMPORTANT TO YOU. YOU TREAT HER SO SPECIAL.
THAT WHAT MAKES ME THINK...
...IF YOU FELL IN LOVE WITH ME...
...YOU'D TREAT ME REALLY SPECIAL TOO.

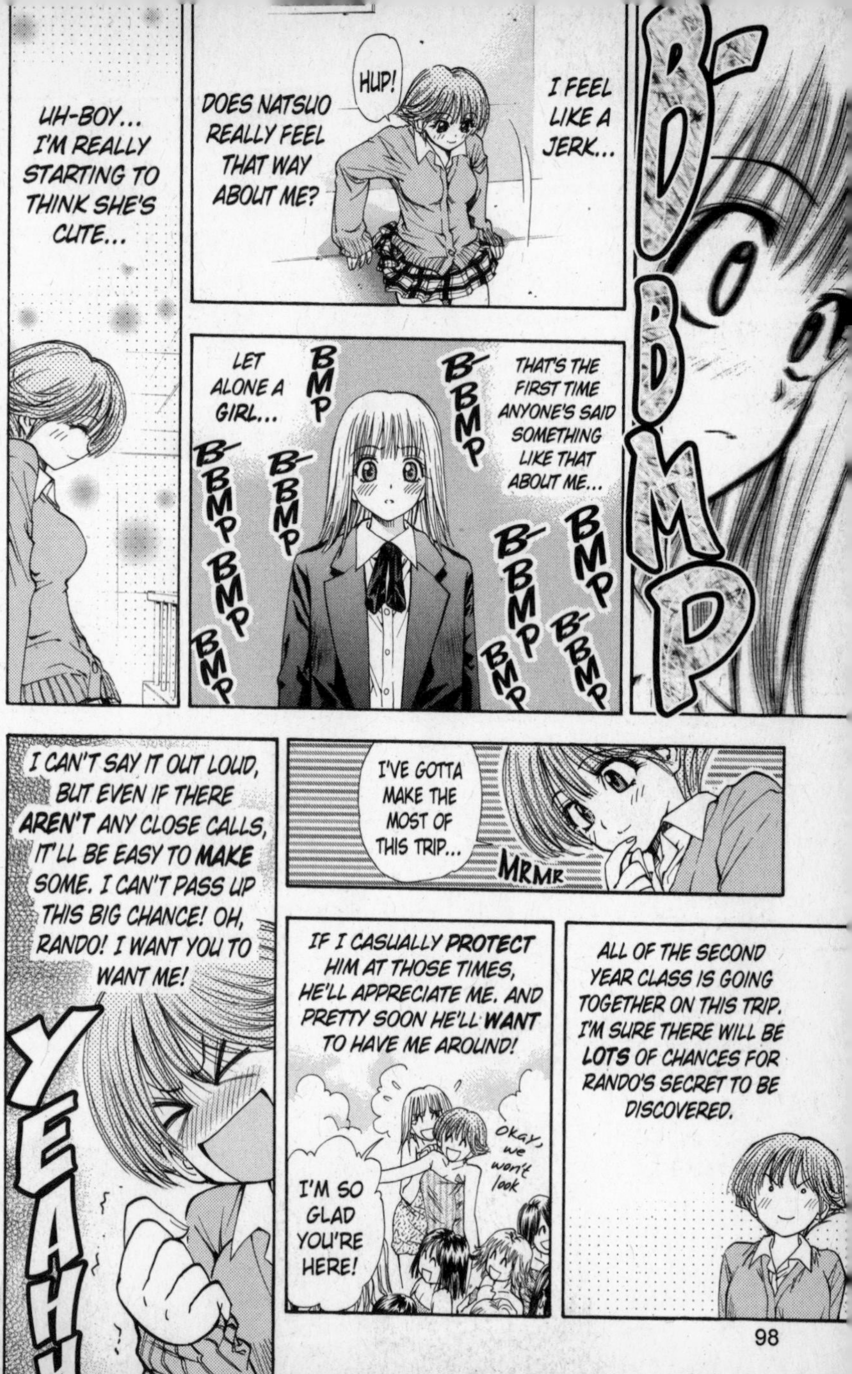
B-BMP
I FEEL LIKE A JERK...
DOES NATSUO REALLY FEEL THAT WAY ABOUT ME?
HUP!
THAT'S THE FIRST TIME ANYONE'S SAID SOMETHING LIKE THAT ABOUT ME...
BMP B-BMP B-BMP BMP B-BMP BMP B-BMP BMP BMP B-BMP BMP BMP
LET ALONE A GIRL...
UH-BOY... I'M REALLY STARTING TO THINK SHE'S CUTE...
I'VE GOTTA MAKE THE MOST OF THIS TRIP...
MRMR
ALL OF THE SECOND YEAR CLASS IS GOING TOGETHER ON THIS TRIP. I'M SURE THERE WILL BE LOTS OF CHANCES FOR RANDO'S SECRET TO BE DISCOVERED.
IF I CASUALLY PROTECT HIM AT THOSE TIMES, HE'LL APPRECIATE ME. AND PRETTY SOON HE'LL WANT TO HAVE ME AROUND!
Okay, we won't look
I'M SO GLAD YOU'RE HERE!
I CAN'T SAY IT OUT LOUD, BUT EVEN IF THERE AREN'T ANY CLOSE CALLS, IT'LL BE EASY TO MAKE SOME. I CAN'T PASS UP THIS BIG CHANCE! OH, RANDO! I WANT YOU TO WANT ME!
YEAHH

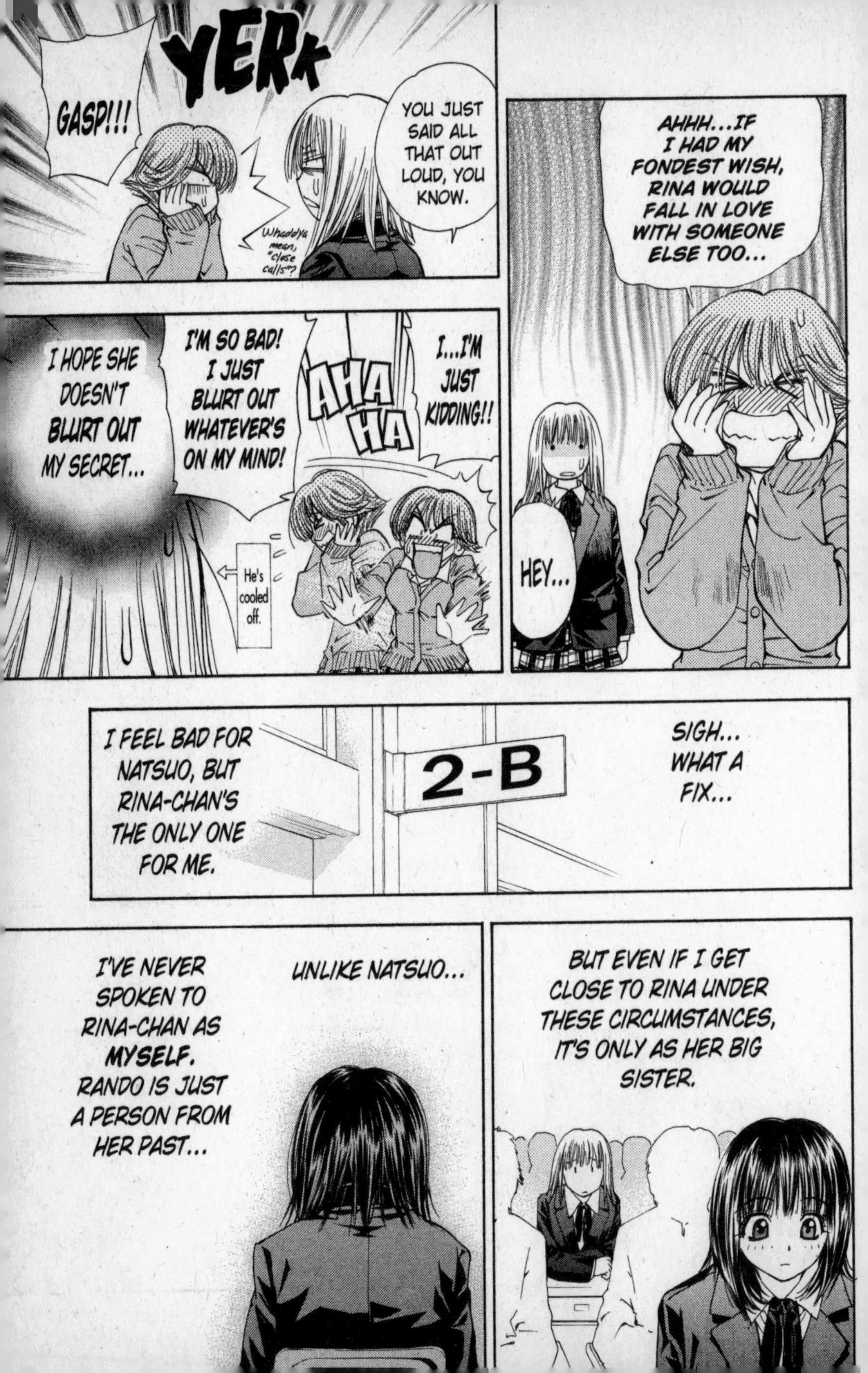
AHHH...IF I HAD MY FONDEST WISH, RINA WOULD FALL IN LOVE WITH SOMEONE ELSE TOO...
HEY...
YOU JUST SAID ALL THAT OUT LOUD, YOU KNOW.
Whaddya mean, "close calls"?
YERK
GASP!!!
I...I'M JUST KIDDING!!
AHA HA
I'M SO BAD! I JUST BLURT OUT WHATEVER'S ON MY MIND!
He's cooled off.
I HOPE SHE DOESN'T BLURT OUT MY SECRET...
SIGH... WHAT A FIX...
2-B
I FEEL BAD FOR NATSUO, BUT RINA-CHAN'S THE ONLY ONE FOR ME.
BUT EVEN IF I GET CLOSE TO RINA UNDER THESE CIRCUMSTANCES, IT'S ONLY AS HER BIG SISTER.
UNLIKE NATSUO...
I'VE NEVER SPOKEN TO RINA-CHAN AS MYSELF. RANDO IS JUST A PERSON FROM HER PAST...

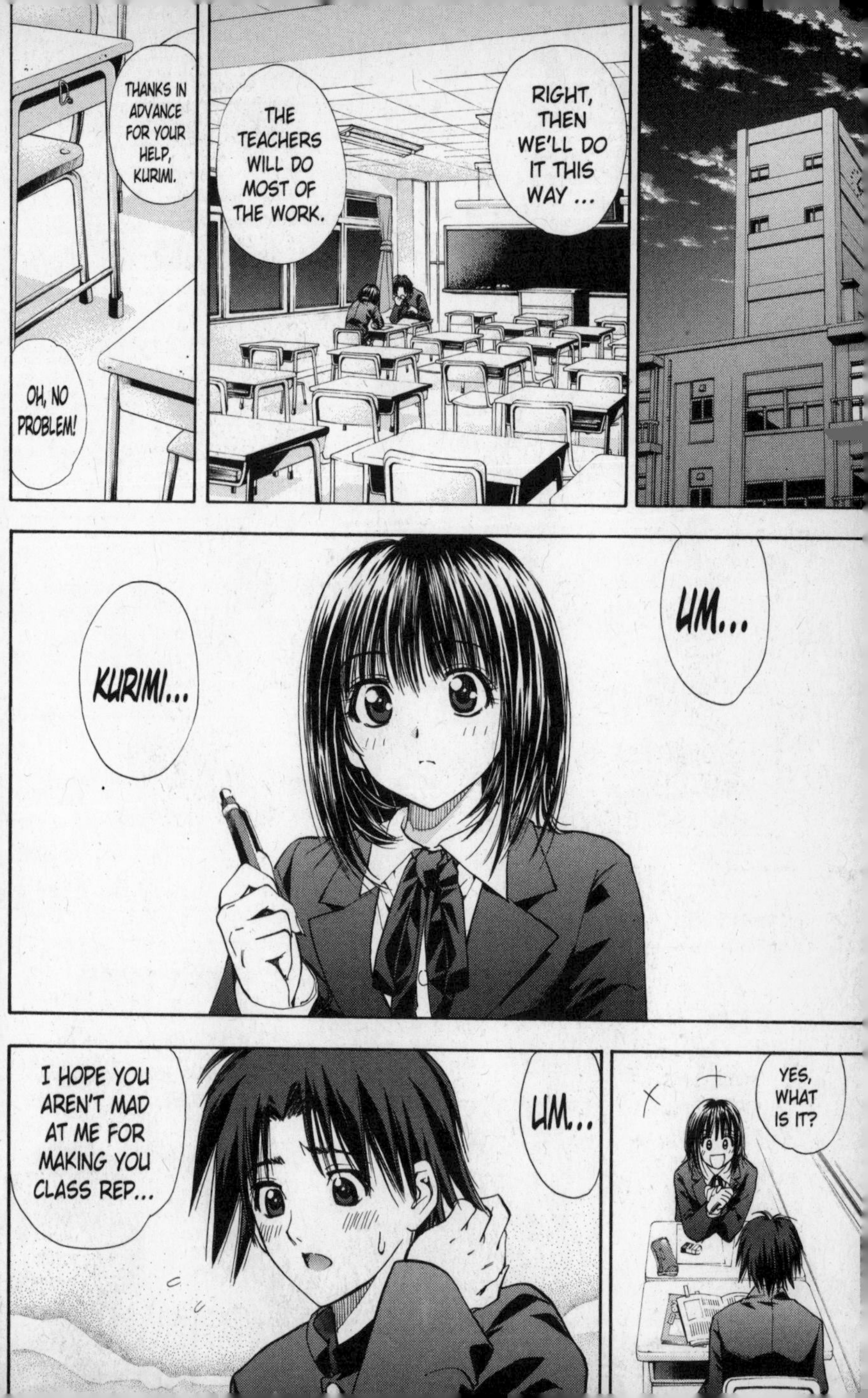
RIGHT, THEN WE'LL DO IT THIS WAY ...
THE TEACHERS WILL DO MOST OF THE WORK.
THANKS IN ADVANCE FOR YOUR HELP, KURIMI.
OH, NO PROBLEM!
UM...
KURIMI...
YES, WHAT IS IT?
UM...
I HOPE YOU AREN'T MAD AT ME FOR MAKING YOU CLASS REP...

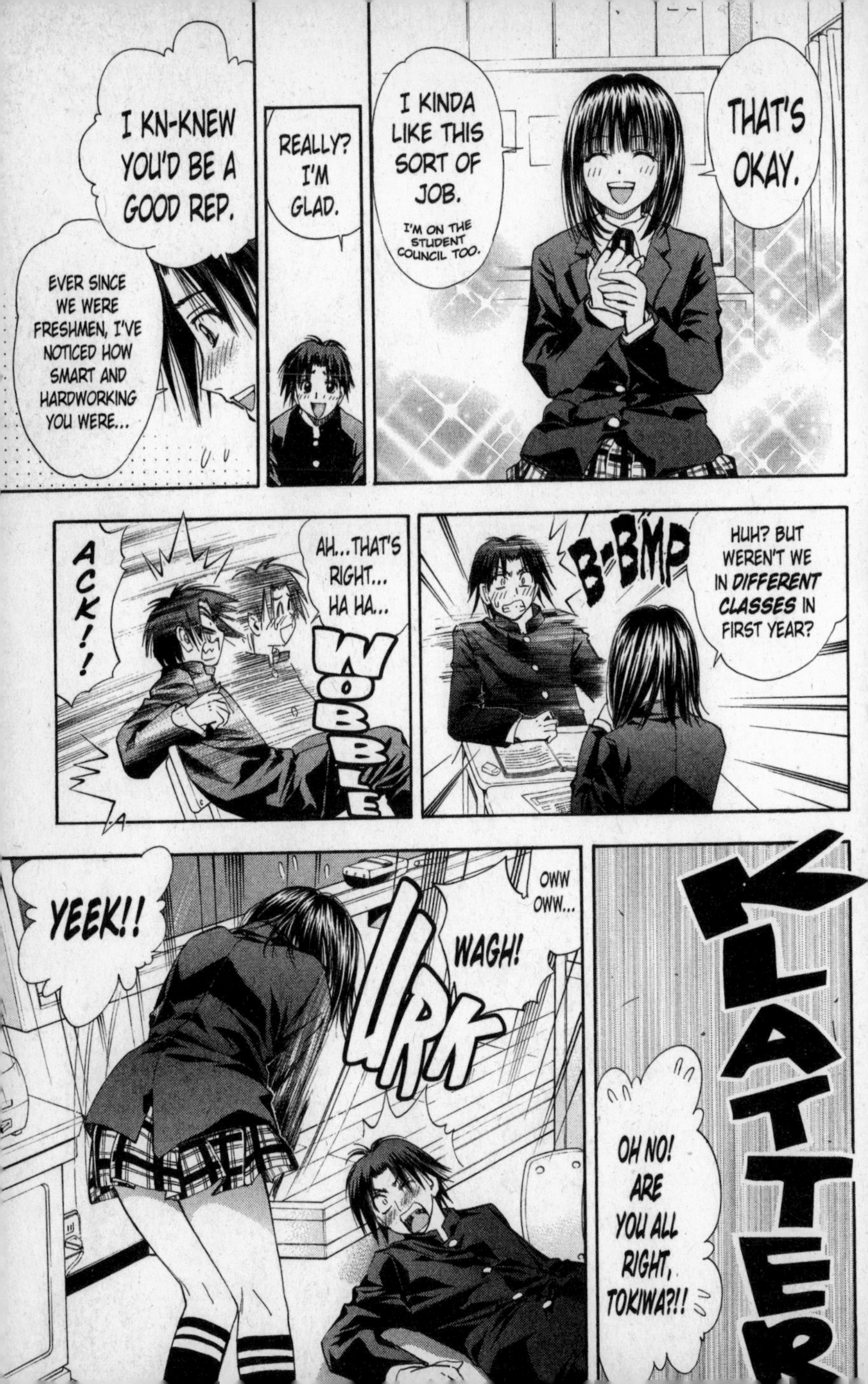
THAT'S OKAY.
I KINDA LIKE THIS SORT OF JOB.
I'M ON THE STUDENT COUNCIL TOO.
REALLY? I'M GLAD.
I KN-KNEW YOU'D BE A GOOD REP.
EVER SINCE WE WERE FRESHMEN, I'VE NOTICED HOW SMART AND HARDWORKING YOU WERE...
B-BMP
HUH? BUT WEREN'T WE IN *DIFFERENT CLASSES* IN FIRST YEAR?
AH...THAT'S RIGHT... HA HA...
WOBBLE
ACK!!
KLATTER
OH NO! ARE YOU ALL RIGHT, TOKIWA?!!
OWW OWW...
WAGH!
URK
YEEK!!

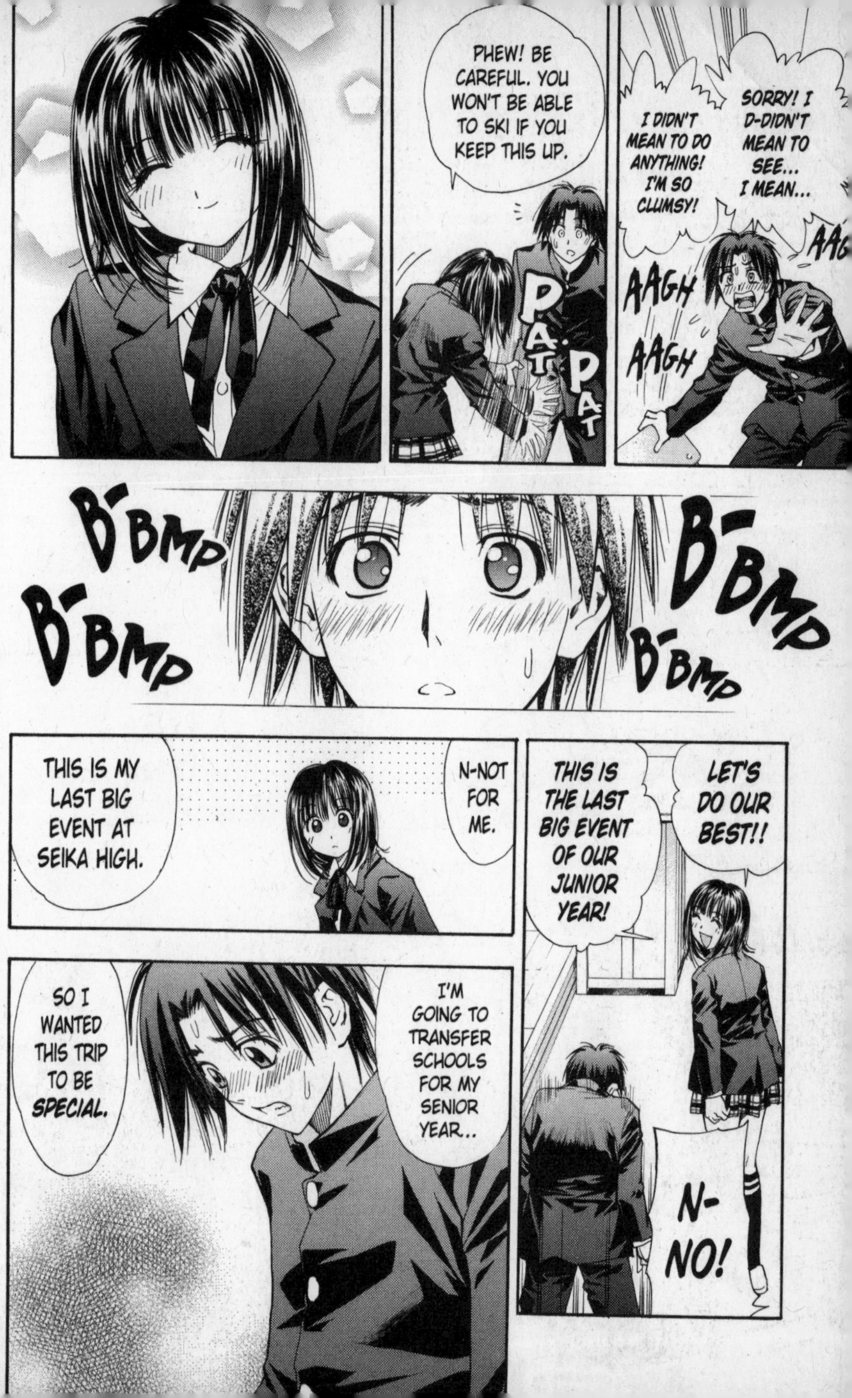
SORRY! I D-DIDN'T MEAN TO SEE... I MEAN...
I DIDN'T MEAN TO DO ANYTHING! I'M SO CLUMSY!
AAG
AAGH
AAGH
PHEW! BE CAREFUL. YOU WON'T BE ABLE TO SKI IF YOU KEEP THIS UP.
PAT PAT
B-BMP
B-BMP
B-BMP
B-BMP
LET'S DO OUR BEST!!
THIS IS THE LAST BIG EVENT OF OUR JUNIOR YEAR!
N-NO!
N-NOT FOR ME.
THIS IS MY LAST BIG EVENT AT SEIKA HIGH.
I'M GOING TO TRANSFER SCHOOLS FOR MY SENIOR YEAR...
SO I WANTED THIS TRIP TO BE SPECIAL.

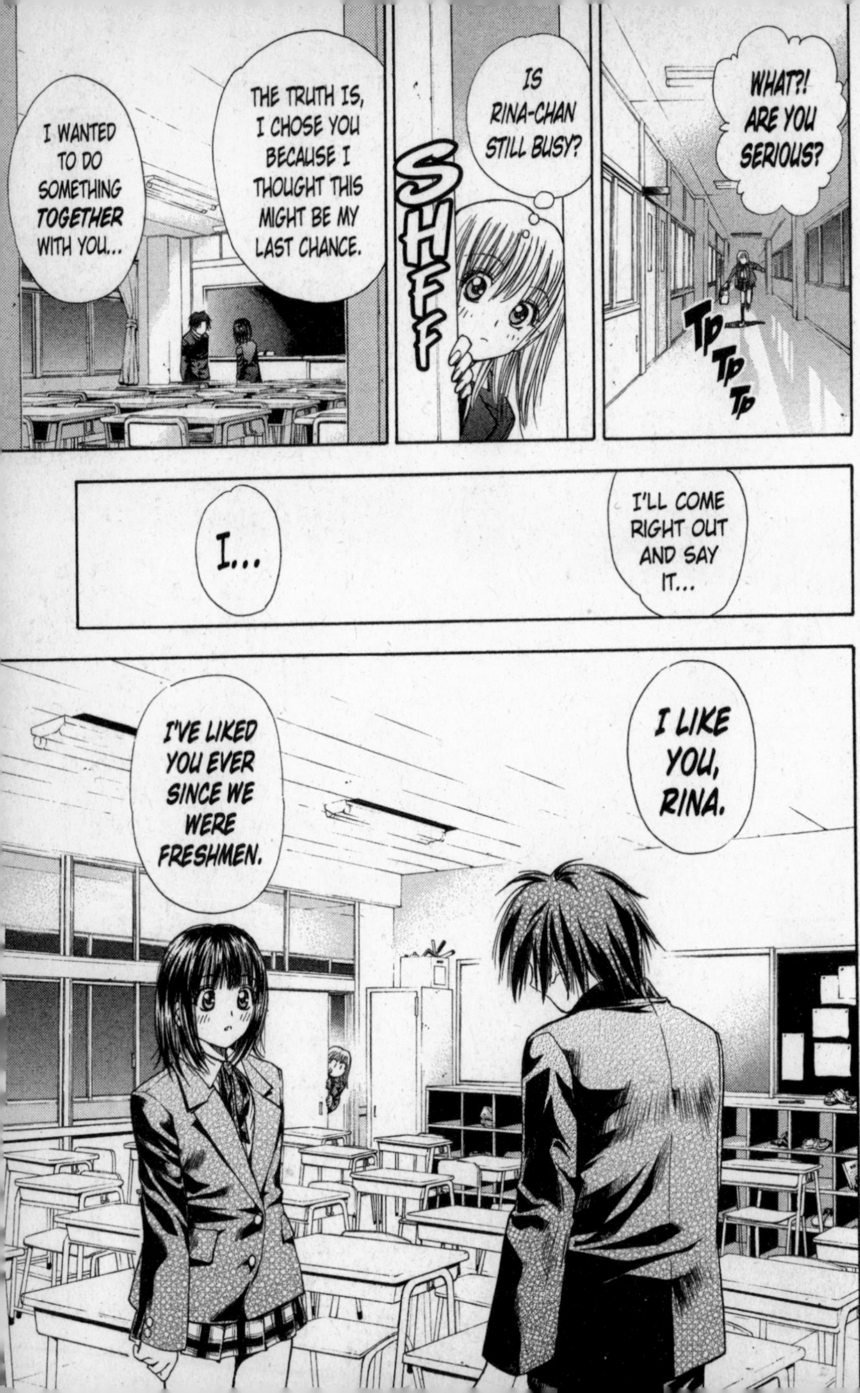
WHAT?! ARE YOU SERIOUS?
TP TP TP
IS RINA-CHAN STILL BUSY?
SHFF
THE TRUTH IS, I CHOSE YOU BECAUSE I THOUGHT THIS MIGHT BE MY LAST CHANCE.
I WANTED TO DO SOMETHING *TOGETHER* WITH YOU...
I'LL COME RIGHT OUT AND SAY IT...
I...
I LIKE YOU, RINA.
I'VE LIKED YOU EVER SINCE WE WERE FRESHMEN.

Ms. Masuko

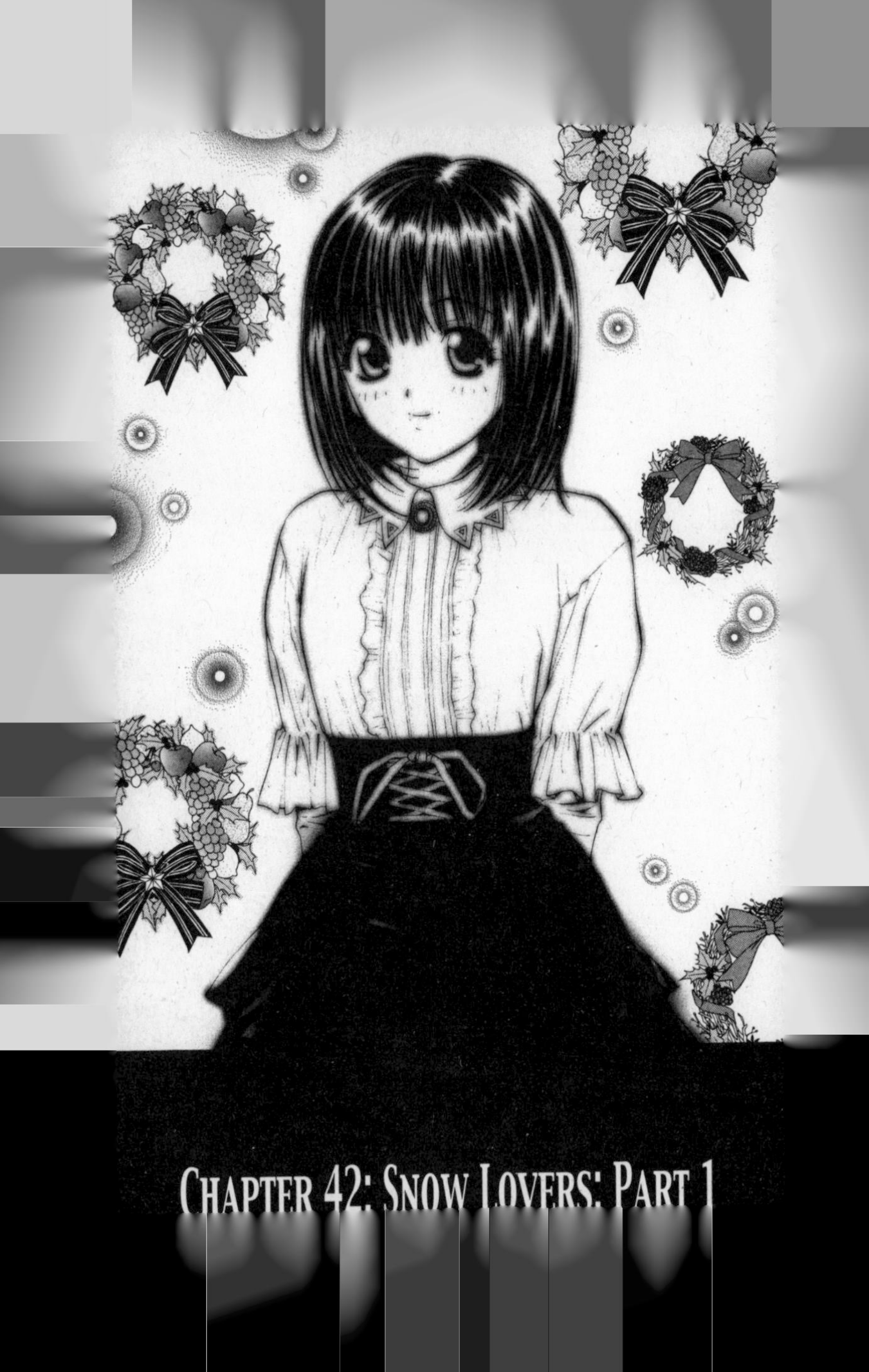

Chapter 42: Snow Lovers: Part 1

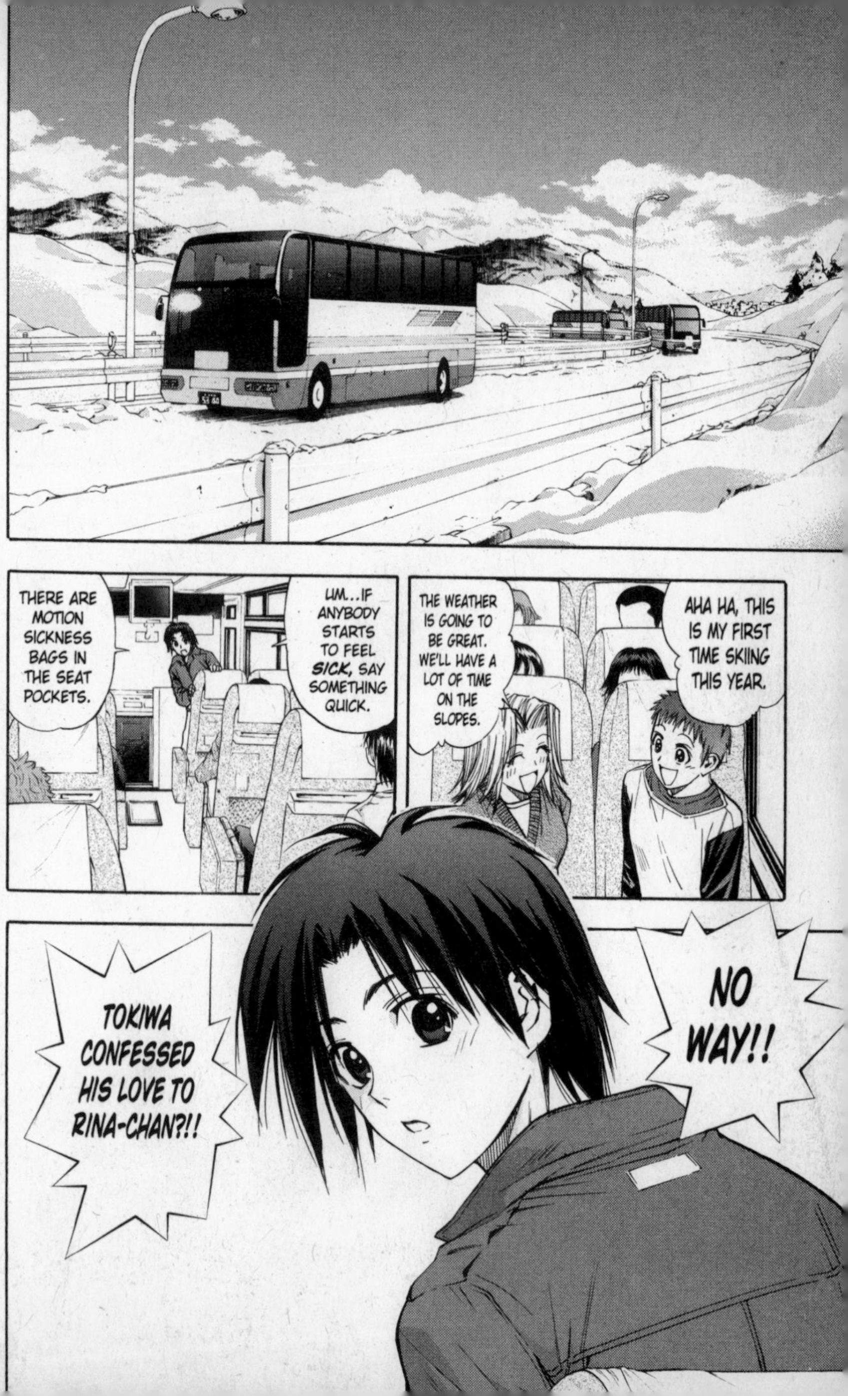
AHA HA, THIS IS MY FIRST TIME SKIING THIS YEAR.
THE WEATHER IS GOING TO BE GREAT. WE'LL HAVE A LOT OF TIME ON THE SLOPES.
UM...IF ANYBODY STARTS TO FEEL *SICK*, SAY SOMETHING QUICK.
THERE ARE MOTION SICKNESS BAGS IN THE SEAT POCKETS.
NO WAY!!
TOKIWA CONFESSED HIS LOVE TO RINA-CHAN?!!

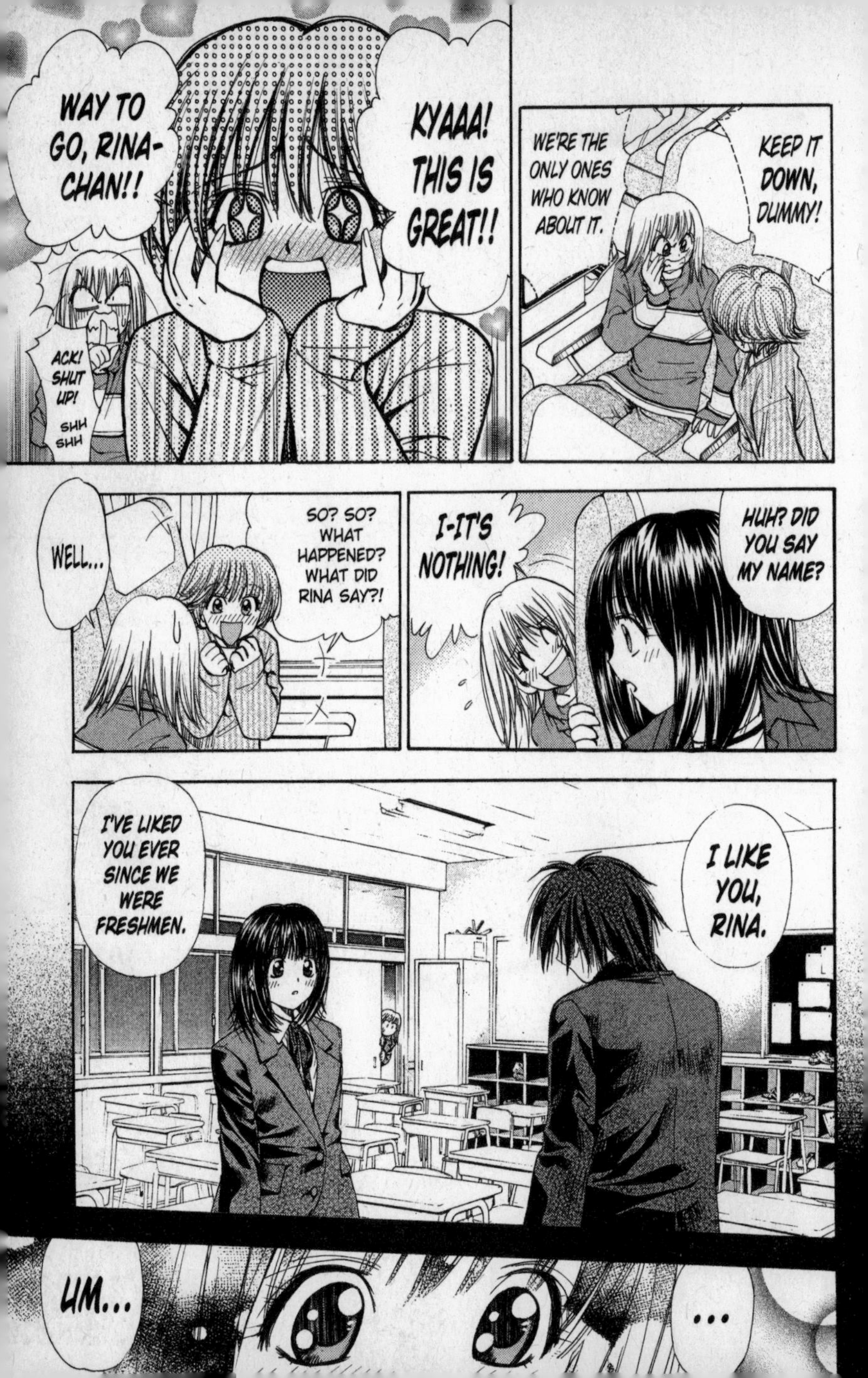
KEEP IT DOWN, DUMMY!
WE'RE THE ONLY ONES WHO KNOW ABOUT IT.
KYAAA! THIS IS GREAT!!
WAY TO GO, RINA-CHAN!!
ACK! SHUT UP!
SHH SHH
HUH? DID YOU SAY MY NAME?
I-IT'S NOTHING!
SO? SO? WHAT HAPPENED? WHAT DID RINA SAY?!
WELL...
I LIKE YOU, RINA.
I'VE LIKED YOU EVER SINCE WE WERE FRESHMEN.
...
UM...

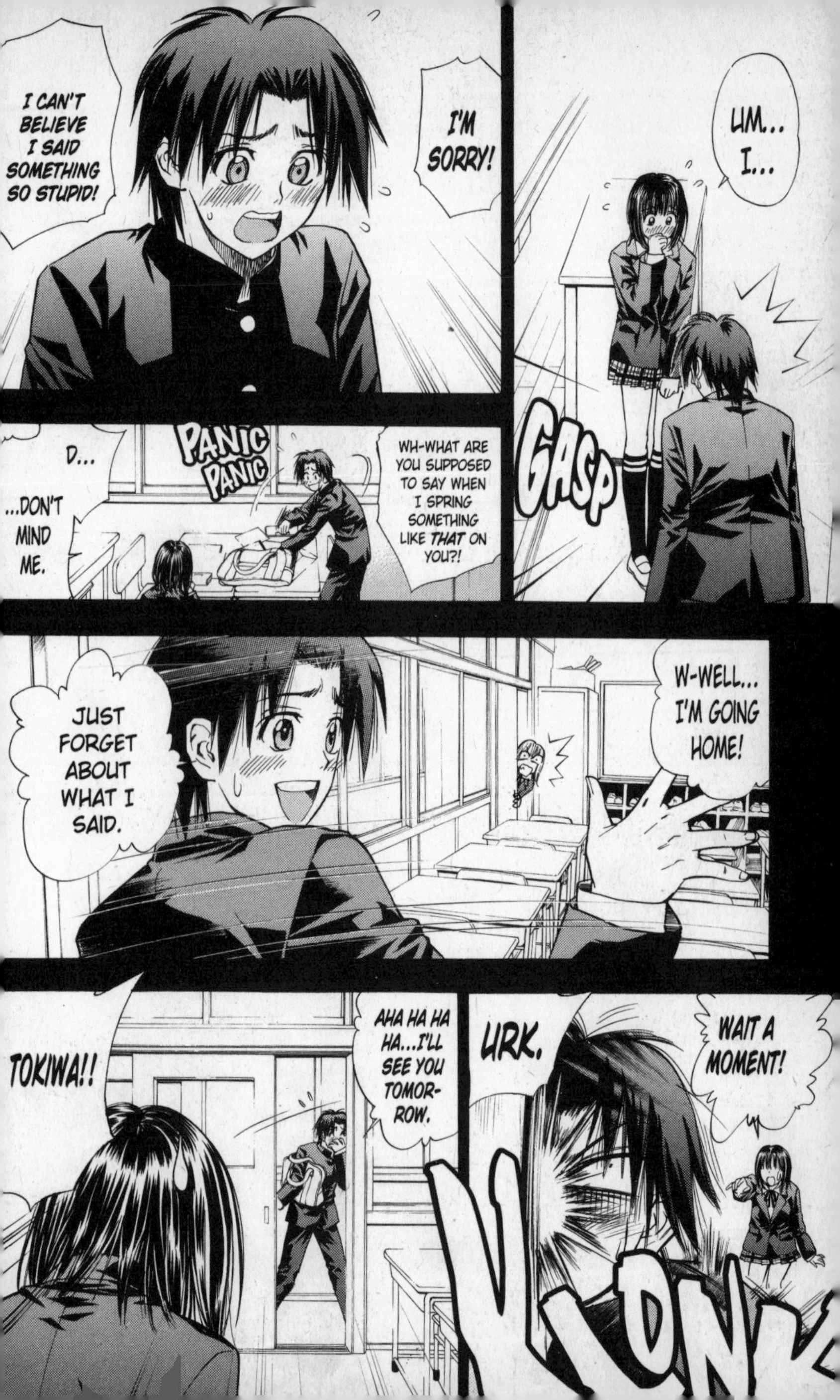
UM... I...
GASP
I'M SORRY!
I CAN'T BELIEVE I SAID SOMETHING SO STUPID!
WH-WHAT ARE YOU SUPPOSED TO SAY WHEN I SPRING SOMETHING LIKE THAT ON YOU?!
PANIC PANIC
D...
...DON'T MIND ME.
W-WELL... I'M GOING HOME!
JUST FORGET ABOUT WHAT I SAID.
WAIT A MOMENT!
URK.
AHA HA HA HA...I'LL SEE YOU TOMOR-ROW.
TOKIWA!!

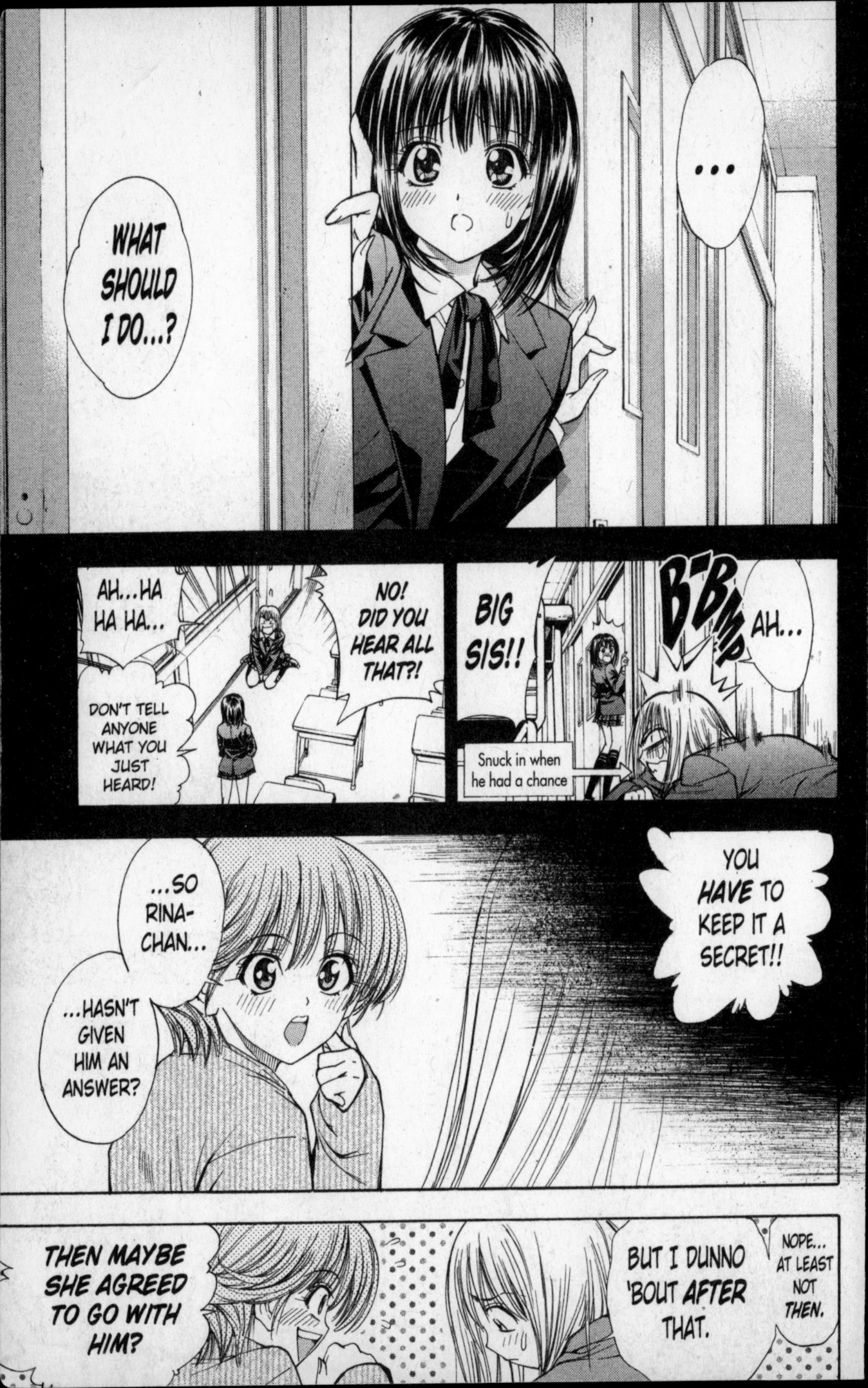
...
WHAT SHOULD I DO...?
B-BMP
AH...
BIG SIS!!
Snuck in when he had a chance
NO! DID YOU HEAR ALL THAT?!
AH...HA HA HA...
DON'T TELL ANYONE WHAT YOU JUST HEARD!
YOU HAVE TO KEEP IT A SECRET!!
...SO RINA-CHAN...
...HASN'T GIVEN HIM AN ANSWER?
NOPE... AT LEAST NOT THEN.
BUT I DUNNO 'BOUT AFTER THAT.
THEN MAYBE SHE AGREED TO GO WITH HIM?

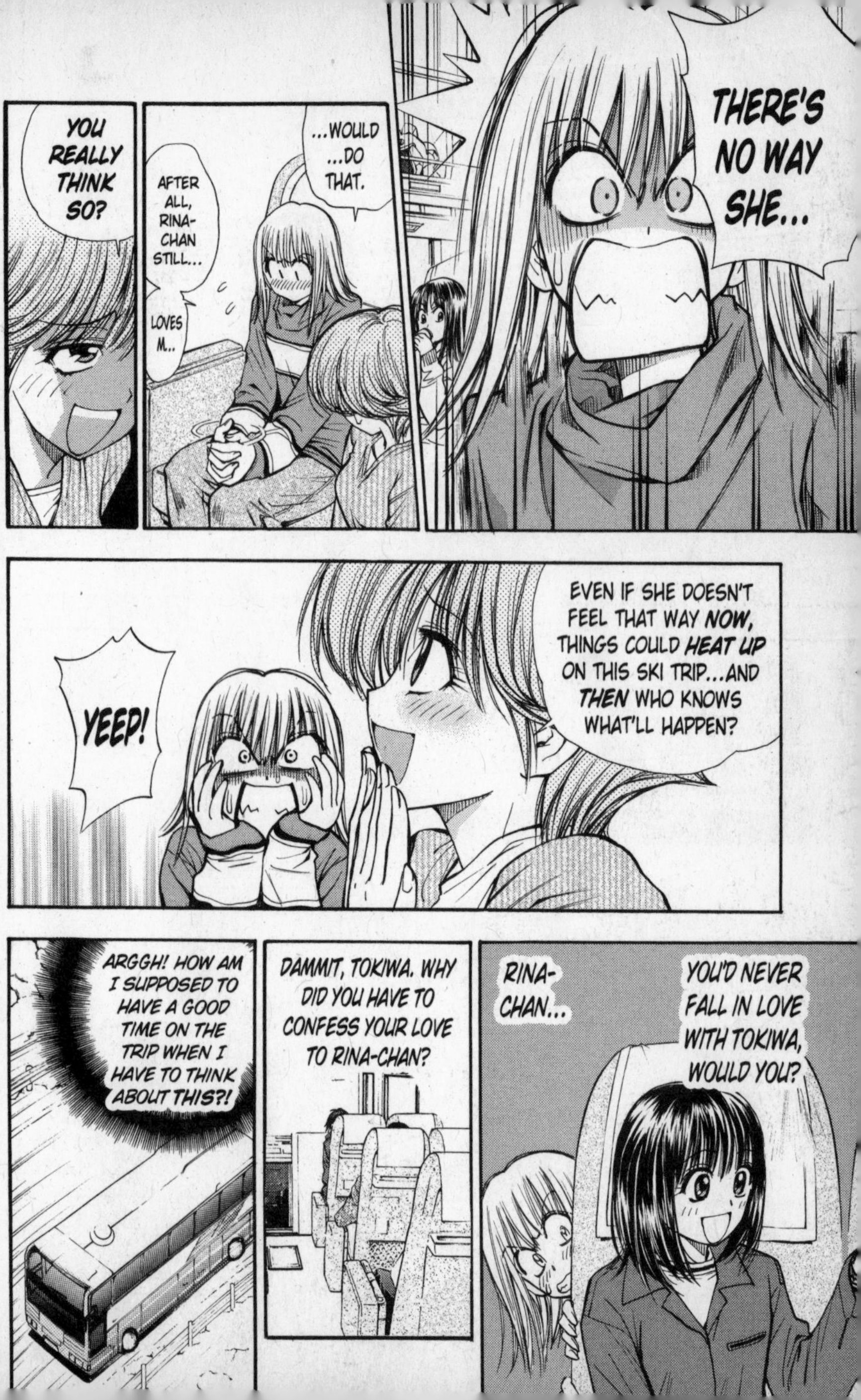
THERE'S NO WAY SHE...
...WOULD ...DO THAT.
AFTER ALL, RINA-CHAN STILL...
LOVES M...
YOU REALLY THINK SO?
EVEN IF SHE DOESN'T FEEL THAT WAY *NOW*, THINGS COULD *HEAT UP* ON THIS SKI TRIP...AND *THEN* WHO KNOWS WHAT'LL HAPPEN?
YEEP!
RINA-CHAN...
YOU'D NEVER FALL IN LOVE WITH TOKIWA, WOULD YOU?
DAMMIT, TOKIWA. WHY DID YOU HAVE TO CONFESS YOUR LOVE TO RINA-CHAN?
ARGGH! HOW AM I SUPPOSED TO HAVE A GOOD TIME ON THE TRIP WHEN I HAVE TO THINK ABOUT THIS?!

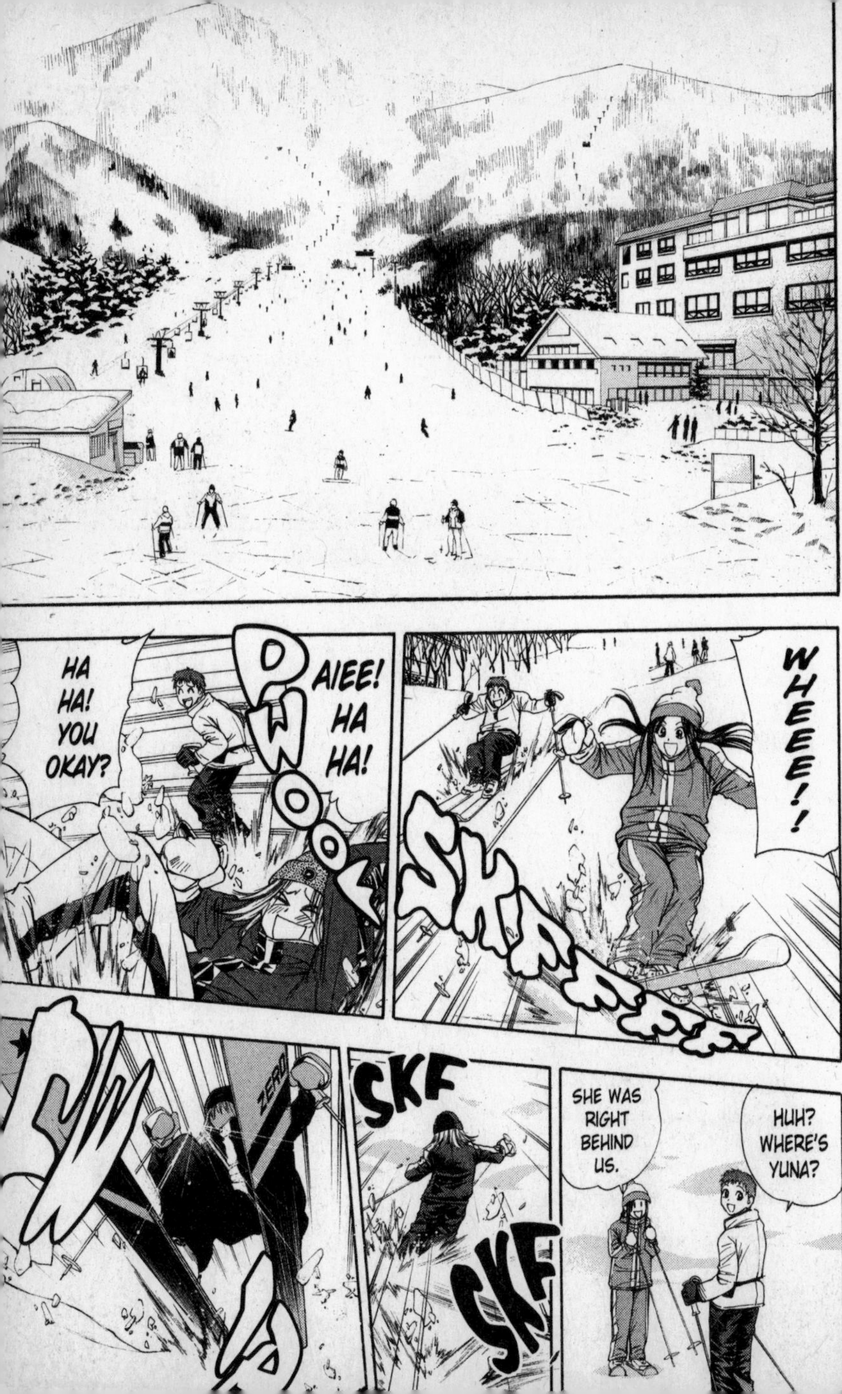
WHEEEE!!
DWOOOM
AIEE! HA HA!
HA HA! YOU OKAY?
HUH? WHERE'S YUNA?
SHE WAS RIGHT BEHIND US.
SKF
SKF
ZERO

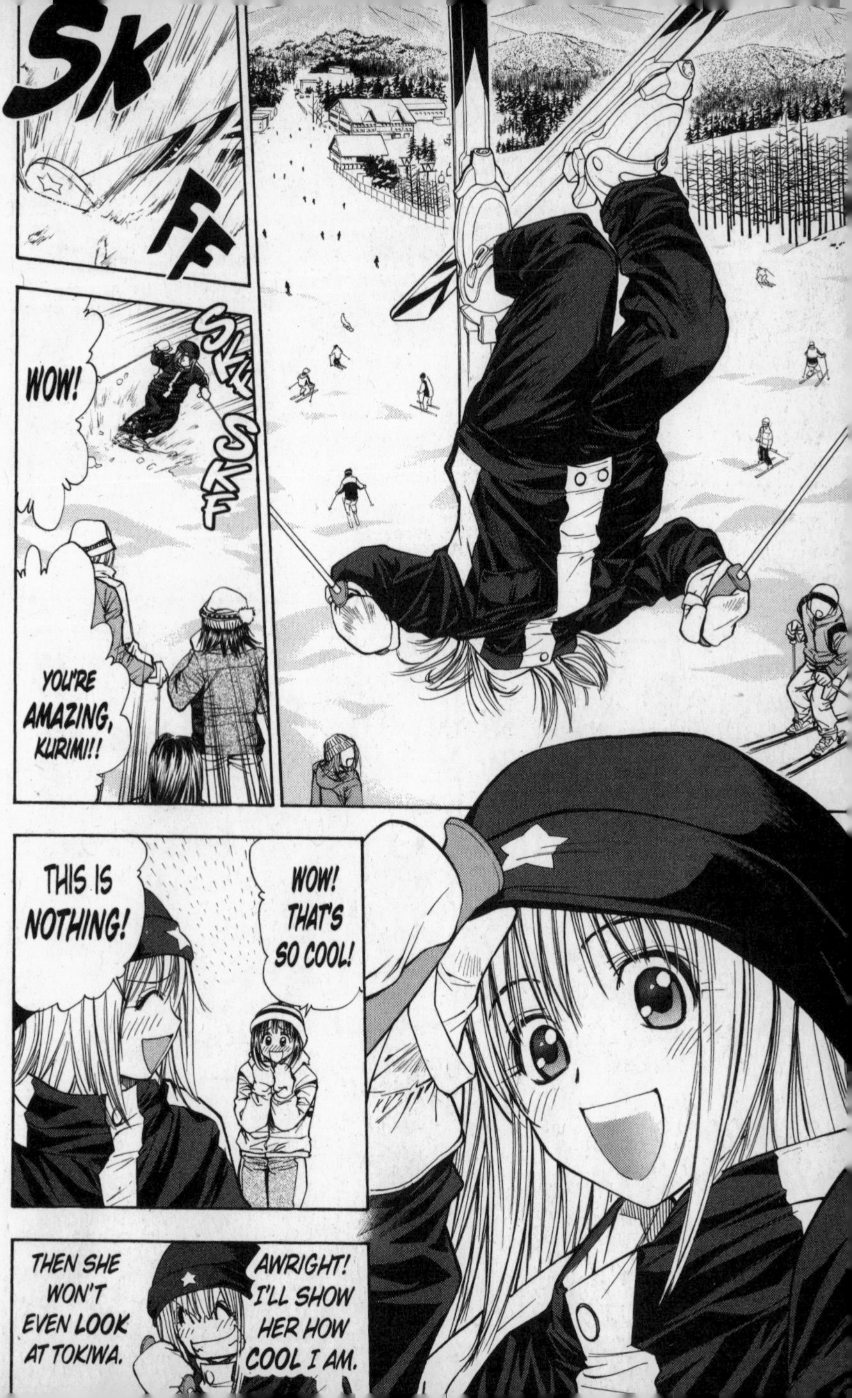
SKFF
SKF
SKF
WOW!
YOU'RE AMAZING, KURIMI!!
WOW! THAT'S SO COOL!
THIS IS NOTHING!
AWRIGHT! I'LL SHOW HER HOW COOL I AM.
THEN SHE WON'T EVEN LOOK AT TOKIWA.

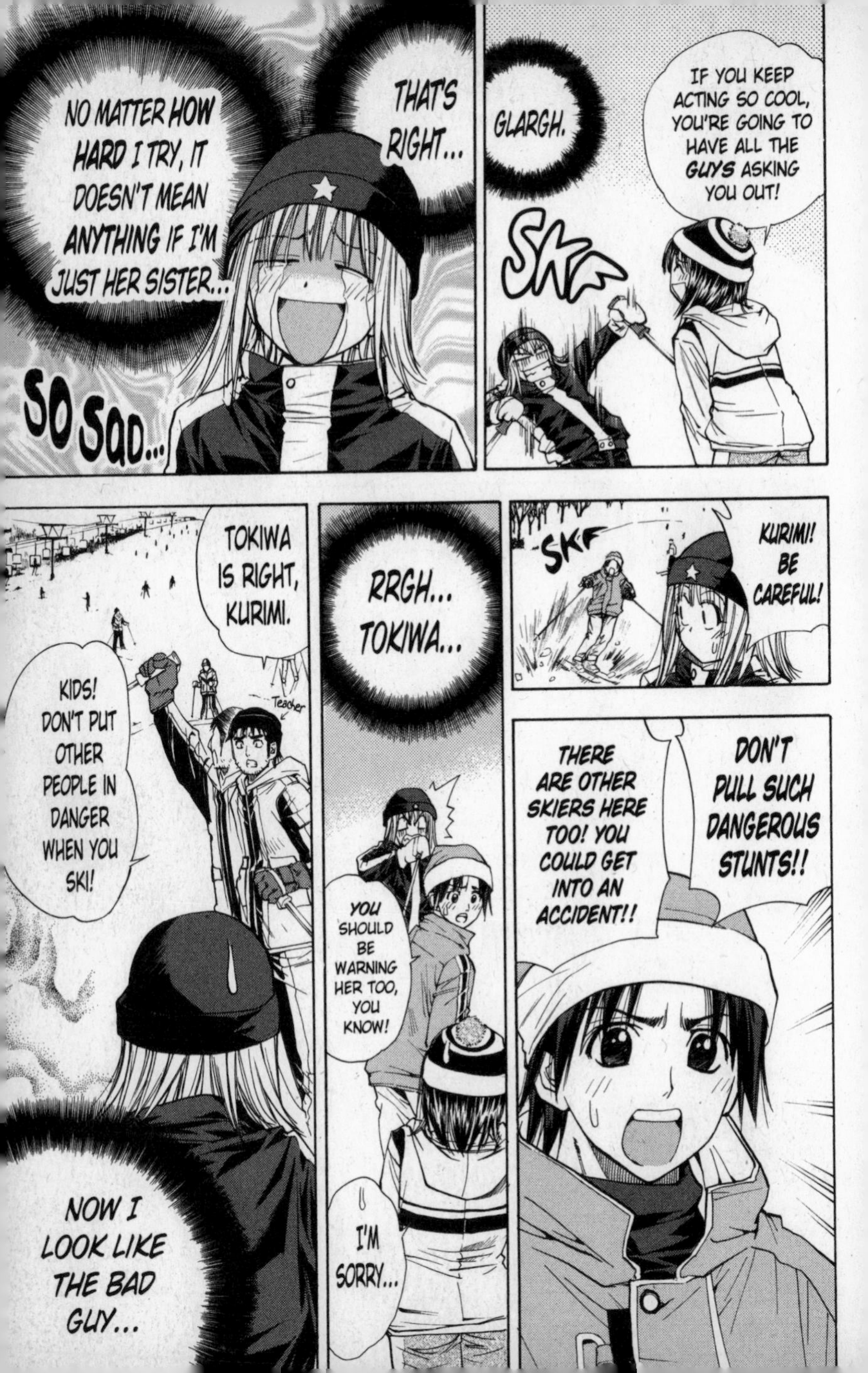
IF YOU KEEP ACTING SO COOL, YOU'RE GOING TO HAVE ALL THE GUYS ASKING YOU OUT!
SKF
GLARGH.
THAT'S RIGHT...
NO MATTER HOW HARD I TRY, IT DOESN'T MEAN ANYTHING IF I'M JUST HER SISTER...
SO SAD...
KURIMI! BE CAREFUL!
SKF
DON'T PULL SUCH DANGEROUS STUNTS!!
THERE ARE OTHER SKIERS HERE TOO! YOU COULD GET INTO AN ACCIDENT!!
RRGH... TOKIWA...
YOU SHOULD BE WARNING HER TOO, YOU KNOW!
I'M SORRY...
TOKIWA IS RIGHT, KURIMI.
KIDS! DON'T PUT OTHER PEOPLE IN DANGER WHEN YOU SKI!
Teacher
NOW I LOOK LIKE THE BAD GUY...

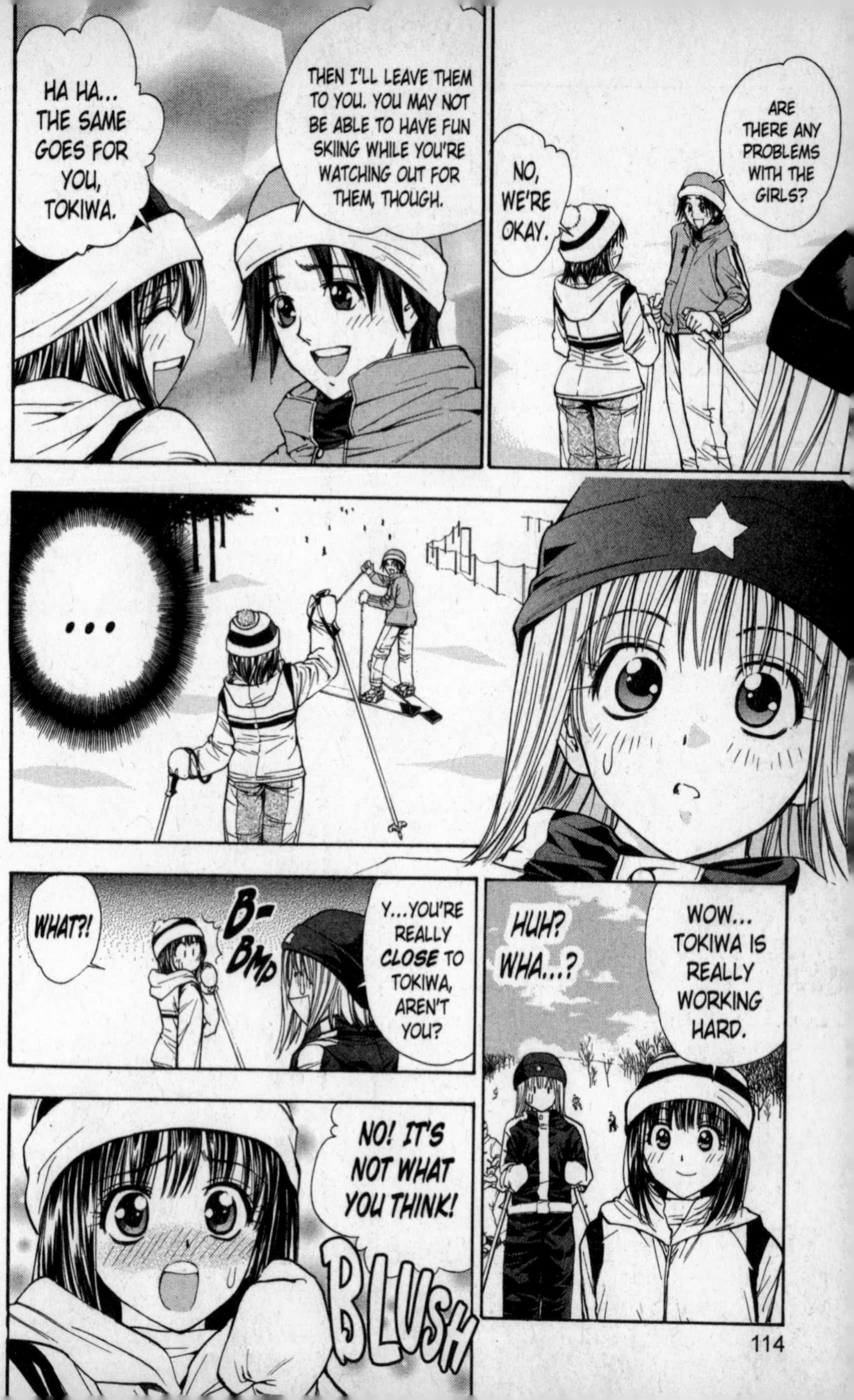
ARE THERE ANY PROBLEMS WITH THE GIRLS?
NO, WE'RE OKAY.
THEN I'LL LEAVE THEM TO YOU. YOU MAY NOT BE ABLE TO HAVE FUN SKIING WHILE YOU'RE WATCHING OUT FOR THEM, THOUGH.
HA HA... THE SAME GOES FOR YOU, TOKIWA.
...
WOW... TOKIWA IS REALLY WORKING HARD.
HUH? WHA...?
Y...YOU'RE REALLY CLOSE TO TOKIWA, AREN'T YOU?
B-BMP
WHAT?!
NO! IT'S NOT WHAT YOU THINK!
BLUSH

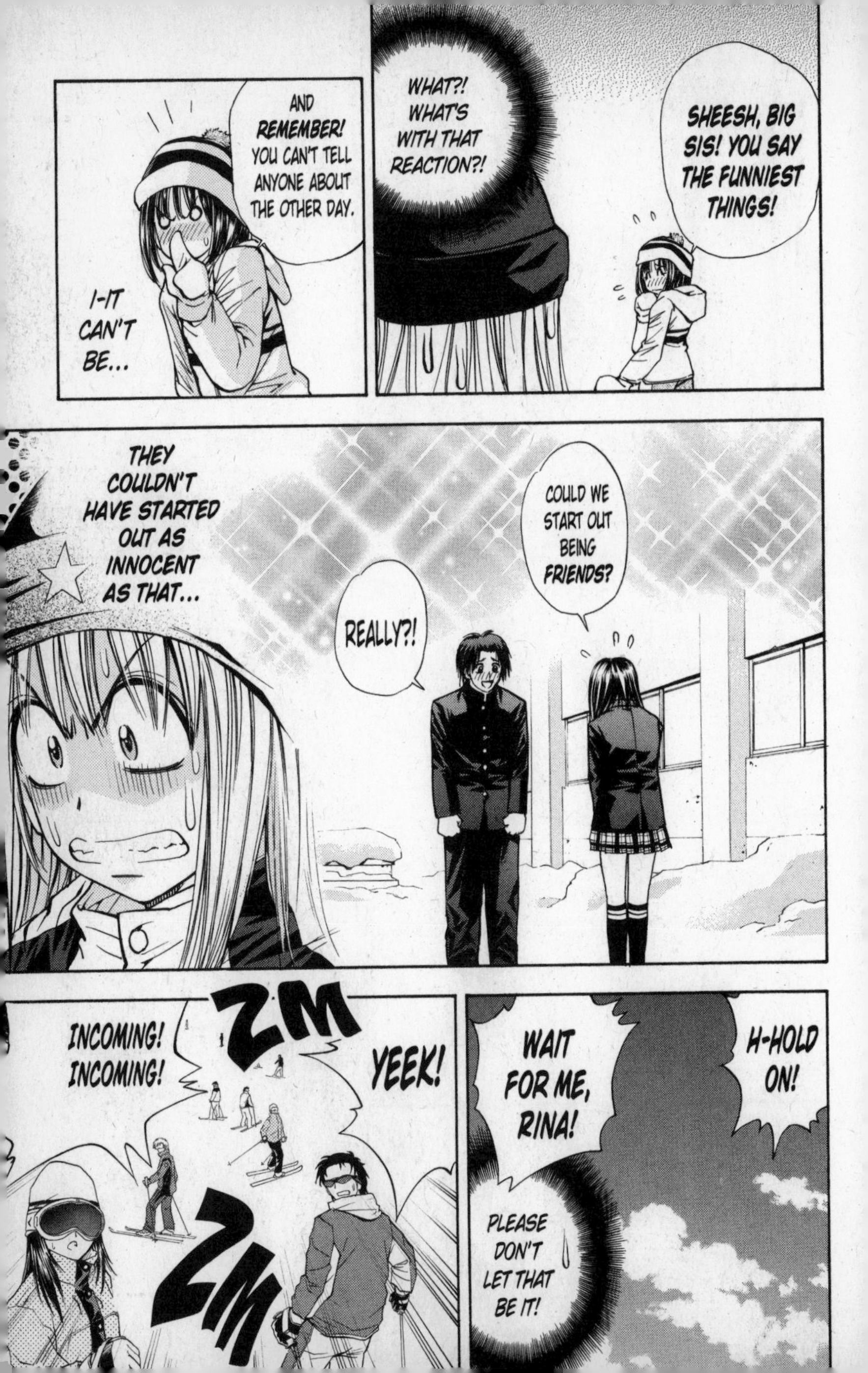

SHEESH, BIG SIS! YOU SAY THE FUNNIEST THINGS!
WHAT?! WHAT'S WITH THAT REACTION?!
AND REMEMBER! YOU CAN'T TELL ANYONE ABOUT THE OTHER DAY.
I-IT CAN'T BE...
COULD WE START OUT BEING FRIENDS?
REALLY?!
THEY COULDN'T HAVE STARTED OUT AS INNOCENT AS THAT...
H-HOLD ON!
WAIT FOR ME, RINA!
PLEASE DON'T LET THAT BE IT!
YEEK!
ZM
INCOMING! INCOMING!
ZM

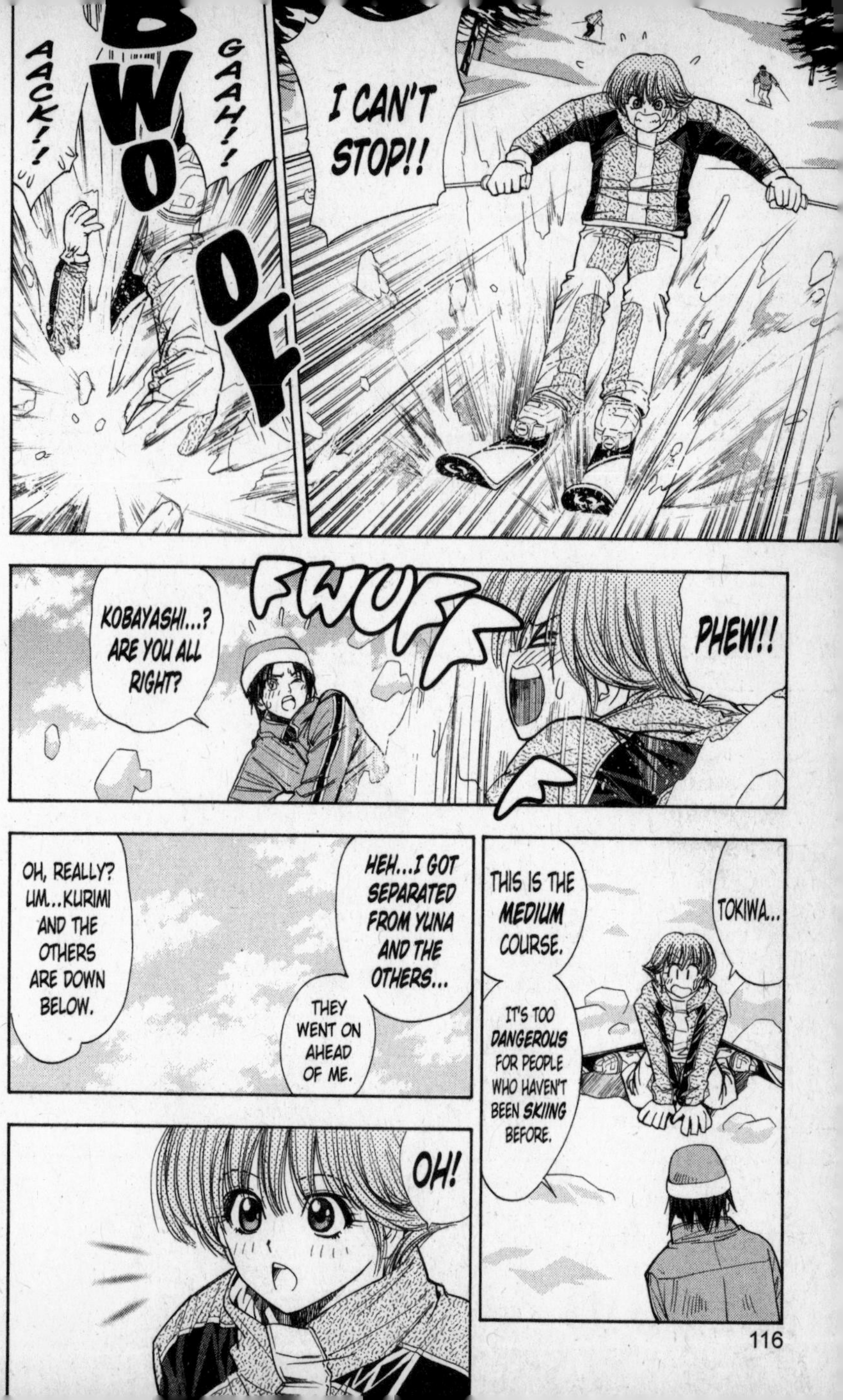
I CAN'T STOP!!
GAAH!!
BWOOF
AACK!!
PHEW!!
FWUF
KOBAYASHI...? ARE YOU ALL RIGHT?
TOKIWA...
THIS IS THE MEDIUM COURSE.
IT'S TOO DANGEROUS FOR PEOPLE WHO HAVEN'T BEEN SKIING BEFORE.
HEH...I GOT SEPARATED FROM YUNA AND THE OTHERS...
THEY WENT ON AHEAD OF ME.
OH, REALLY? UM...KURIMI AND THE OTHERS ARE DOWN BELOW.
OH!

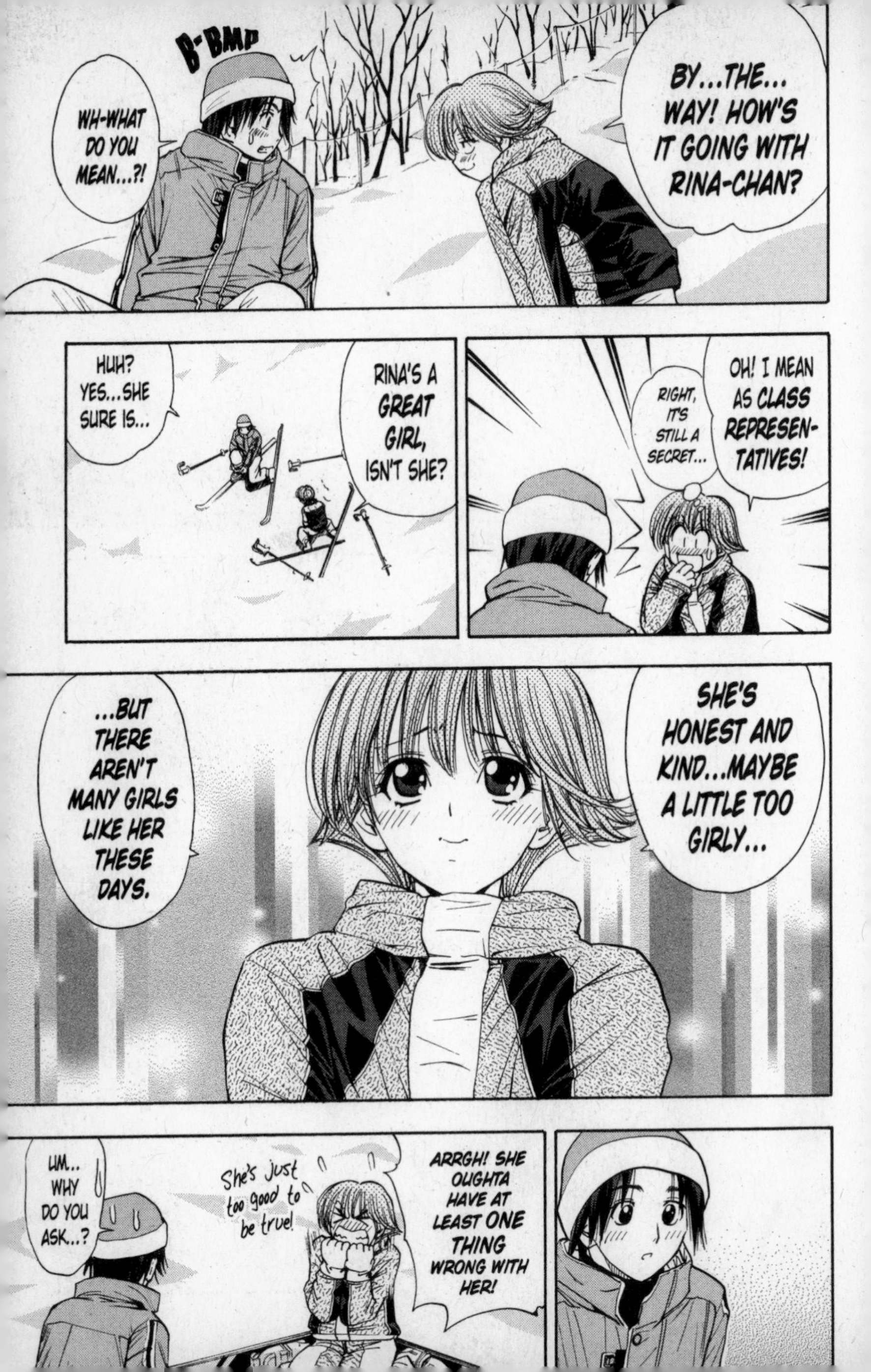
BY...THE... WAY! HOW'S IT GOING WITH RINA-CHAN?
B-BMP
WH-WHAT DO YOU MEAN...?!
OH! I MEAN AS CLASS REPRESEN-TATIVES!
RIGHT, IT'S STILL A SECRET...
RINA'S A GREAT GIRL, ISN'T SHE?
HUH? YES...SHE SURE IS...
SHE'S HONEST AND KIND...MAYBE A LITTLE TOO GIRLY...
...BUT THERE AREN'T MANY GIRLS LIKE HER THESE DAYS.
ARRGH! SHE OUGHTA HAVE AT LEAST ONE THING WRONG WITH HER!
She's just too good to be true!
UM... WHY DO YOU ASK...?

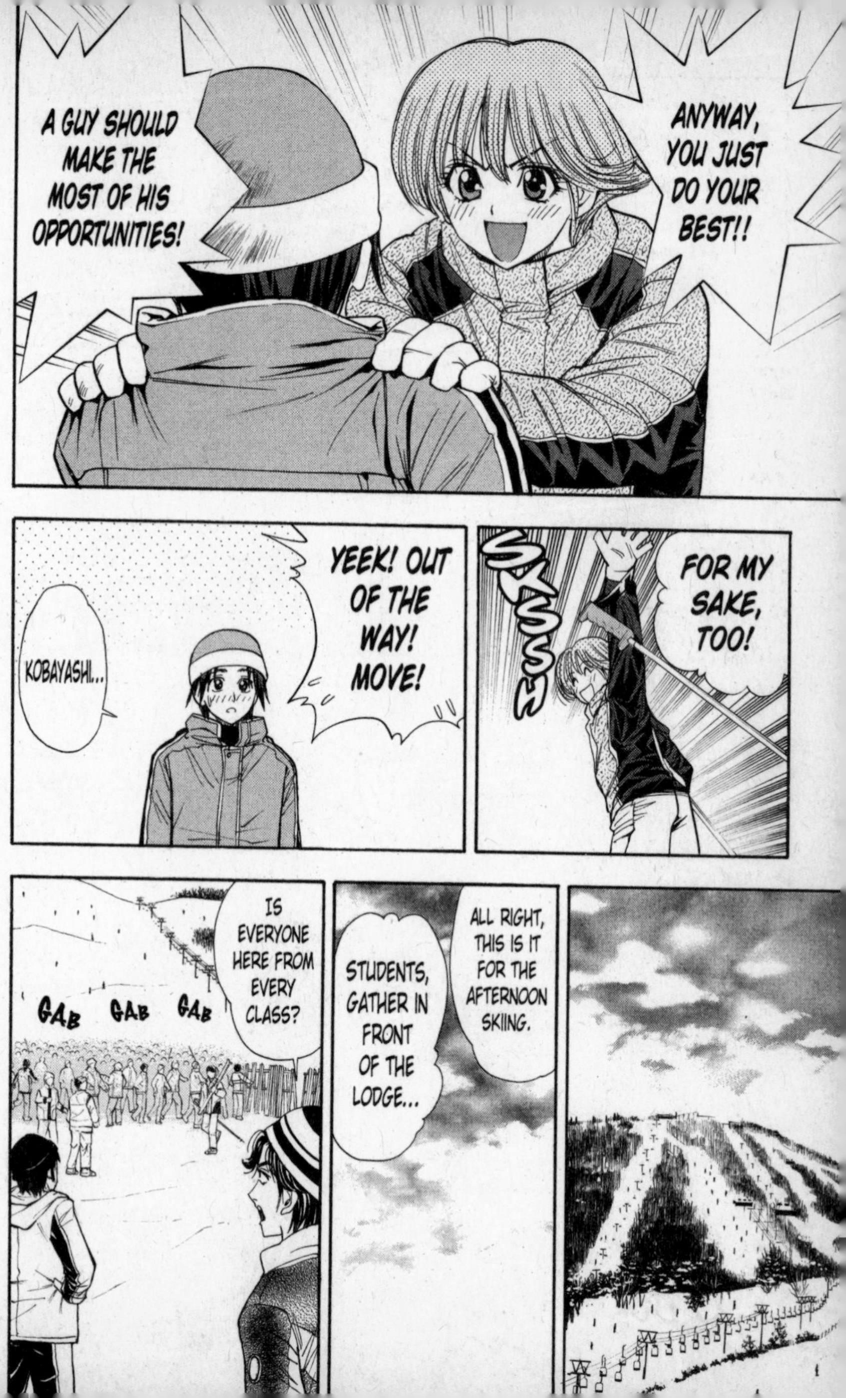
ANYWAY, YOU JUST DO YOUR BEST!!
A GUY SHOULD MAKE THE MOST OF HIS OPPORTUNITIES!
FOR MY SAKE, TOO!
YEEK! OUT OF THE WAY! MOVE!
KOBAYASHI...
ALL RIGHT, THIS IS IT FOR THE AFTERNOON SKIING.
STUDENTS, GATHER IN FRONT OF THE LODGE...
IS EVERYONE HERE FROM EVERY CLASS?
GAB
GAB
GAB

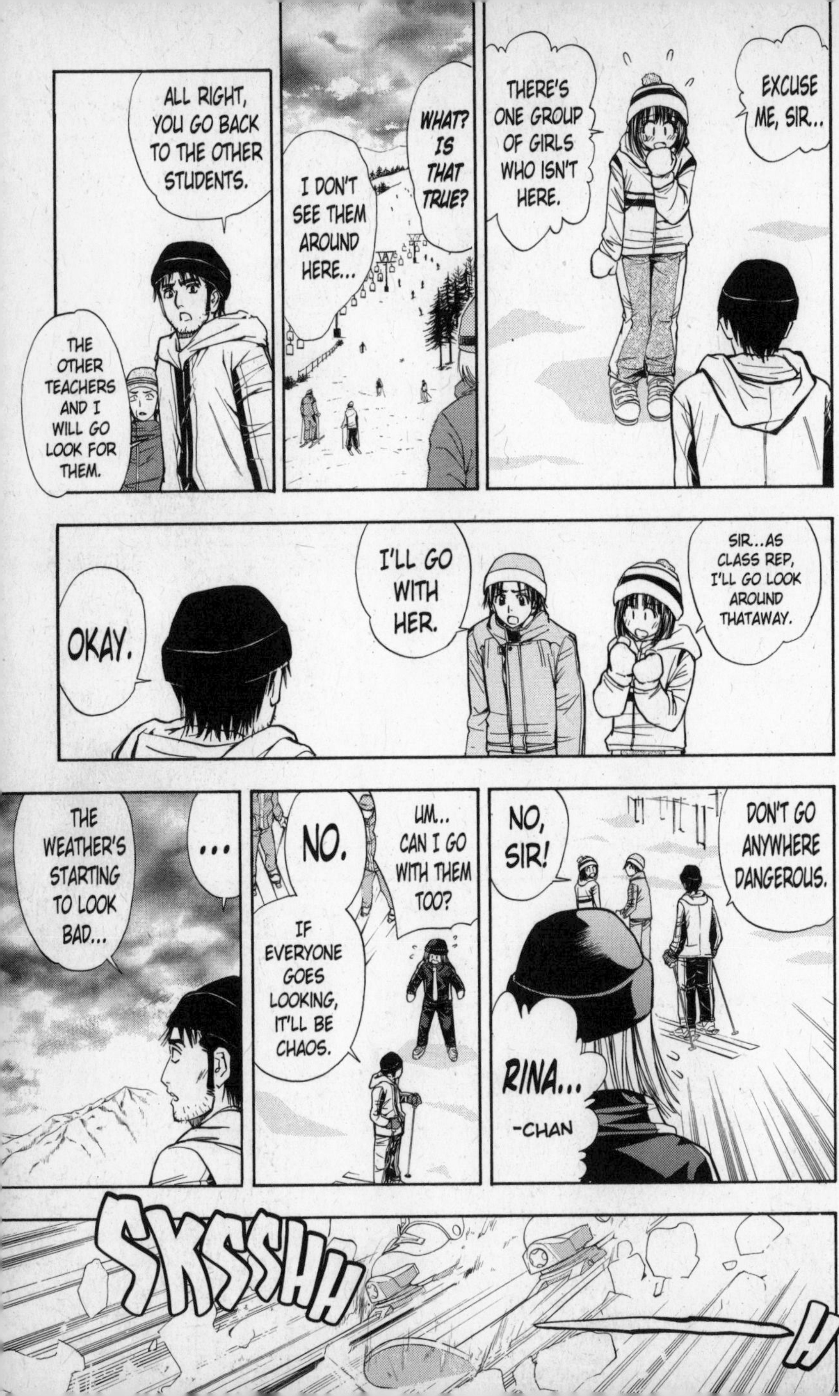
EXCUSE ME, SIR...
THERE'S ONE GROUP OF GIRLS WHO ISN'T HERE.
WHAT? IS THAT TRUE?
I DON'T SEE THEM AROUND HERE...
ALL RIGHT, YOU GO BACK TO THE OTHER STUDENTS.
THE OTHER TEACHERS AND I WILL GO LOOK FOR THEM.
SIR...AS CLASS REP, I'LL GO LOOK AROUND THATAWAY.
I'LL GO WITH HER.
OKAY.
DON'T GO ANYWHERE DANGEROUS.
NO, SIR!
RINA... -CHAN
UM... CAN I GO WITH THEM TOO?
NO.
IF EVERYONE GOES LOOKING, IT'LL BE CHAOS.
...
THE WEATHER'S STARTING TO LOOK BAD...
SKSSHH
H

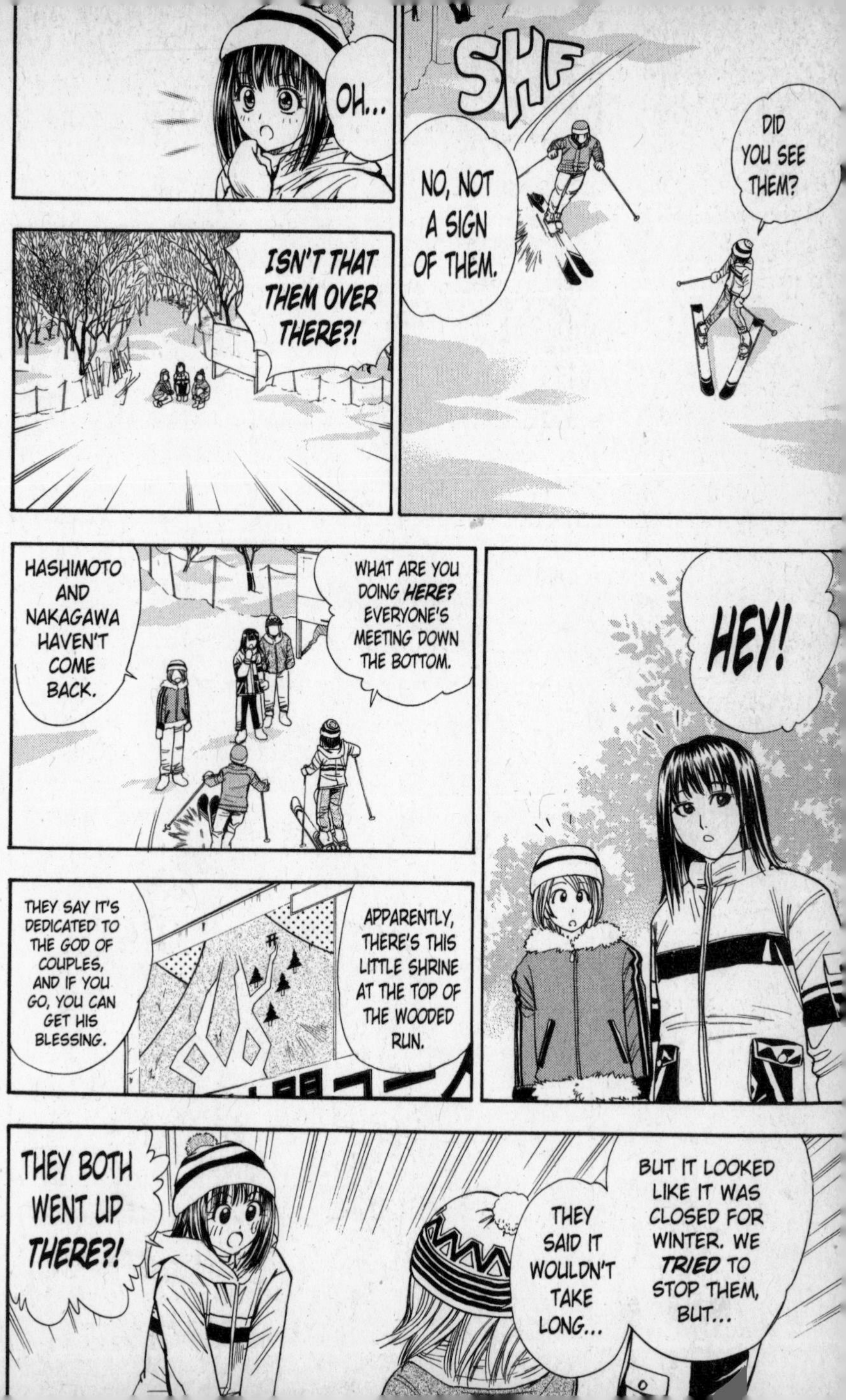
SHF
DID YOU SEE THEM?
NO, NOT A SIGN OF THEM.
OH...
ISN'T THAT THEM OVER THERE?!
HEY!
WHAT ARE YOU DOING *HERE?* EVERYONE'S MEETING DOWN THE BOTTOM.
HASHIMOTO AND NAKAGAWA HAVEN'T COME BACK.
APPARENTLY, THERE'S THIS LITTLE SHRINE AT THE TOP OF THE WOODED RUN.
THEY SAY IT'S DEDICATED TO THE GOD OF COUPLES, AND IF YOU GO, YOU CAN GET HIS BLESSING.
BUT IT LOOKED LIKE IT WAS CLOSED FOR WINTER. WE *TRIED* TO STOP THEM, BUT...
THEY SAID IT WOULDN'T TAKE LONG...
THEY BOTH WENT UP *THERE?!*

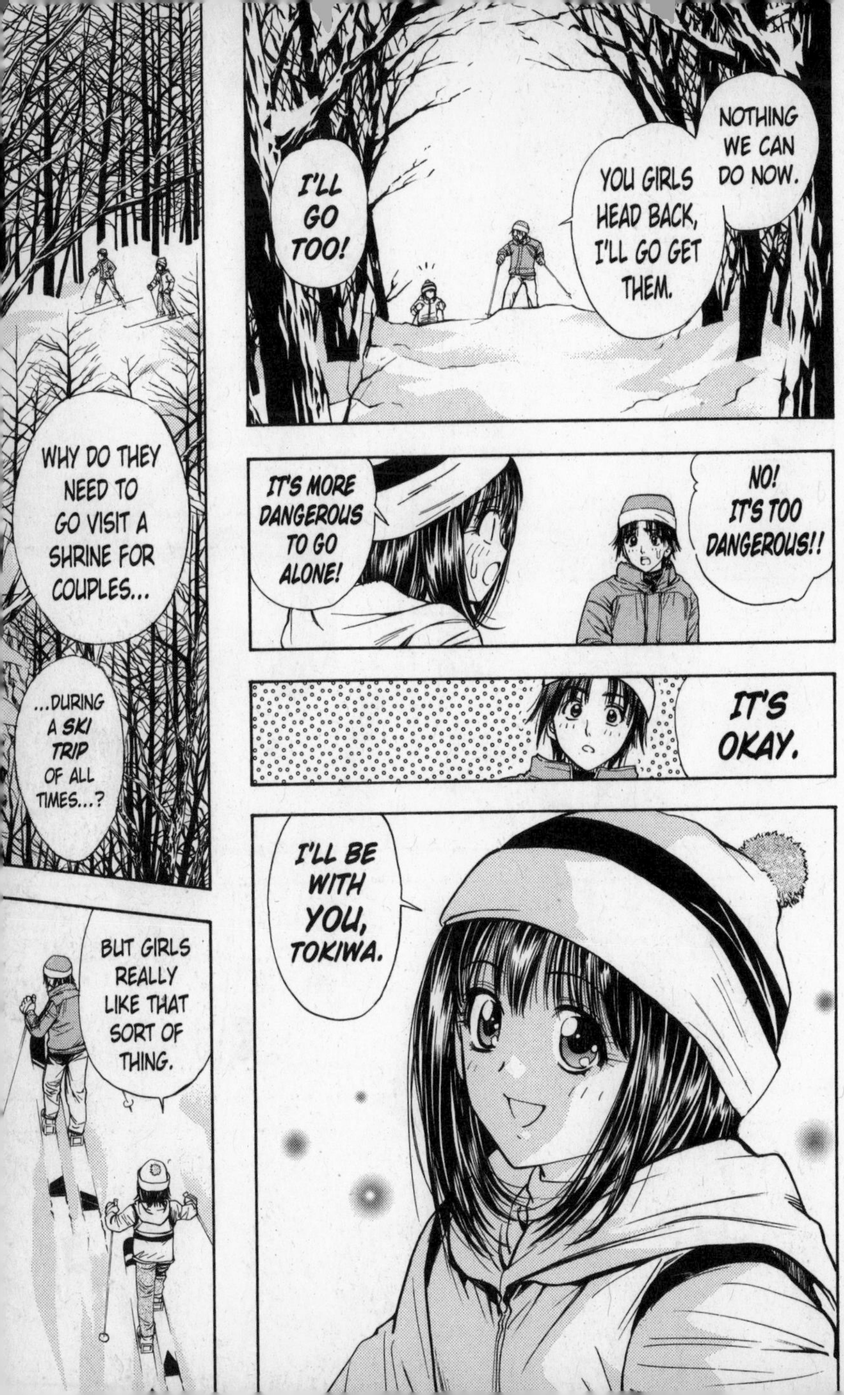
NOTHING WE CAN DO NOW.
YOU GIRLS HEAD BACK, I'LL GO GET THEM.
I'LL GO TOO!
NO! IT'S TOO DANGEROUS!!
IT'S MORE DANGEROUS TO GO ALONE!
IT'S OKAY.
I'LL BE WITH YOU, TOKIWA.
WHY DO THEY NEED TO GO VISIT A SHRINE FOR COUPLES...
...DURING A SKI TRIP OF ALL TIMES...?
BUT GIRLS REALLY LIKE THAT SORT OF THING.

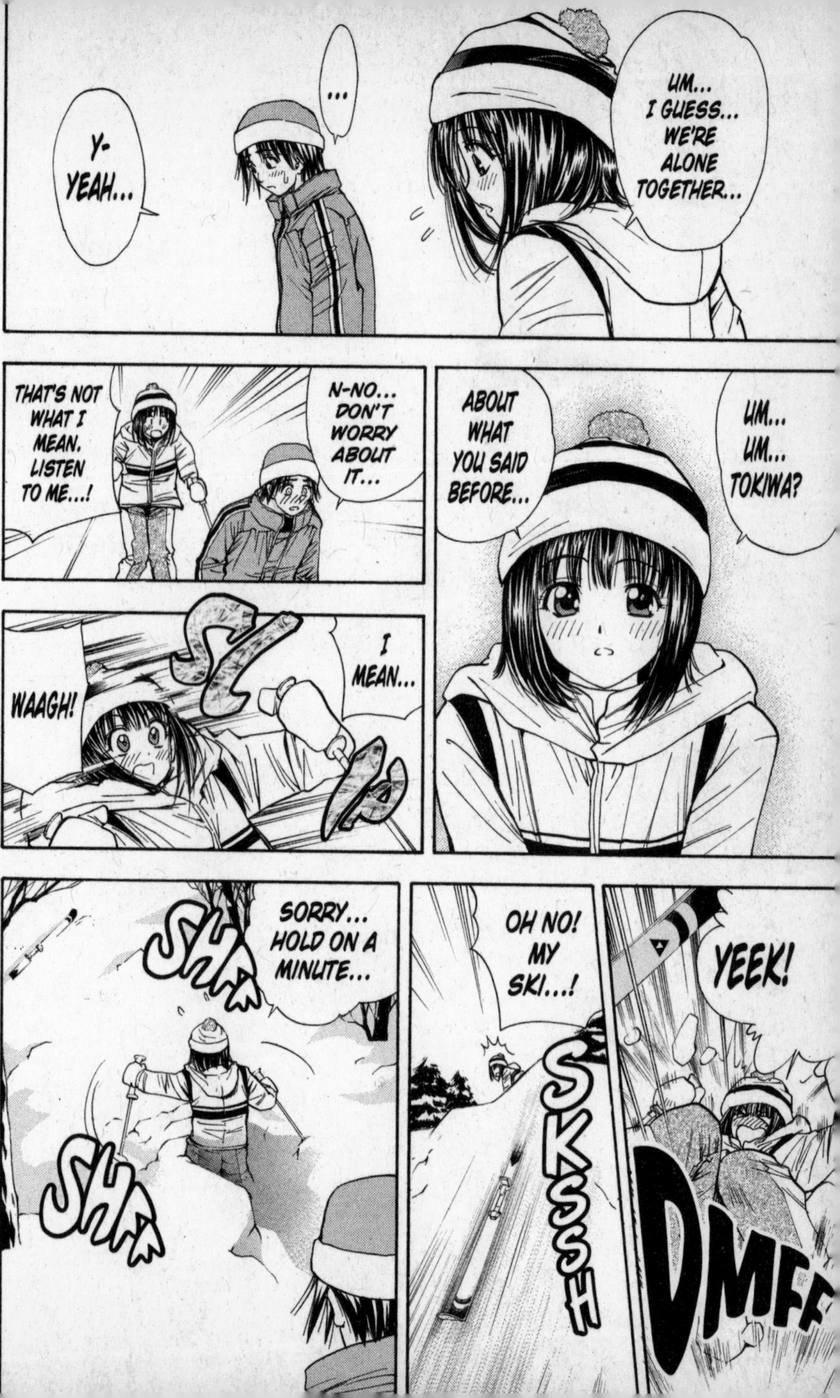
UM... I GUESS... WE'RE ALONE TOGETHER...
...
Y-YEAH...
UM... UM... TOKIWA?
ABOUT WHAT YOU SAID BEFORE...
N-NO... DON'T WORRY ABOUT IT...
THAT'S NOT WHAT I MEAN. LISTEN TO ME...!
I MEAN...
WAAGH!
YEEK!
DMFF
OH NO! MY SKI...!
SKSSH
SORRY... HOLD ON A MINUTE...
SHA
SHA

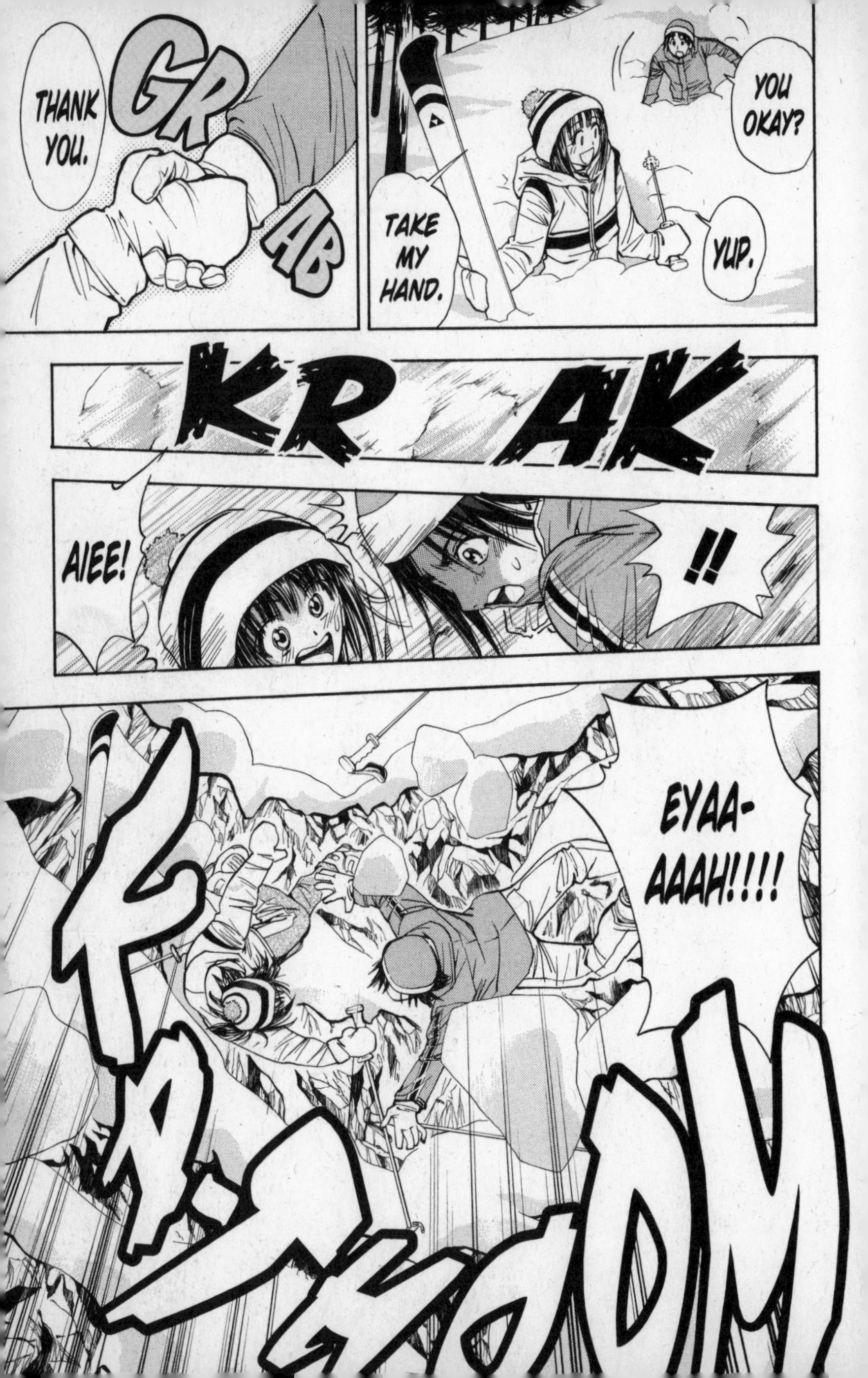
YOU OKAY?
YUP.
TAKE MY HAND.
GRAB
THANK YOU.
KRAK
!!
AIEE!
EYAA-AAAH!!!!

Rough sketch for a pin-up poster

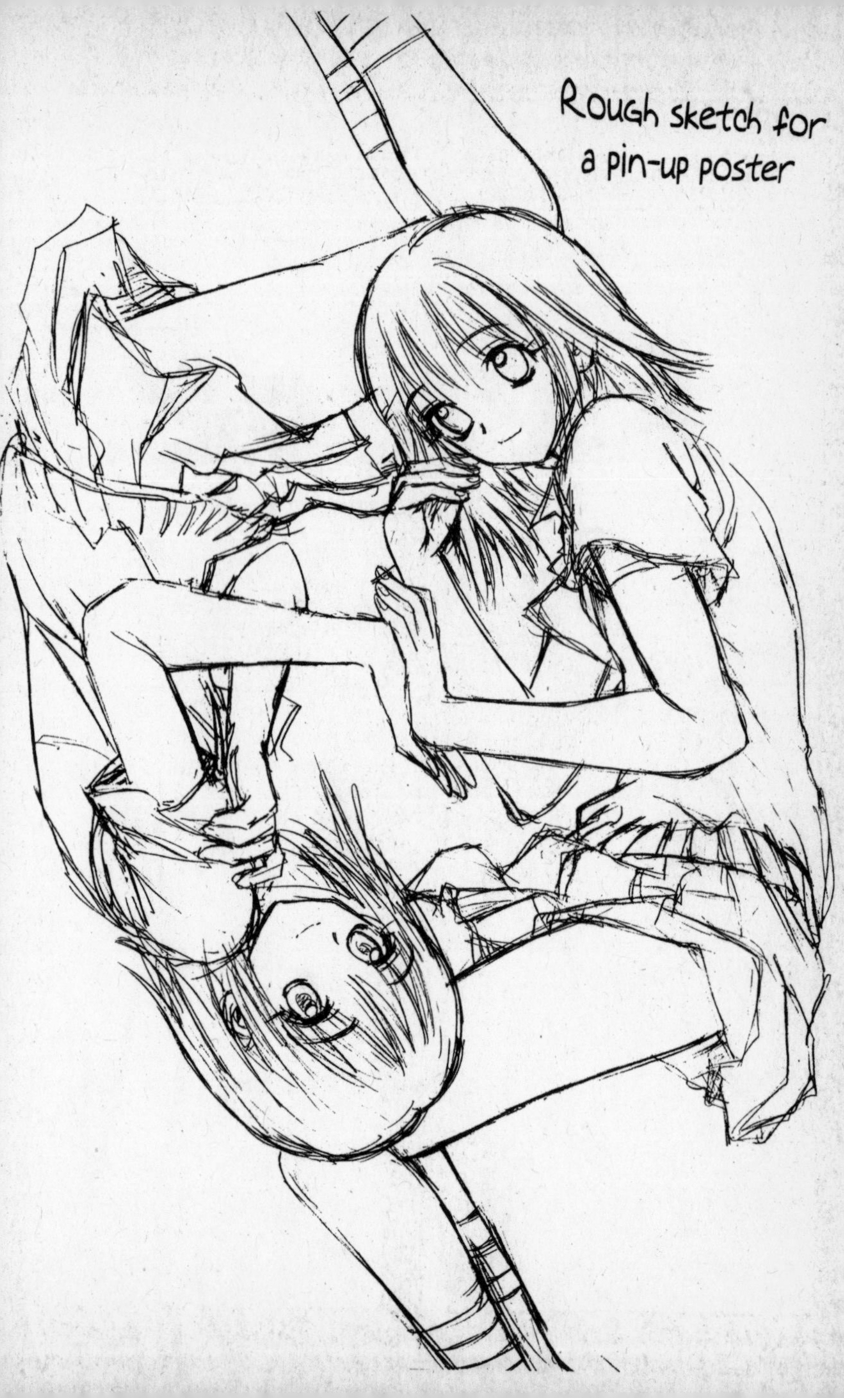

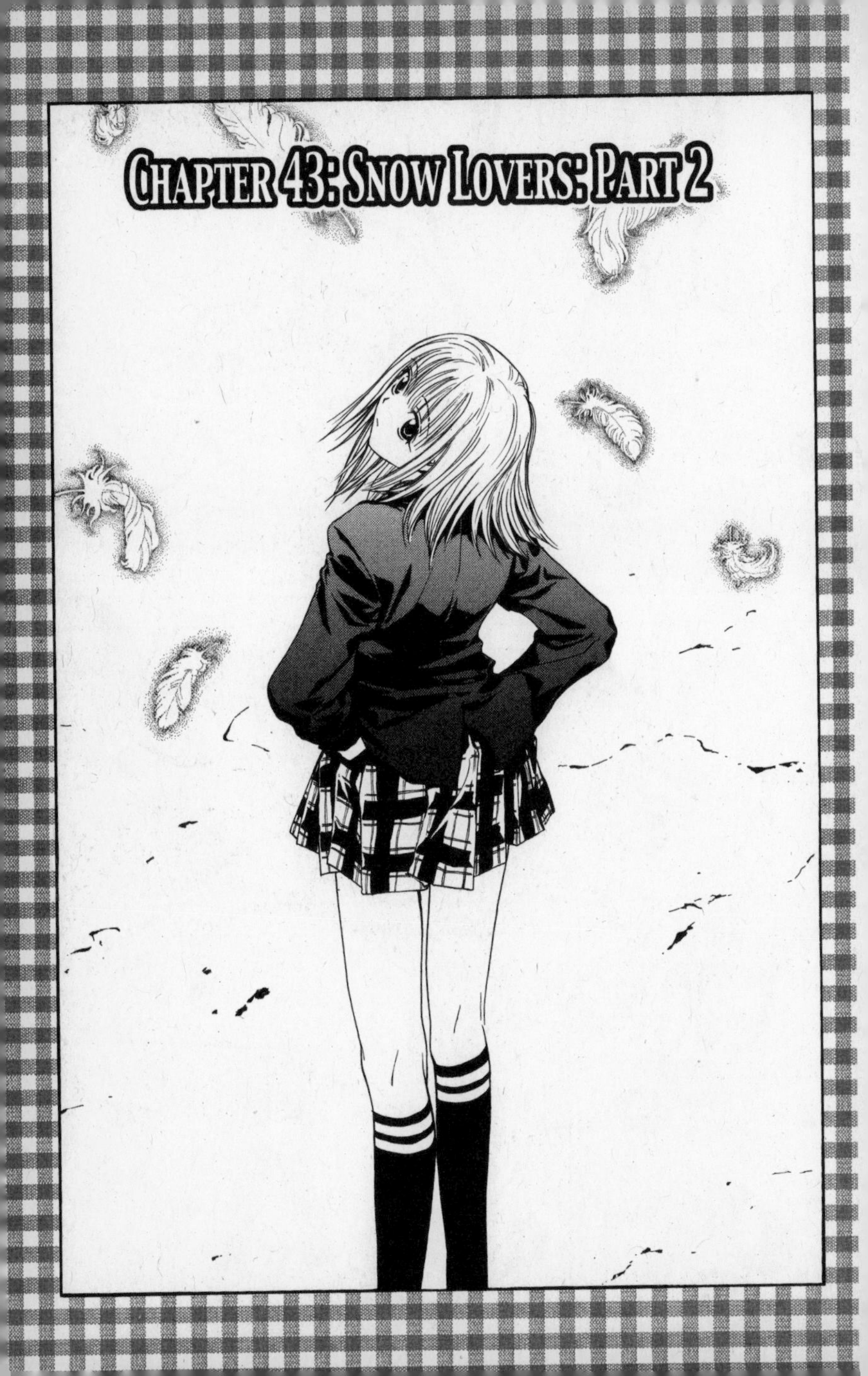
CHAPTER 43: SNOW LOVERS: PART 2

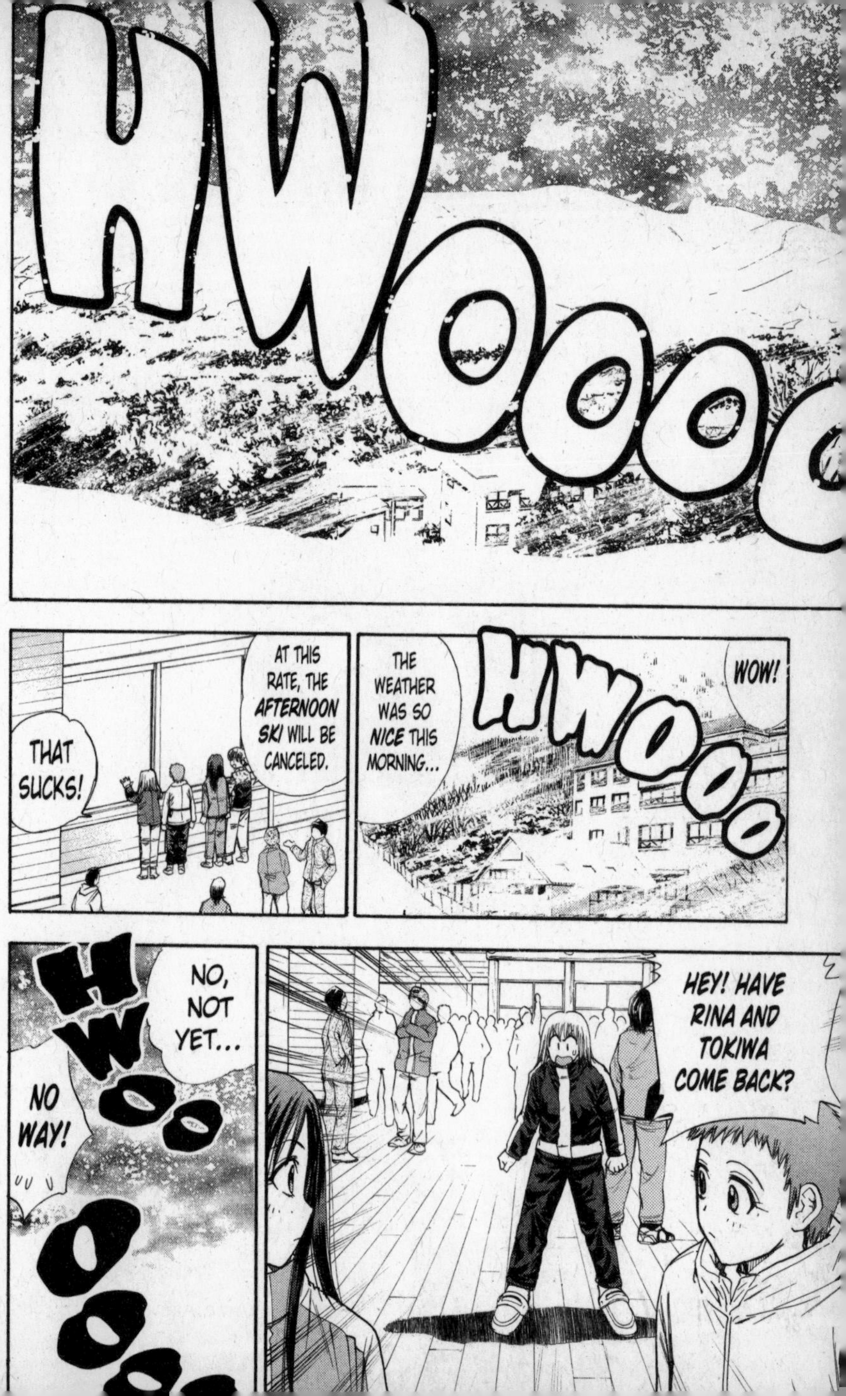
HWOOOOO
WOW!
HWOOOO
THE WEATHER WAS SO NICE THIS MORNING...
AT THIS RATE, THE AFTERNOON SKI WILL BE CANCELED.
THAT SUCKS!
HEY! HAVE RINA AND TOKIWA COME BACK?
NO, NOT YET...
HWOOOOOOO
NO WAY!

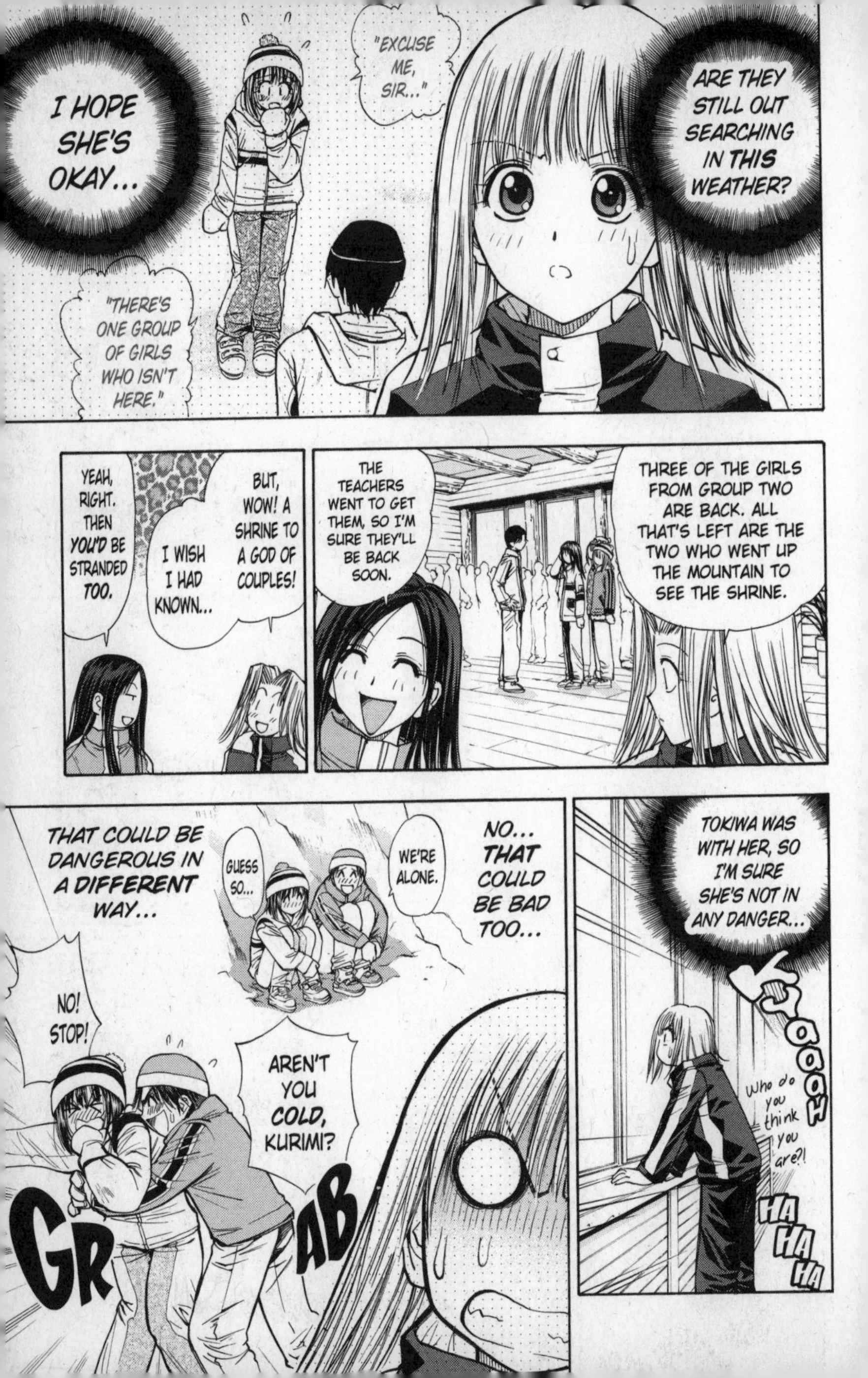
ARE THEY STILL OUT SEARCHING IN THIS WEATHER?
"EXCUSE ME, SIR..."
I HOPE SHE'S OKAY...
"THERE'S ONE GROUP OF GIRLS WHO ISN'T HERE."
THREE OF THE GIRLS FROM GROUP TWO ARE BACK. ALL THAT'S LEFT ARE THE TWO WHO WENT UP THE MOUNTAIN TO SEE THE SHRINE.
THE TEACHERS WENT TO GET THEM, SO I'M SURE THEY'LL BE BACK SOON.
BUT, WOW! A SHRINE TO A GOD OF COUPLES!
I WISH I HAD KNOWN...
YEAH, RIGHT. THEN YOU'D BE STRANDED TOO.
TOKIWA WAS WITH HER, SO I'M SURE SHE'S NOT IN ANY DANGER...
KYOOOOH
Who do you think you are?!
HA HA HA
NO... THAT COULD BE BAD TOO...
WE'RE ALONE.
GUESS SO...
THAT COULD BE DANGEROUS IN A DIFFERENT WAY...
AREN'T YOU COLD, KURIMI?
NO! STOP!
GRAB

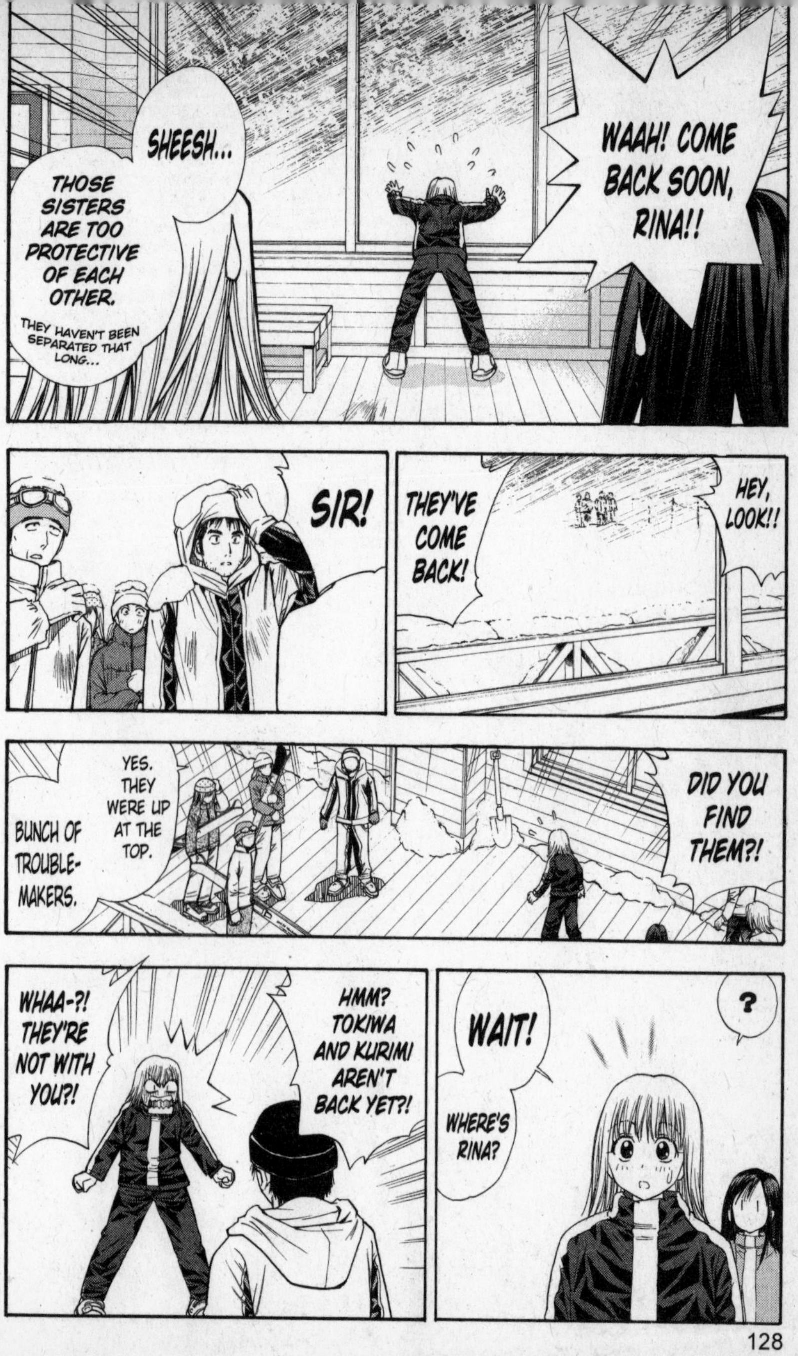
WAAH! COME BACK SOON, RINA!!
SHEESH...
THOSE SISTERS ARE TOO PROTECTIVE OF EACH OTHER.
THEY HAVEN'T BEEN SEPARATED THAT LONG...
HEY, LOOK!!
THEY'VE COME BACK!
SIR!
DID YOU FIND THEM?!
YES. THEY WERE UP AT THE TOP.
BUNCH OF TROUBLE-MAKERS.
?
WAIT!
WHERE'S RINA?
HMM? TOKIWA AND KURIMI AREN'T BACK YET?!
WHAA-?! THEY'RE NOT WITH YOU?!

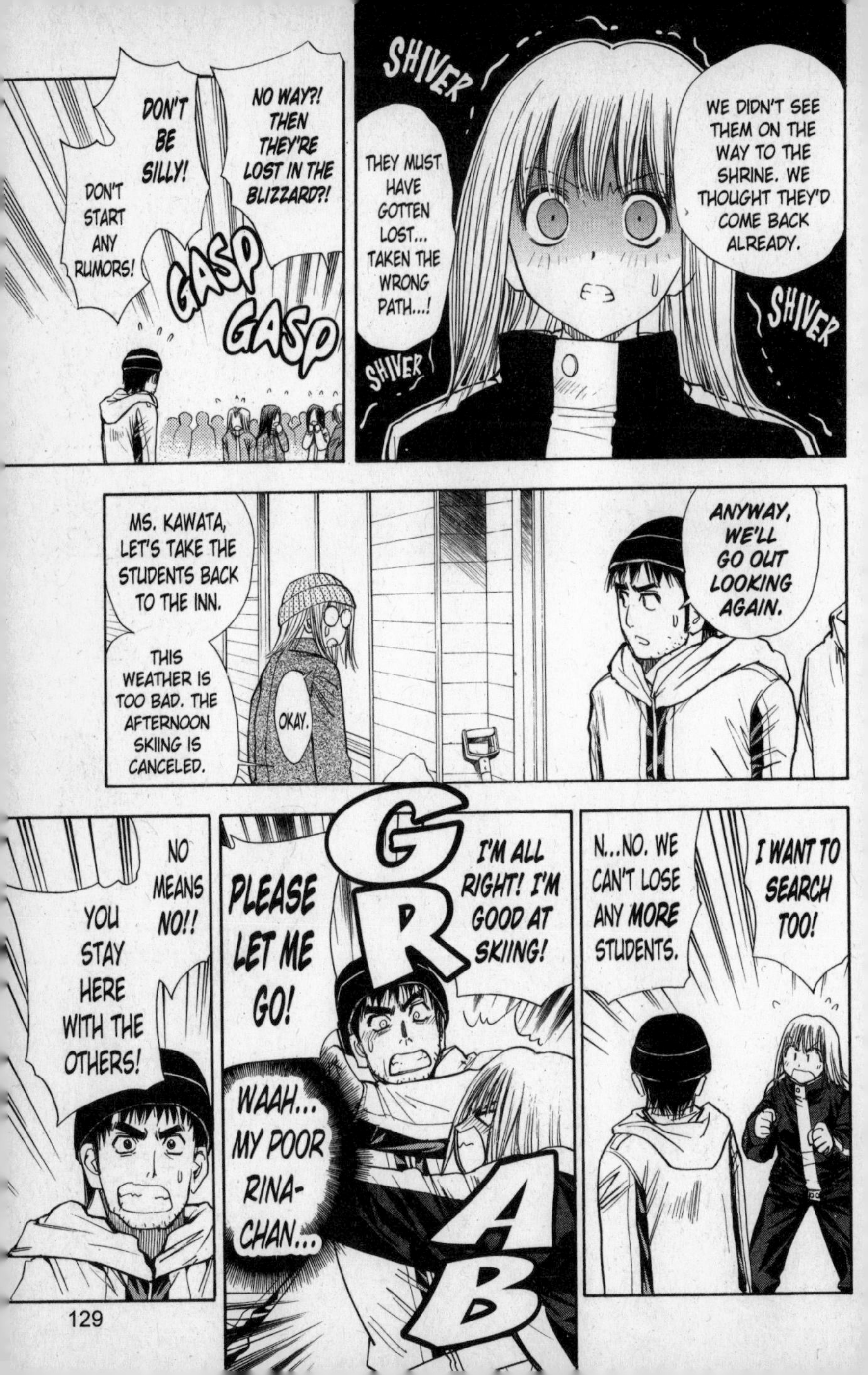
SHIVER
WE DIDN'T SEE THEM ON THE WAY TO THE SHRINE. WE THOUGHT THEY'D COME BACK ALREADY.
THEY MUST HAVE GOTTEN LOST... TAKEN THE WRONG PATH...!
SHIVER
SHIVER
NO WAY?! THEN THEY'RE LOST IN THE BLIZZARD?!
DON'T BE SILLY!
DON'T START ANY RUMORS!
GASP
GASP
ANYWAY, WE'LL GO OUT LOOKING AGAIN.
MS. KAWATA, LET'S TAKE THE STUDENTS BACK TO THE INN.
THIS WEATHER IS TOO BAD. THE AFTERNOON SKIING IS CANCELED.
OKAY.
I WANT TO SEARCH TOO!
N...NO. WE CAN'T LOSE ANY MORE STUDENTS.
I'M ALL RIGHT! I'M GOOD AT SKIING!
PLEASE LET ME GO!
GRAB
WAAH... MY POOR RINA-CHAN...
NO MEANS NO!!
YOU STAY HERE WITH THE OTHERS!

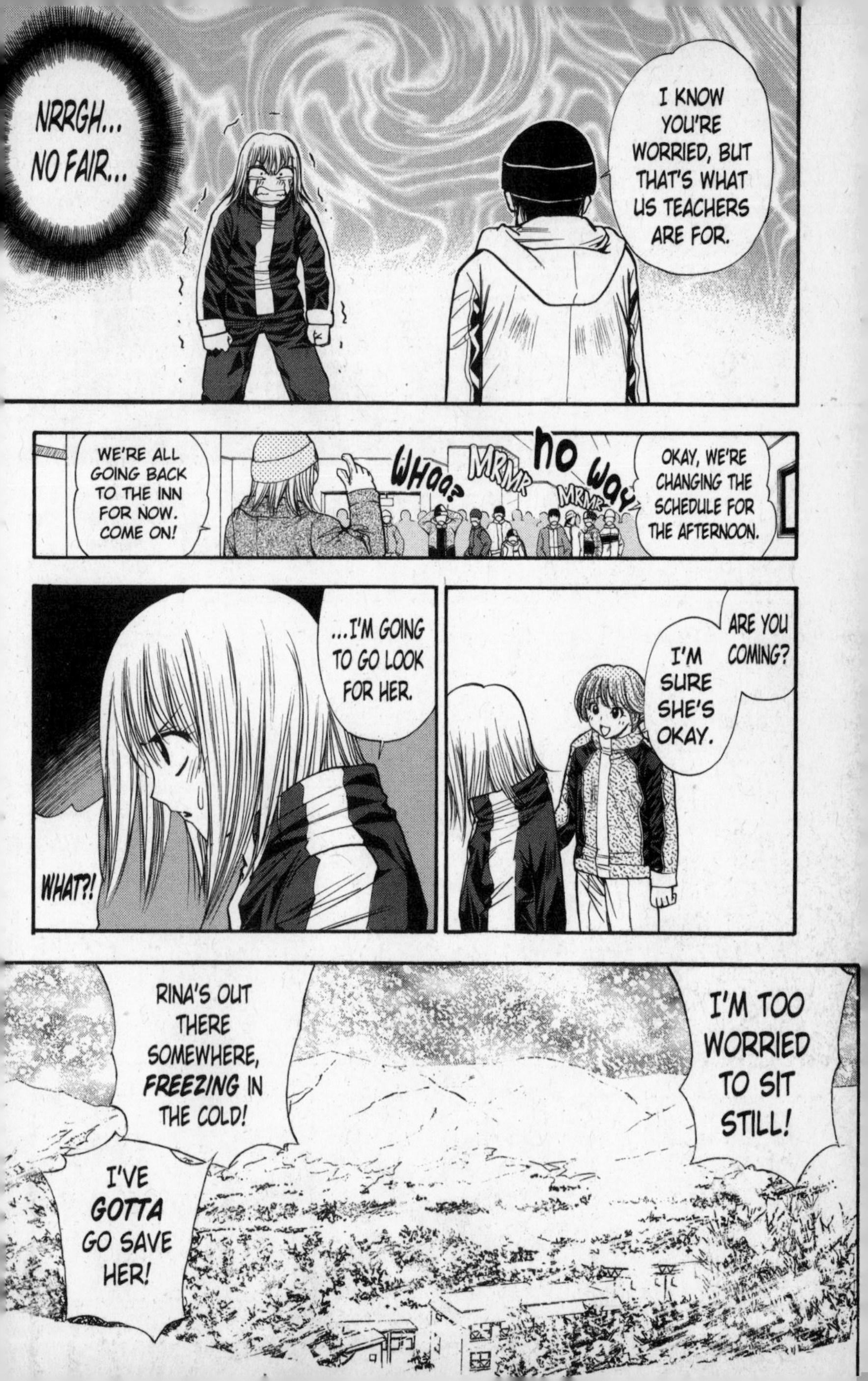
I KNOW YOU'RE WORRIED, BUT THAT'S WHAT US TEACHERS ARE FOR.
NRRGH... NO FAIR...
OKAY, WE'RE CHANGING THE SCHEDULE FOR THE AFTERNOON.
no way
MRMR
MRMR
Whaa?
WE'RE ALL GOING BACK TO THE INN FOR NOW. COME ON!
ARE YOU COMING?
I'M SURE SHE'S OKAY.
...I'M GOING TO GO LOOK FOR HER.
WHAT?!
I'M TOO WORRIED TO SIT STILL!
RINA'S OUT THERE SOMEWHERE, FREEZING IN THE COLD!
I'VE GOTTA GO SAVE HER!

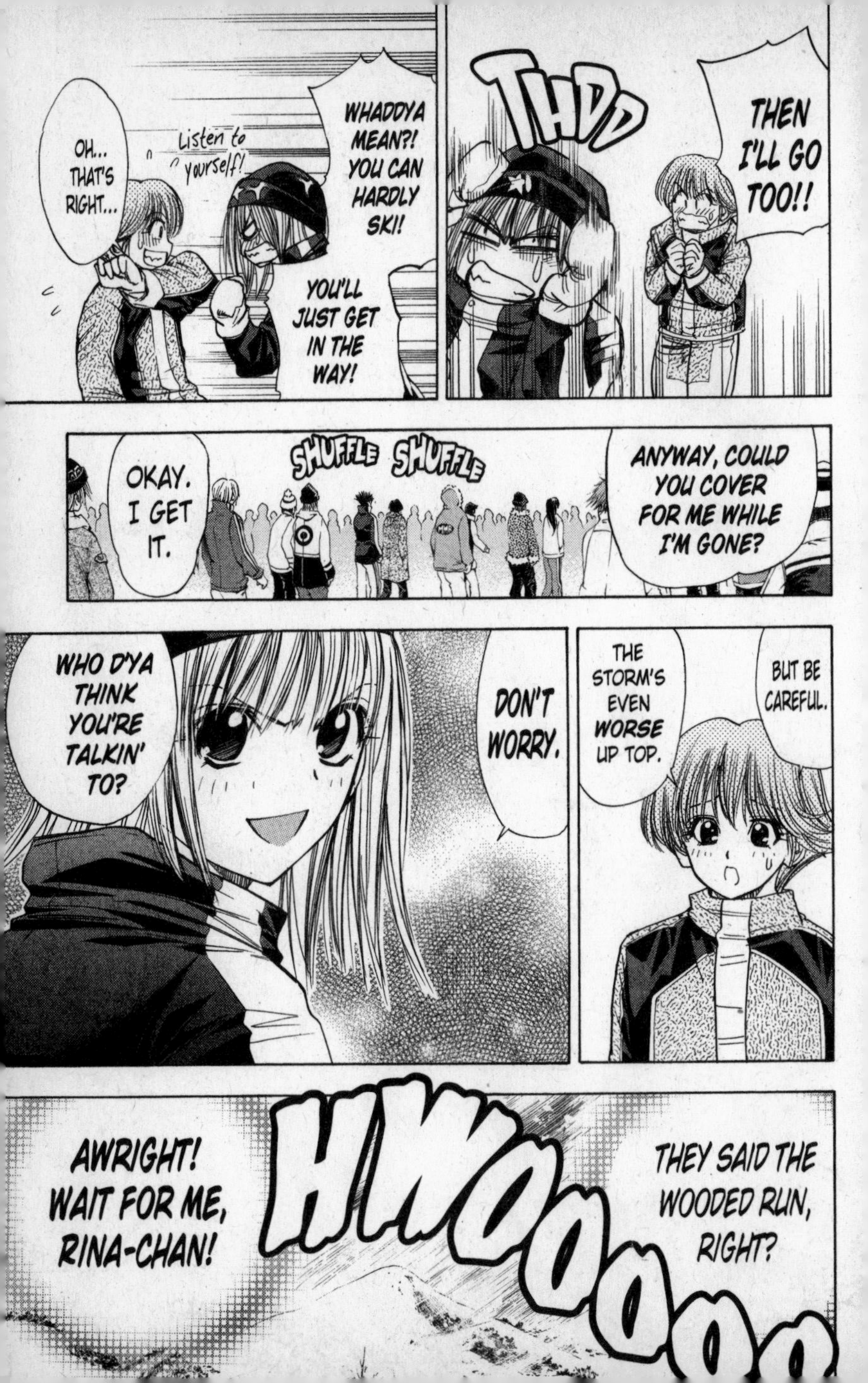
THDD
THEN I'LL GO TOO!!
WHADDYA MEAN?! YOU CAN HARDLY SKI!
YOU'LL JUST GET IN THE WAY!
Listen to yourself!
OH... THAT'S RIGHT...
ANYWAY, COULD YOU COVER FOR ME WHILE I'M GONE?
SHUFFLE SHUFFLE
OKAY. I GET IT.
BUT BE CAREFUL.
THE STORM'S EVEN WORSE UP TOP.
DON'T WORRY.
WHO D'YA THINK YOU'RE TALKIN' TO?
THEY SAID THE WOODED RUN, RIGHT?
HWOOOOOO
AWRIGHT! WAIT FOR ME, RINA-CHAN!

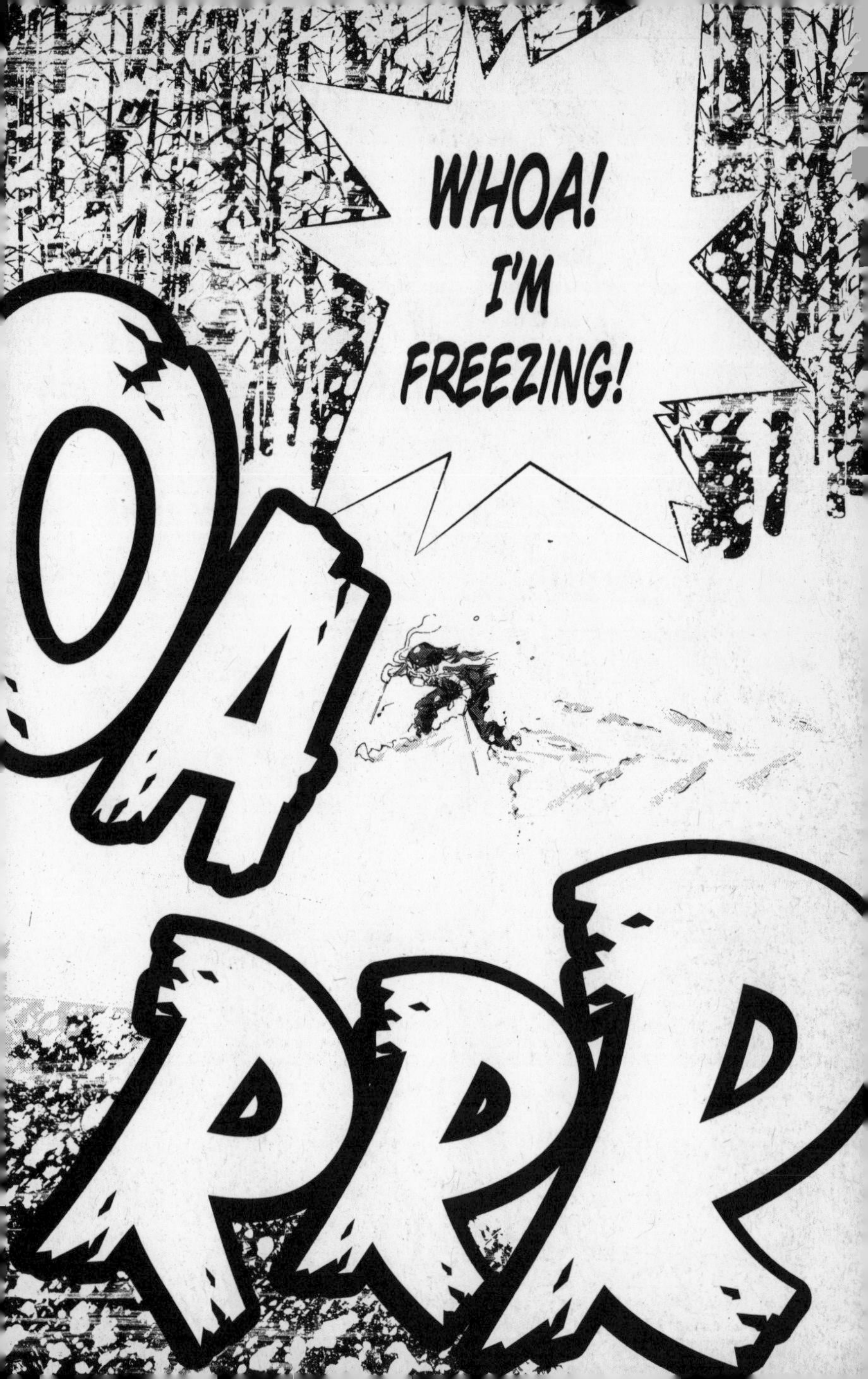
WHOA! I'M FREEZING!

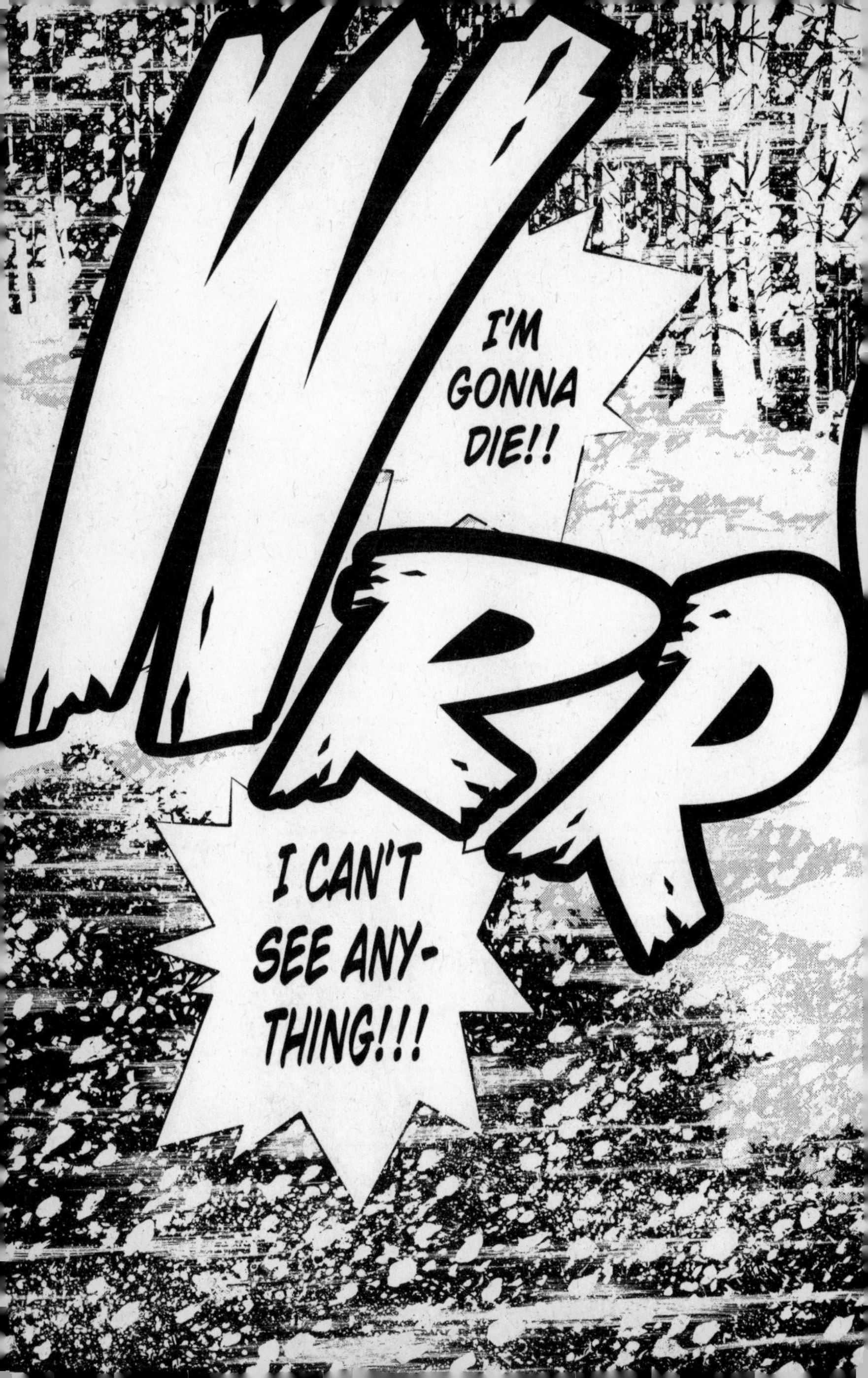
I'M GONNA DIE!!
I CAN'T SEE ANYTHING!!!

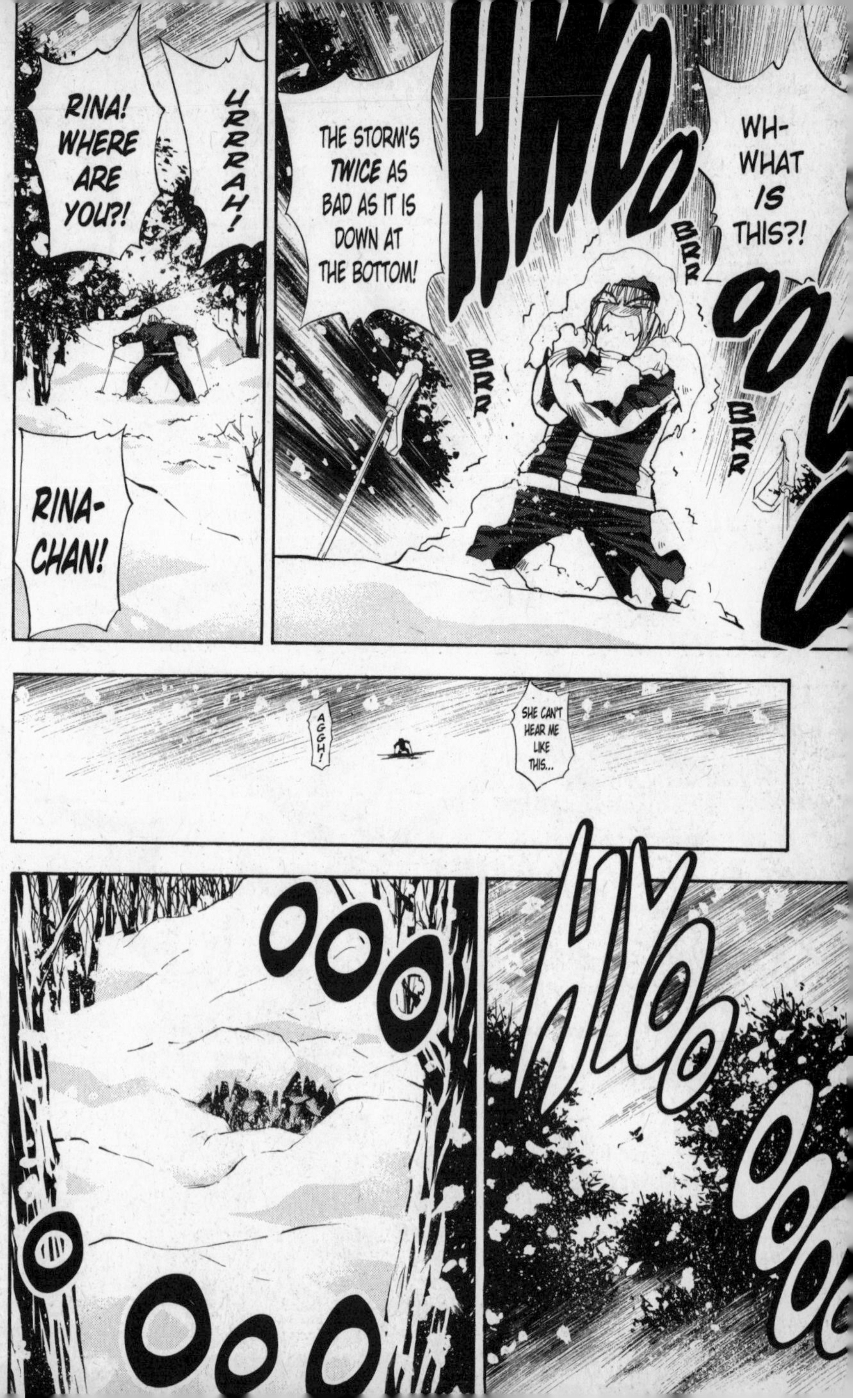
WH-WHAT IS THIS?!
HWOOOOOOO
BRR
BRR
BRR
THE STORM'S TWICE AS BAD AS IT IS DOWN AT THE BOTTOM!
URRRAH!
RINA! WHERE ARE YOU?!
RINA-CHAN!
SHE CAN'T HEAR ME LIKE THIS...
AGGH!
HWOOOOOOO
OOOOOO

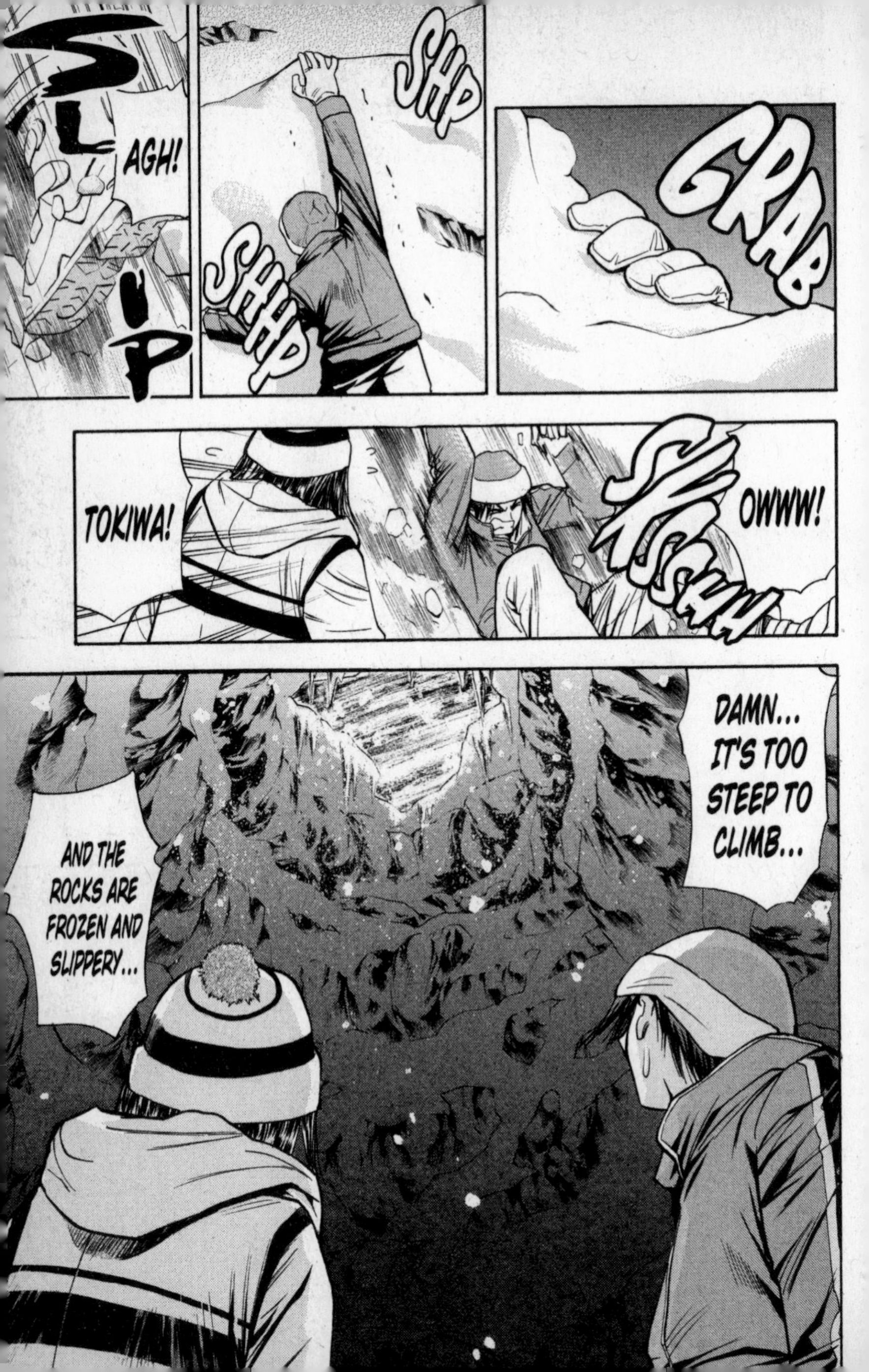
GRAB
SHIP
SHHP
SLIP
AGH!
SKSHH
OWWW!
TOKIWA!
DAMN... IT'S TOO STEEP TO CLIMB...
AND THE ROCKS ARE FROZEN AND SLIPPERY...

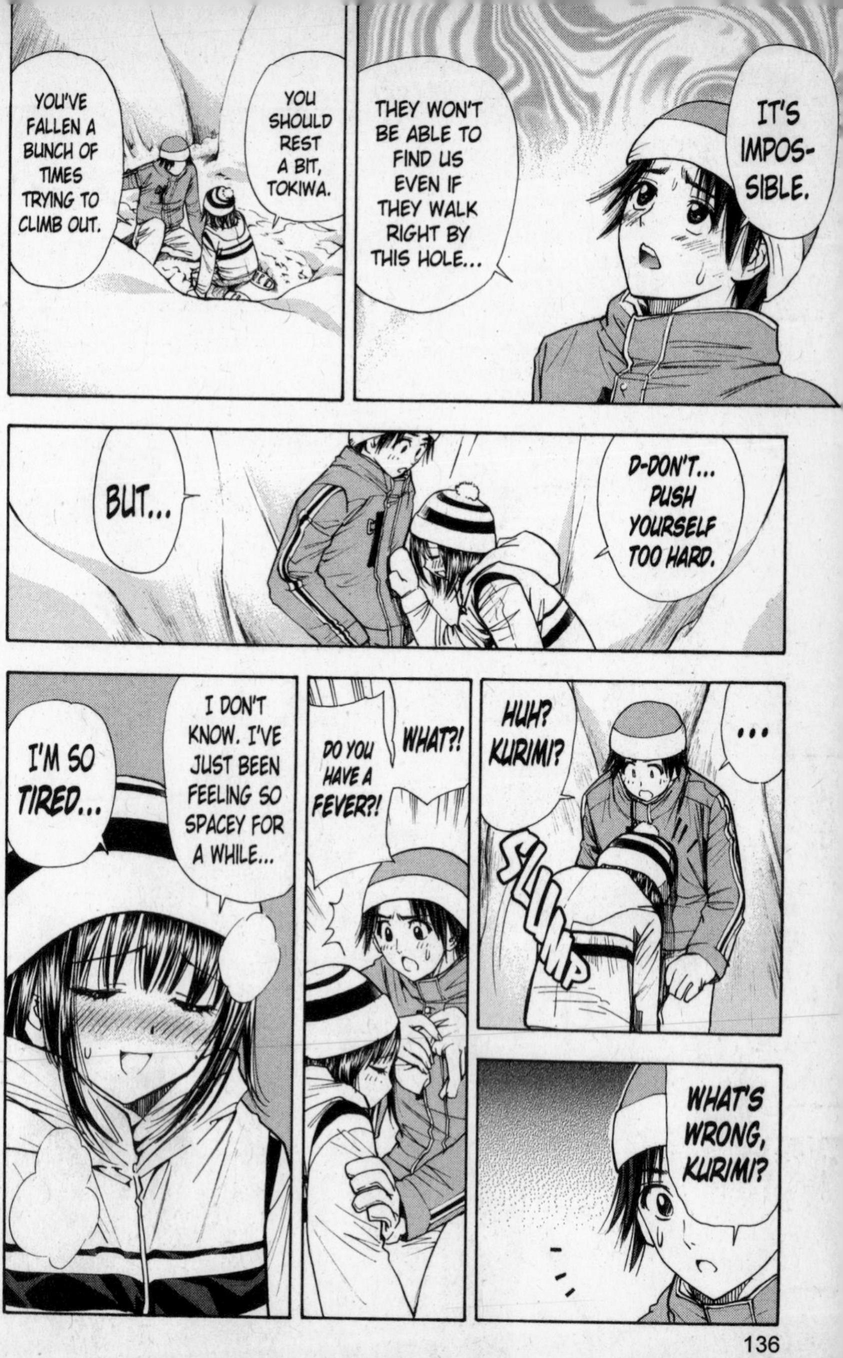
IT'S IMPOS-SIBLE.
THEY WON'T BE ABLE TO FIND US EVEN IF THEY WALK RIGHT BY THIS HOLE...
YOU SHOULD REST A BIT, TOKIWA.
YOU'VE FALLEN A BUNCH OF TIMES TRYING TO CLIMB OUT.
D-DON'T... PUSH YOURSELF TOO HARD.
BUT...
...
HUH? KURIMI?
SLUMP
WHAT'S WRONG, KURIMI?
WHAT?!
DO YOU HAVE A FEVER?!
I DON'T KNOW. I'VE JUST BEEN FEELING SO SPACEY FOR A WHILE...
I'M SO TIRED...

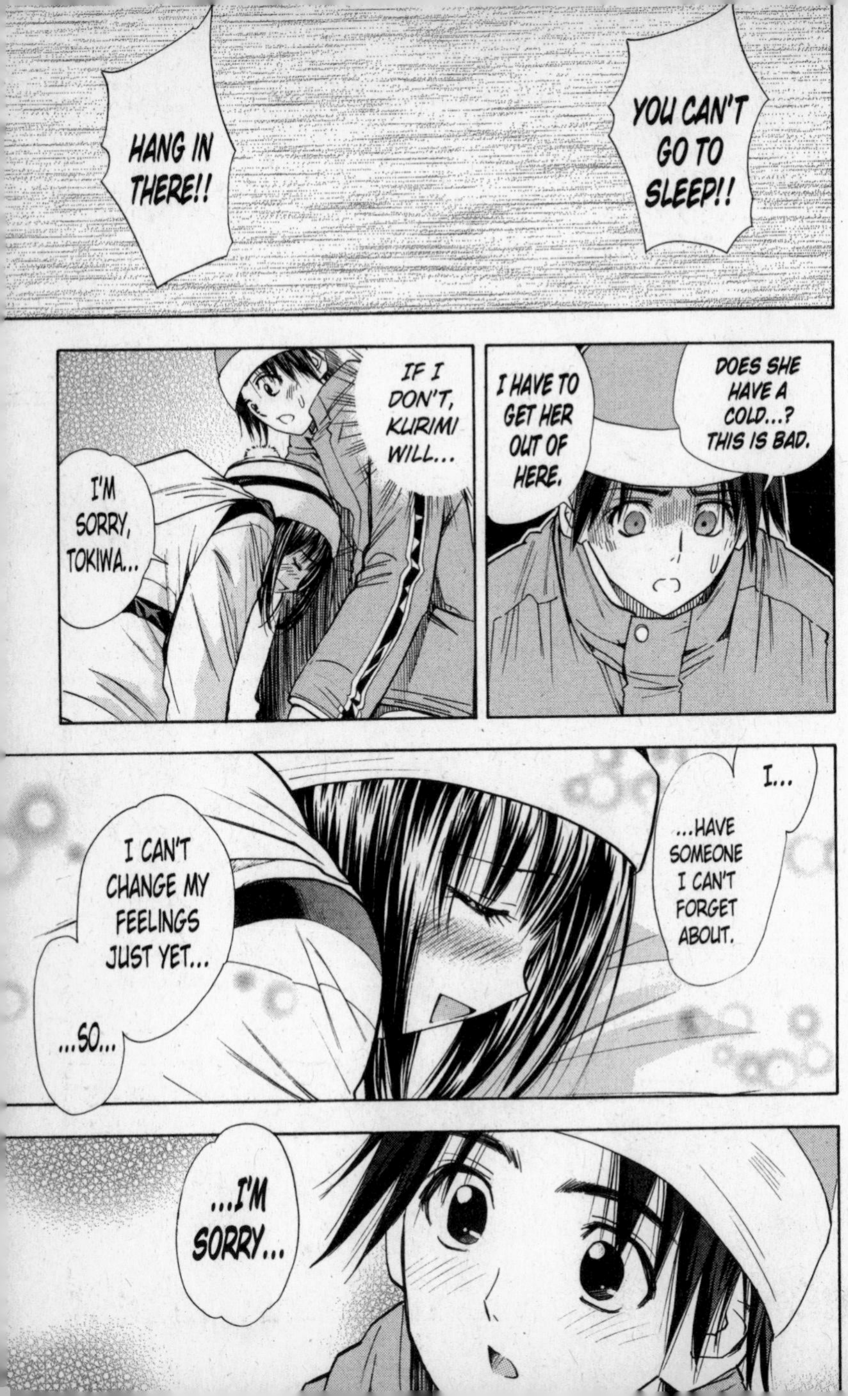
YOU CAN'T GO TO SLEEP!!
HANG IN THERE!!
DOES SHE HAVE A COLD...? THIS IS BAD.
I HAVE TO GET HER OUT OF HERE.
IF I DON'T, KURIMI WILL...
I'M SORRY, TOKIWA...
I...
...HAVE SOMEONE I CAN'T FORGET ABOUT.
I CAN'T CHANGE MY FEELINGS JUST YET...
...SO...
...I'M SORRY...

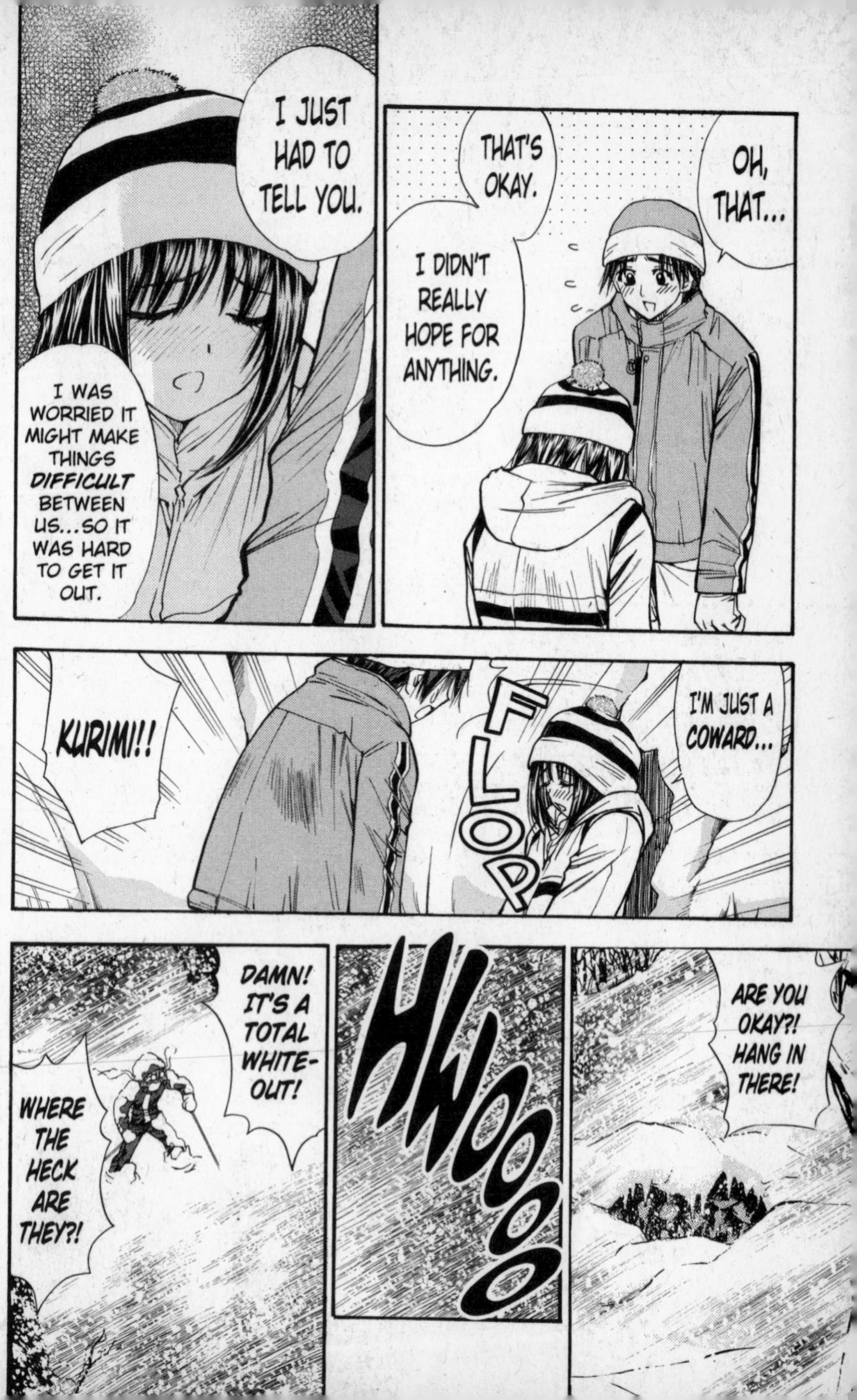
OH, THAT...
THAT'S OKAY.
I DIDN'T REALLY HOPE FOR ANYTHING.
I JUST HAD TO TELL YOU.
I WAS WORRIED IT MIGHT MAKE THINGS DIFFICULT BETWEEN US...SO IT WAS HARD TO GET IT OUT.
I'M JUST A COWARD...
FLLOP
KURIMI!!
ARE YOU OKAY?! HANG IN THERE!
HWOOOOO
DAMN! IT'S A TOTAL WHITE-OUT!
WHERE THE HECK ARE THEY?!

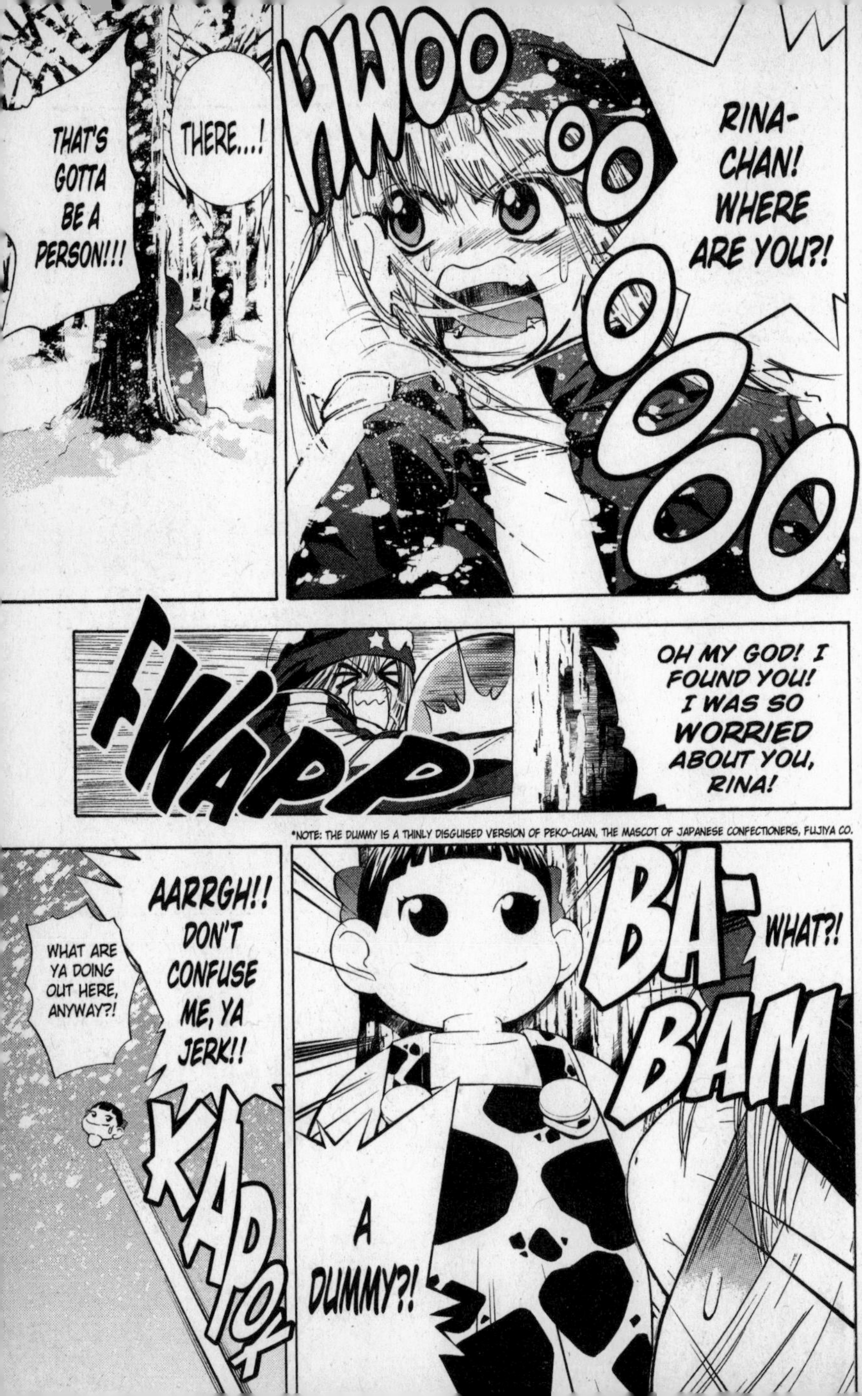
HWOOOOOOOOOO
RINA-CHAN! WHERE ARE YOU?!
THERE...!
THAT'S GOTTA BE A PERSON!!!
OH MY GOD! I FOUND YOU! I WAS SO WORRIED ABOUT YOU, RINA!
FWAPP
*NOTE: THE DUMMY IS A THINLY DISGUISED VERSION OF PEKO-CHAN, THE MASCOT OF JAPANESE CONFECTIONERS, FUJIYA CO.
WHAT?!
BA-BAM
A DUMMY?!
AARRGH!! DON'T CONFUSE ME, YA JERK!!
WHAT ARE YA DOING OUT HERE, ANYWAY?!
KAPOK

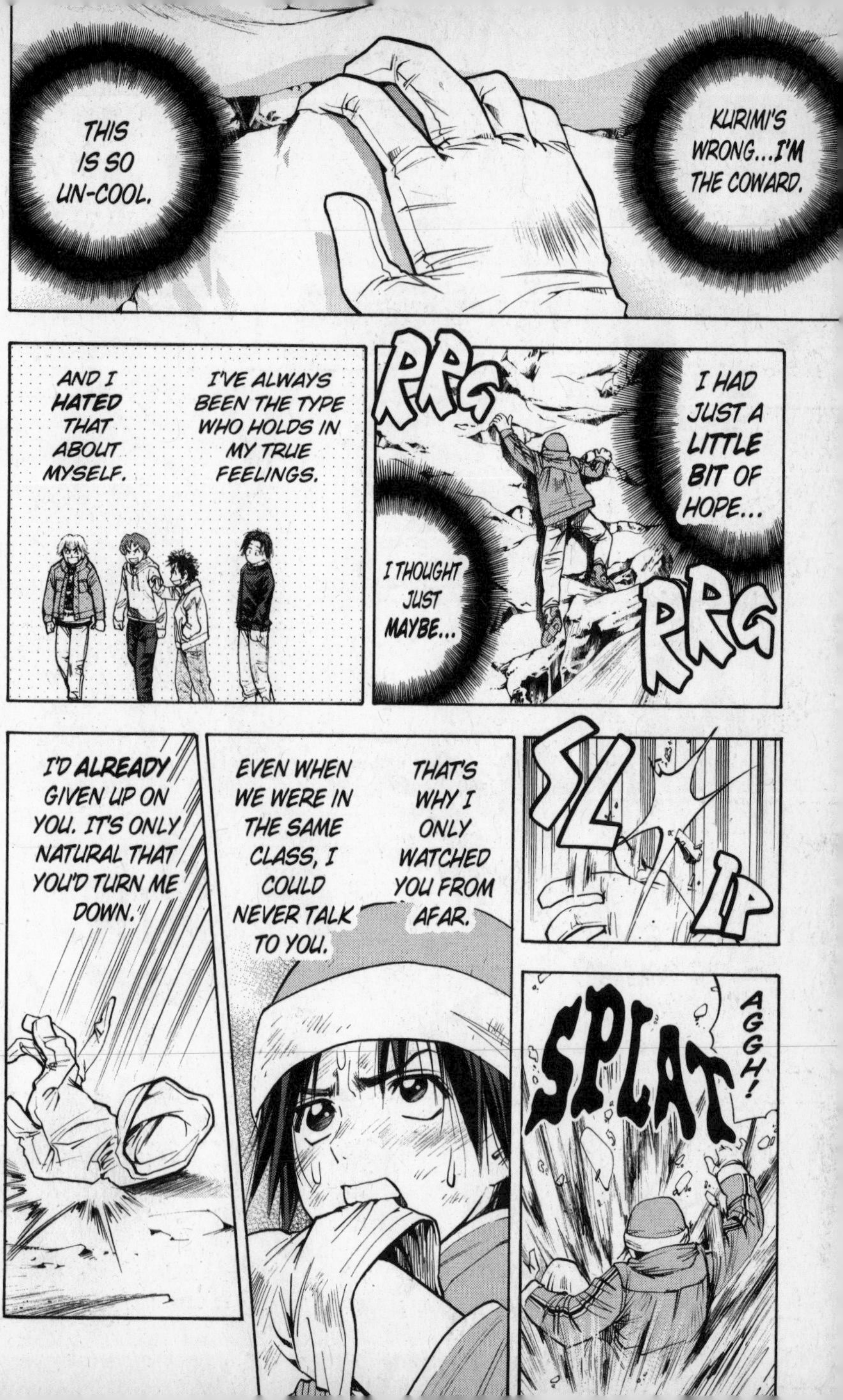
KURIMI'S WRONG...I'M THE COWARD.
THIS IS SO UN-COOL.
I HAD JUST A LITTLE BIT OF HOPE...
RRG
I THOUGHT JUST MAYBE...
RRG
I'VE ALWAYS BEEN THE TYPE WHO HOLDS IN MY TRUE FEELINGS.
AND I HATED THAT ABOUT MYSELF.
SLIP
AGGH!
SPLAT
THAT'S WHY I ONLY WATCHED YOU FROM AFAR.
EVEN WHEN WE WERE IN THE SAME CLASS, I COULD NEVER TALK TO YOU.
I'D ALREADY GIVEN UP ON YOU. IT'S ONLY NATURAL THAT YOU'D TURN ME DOWN.

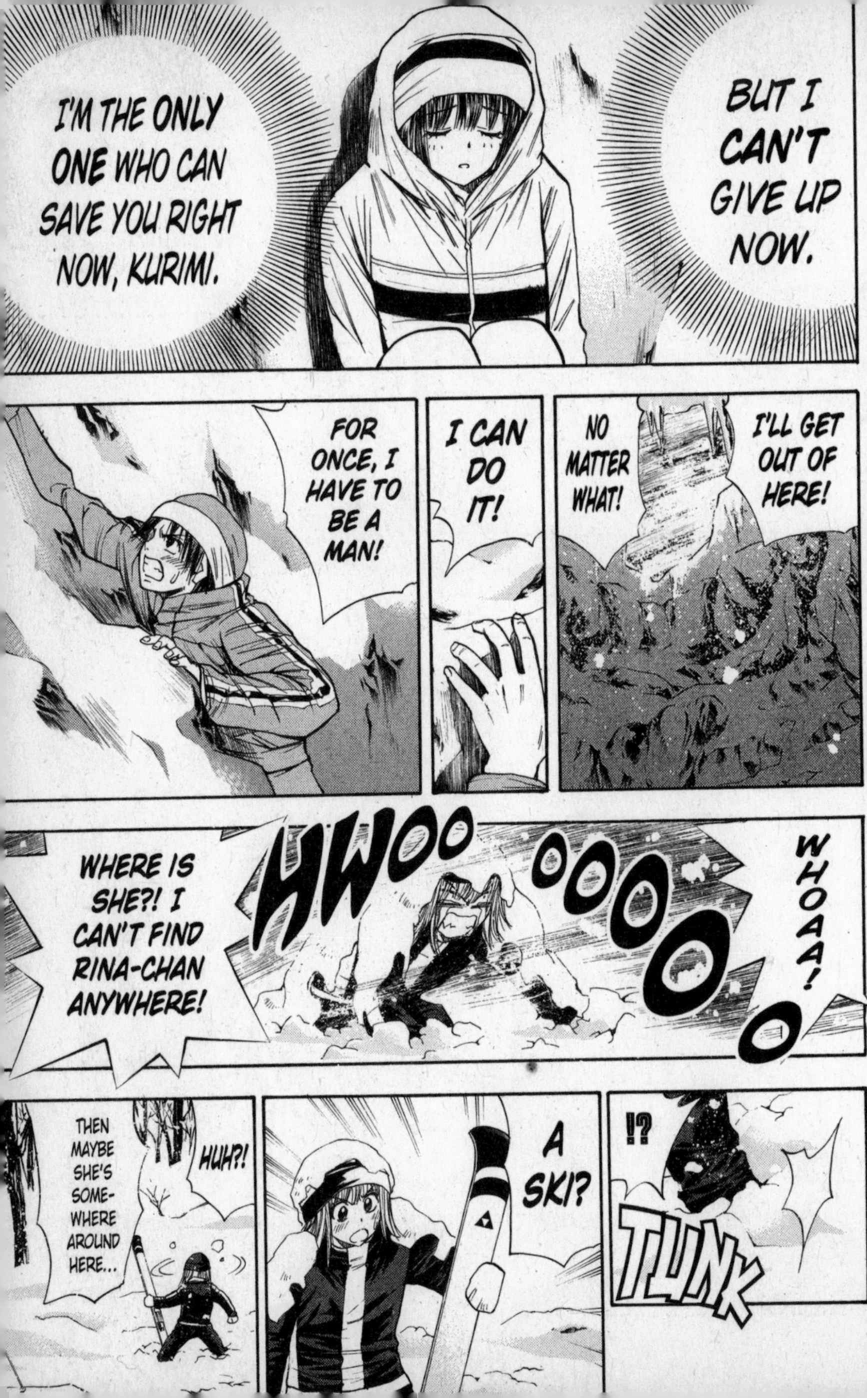
BUT I CAN'T GIVE UP NOW.
I'M THE ONLY ONE WHO CAN SAVE YOU RIGHT NOW, KURIMI.
I'LL GET OUT OF HERE!
NO MATTER WHAT!
I CAN DO IT!
FOR ONCE, I HAVE TO BE A MAN!
WHOAAA!
HWOOOOOOOOO
WHERE IS SHE?! I CAN'T FIND RINA-CHAN ANYWHERE!
!?
TUNK
A SKI?
HUH?!
THEN MAYBE SHE'S SOME-WHERE AROUND HERE...

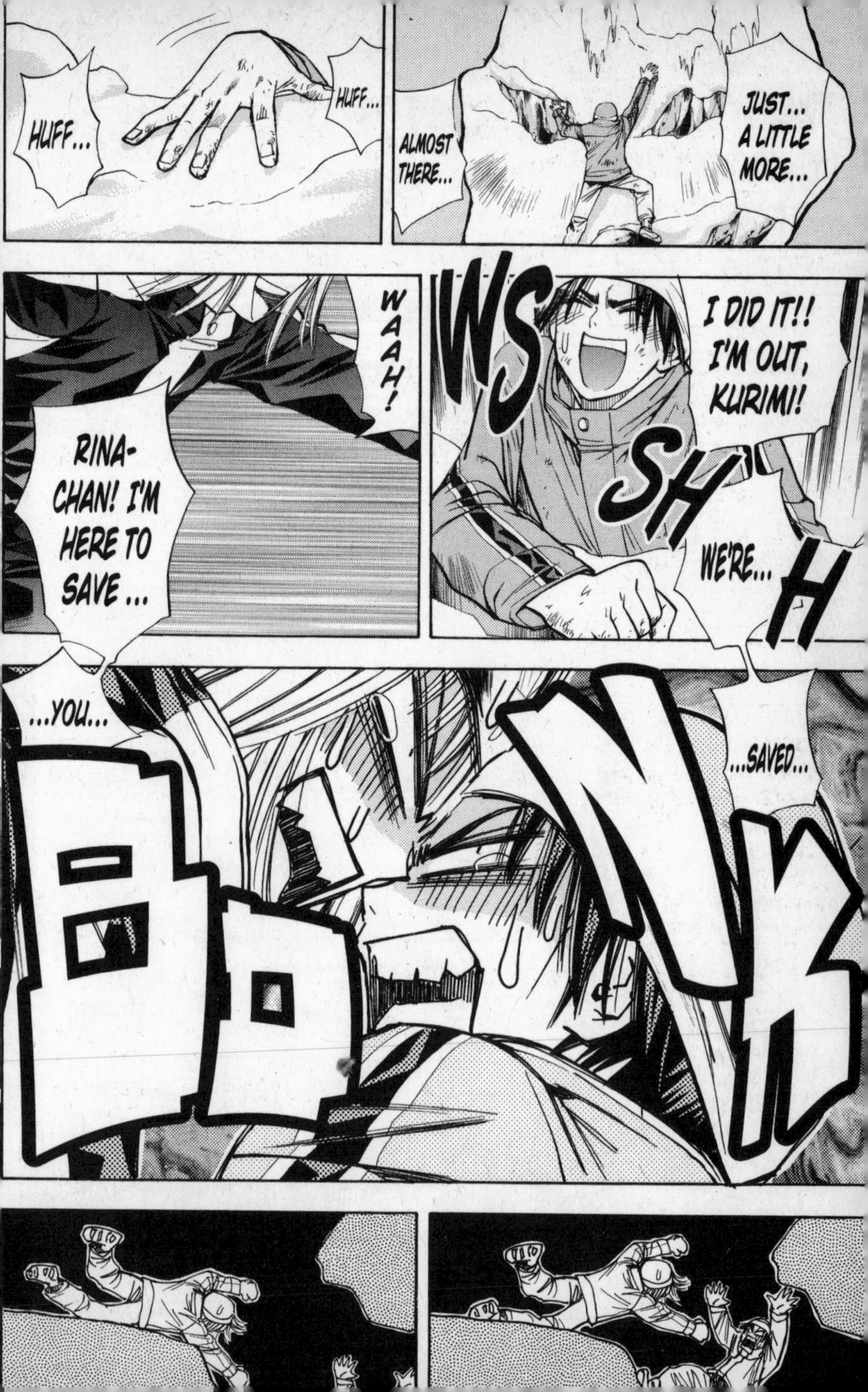
JUST... A LITTLE MORE...
ALMOST THERE...
HUFF...
HUFF...
I DID IT!! I'M OUT, KURIMI!
WS
SH
H
WE'RE...
...SAVED...
WAAH!
RINA-CHAN! I'M HERE TO SAVE ...
...YOU...
BONK

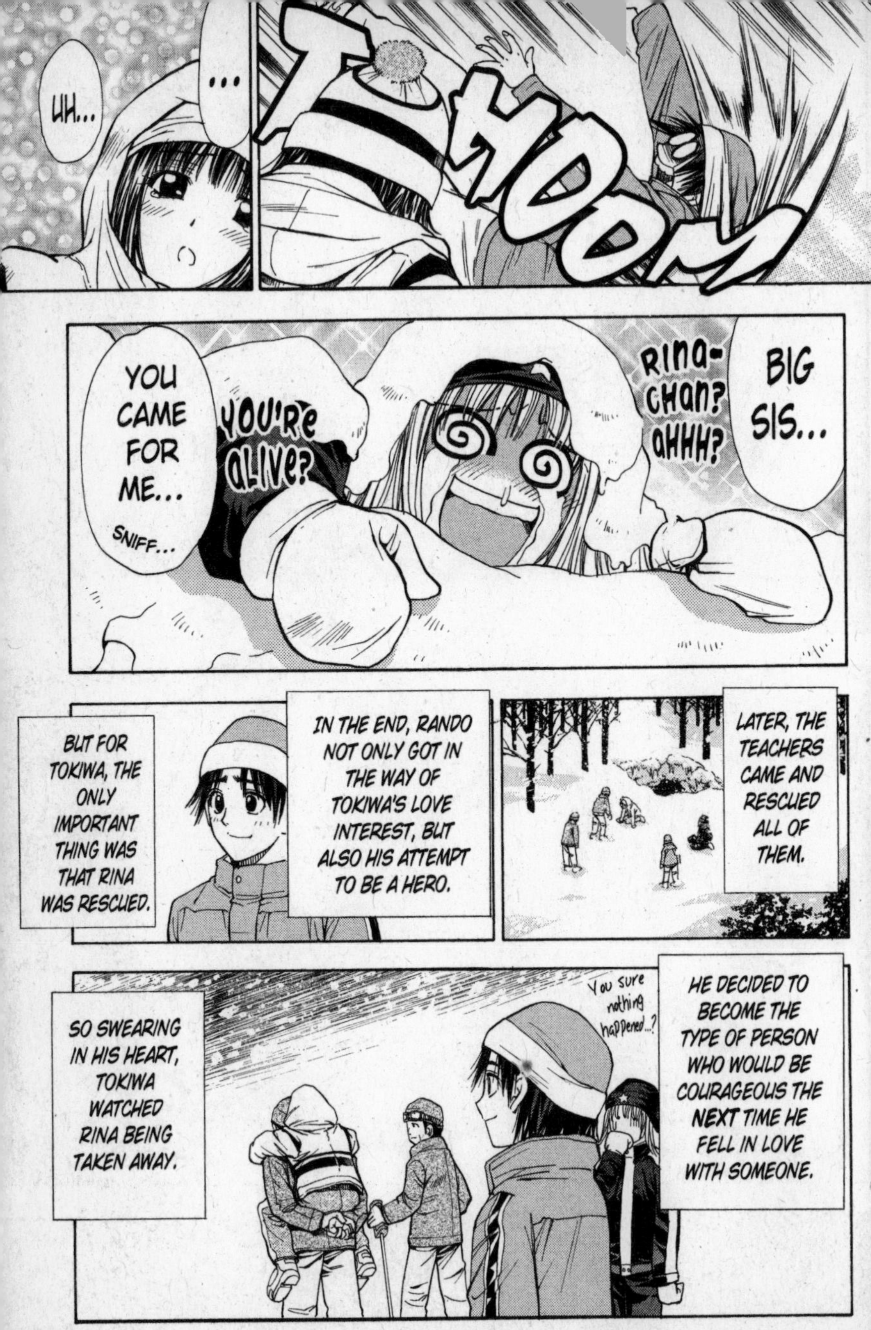
THOOM
...
UH...
BIG SIS...
RINA-CHAN? AHHH?
YOU'RE ALIVE?
YOU CAME FOR ME...
SNIFF...
LATER, THE TEACHERS CAME AND RESCUED ALL OF THEM.
IN THE END, RANDO NOT ONLY GOT IN THE WAY OF TOKIWA'S LOVE INTEREST, BUT ALSO HIS ATTEMPT TO BE A HERO.
BUT FOR TOKIWA, THE ONLY IMPORTANT THING WAS THAT RINA WAS RESCUED.
HE DECIDED TO BECOME THE TYPE OF PERSON WHO WOULD BE COURAGEOUS THE NEXT TIME HE FELL IN LOVE WITH SOMEONE.
You sure nothing happened...?
SO SWEARING IN HIS HEART, TOKIWA WATCHED RINA BEING TAKEN AWAY.

Art for the mugs for Pretty Face's one-year anniversary

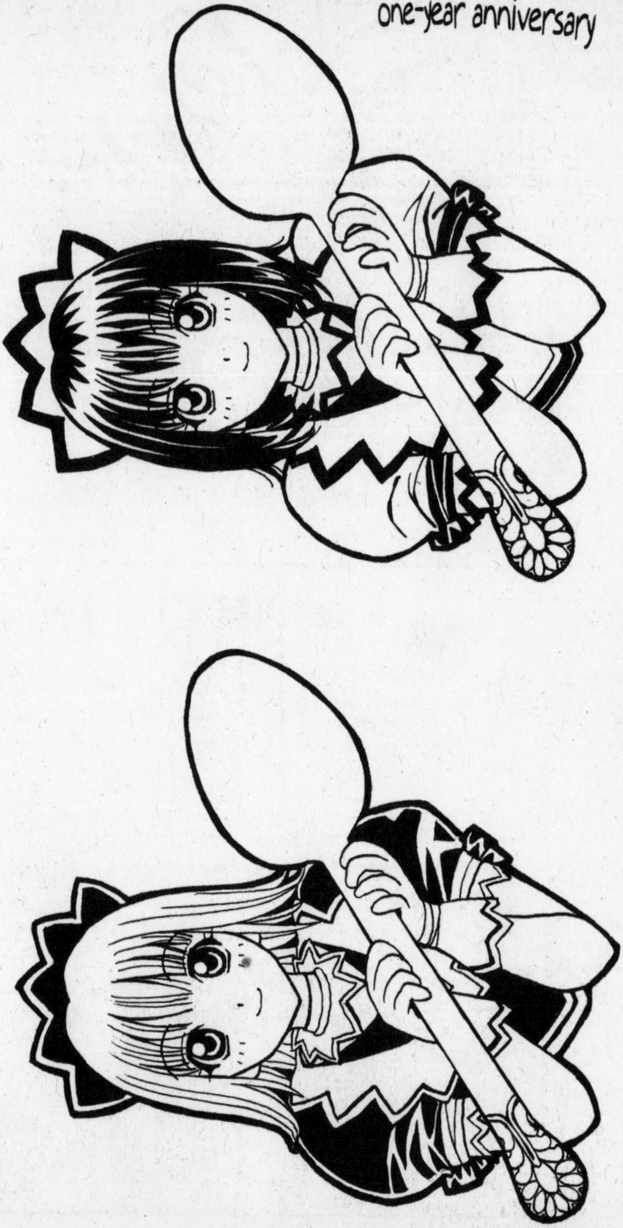

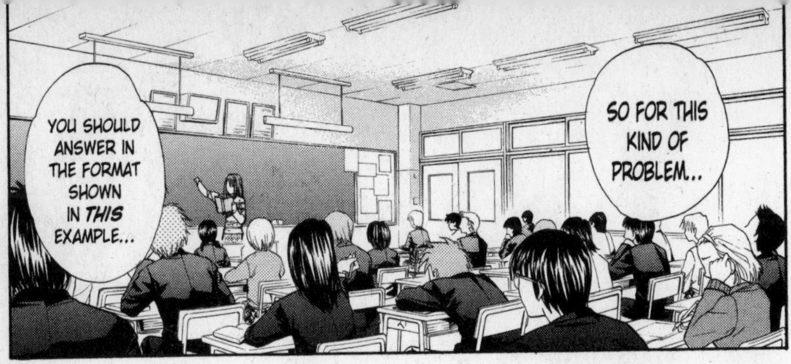
SO FOR THIS KIND OF PROBLEM...
YOU SHOULD ANSWER IN THE FORMAT SHOWN IN *THIS* EXAMPLE...

Chapter 44: Yukie-chan in Love

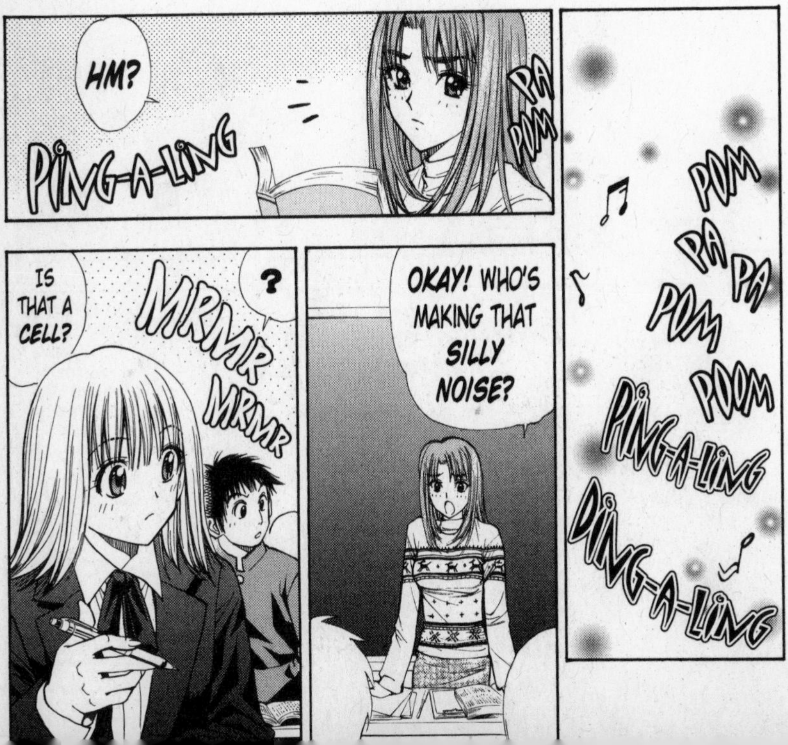
POM
PA PA
POM
POOM
PING-A-LING
DING-A-LING
PA POM
HM?
PING-A-LING
OKAY! WHO'S MAKING THAT SILLY NOISE?
?
IS THAT A CELL?
MRMR
MRMR

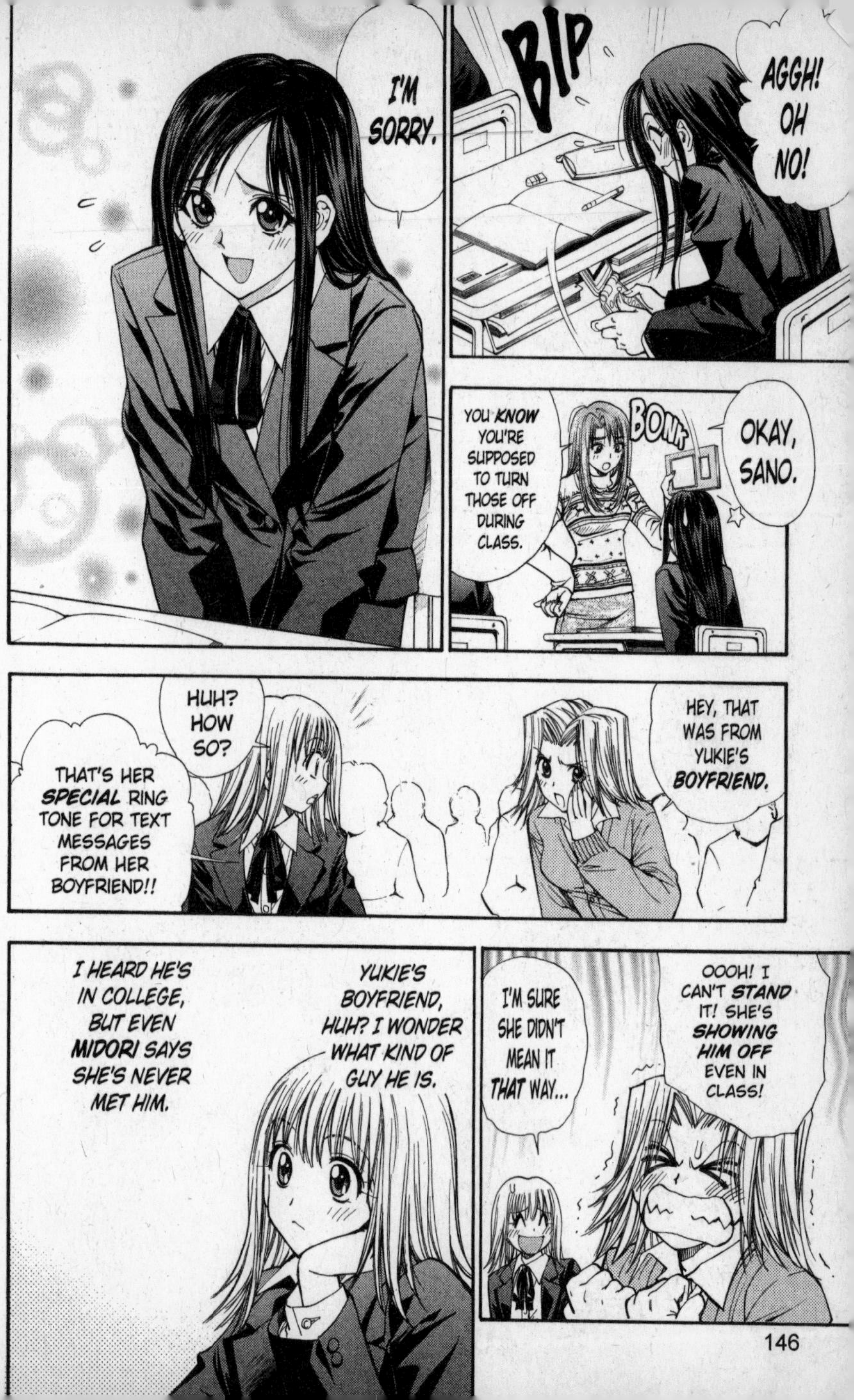
BIP
AGGH! OH NO!
OKAY, SANO.
BONK
YOU KNOW YOU'RE SUPPOSED TO TURN THOSE OFF DURING CLASS.
I'M SORRY.
HEY, THAT WAS FROM YUKIE'S BOYFRIEND.
HUH? HOW SO?
THAT'S HER SPECIAL RING TONE FOR TEXT MESSAGES FROM HER BOYFRIEND!!
OOOH! I CAN'T STAND IT! SHE'S SHOWING HIM OFF EVEN IN CLASS!
I'M SURE SHE DIDN'T MEAN IT THAT WAY...
YUKIE'S BOYFRIEND, HUH? I WONDER WHAT KIND OF GUY HE IS.
I HEARD HE'S IN COLLEGE, BUT EVEN MIDORI SAYS SHE'S NEVER MET HIM.

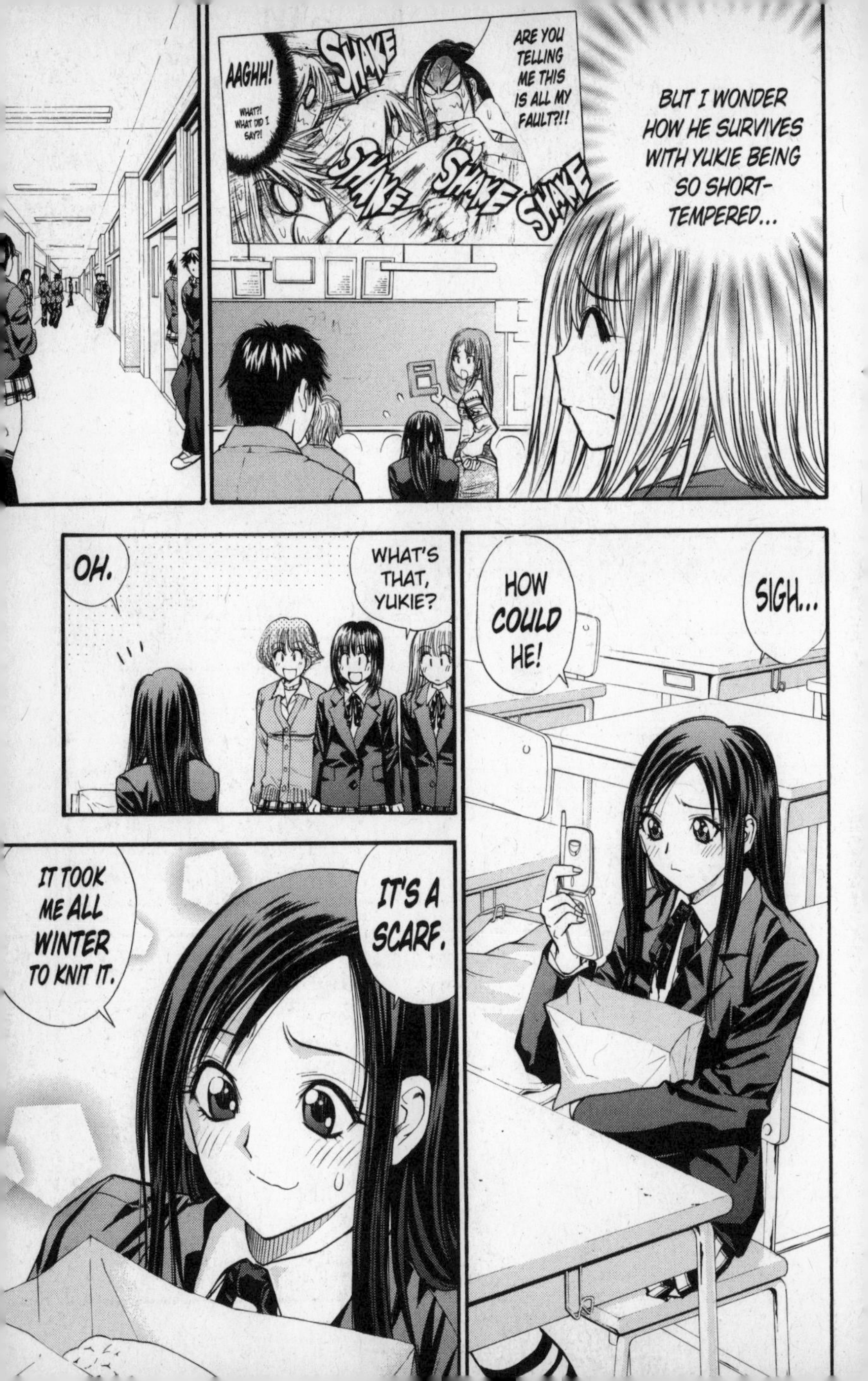
BUT I WONDER HOW HE SURVIVES WITH YUKIE BEING SO SHORT-TEMPERED...
ARE YOU TELLING ME THIS IS ALL MY FAULT?!!
SHAKE
SHAKE
SHAKE
SHAKE
AAGHH!
WHAT?! WHAT DID I SAY?!
SIGH...
HOW COULD HE!
WHAT'S THAT, YUKIE?
OH.
IT'S A SCARF.
IT TOOK ME ALL WINTER TO KNIT IT.

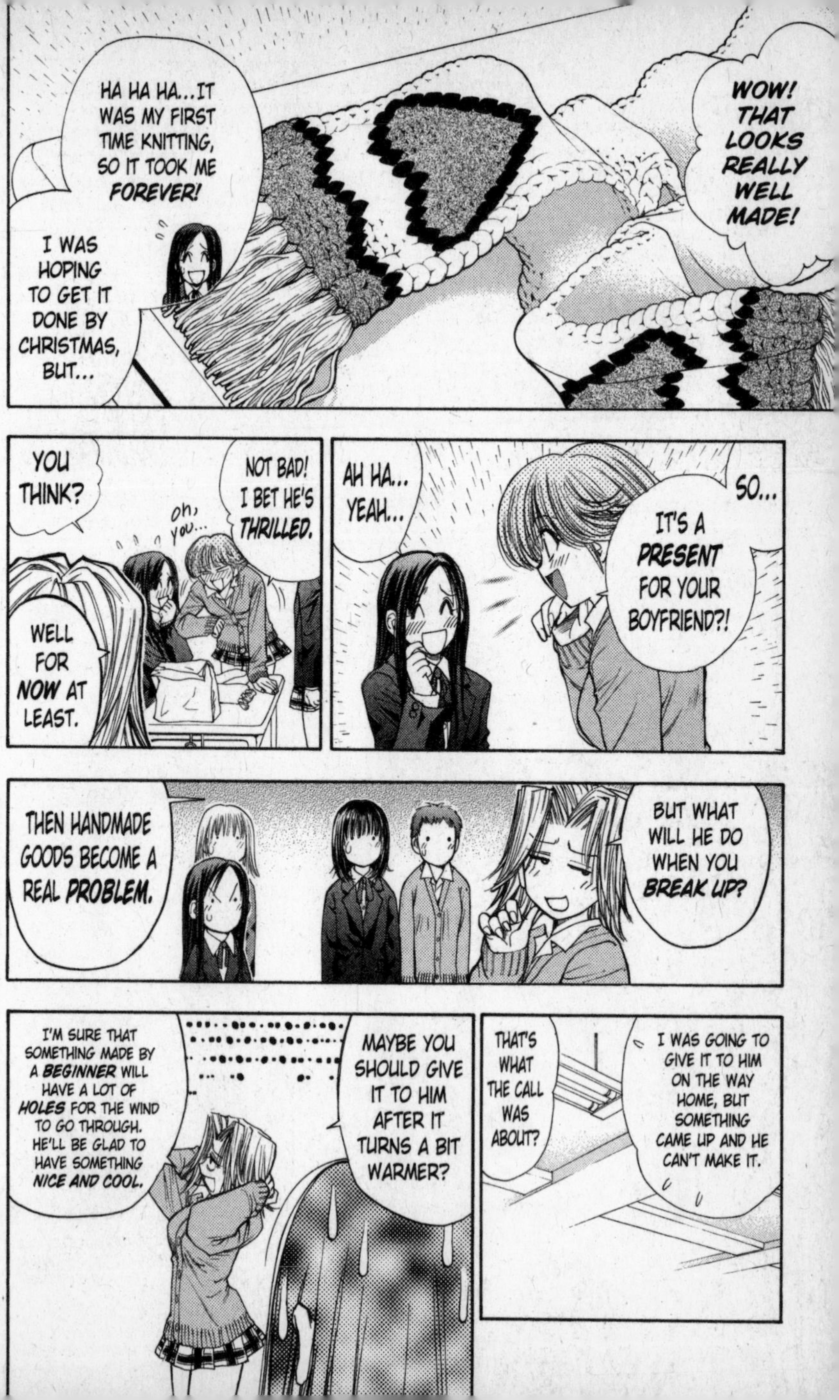
WOW! THAT LOOKS REALLY WELL MADE!
HA HA HA...IT WAS MY FIRST TIME KNITTING, SO IT TOOK ME FOREVER!
I WAS HOPING TO GET IT DONE BY CHRISTMAS, BUT...
SO...
IT'S A PRESENT FOR YOUR BOYFRIEND?!
AH HA... YEAH...
NOT BAD! I BET HE'S THRILLED.
Oh, you...
YOU THINK?
WELL FOR NOW AT LEAST.
BUT WHAT WILL HE DO WHEN YOU BREAK UP?
THEN HANDMADE GOODS BECOME A REAL PROBLEM.
I WAS GOING TO GIVE IT TO HIM ON THE WAY HOME, BUT SOMETHING CAME UP AND HE CAN'T MAKE IT.
THAT'S WHAT THE CALL WAS ABOUT?
MAYBE YOU SHOULD GIVE IT TO HIM AFTER IT TURNS A BIT WARMER?
I'M SURE THAT SOMETHING MADE BY A BEGINNER WILL HAVE A LOT OF HOLES FOR THE WIND TO GO THROUGH. HE'LL BE GLAD TO HAVE SOMETHING NICE AND COOL.

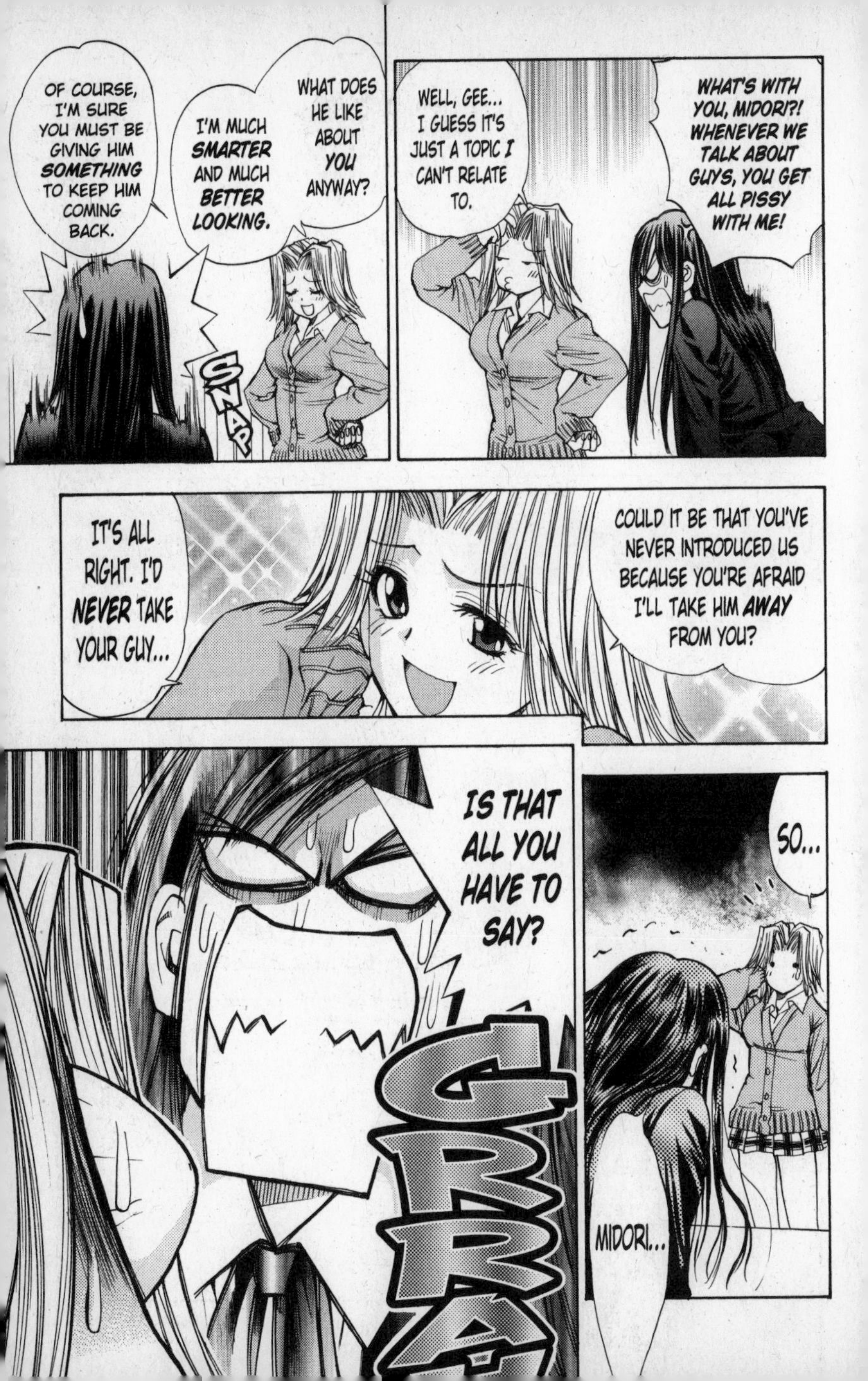
WHAT'S WITH YOU, MIDORI?! WHENEVER WE TALK ABOUT GUYS, YOU GET ALL PISSY WITH ME!
WELL, GEE... I GUESS IT'S JUST A TOPIC I CAN'T RELATE TO.
WHAT DOES HE LIKE ABOUT YOU ANYWAY?
I'M MUCH SMARTER AND MUCH BETTER LOOKING.
OF COURSE, I'M SURE YOU MUST BE GIVING HIM SOMETHING TO KEEP HIM COMING BACK.
SNAP
COULD IT BE THAT YOU'VE NEVER INTRODUCED US BECAUSE YOU'RE AFRAID I'LL TAKE HIM AWAY FROM YOU?
IT'S ALL RIGHT. I'D NEVER TAKE YOUR GUY...
SO...
MIDORI...
IS THAT ALL YOU HAVE TO SAY?
GRRA

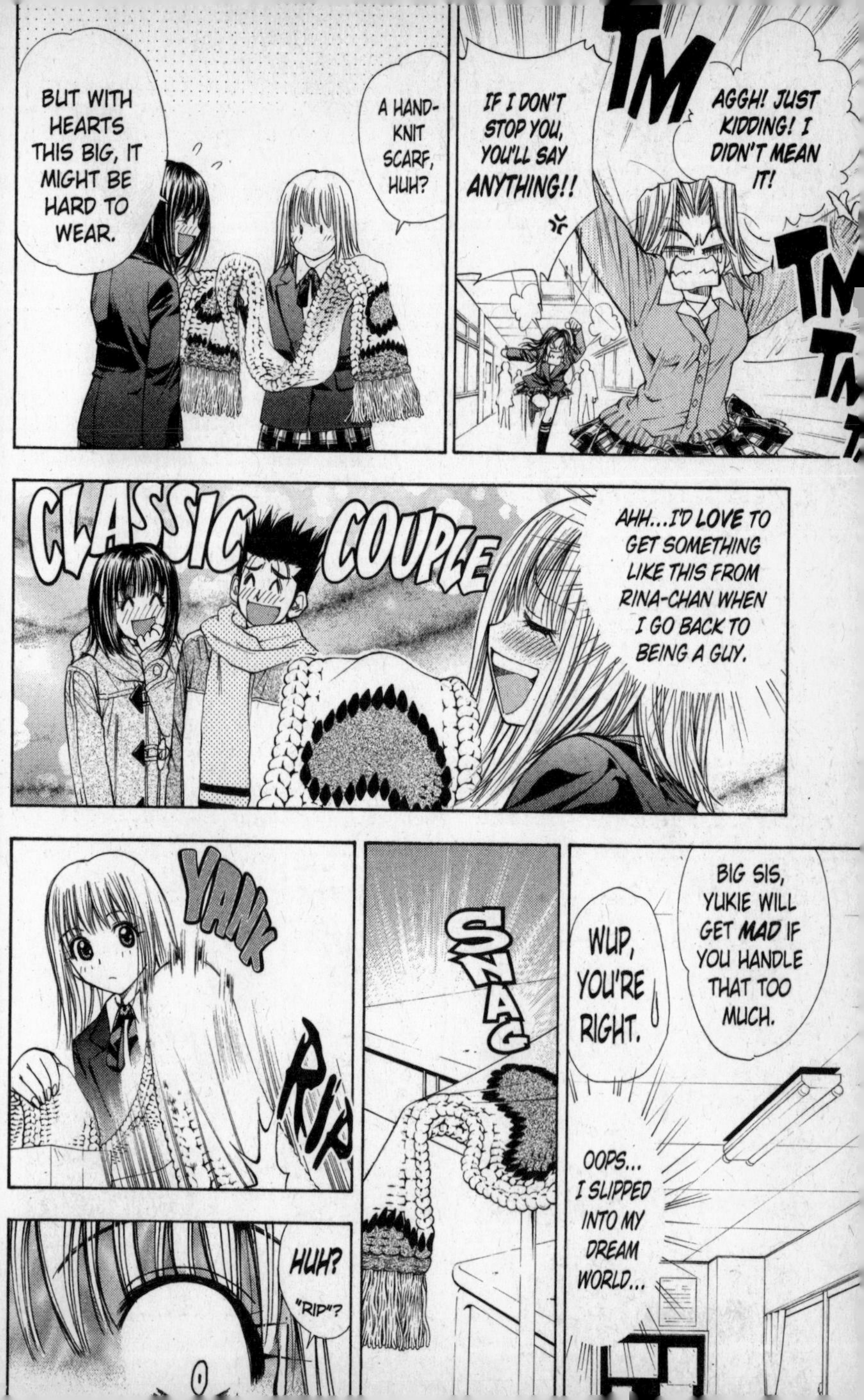
TM
AGGH! JUST KIDDING! I DIDN'T MEAN IT!
TM
TM
T
IF I DON'T STOP YOU, YOU'LL SAY ANYTHING!!
A HAND-KNIT SCARF, HUH?
BUT WITH HEARTS THIS BIG, IT MIGHT BE HARD TO WEAR.
AHH...I'D LOVE TO GET SOMETHING LIKE THIS FROM RINA-CHAN WHEN I GO BACK TO BEING A GUY.
CLASSIC COUPLE
BIG SIS, YUKIE WILL GET MAD IF YOU HANDLE THAT TOO MUCH.
WUP, YOU'RE RIGHT.
OOPS... I SLIPPED INTO MY DREAM WORLD...
SNAG
YANK
RIP
HUH?
"RIP"?

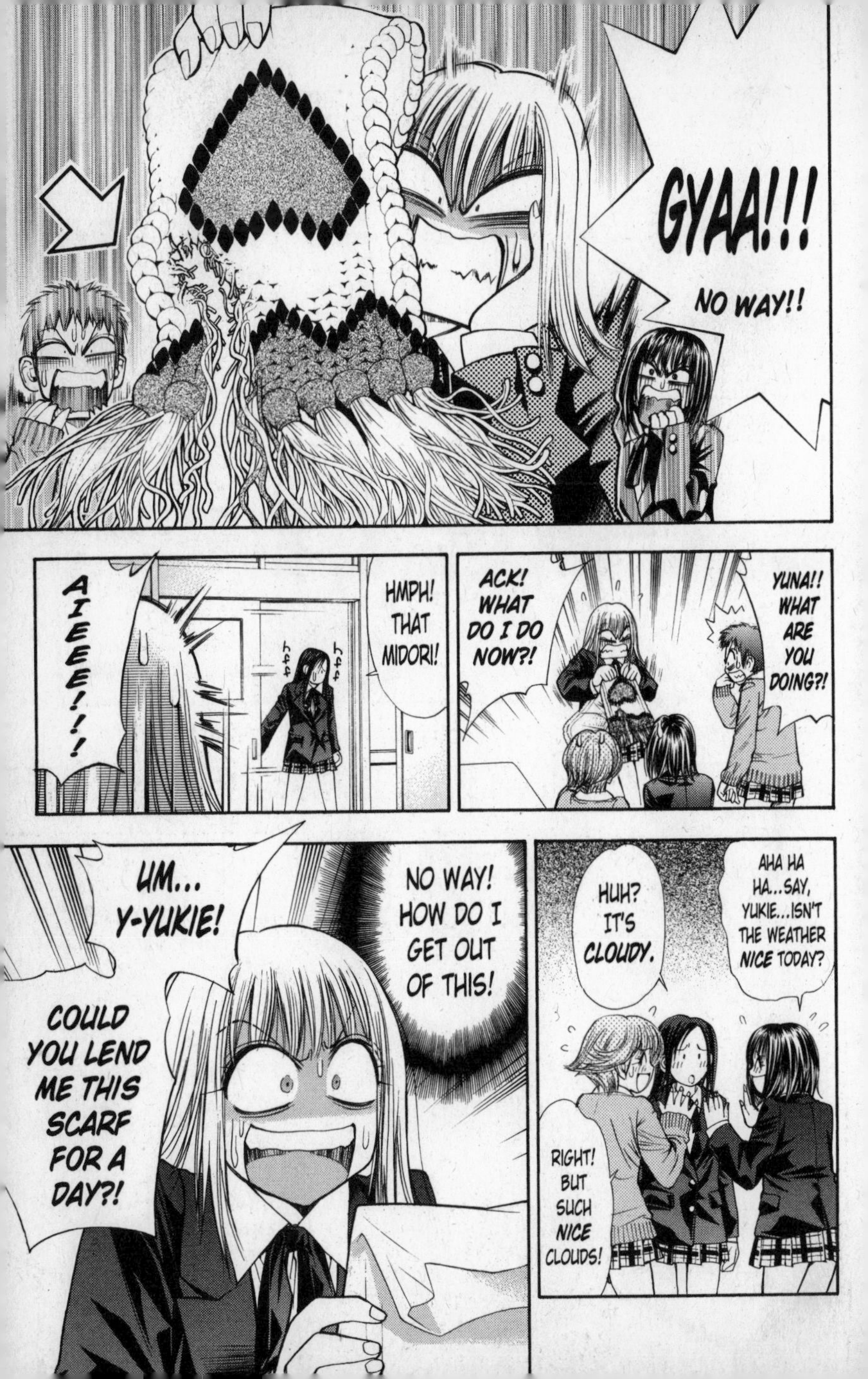
GYAA!!!
NO WAY!!
YUNA!! WHAT ARE YOU DOING?!
ACK! WHAT DO I DO NOW?!
HMPH! THAT MIDORI!
AIEEEE!!!
AHA HA HA...SAY, YUKIE...ISN'T THE WEATHER NICE TODAY?
HUH? IT'S CLOUDY.
RIGHT! BUT SUCH NICE CLOUDS!
NO WAY! HOW DO I GET OUT OF THIS!
UM... Y-YUKIE!
COULD YOU LEND ME THIS SCARF FOR A DAY?!

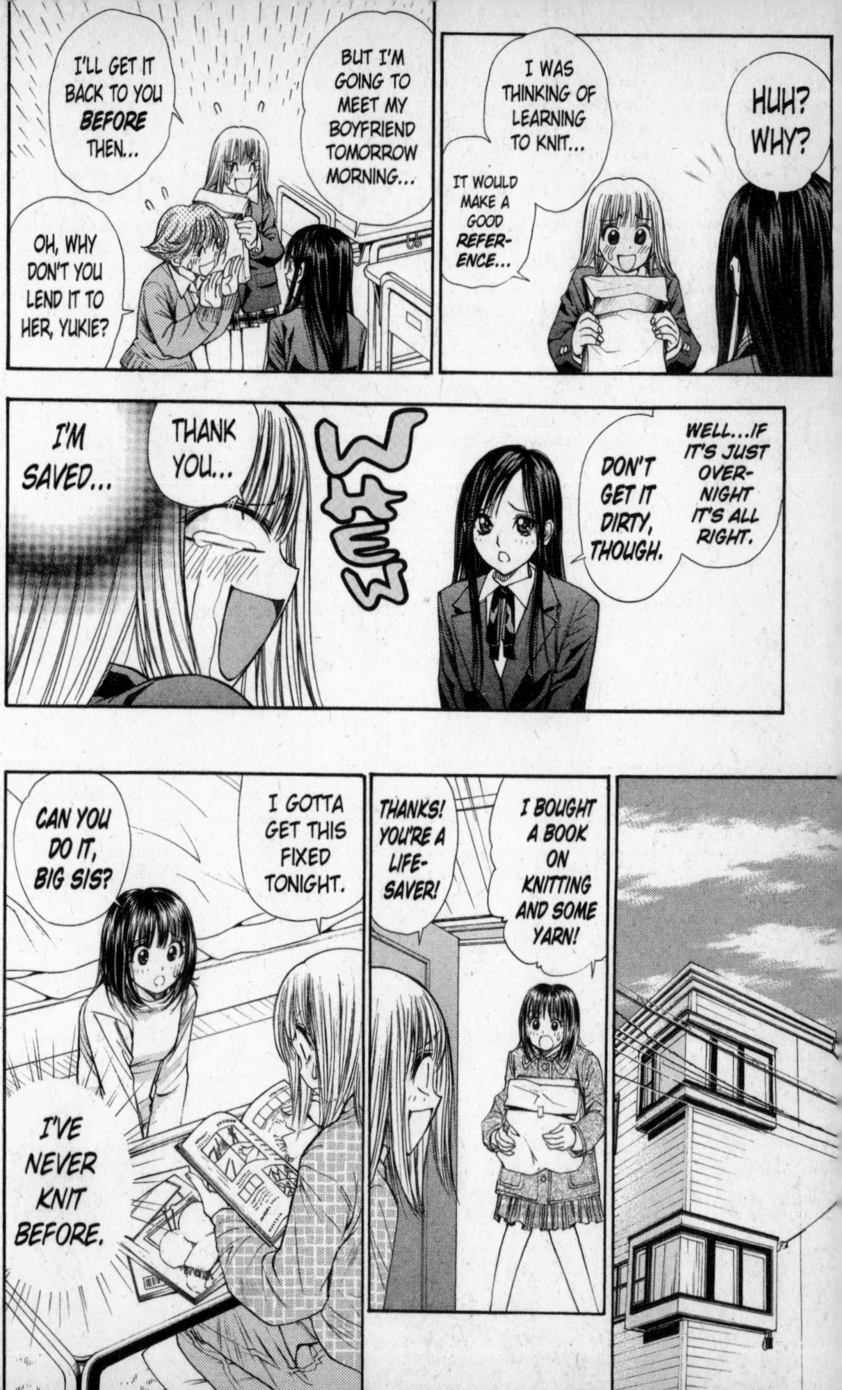
HUH? WHY?
I WAS THINKING OF LEARNING TO KNIT...
IT WOULD MAKE A GOOD REFER-ENCE...
BUT I'M GOING TO MEET MY BOYFRIEND TOMORROW MORNING...
I'LL GET IT BACK TO YOU BEFORE THEN...
OH, WHY DON'T YOU LEND IT TO HER, YUKIE?
WELL...IF IT'S JUST OVER-NIGHT IT'S ALL RIGHT.
DON'T GET IT DIRTY, THOUGH.
WHEW
THANK YOU...
I'M SAVED...
I BOUGHT A BOOK ON KNITTING AND SOME YARN!
THANKS! YOU'RE A LIFE-SAVER!
I GOTTA GET THIS FIXED TONIGHT.
CAN YOU DO IT, BIG SIS?
I'VE NEVER KNIT BEFORE.

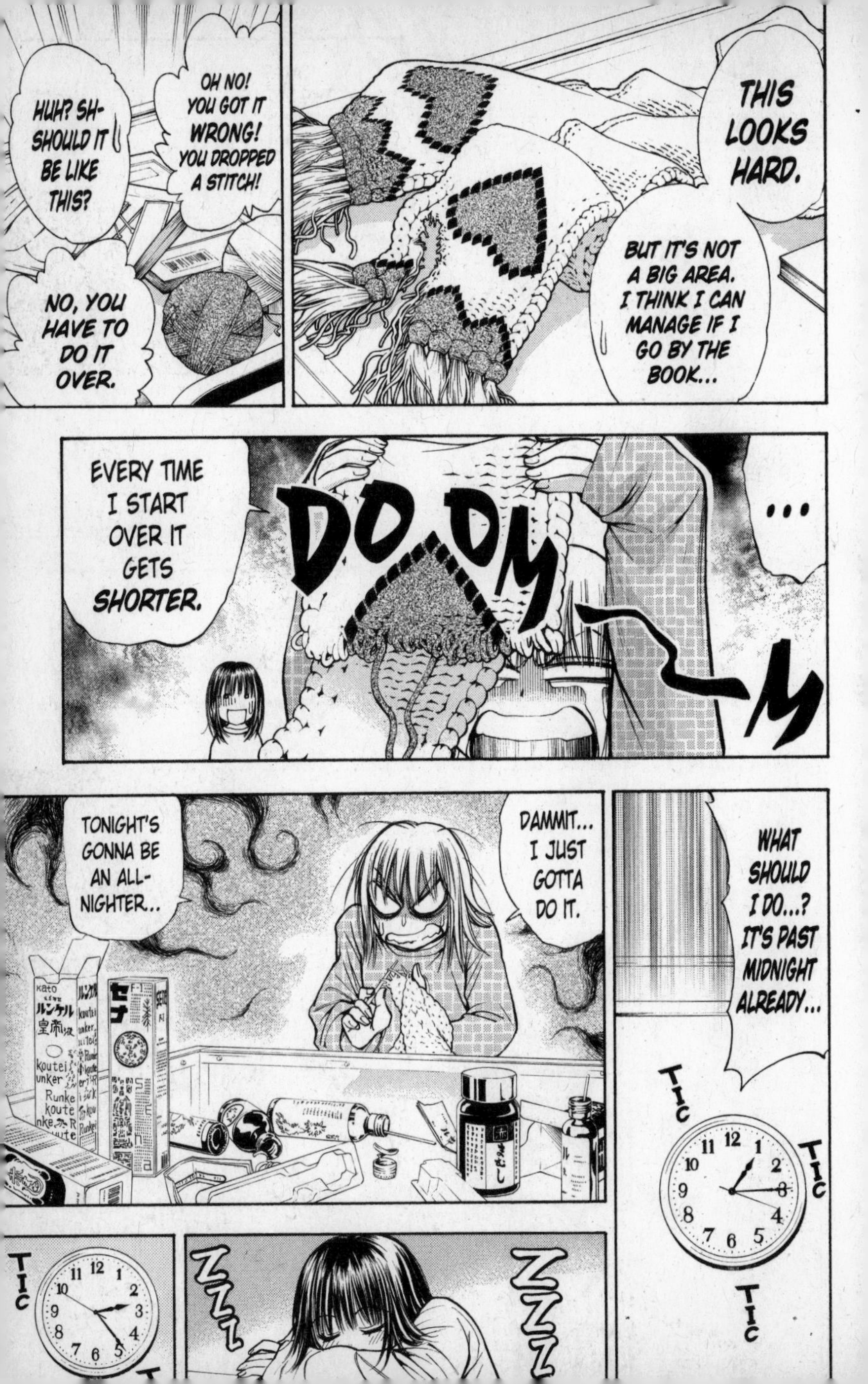
THIS LOOKS HARD.
BUT IT'S NOT A BIG AREA. I THINK I CAN MANAGE IF I GO BY THE BOOK...
OH NO! YOU GOT IT WRONG! YOU DROPPED A STITCH!
HUH? SH-SHOULD IT BE LIKE THIS?
NO, YOU HAVE TO DO IT OVER.
...
DOOOM
EVERY TIME I START OVER IT GETS SHORTER.
WHAT SHOULD I DO...? IT'S PAST MIDNIGHT ALREADY...
TIC
TIC
TIC
DAMMIT... I JUST GOTTA DO IT.
TONIGHT'S GONNA BE AN ALL-NIGHTER...
ZZZ
ZZZ
TIC

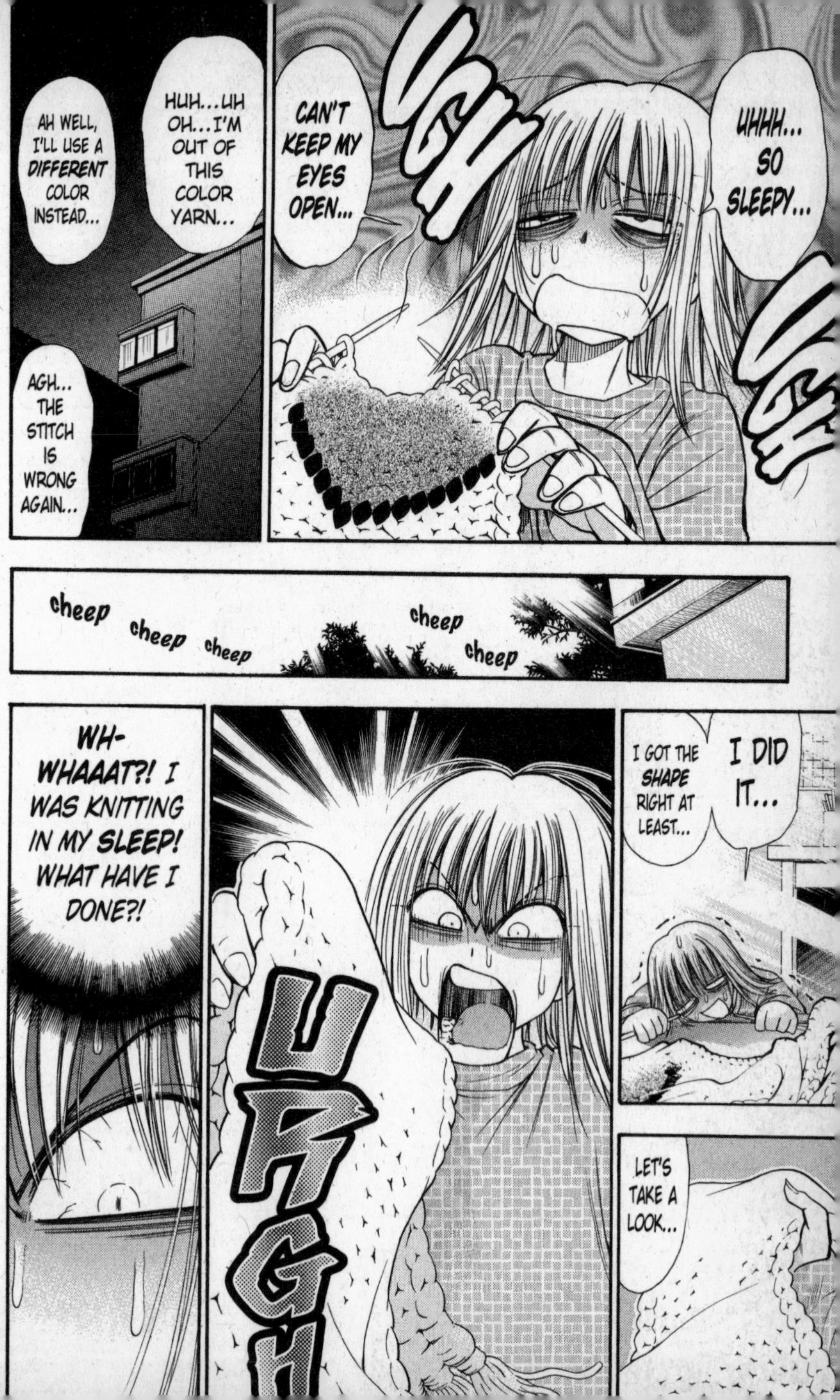

UHHH... SO SLEEPY...
UGH
UGH
CAN'T KEEP MY EYES OPEN...
HUH...UH OH...I'M OUT OF THIS COLOR YARN...
AH WELL, I'LL USE A DIFFERENT COLOR INSTEAD...
AGH... THE STITCH IS WRONG AGAIN...
cheep
cheep
cheep
cheep
cheep
I DID IT...
I GOT THE SHAPE RIGHT AT LEAST...
LET'S TAKE A LOOK...
URGH
WH-WHAAAT?! I WAS KNITTING IN MY SLEEP! WHAT HAVE I DONE?!

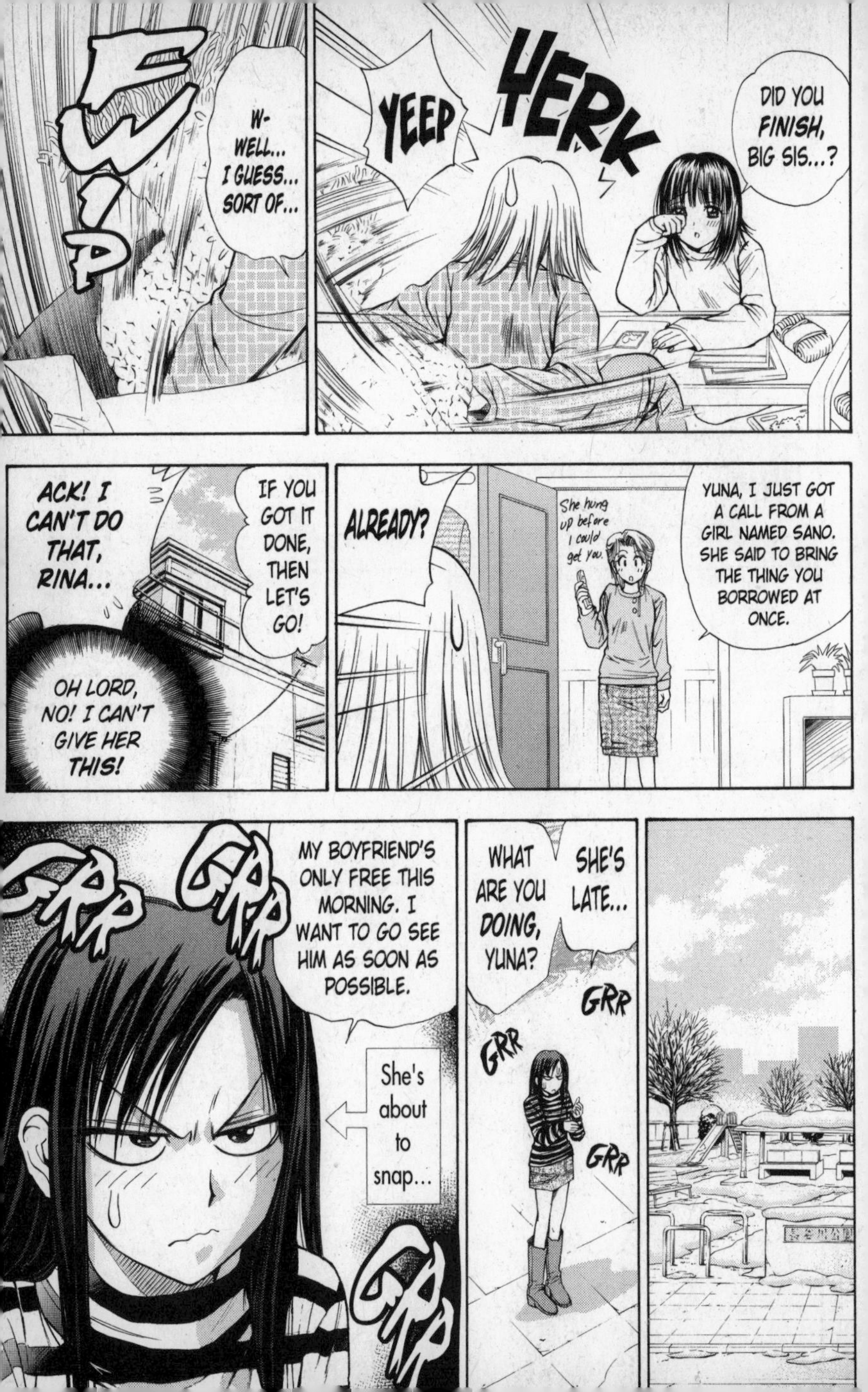
DID YOU FINISH, BIG SIS...?
HERK
YEEP
W-WELL... I GUESS... SORT OF...
WIP
YUNA, I JUST GOT A CALL FROM A GIRL NAMED SANO. SHE SAID TO BRING THE THING YOU BORROWED AT ONCE.
She hung up before I could get you.
ALREADY?
IF YOU GOT IT DONE, THEN LET'S GO!
ACK! I CAN'T DO THAT, RINA...
OH LORD, NO! I CAN'T GIVE HER THIS!
SHE'S LATE...
WHAT ARE YOU DOING, YUNA?
GRR
GRR
GRR
MY BOYFRIEND'S ONLY FREE THIS MORNING. I WANT TO GO SEE HIM AS SOON AS POSSIBLE.
She's about to snap...
GRR
GRR
GRR

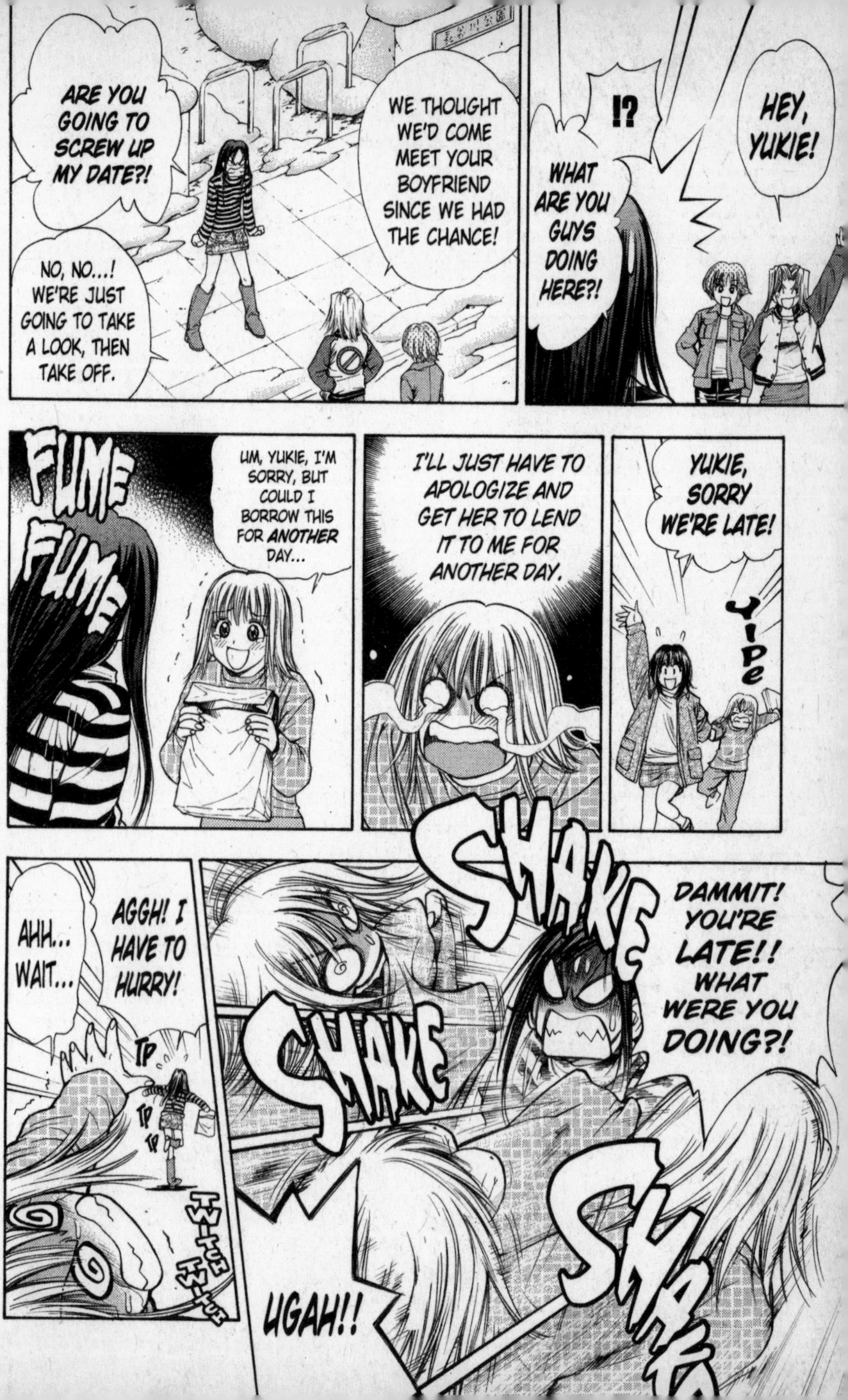
HEY, YUKIE!
!?
WHAT ARE YOU GUYS DOING HERE?!
WE THOUGHT WE'D COME MEET YOUR BOYFRIEND SINCE WE HAD THE CHANCE!
ARE YOU GOING TO SCREW UP MY DATE?!
NO, NO...! WE'RE JUST GOING TO TAKE A LOOK, THEN TAKE OFF.
YUKIE, SORRY WE'RE LATE!
YIPE
I'LL JUST HAVE TO APOLOGIZE AND GET HER TO LEND IT TO ME FOR ANOTHER DAY.
UM, YUKIE, I'M SORRY, BUT COULD I BORROW THIS FOR ANOTHER DAY...
FUME
FUME
SHAKE
DAMMIT! YOU'RE LATE!! WHAT WERE YOU DOING?!
SHAKE
UGAH!!
AGGH! I HAVE TO HURRY!
AHH... WAIT...
TP
TP
TP
TWITCH
TWITCH

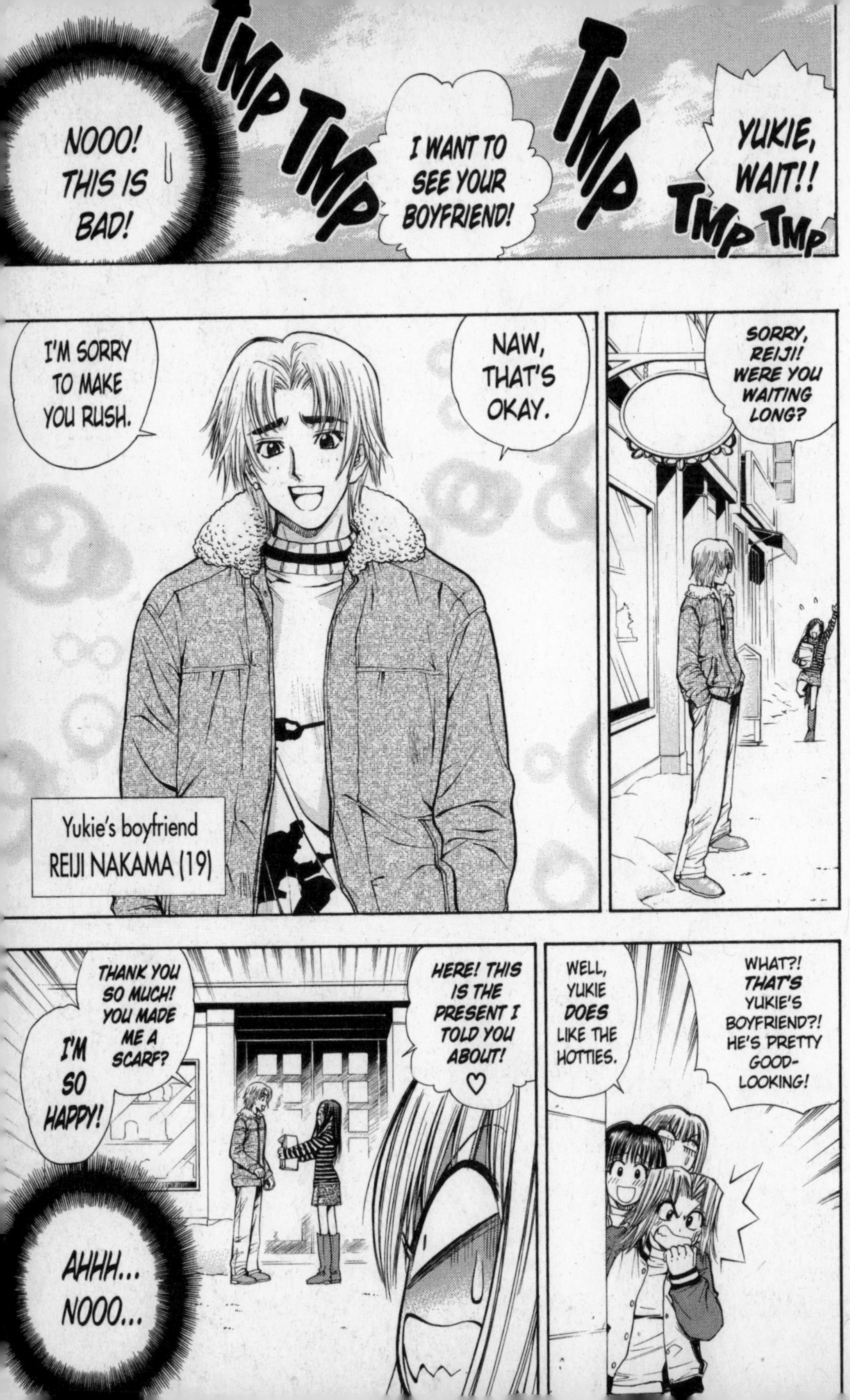
YUKIE, WAIT!!
TMP TMP
TMP
I WANT TO SEE YOUR BOYFRIEND!
TMP TMP
NOOO! THIS IS BAD!
SORRY, REIJI! WERE YOU WAITING LONG?
NAW, THAT'S OKAY.
I'M SORRY TO MAKE YOU RUSH.
Yukie's boyfriend REIJI NAKAMA (19)
WHAT?! **THAT'S** YUKIE'S BOYFRIEND?! HE'S PRETTY GOOD-LOOKING!
WELL, YUKIE **DOES** LIKE THE HOTTIES.
HERE! THIS IS THE PRESENT I TOLD YOU ABOUT! ♡
THANK YOU SO MUCH! YOU MADE ME A SCARF?
I'M SO HAPPY!
AHHH... NOOO...

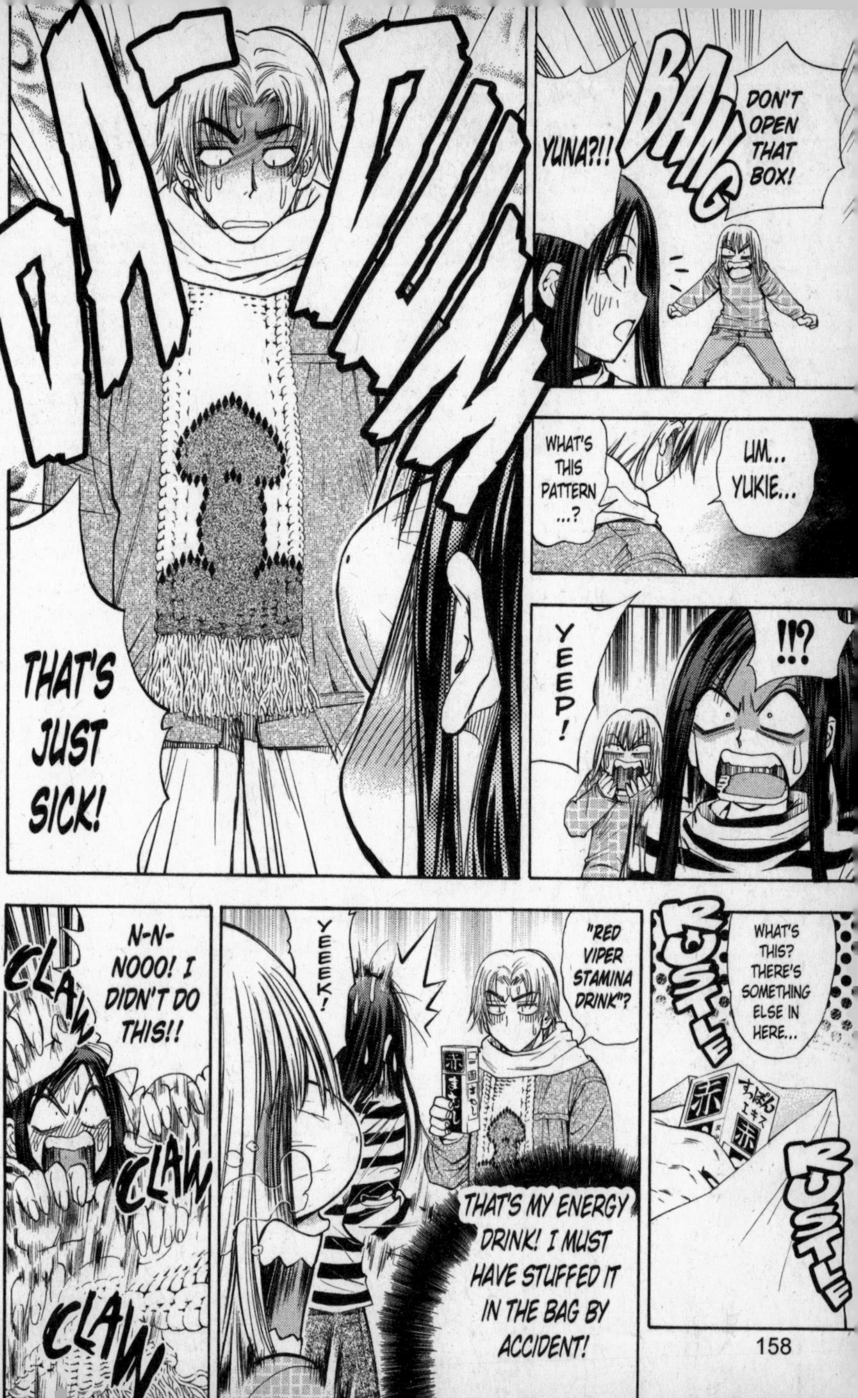
BANG
DON'T OPEN THAT BOX!
YUNA?!!
UM.. YUKIE...
WHAT'S THIS PATTERN ...?
!!?
YEEP!
DA-DUM
THAT'S JUST SICK!
RUSTLE
WHAT'S THIS? THERE'S SOMETHING ELSE IN HERE...
RUSTLE
"RED VIPER STAMINA DRINK"?
YEEEK!
THAT'S MY ENERGY DRINK! I MUST HAVE STUFFED IT IN THE BAG BY ACCIDENT!
N-N-NOOO! I DIDN'T DO THIS!!
CLAW
CLAW
CLAW

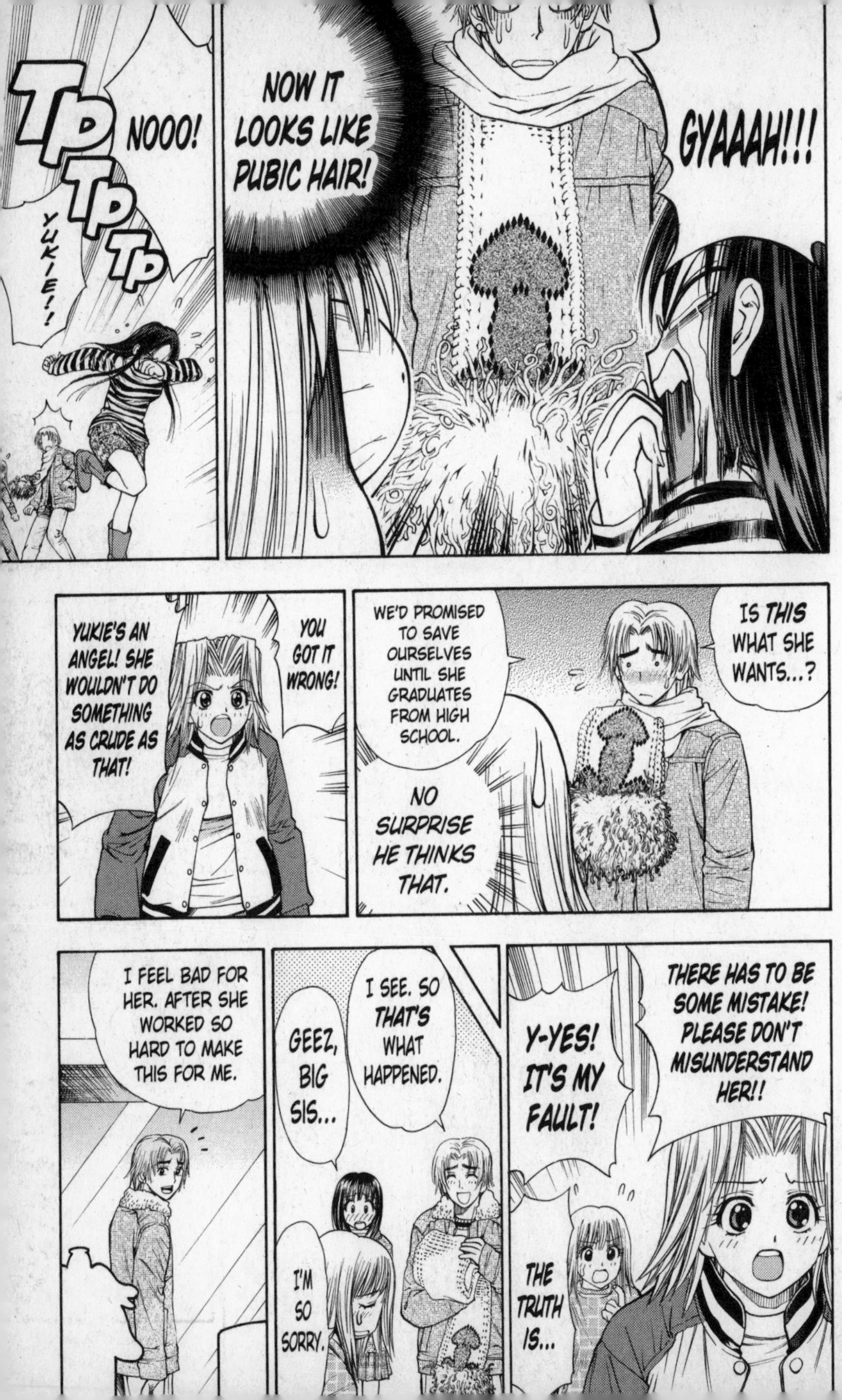
GYAAAH!!!
NOW IT LOOKS LIKE PUBIC HAIR!
NOOO!
Tp Tp Tp
YUKIE!!
IS THIS WHAT SHE WANTS...?
WE'D PROMISED TO SAVE OURSELVES UNTIL SHE GRADUATES FROM HIGH SCHOOL.
NO SURPRISE HE THINKS THAT.
YOU GOT IT WRONG!
YUKIE'S AN ANGEL! SHE WOULDN'T DO SOMETHING AS CRUDE AS THAT!
THERE HAS TO BE SOME MISTAKE! PLEASE DON'T MISUNDERSTAND HER!!
Y-YES! IT'S MY FAULT!
THE TRUTH IS...
I SEE. SO THAT'S WHAT HAPPENED.
GEEZ, BIG SIS...
I'M SO SORRY.
I FEEL BAD FOR HER. AFTER SHE WORKED SO HARD TO MAKE THIS FOR ME.

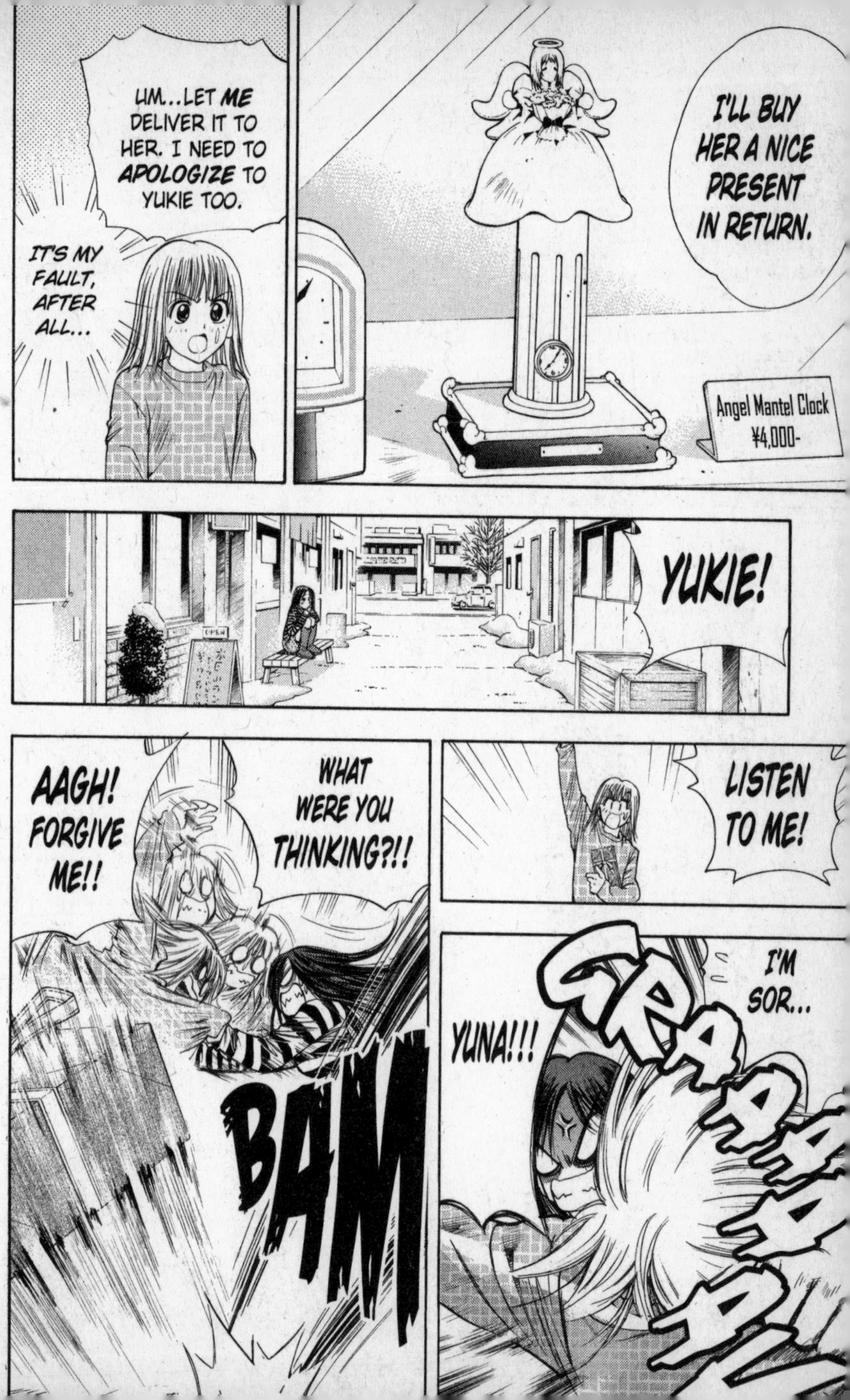
I'LL BUY HER A NICE PRESENT IN RETURN.
Angel Mantel Clock ¥4,000-
UM...LET ME DELIVER IT TO HER. I NEED TO APOLOGIZE TO YUKIE TOO.
IT'S MY FAULT, AFTER ALL...
YUKIE!
LISTEN TO ME!
I'M SOR...
YUNA!!!
WHAT WERE YOU THINKING?!!
AAGH! FORGIVE ME!!
BAM

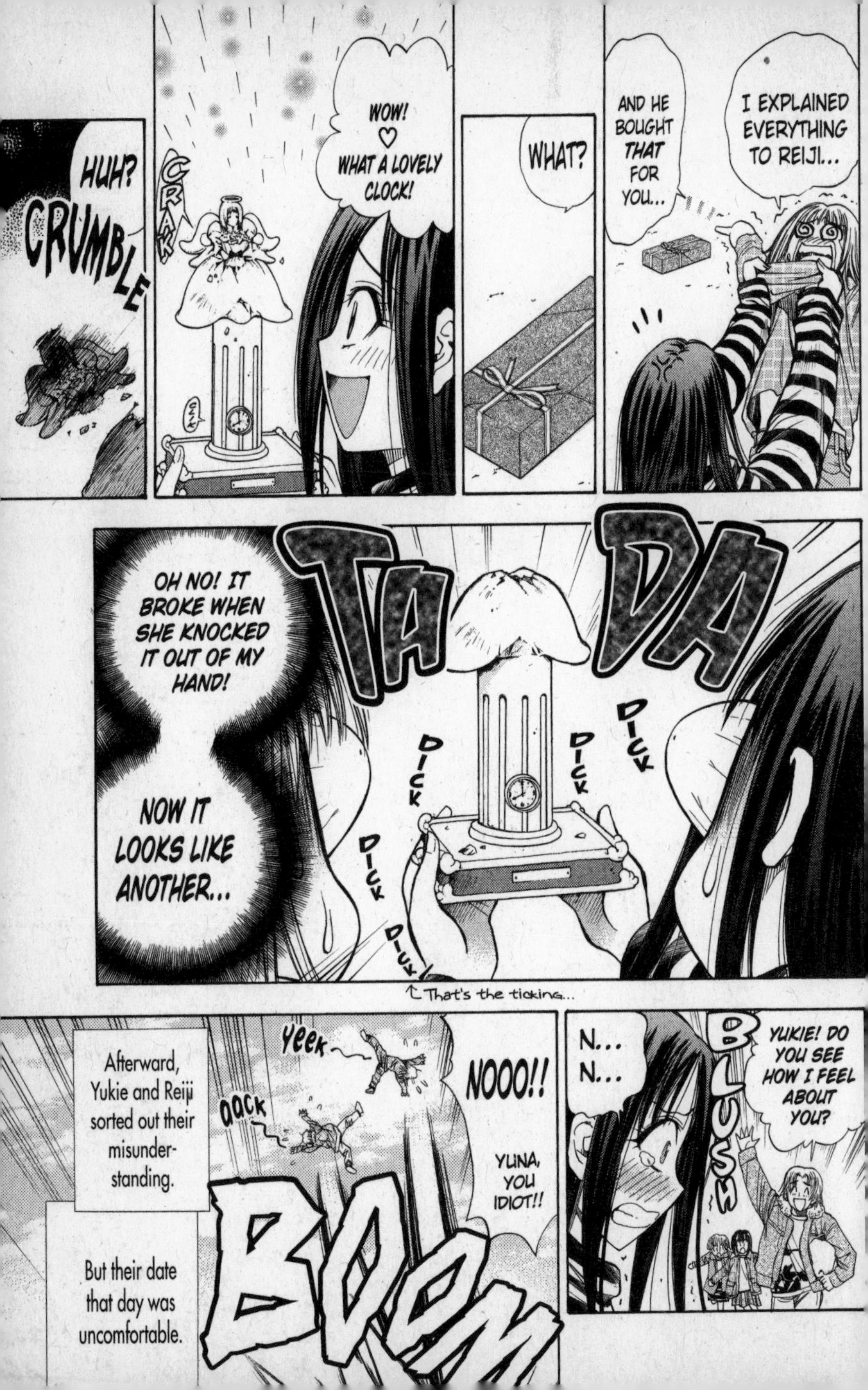
I EXPLAINED EVERYTHING TO REIJI...
AND HE BOUGHT THAT FOR YOU...
WHAT?
WOW! ♡ WHAT A LOVELY CLOCK!
CRAK
HUH?
CRUMBLE
TA DA
OH NO! IT BROKE WHEN SHE KNOCKED IT OUT OF MY HAND!
NOW IT LOOKS LIKE ANOTHER...
DICK
DICK
DICK
DICK
DICK
That's the ticking...
YUKIE! DO YOU SEE HOW I FEEL ABOUT YOU?
BLUSH
N... N...
NOOO!!
YUNA, YOU IDIOT!!
yeek
aack
BOOM
Afterward, Yukie and Reiji sorted out their misunder-standing.
But their date that day was uncomfortable.

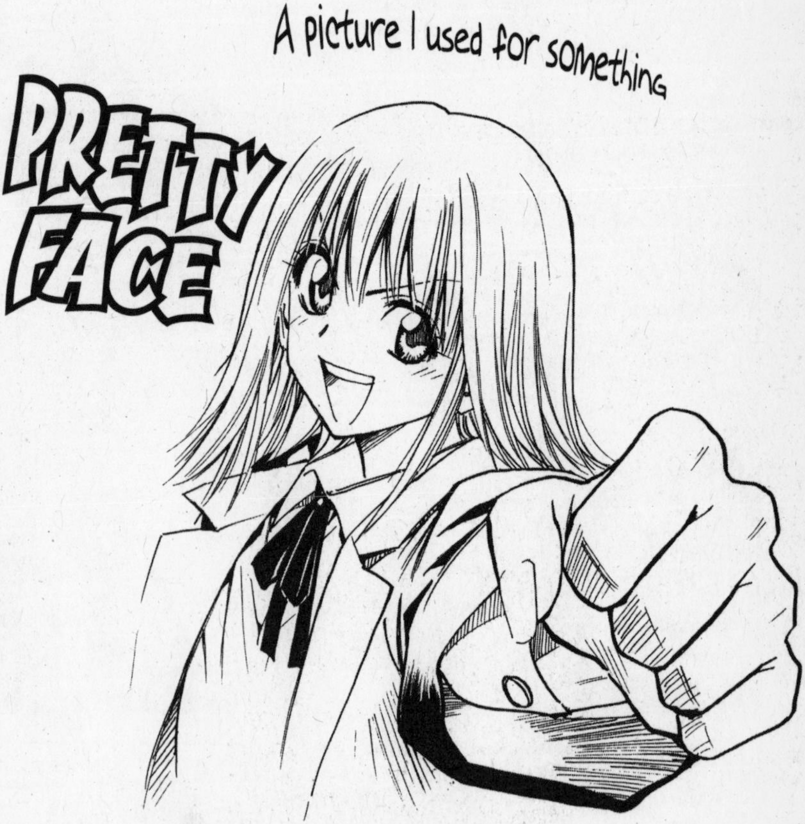
A picture I used for something
PRETTY FACE

CHAPTER 45: THE GRADUATION TREE

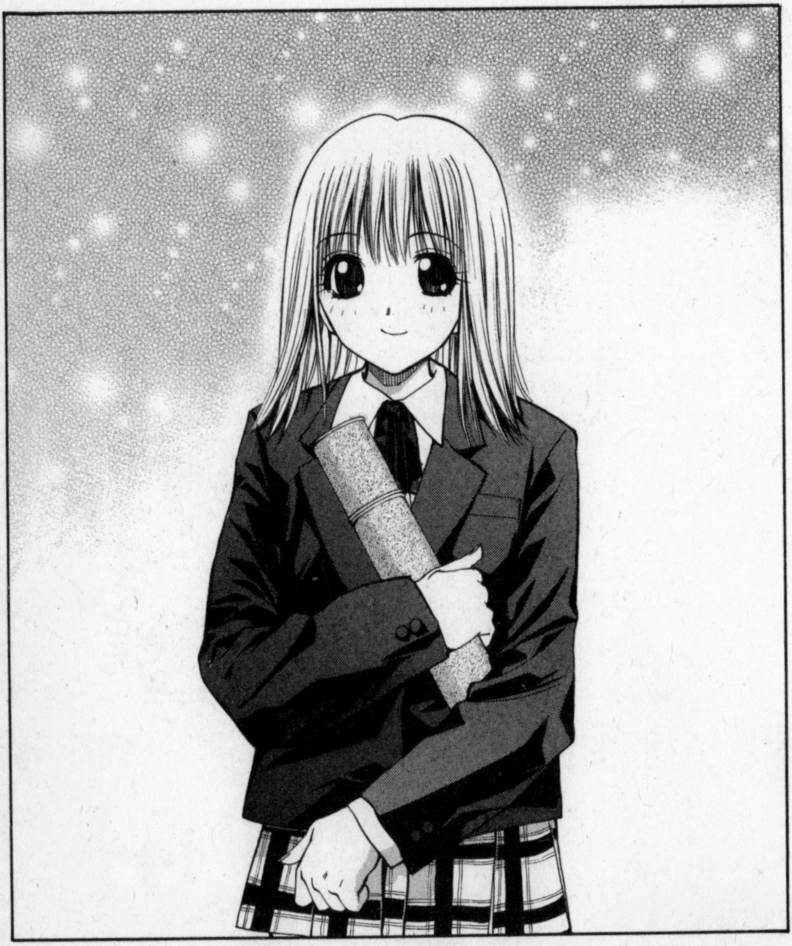

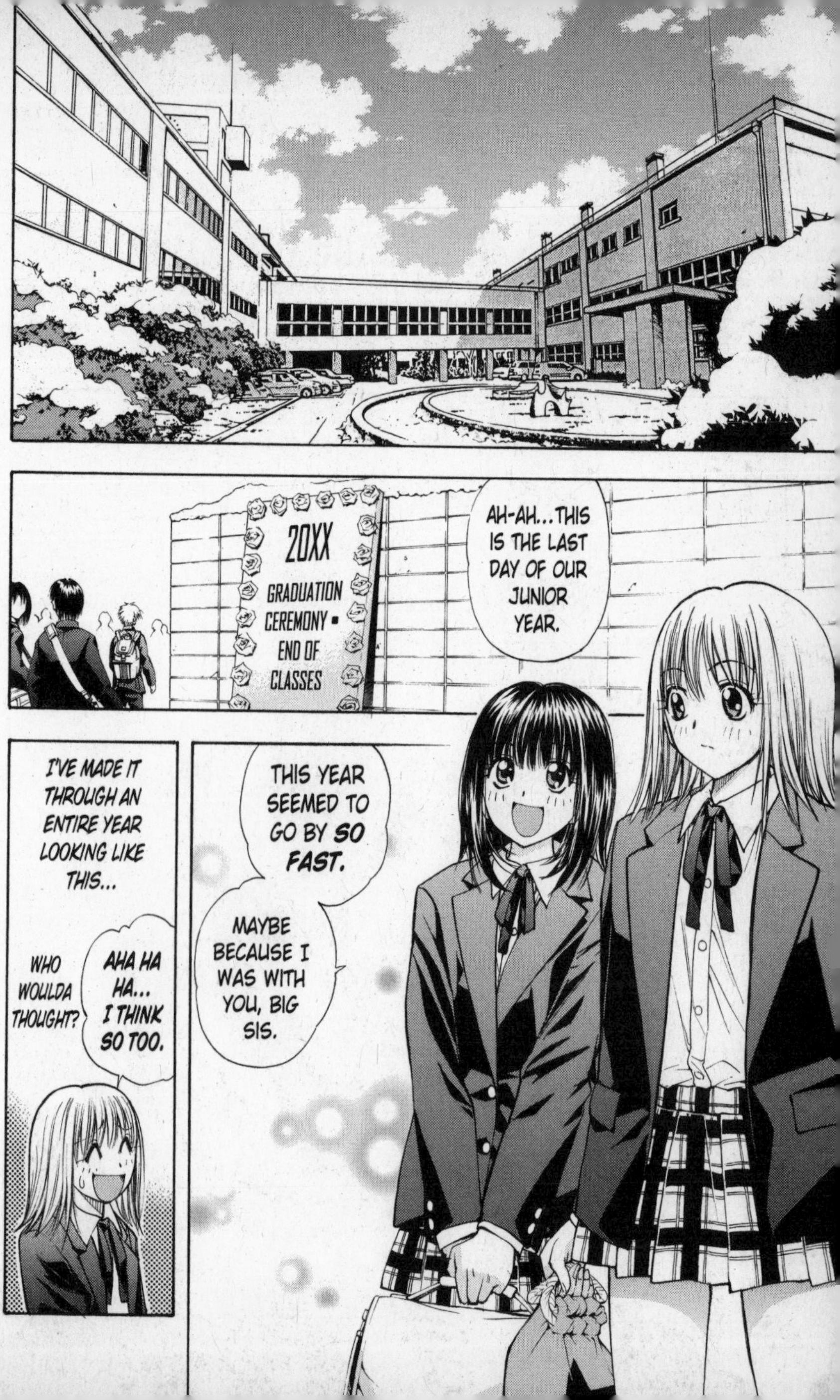
AH-AH...THIS IS THE LAST DAY OF OUR JUNIOR YEAR.
20XX
GRADUATION CEREMONY ▪ END OF CLASSES
THIS YEAR SEEMED TO GO BY **SO FAST.**
MAYBE BECAUSE I WAS WITH YOU, BIG SIS.
I'VE MADE IT THROUGH AN ENTIRE YEAR LOOKING LIKE THIS...
AHA HA HA... I THINK SO TOO.
WHO WOULDA THOUGHT?

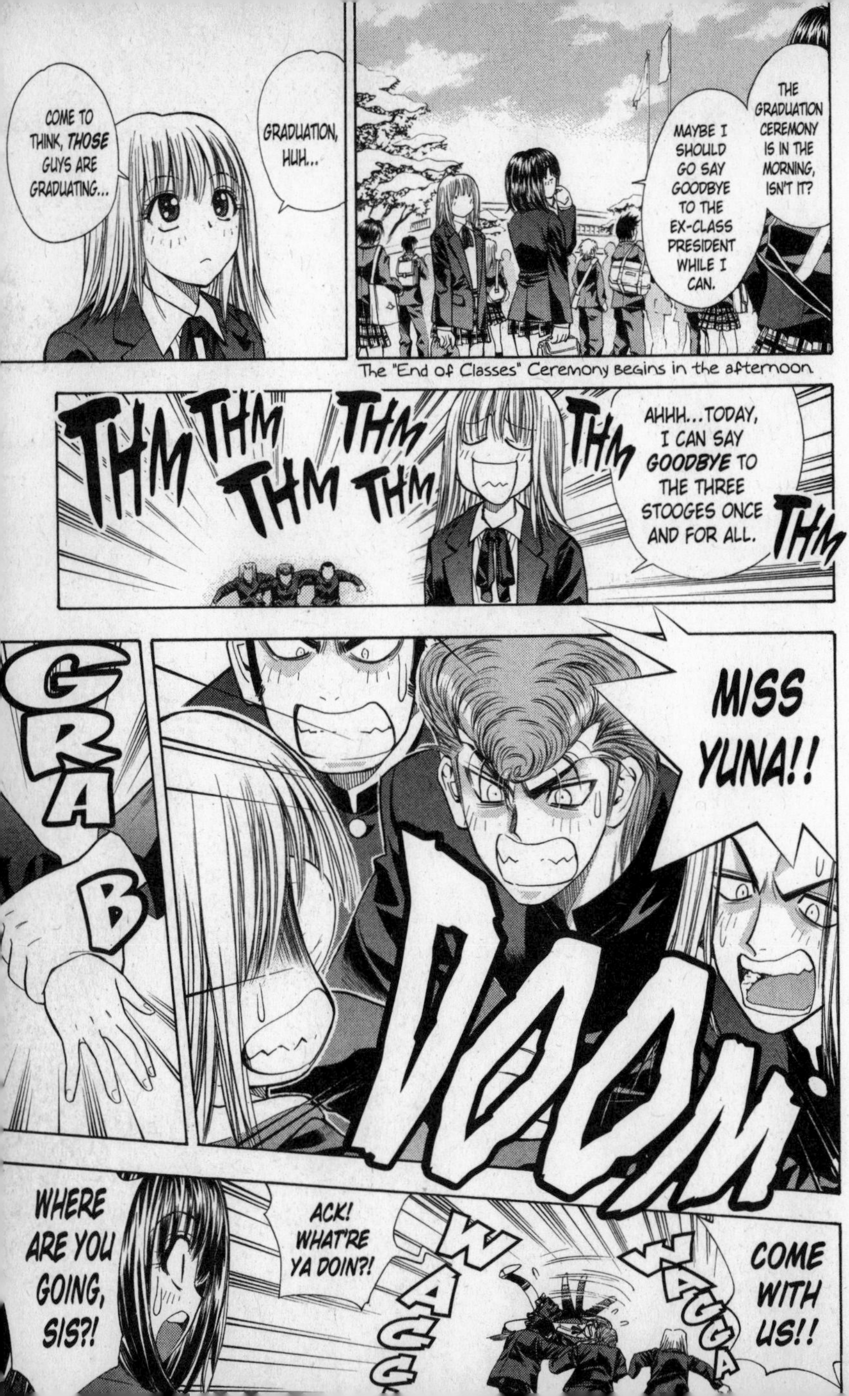
THE GRADUATION CEREMONY IS IN THE MORNING, ISN'T IT?
MAYBE I SHOULD GO SAY GOODBYE TO THE EX-CLASS PRESIDENT WHILE I CAN.
GRADUATION, HUH...
COME TO THINK, *THOSE* GUYS ARE GRADUATING...
The "End of Classes" Ceremony begins in the afternoon.
THM
AHHH...TODAY, I CAN SAY **GOODBYE** TO THE THREE STOOGES ONCE AND FOR ALL.
THM THM THM THM THM THM
MISS YUNA!!
DOOM
GRAB
COME WITH US!!
WAGGA
WAGG
ACK! WHAT'RE YA DOIN?!
WHERE ARE YOU GOING, SIS?!

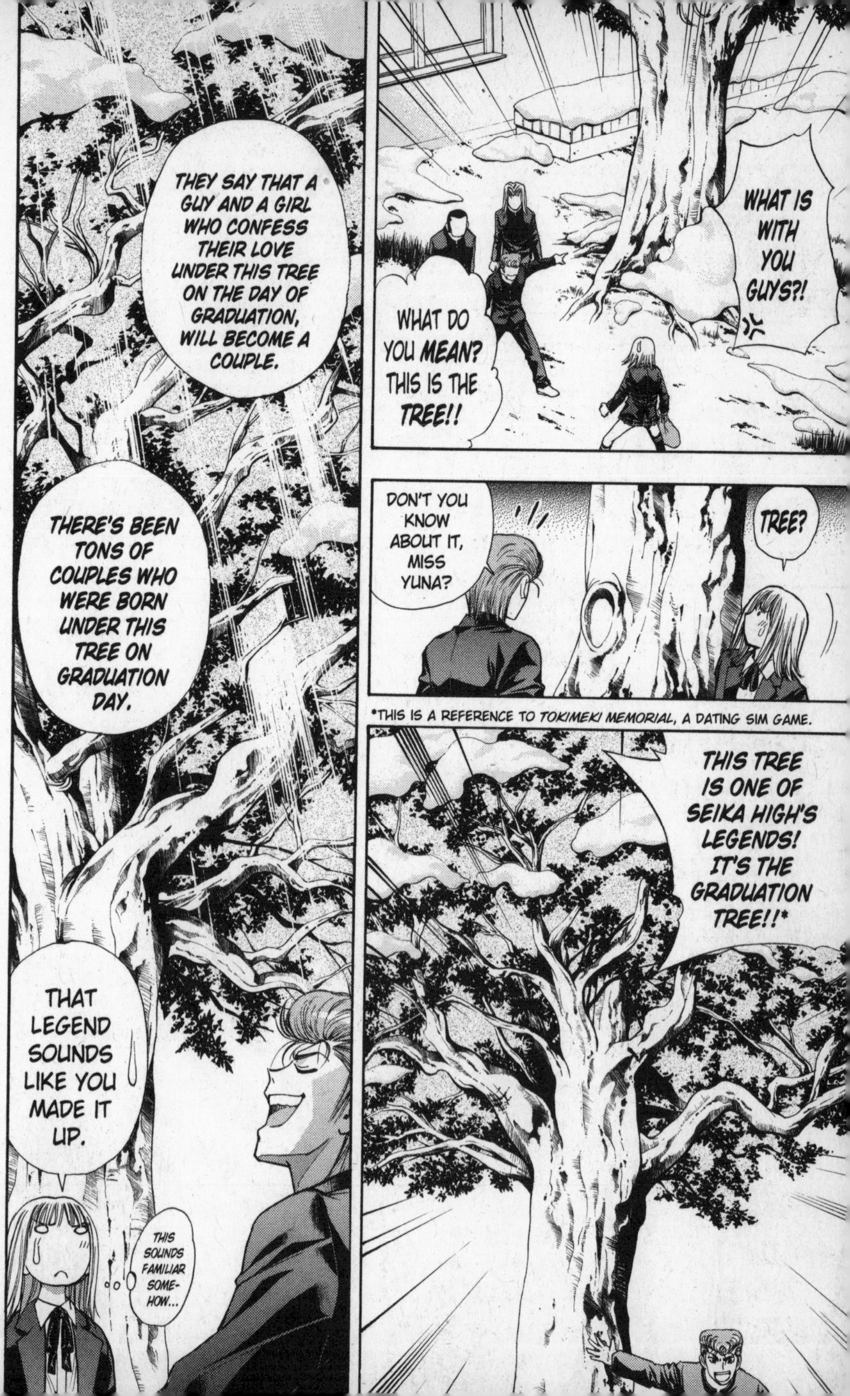
WHAT IS WITH YOU GUYS?!
WHAT DO YOU MEAN? THIS IS THE TREE!!
TREE?
DON'T YOU KNOW ABOUT IT, MISS YUNA?
THIS TREE IS ONE OF SEIKA HIGH'S LEGENDS! IT'S THE GRADUATION TREE!!*
THEY SAY THAT A GUY AND A GIRL WHO CONFESS THEIR LOVE UNDER THIS TREE ON THE DAY OF GRADUATION, WILL BECOME A COUPLE.
THERE'S BEEN TONS OF COUPLES WHO WERE BORN UNDER THIS TREE ON GRADUATION DAY.
THAT LEGEND SOUNDS LIKE YOU MADE IT UP.
THIS SOUNDS FAMILIAR SOMEHOW...
*THIS IS A REFERENCE TO *TOKIMEKI MEMORIAL*, A DATING SIM GAME.

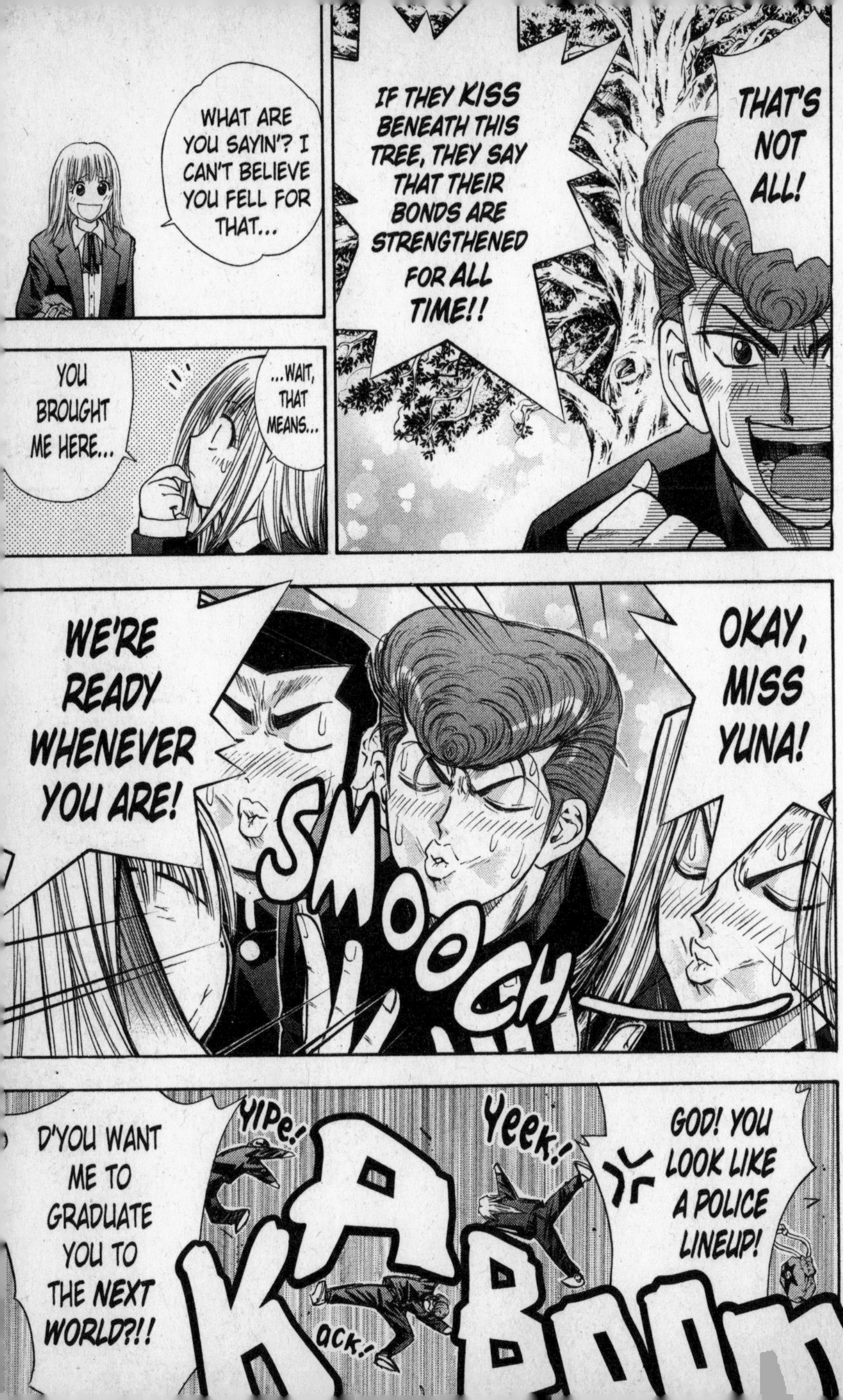
THAT'S NOT ALL!
IF THEY KISS BENEATH THIS TREE, THEY SAY THAT THEIR BONDS ARE STRENGTHENED FOR ALL TIME!!
WHAT ARE YOU SAYIN'? I CAN'T BELIEVE YOU FELL FOR THAT...
...WAIT, THAT MEANS...
YOU BROUGHT ME HERE...
OKAY, MISS YUNA!
WE'RE READY WHENEVER YOU ARE!
SMOOCH
GOD! YOU LOOK LIKE A POLICE LINEUP!
Yeek!
YIPe!
KABOOM
ack!
D'YOU WANT ME TO GRADUATE YOU TO THE NEXT WORLD?!!

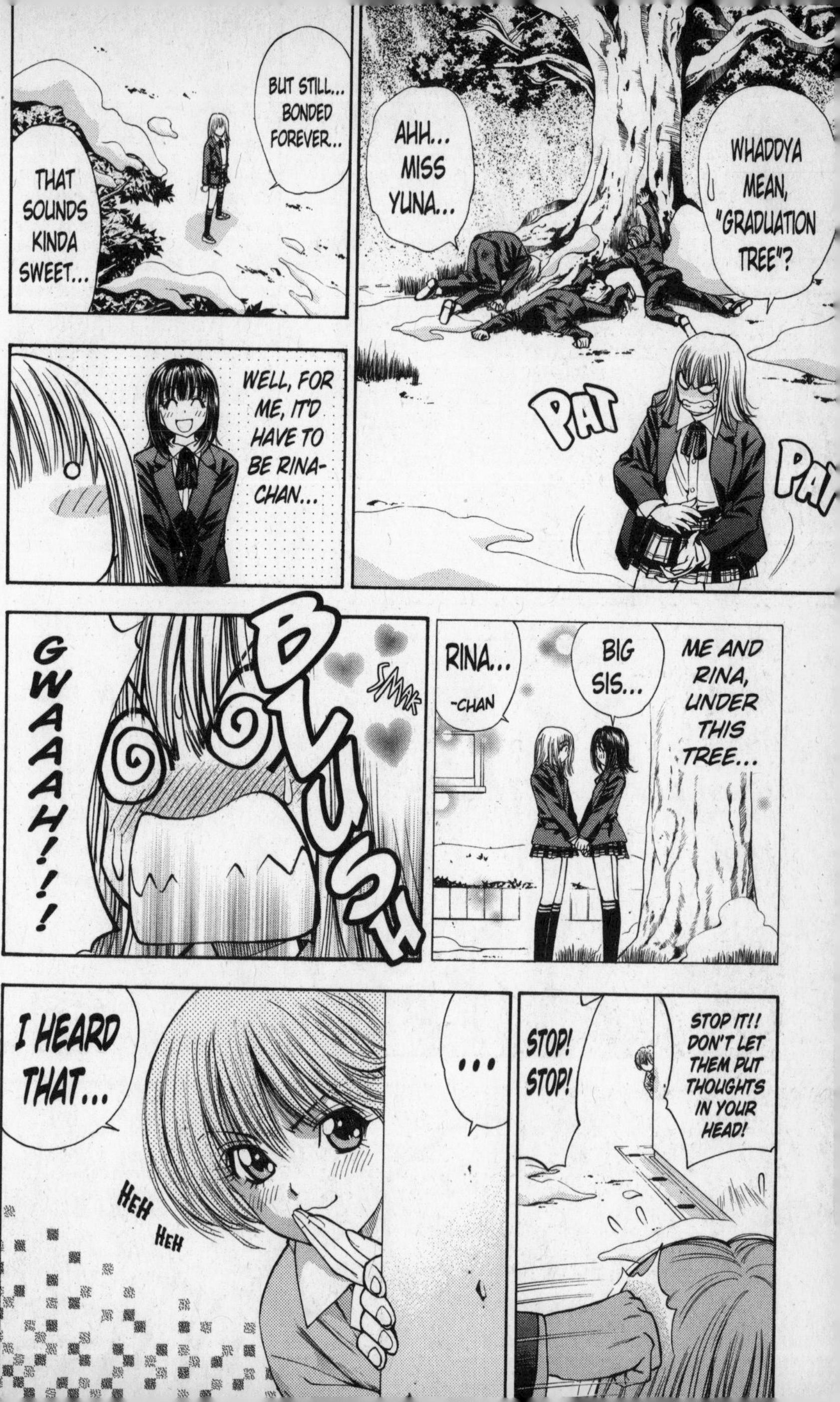
WHADDYA MEAN, "GRADUATION TREE"?
AHH... MISS YUNA...
PAT
PAT
BUT STILL... BONDED FOREVER...
THAT SOUNDS KINDA SWEET...
WELL, FOR ME, IT'D HAVE TO BE RINA-CHAN...
ME AND RINA, UNDER THIS TREE...
BIG SIS...
RINA... -CHAN
SMAK
BLUSH
GWAAAAH!!!
STOP IT!! DON'T LET THEM PUT THOUGHTS IN YOUR HEAD!
STOP! STOP!
...
I HEARD THAT...
HEH HEH

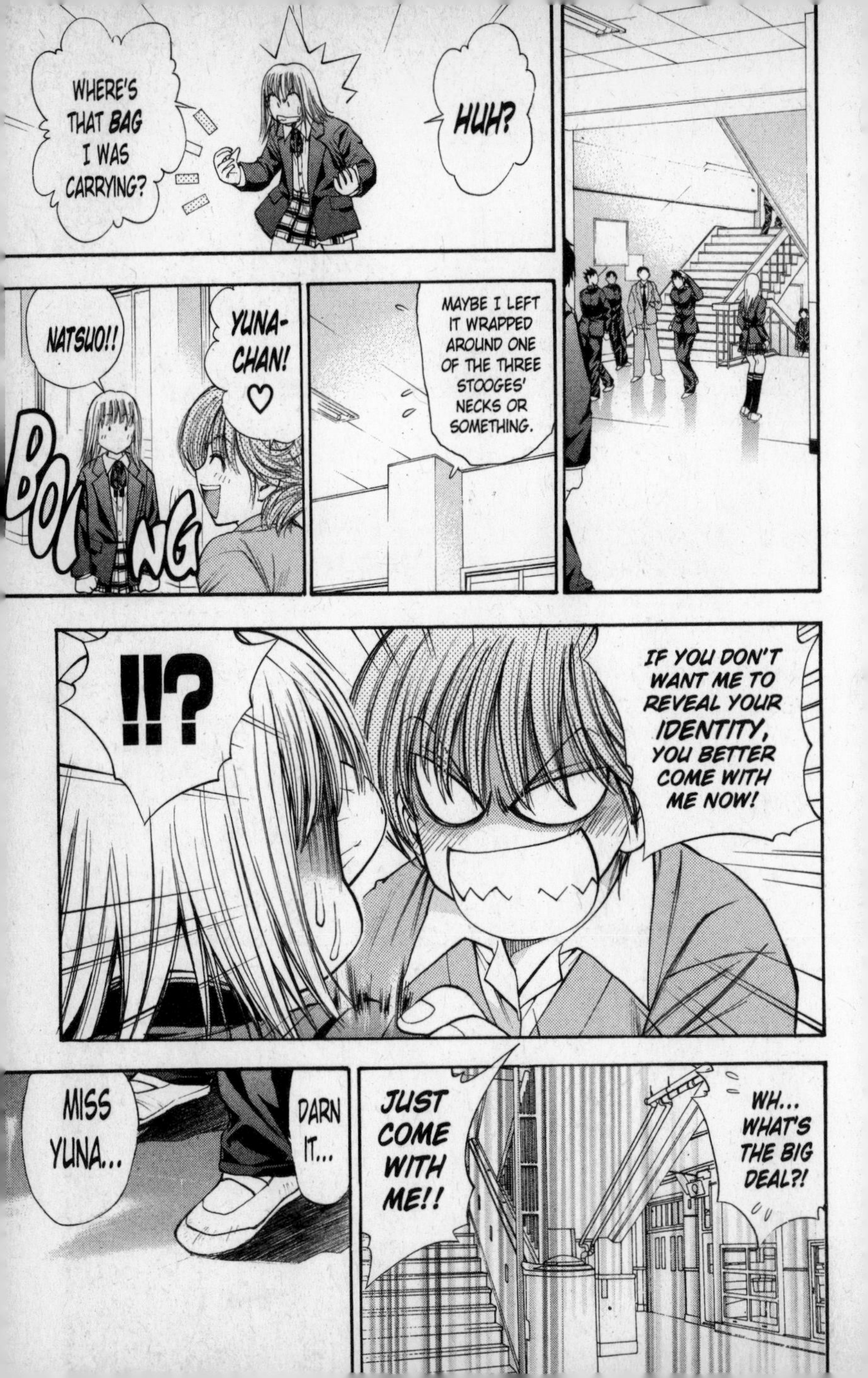
HUH?
WHERE'S THAT BAG I WAS CARRYING?
MAYBE I LEFT IT WRAPPED AROUND ONE OF THE THREE STOOGES' NECKS OR SOMETHING.
YUNA-CHAN! ♥
NATSUO!!
BOING
IF YOU DON'T WANT ME TO REVEAL YOUR IDENTITY, YOU BETTER COME WITH ME NOW!
!!?
WH... WHAT'S THE BIG DEAL?!
JUST COME WITH ME!!
DARN IT...
MISS YUNA...

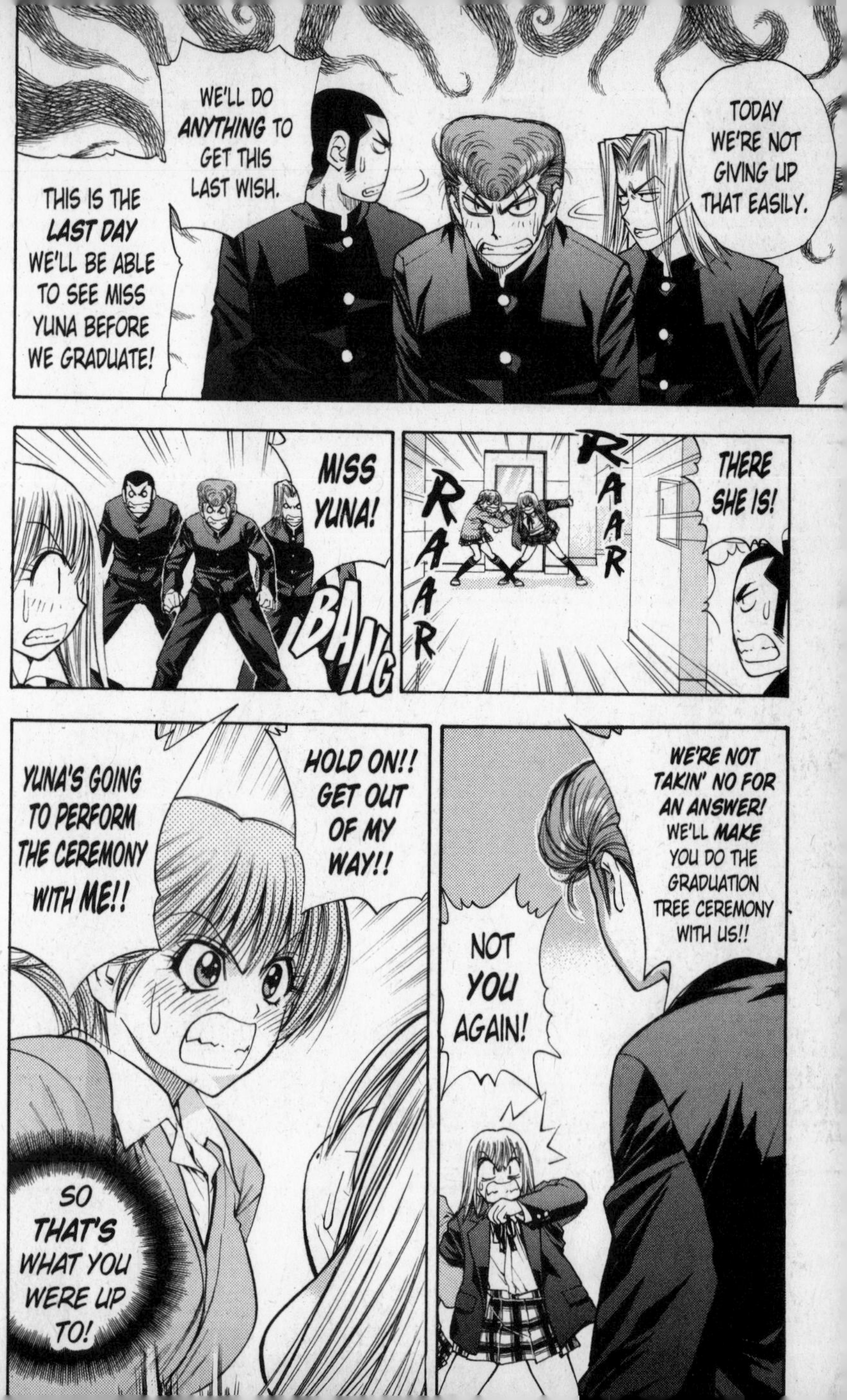
TODAY WE'RE NOT GIVING UP THAT EASILY.
WE'LL DO ANYTHING TO GET THIS LAST WISH.
THIS IS THE LAST DAY WE'LL BE ABLE TO SEE MISS YUNA BEFORE WE GRADUATE!
THERE SHE IS!
RAAR
RAAR
MISS YUNA!
BANG
WE'RE NOT TAKIN' NO FOR AN ANSWER! WE'LL MAKE YOU DO THE GRADUATION TREE CEREMONY WITH US!!
NOT YOU AGAIN!
HOLD ON!! GET OUT OF MY WAY!!
YUNA'S GOING TO PERFORM THE CEREMONY WITH ME!!
SO THAT'S WHAT YOU WERE UP TO!

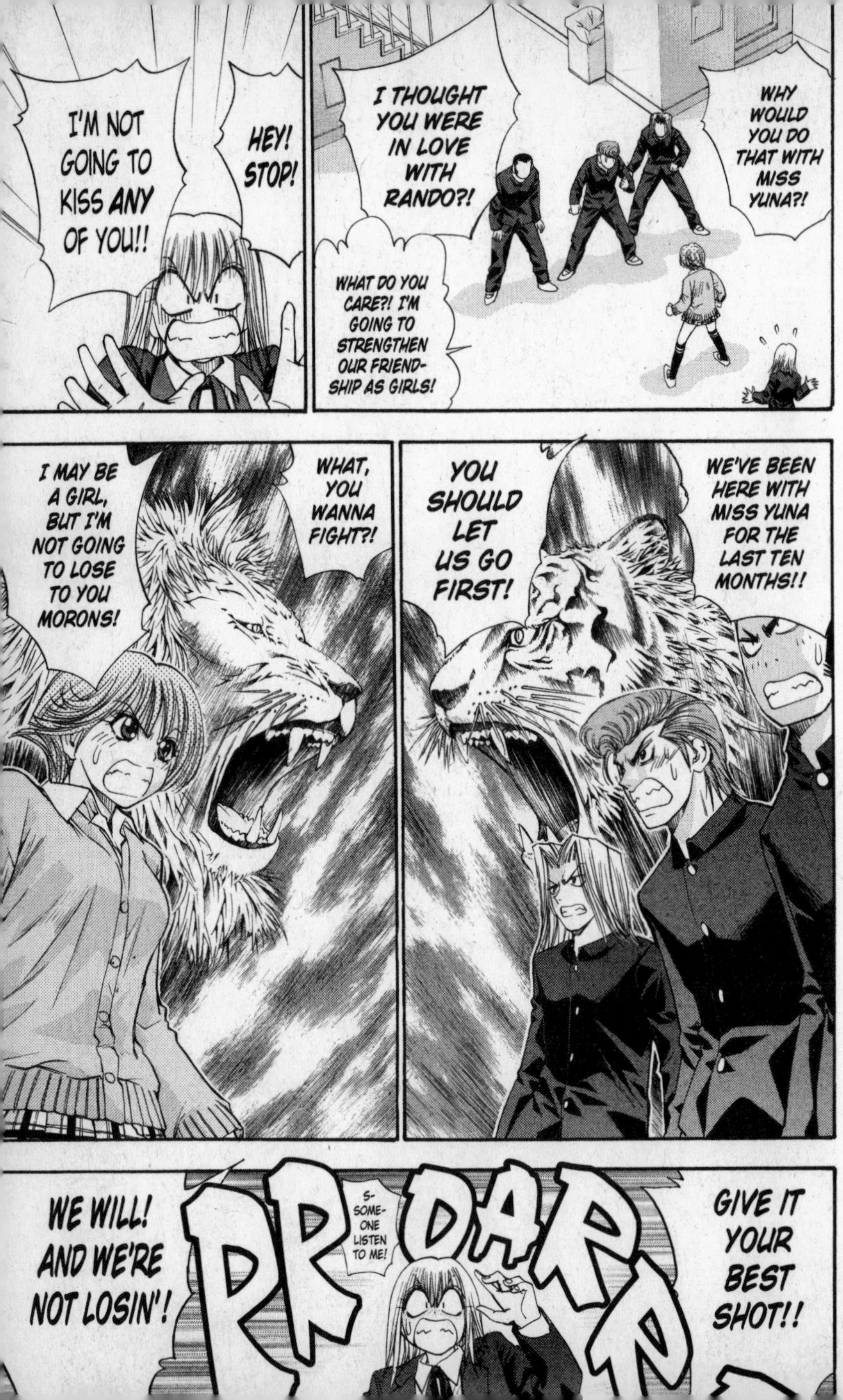
WHY WOULD YOU DO THAT WITH MISS YUNA?!
I THOUGHT YOU WERE IN LOVE WITH RANDO?!
WHAT DO YOU CARE?! I'M GOING TO STRENGTHEN OUR FRIEND-SHIP AS GIRLS!
HEY! STOP!
I'M NOT GOING TO KISS ANY OF YOU!!
WE'VE BEEN HERE WITH MISS YUNA FOR THE LAST TEN MONTHS!!
YOU SHOULD LET US GO FIRST!
WHAT, YOU WANNA FIGHT?!
I MAY BE A GIRL, BUT I'M NOT GOING TO LOSE TO YOU MORONS!
GIVE IT YOUR BEST SHOT!!
S-SOME-ONE LISTEN TO ME!
WE WILL! AND WE'RE NOT LOSIN'!

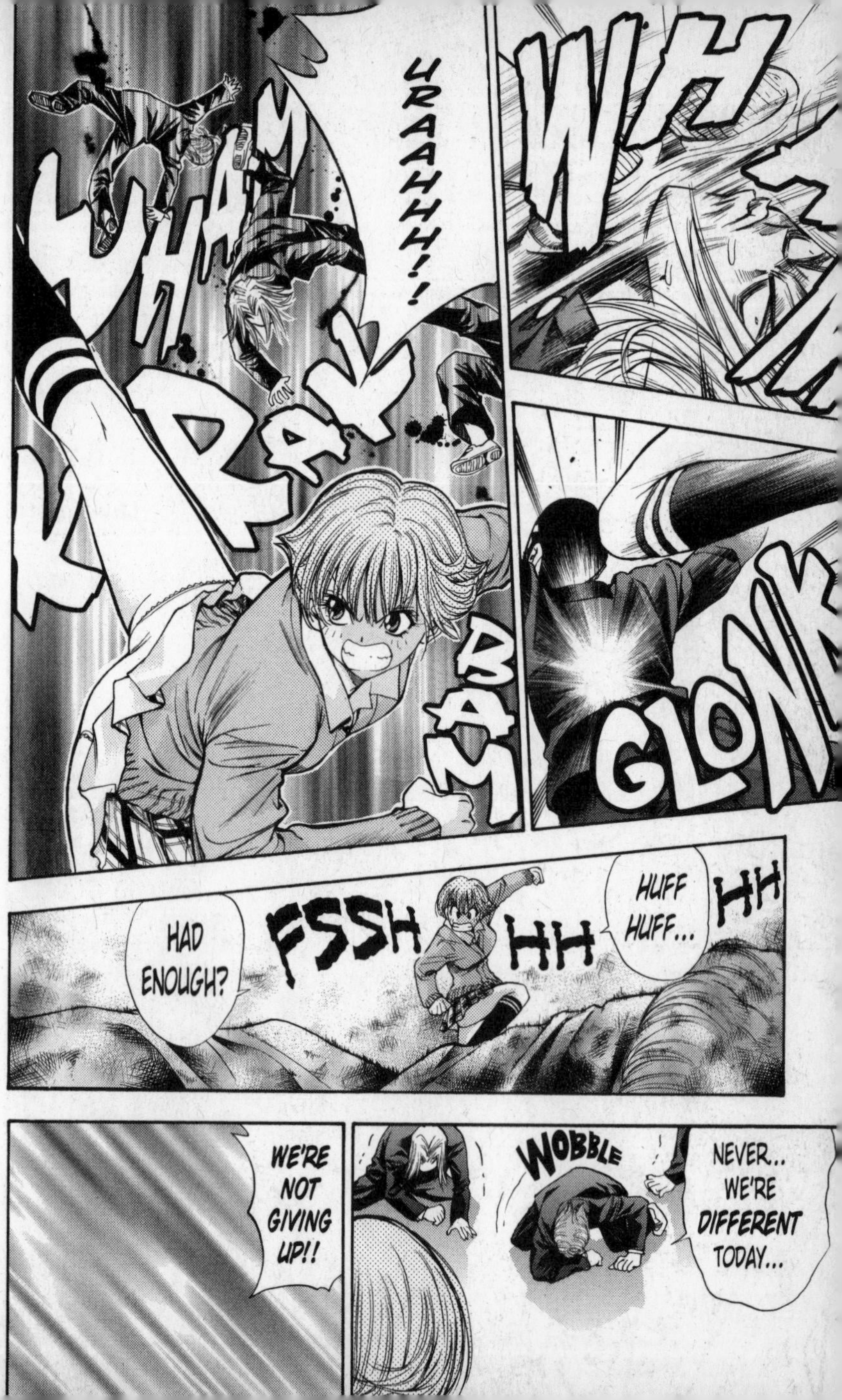
WH
GLONK
WHAM
URAAAHHH!!
KRAK
BAM
HH
HUFF HUFF...
HH
FSSH
HAD ENOUGH?
NEVER... WE'RE DIFFERENT TODAY...
WOBBLE
WE'RE NOT GIVING UP!!

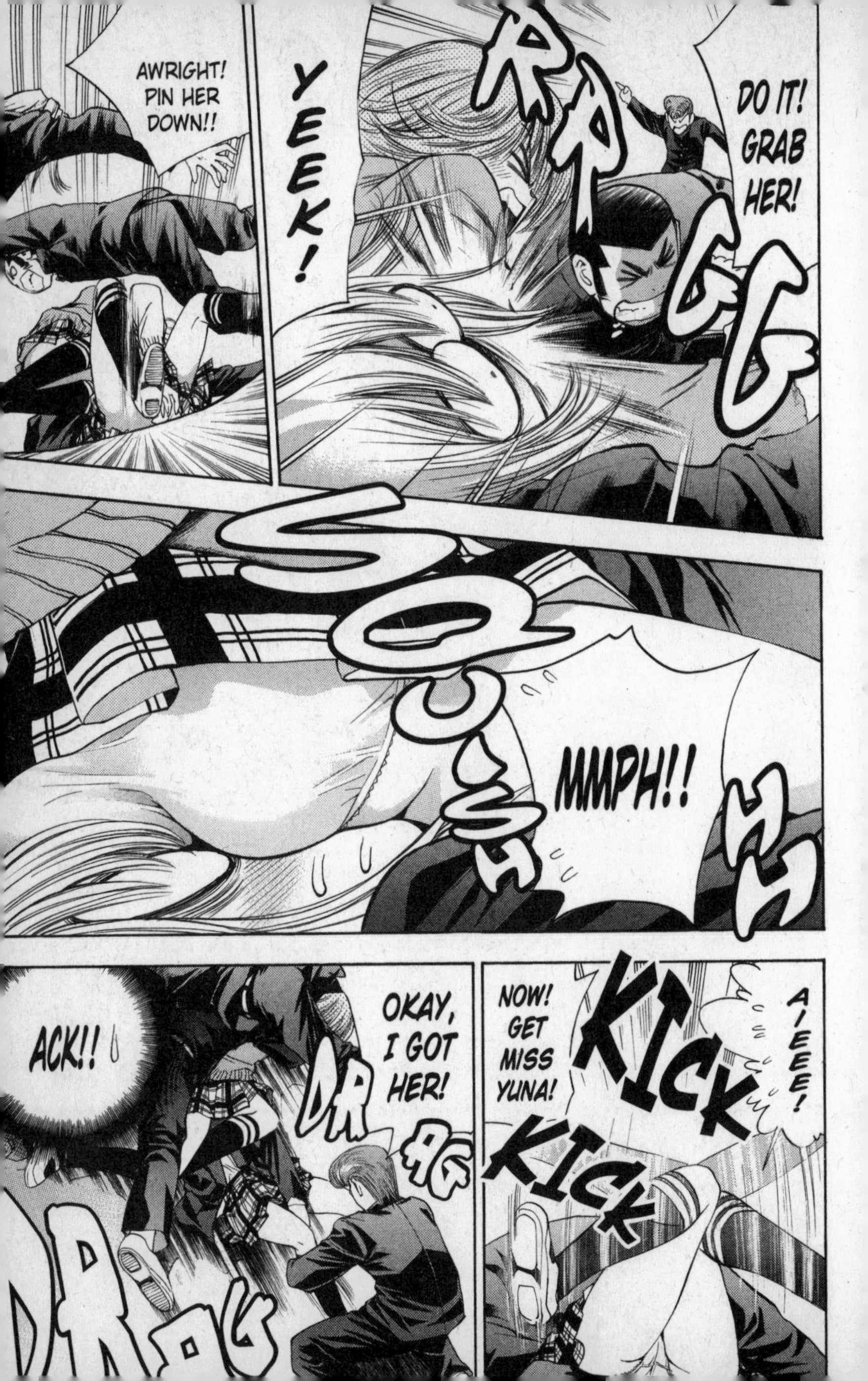
DO IT! GRAB HER!
YEEK!
AWRIGHT! PIN HER DOWN!!
SQUISH
MMPH!!
AIEEEE!
KICK
NOW! GET MISS YUNA!
KICK
OKAY, I GOT HER!
DRAG
ACK!!
DRAG

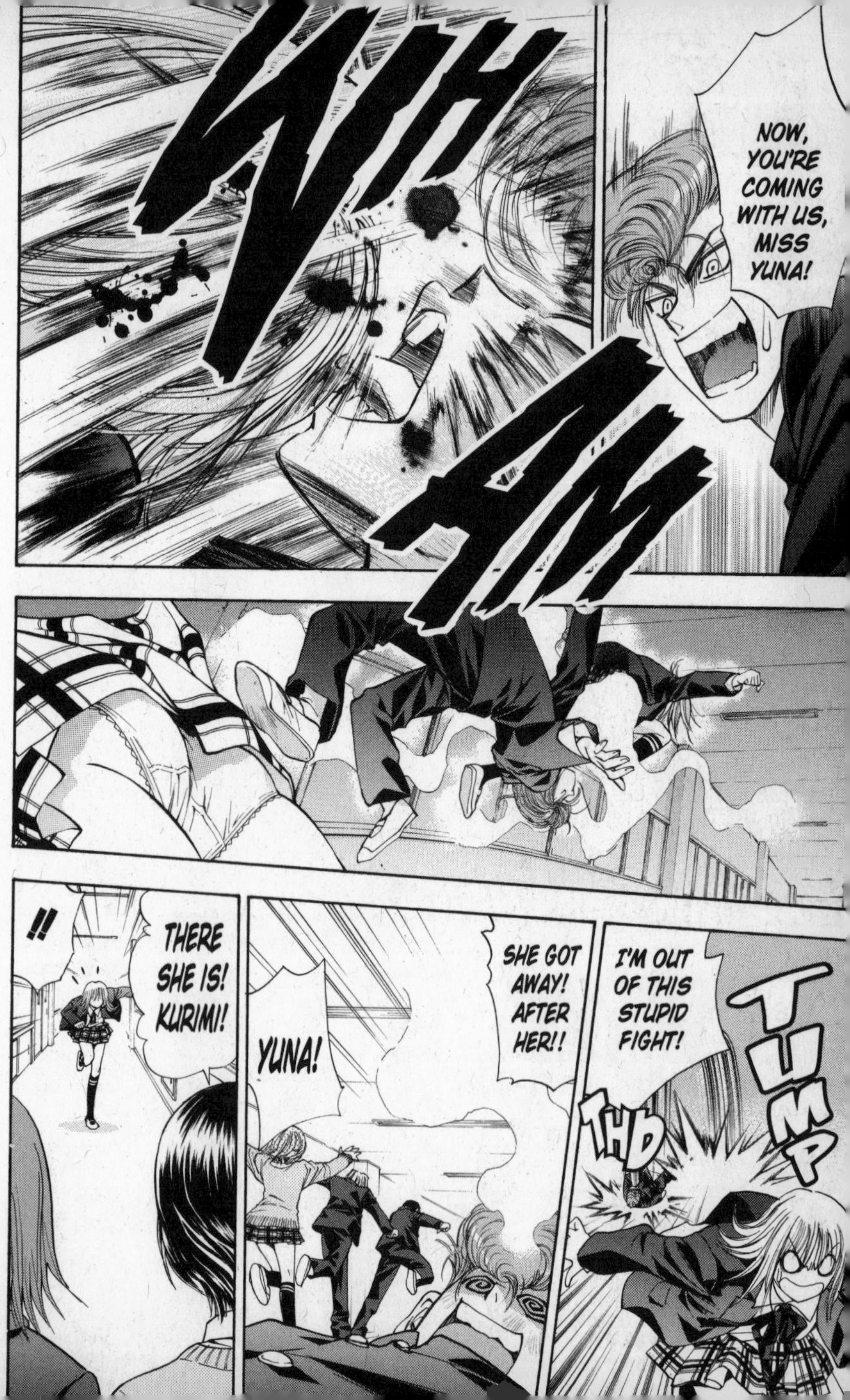
NOW, YOU'RE COMING WITH US, MISS YUNA!
WHAM
I'M OUT OF THIS STUPID FIGHT!
THUMP
THD
SHE GOT AWAY! AFTER HER!!
YUNA!
!!
THERE SHE IS! KURIMI!

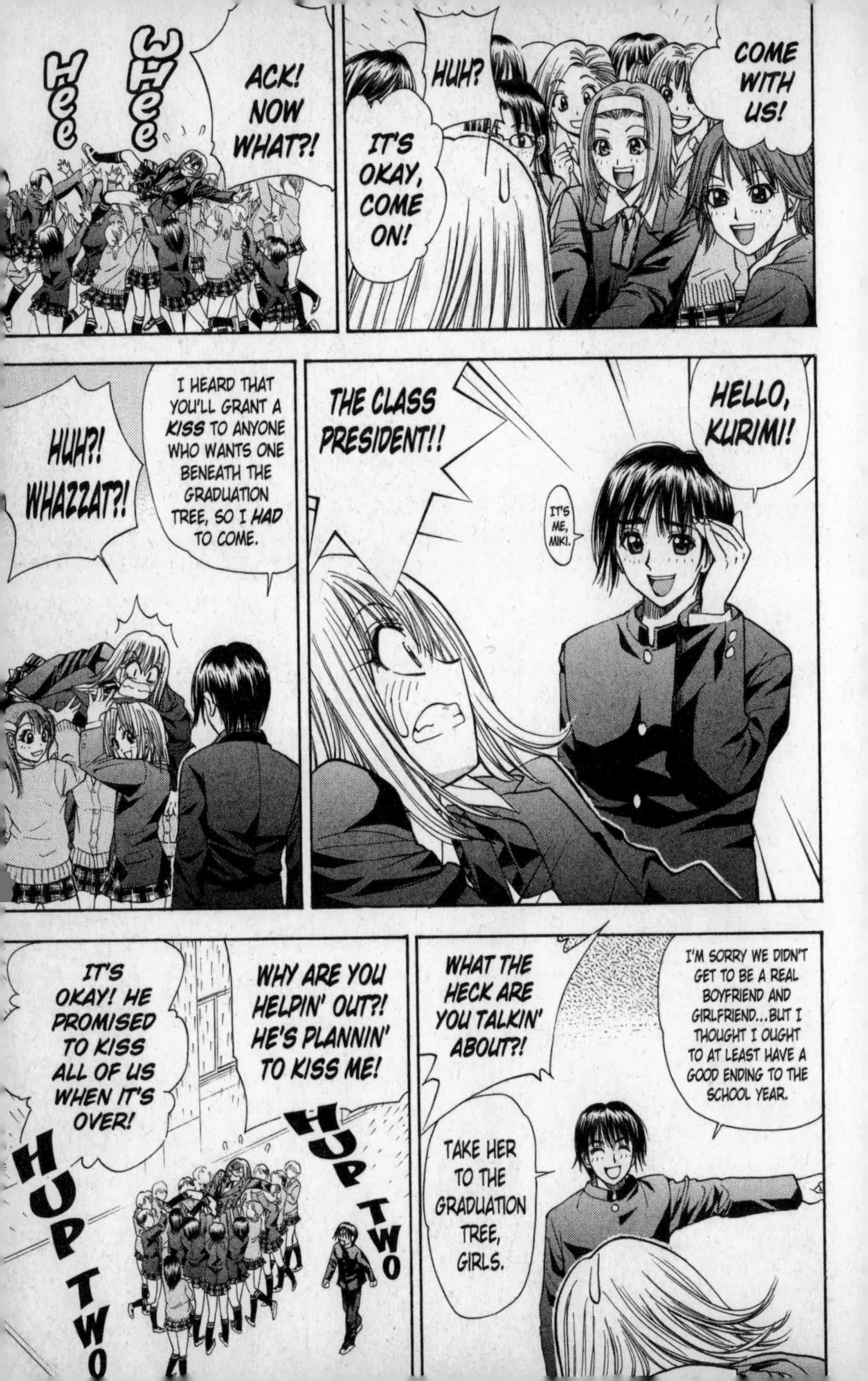
COME WITH US!
HUH?
IT'S OKAY, COME ON!
ACK! NOW WHAT?!
WHEE
HEE
HELLO, KURIMI!
IT'S ME, MIKI.
THE CLASS PRESIDENT!!
I HEARD THAT YOU'LL GRANT A KISS TO ANYONE WHO WANTS ONE BENEATH THE GRADUATION TREE, SO I HAD TO COME.
HUH?! WHAZZAT?!
I'M SORRY WE DIDN'T GET TO BE A REAL BOYFRIEND AND GIRLFRIEND...BUT I THOUGHT I OUGHT TO AT LEAST HAVE A GOOD ENDING TO THE SCHOOL YEAR.
WHAT THE HECK ARE YOU TALKIN' ABOUT?!
TAKE HER TO THE GRADUATION TREE, GIRLS.
WHY ARE YOU HELPIN' OUT?! HE'S PLANNIN' TO KISS ME!
IT'S OKAY! HE PROMISED TO KISS ALL OF US WHEN IT'S OVER!
HUP TWO
HUP TWO

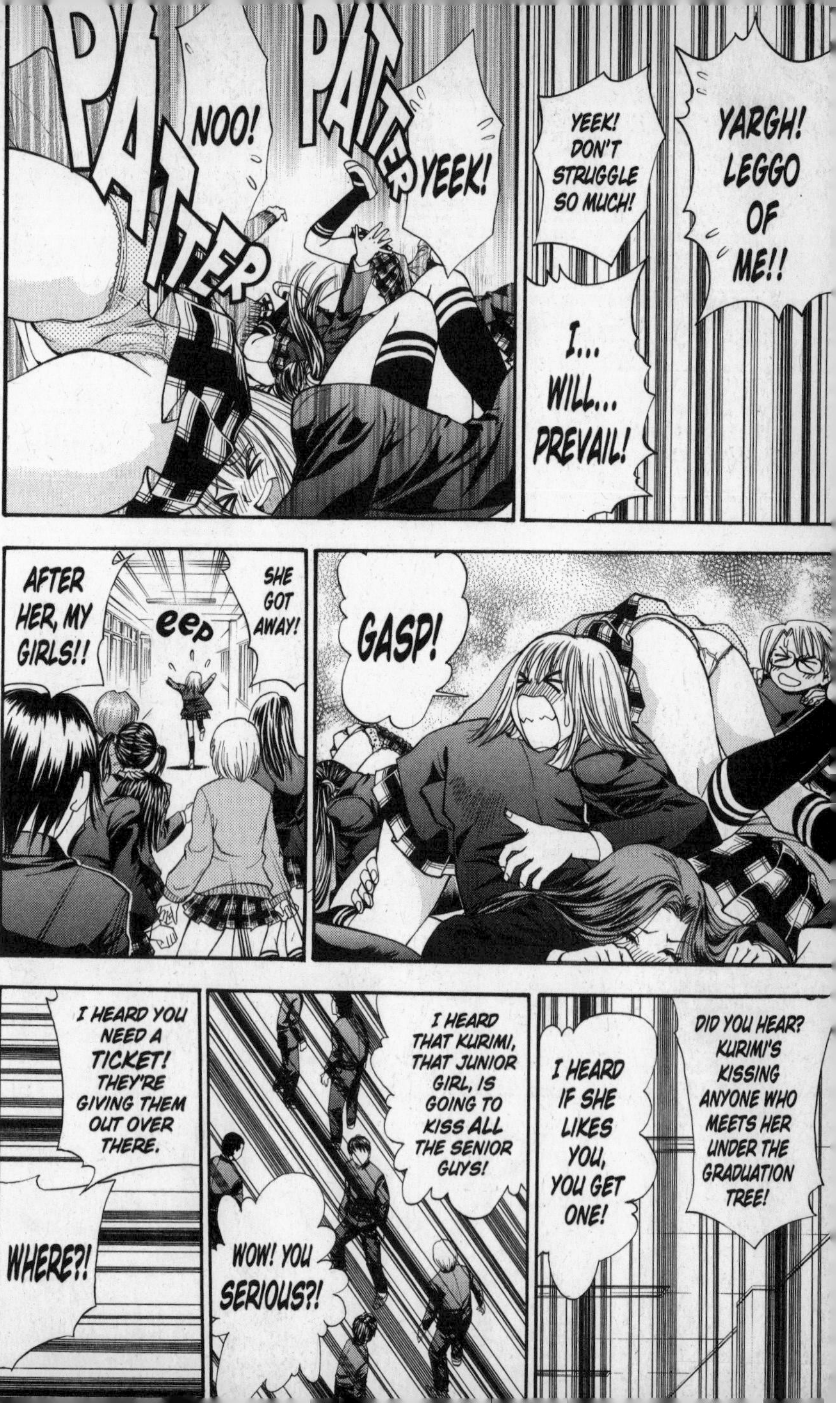
YARGH! LEGGO OF ME!!
YEEK! DON'T STRUGGLE SO MUCH!
I... WILL... PREVAIL!
YEEK!
PATTER
NOO!
PATTER
GASP!
SHE GOT AWAY!
eep
AFTER HER, MY GIRLS!!
DID YOU HEAR? KURIMI'S KISSING ANYONE WHO MEETS HER UNDER THE GRADUATION TREE!
I HEARD IF SHE LIKES YOU, YOU GET ONE!
I HEARD THAT KURIMI, THAT JUNIOR GIRL, IS GOING TO KISS ALL THE SENIOR GUYS!
WOW! YOU SERIOUS?!
I HEARD YOU NEED A TICKET! THEY'RE GIVING THEM OUT OVER THERE.
WHERE?!

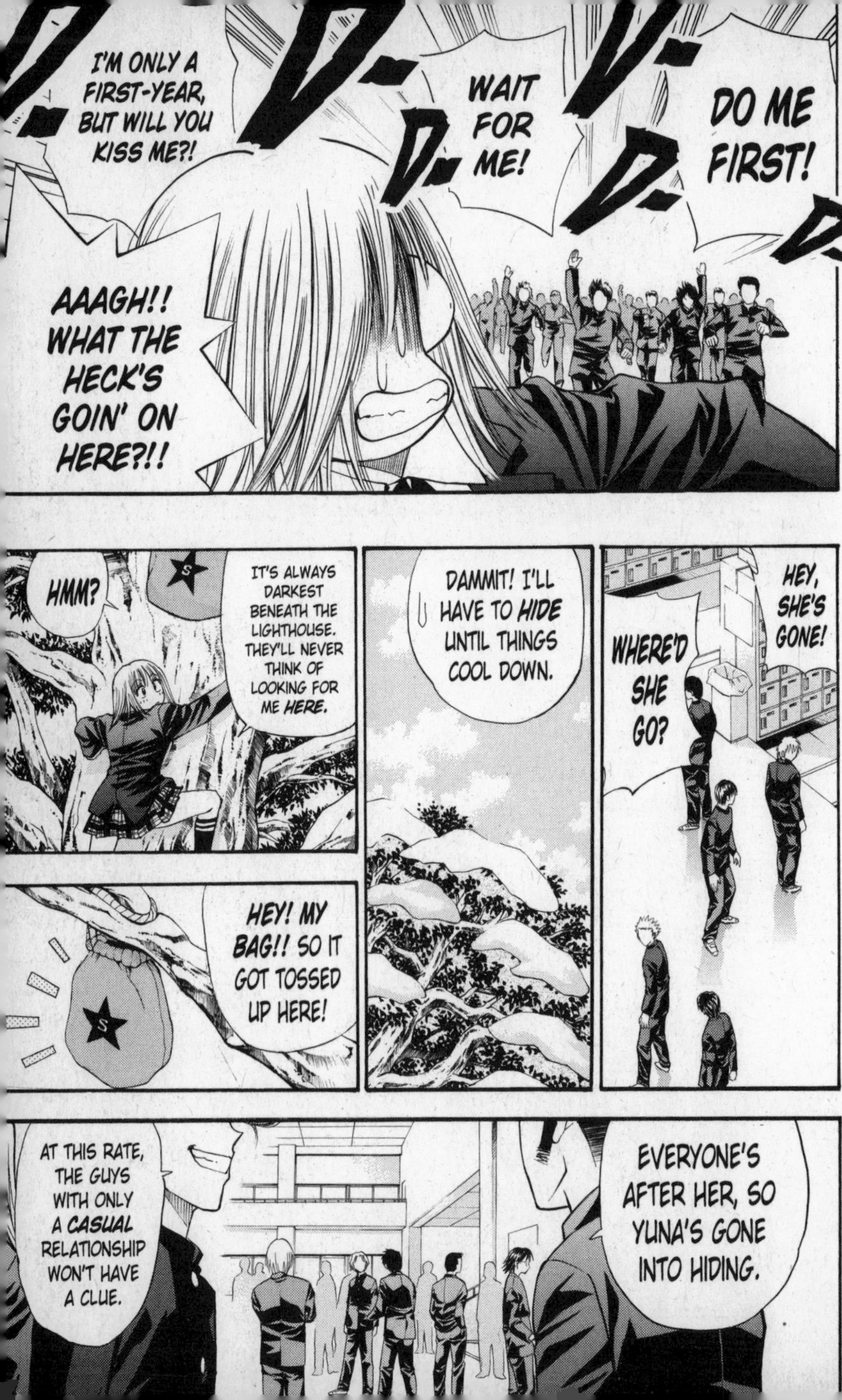
DO ME FIRST!
WAIT FOR ME!
I'M ONLY A FIRST-YEAR, BUT WILL YOU KISS ME?!
AAAGH!! WHAT THE HECK'S GOIN' ON HERE?!!
HEY, SHE'S GONE!
WHERE'D SHE GO?
DAMMIT! I'LL HAVE TO HIDE UNTIL THINGS COOL DOWN.
IT'S ALWAYS DARKEST BENEATH THE LIGHTHOUSE. THEY'LL NEVER THINK OF LOOKING FOR ME HERE.
HMM?
HEY! MY BAG!! SO IT GOT TOSSED UP HERE!
EVERYONE'S AFTER HER, SO YUNA'S GONE INTO HIDING.
AT THIS RATE, THE GUYS WITH ONLY A CASUAL RELATIONSHIP WON'T HAVE A CLUE.

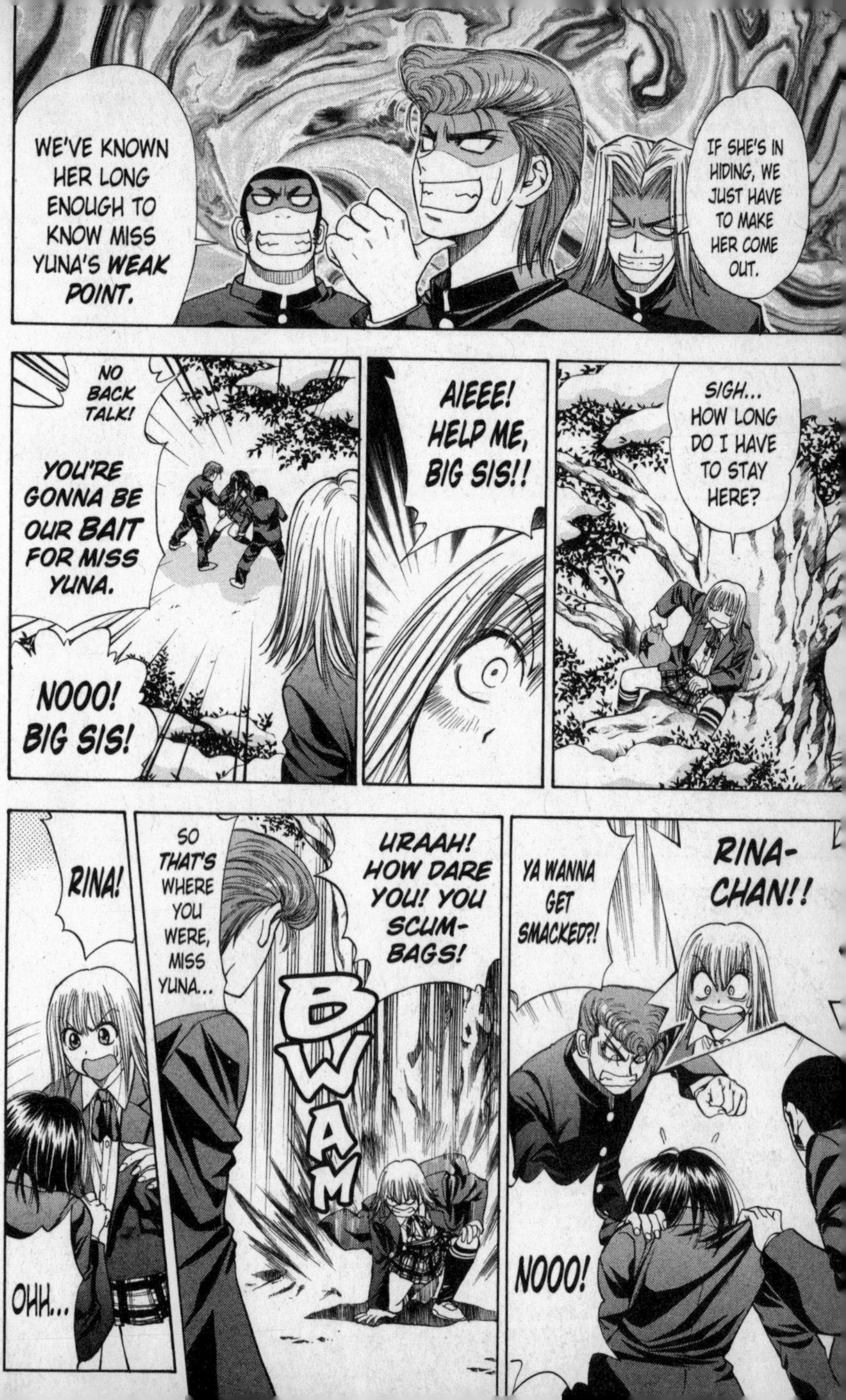
IF SHE'S IN HIDING, WE JUST HAVE TO MAKE HER COME OUT.
WE'VE KNOWN HER LONG ENOUGH TO KNOW MISS YUNA'S WEAK POINT.
SIGH... HOW LONG DO I HAVE TO STAY HERE?
AIEEE! HELP ME, BIG SIS!!
NO BACK TALK!
YOU'RE GONNA BE OUR BAIT FOR MISS YUNA.
NOOO! BIG SIS!
RINA-CHAN!!
YA WANNA GET SMACKED?!
NOOO!
URAAH! HOW DARE YOU! YOU SCUM-BAGS!
SO THAT'S WHERE YOU WERE, MISS YUNA...
BWAM
RINA!
OHH...

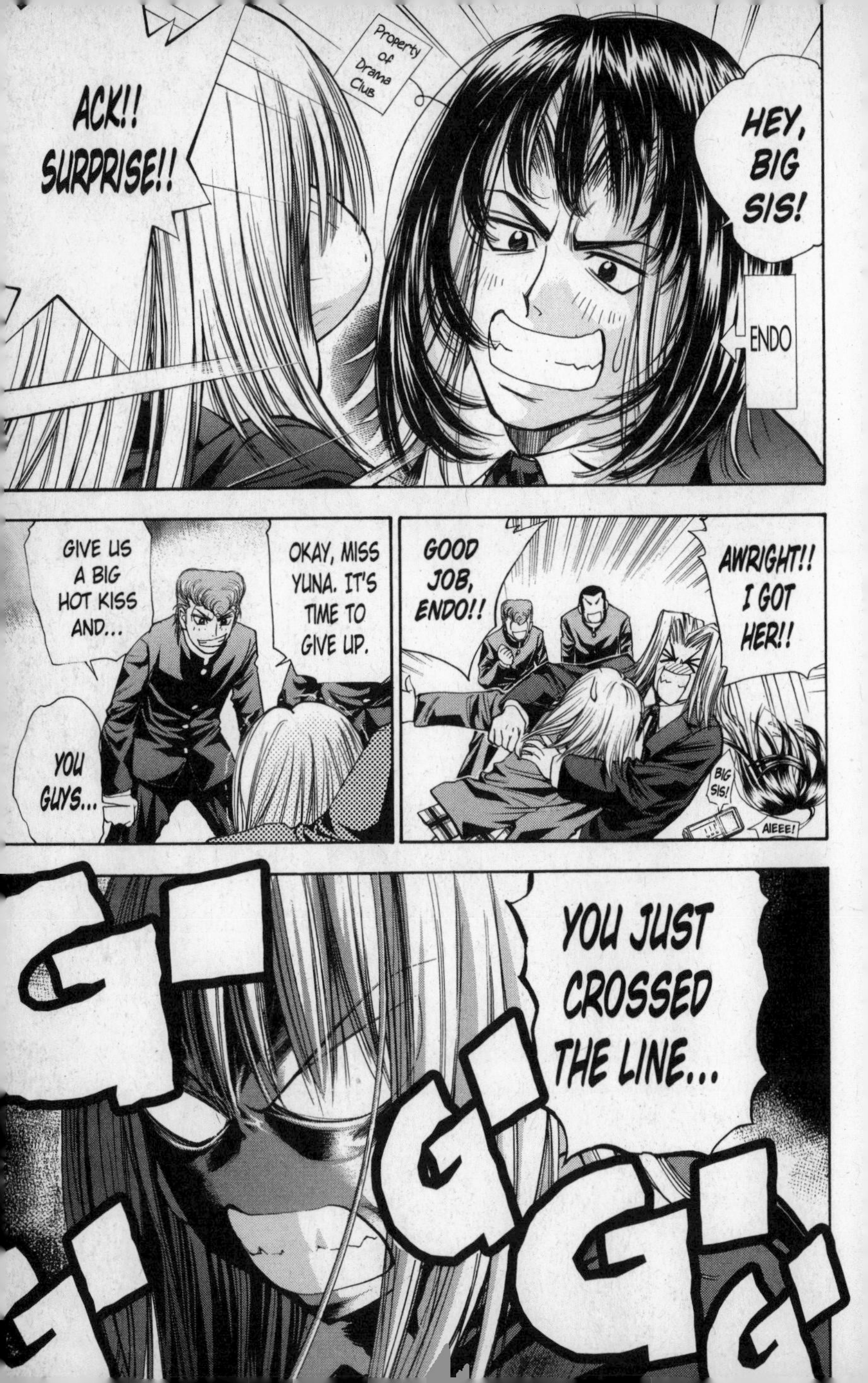
HEY, BIG SIS!
ENDO
Property of Drama Club
ACK!! SURPRISE!!
AWRIGHT!! I GOT HER!!
GOOD JOB, ENDO!!
BIG SIS!
AIEEE!
OKAY, MISS YUNA. IT'S TIME TO GIVE UP.
GIVE US A BIG HOT KISS AND...
YOU GUYS...
YOU JUST CROSSED THE LINE...

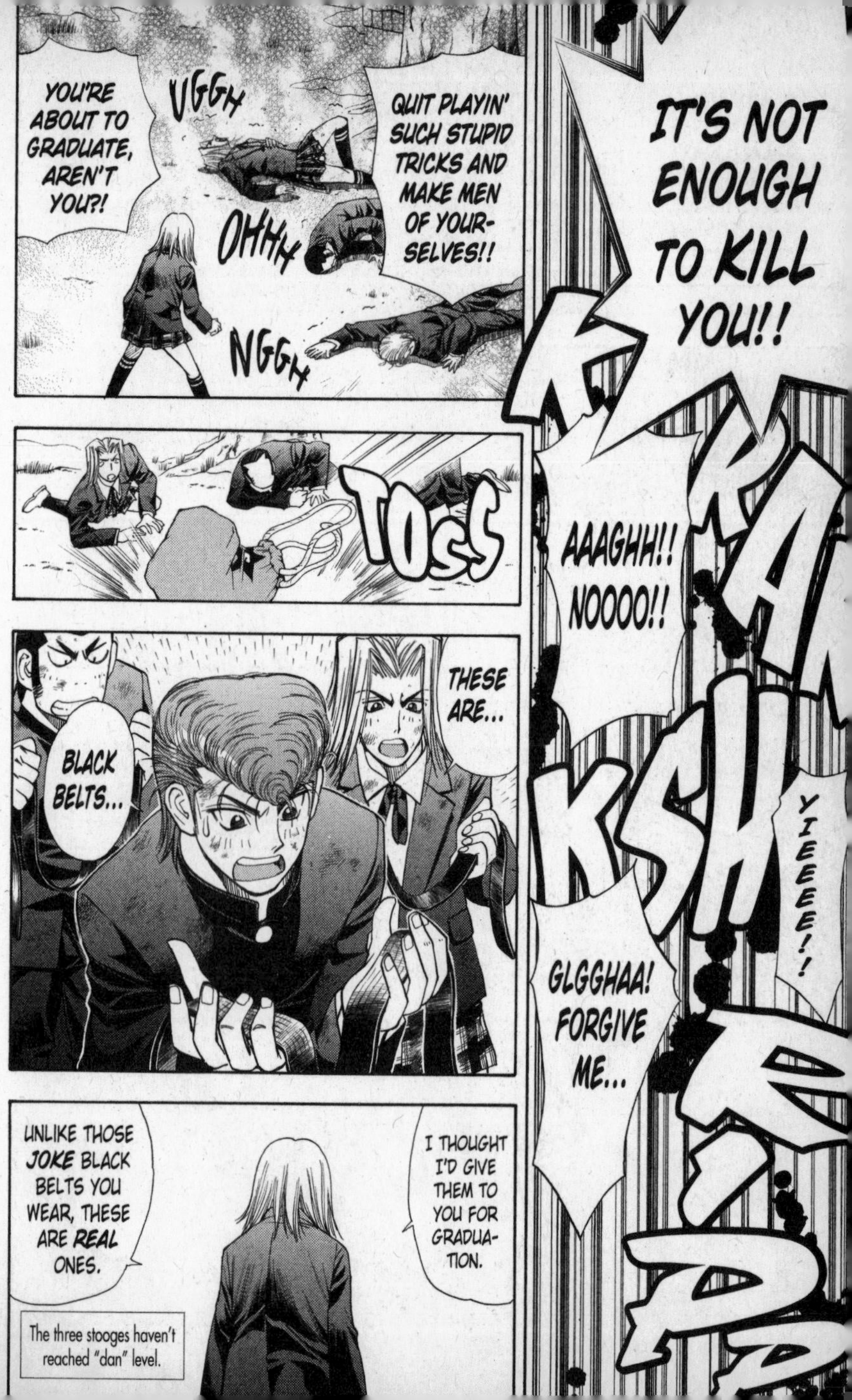

IT'S NOT ENOUGH TO KILL YOU!!
AAAGHH!! NOOOO!!
YIEEEEE!!
GLGGHAA! FORGIVE ME...
QUIT PLAYIN' SUCH STUPID TRICKS AND MAKE MEN OF YOUR-SELVES!!
UGGH
YOU'RE ABOUT TO GRADUATE, AREN'T YOU?!
OHHH
NGGH
TOSS
THESE ARE...
BLACK BELTS...
I THOUGHT I'D GIVE THEM TO YOU FOR GRADUA-TION.
UNLIKE THOSE JOKE BLACK BELTS YOU WEAR, THESE ARE REAL ONES.
The three stooges haven't reached "dan" level.

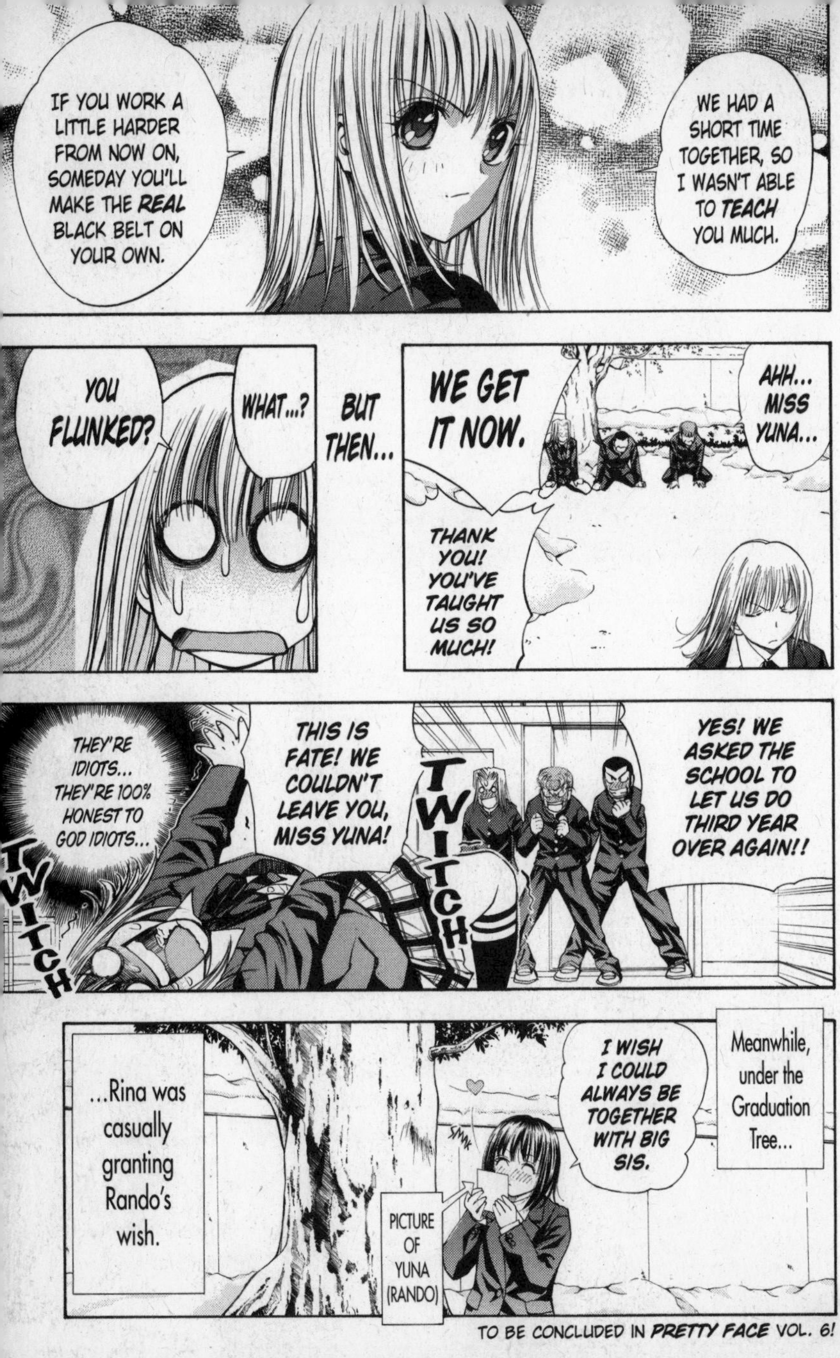
WE HAD A SHORT TIME TOGETHER, SO I WASN'T ABLE TO *TEACH* YOU MUCH.
IF YOU WORK A LITTLE HARDER FROM NOW ON, SOMEDAY YOU'LL MAKE THE *REAL* BLACK BELT ON YOUR OWN.
AHH... MISS YUNA...
WE GET IT NOW.
THANK YOU! YOU'VE TAUGHT US SO MUCH!
BUT THEN...
WHAT...?
YOU FLUNKED?
YES! WE ASKED THE SCHOOL TO LET US DO THIRD YEAR OVER AGAIN!!
THIS IS FATE! WE COULDN'T LEAVE YOU, MISS YUNA!
TWITCH
THEY'RE IDIOTS... THEY'RE 100% HONEST TO GOD IDIOTS...
TWITCH
Meanwhile, under the Graduation Tree...
I WISH I COULD ALWAYS BE TOGETHER WITH BIG SIS.
PICTURE OF YUNA (RANDO)
...Rina was casually granting Rando's wish.

TO BE CONCLUDED IN *PRETTY FACE* VOL. 6!

Pretty Face

FINAL VOLUME!

IN THE NEXT VOLUME...

The war is on for Rando's affections when Natsuo and Nozomi finally meet! Which of the class's toughest girls will have their way with our hero? Then, Rando finally meets the person whose face he's been wearing all this time: Rina's *real* twin sister! Will the return of Yuna spell the end of Rando's womanhood...and when the bandages come off, will his chances with Rina be over?

COMING JUNE 2008!

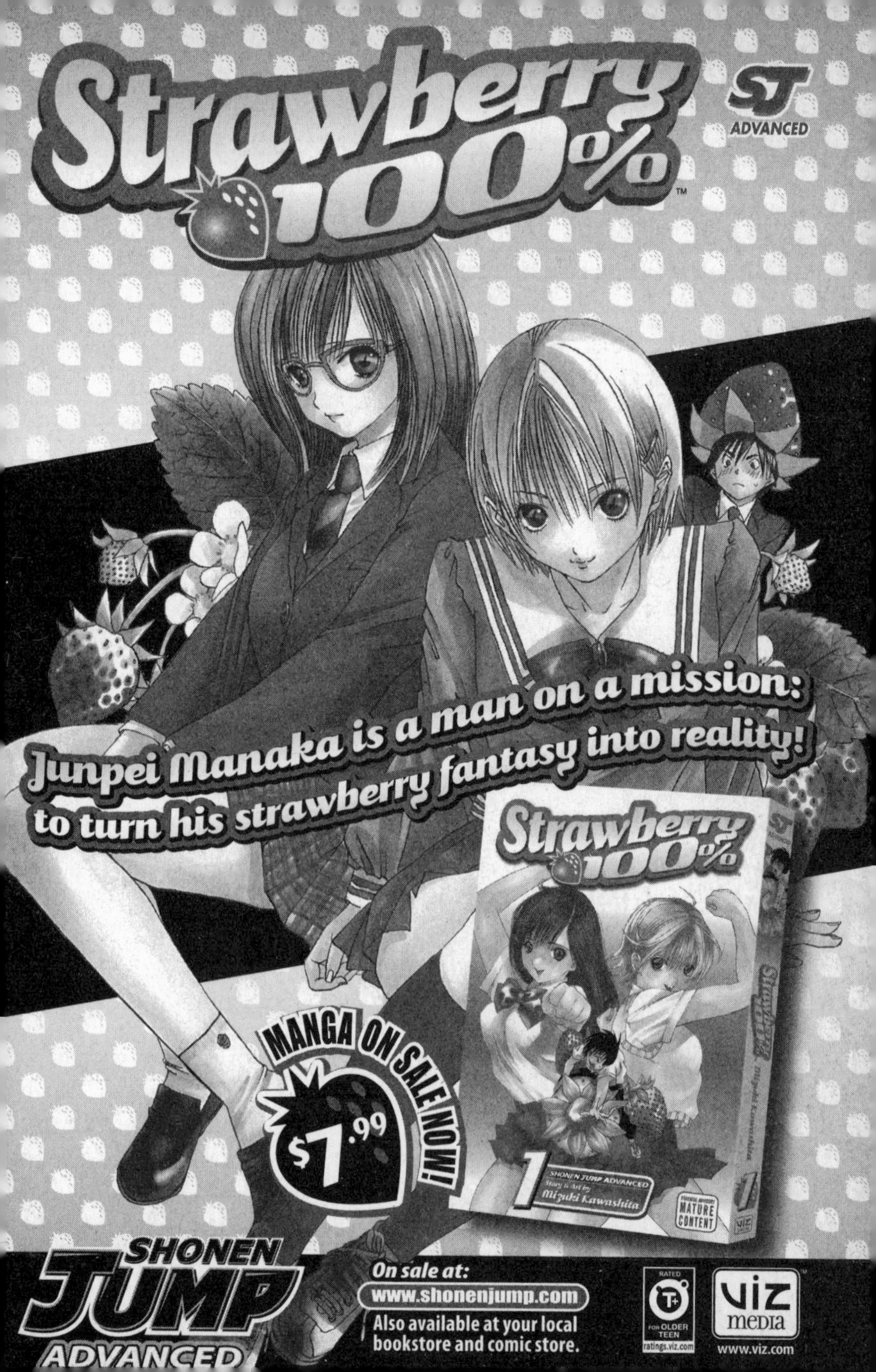

Strawberry 100%™
SJ ADVANCED
Junpei Manaka is a man on a mission: to turn his strawberry fantasy into reality!
Strawberry 100%
1
SHONEN JUMP ADVANCED
Story & Art by Mizuki Kawashita
MATURE CONTENT
MANGA ON SALE NOW!
$7.99
SHONEN JUMP ADVANCED
On sale at:
www.shonenjump.com
Also available at your local bookstore and comic store.
RATED T+ FOR OLDER TEEN
ratings.viz.com
VIZ media
www.viz.com

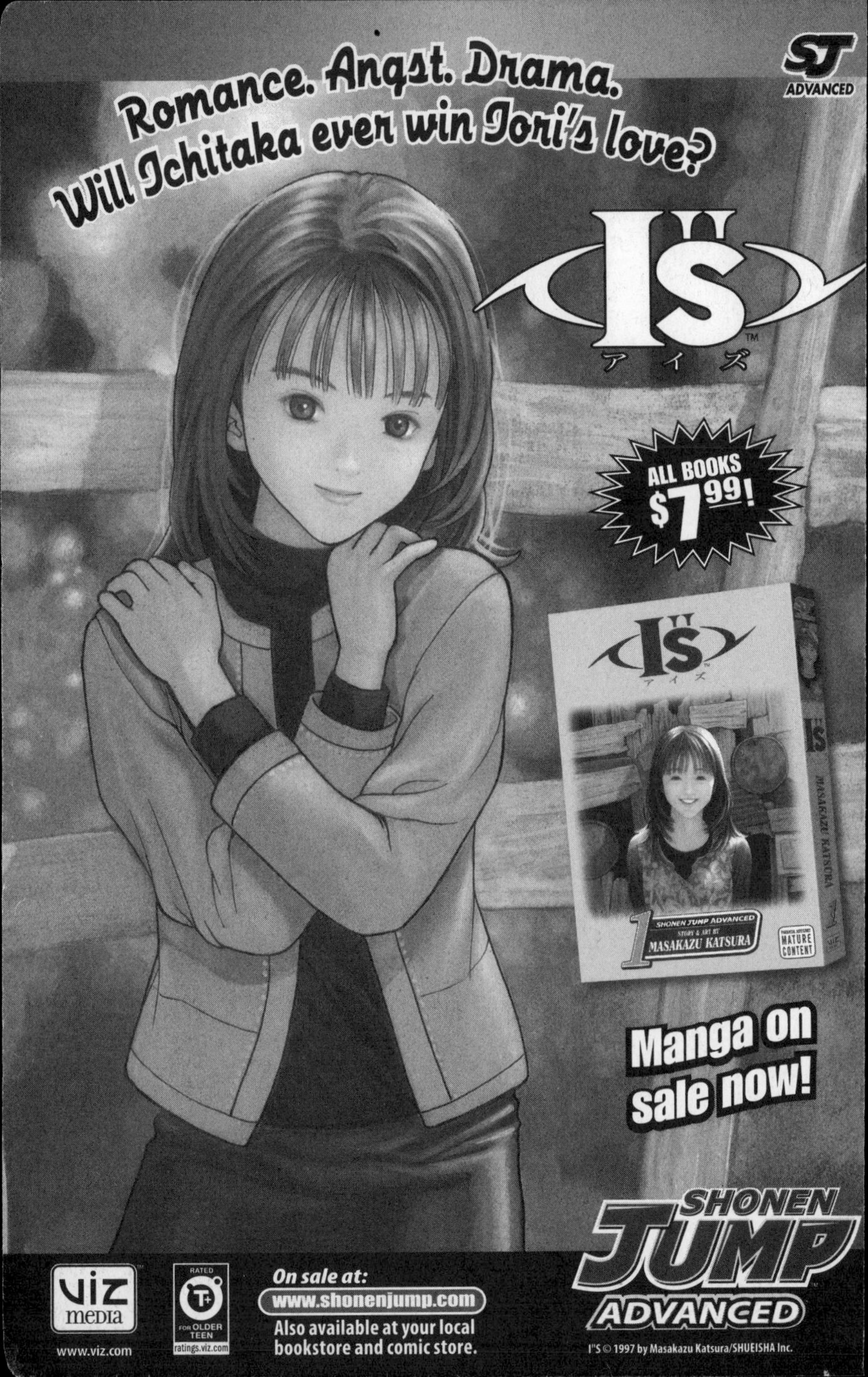
SJ ADVANCED
Romance. Angst. Drama.
Will Ichitaka ever win Iori's love?
I"S
アイズ
ALL BOOKS
$7.99!
I"S
アイズ
SHONEN JUMP ADVANCED
STORY & ART BY
MASAKAZU KATSURA
1
MATURE CONTENT
Manga on sale now!
SHONEN JUMP ADVANCED
viz media
www.viz.com
RATED T+ FOR OLDER TEEN
ratings.viz.com
On sale at:
www.shonenjump.com
Also available at your local bookstore and comic store.
I"S © 1997 by Masakazu Katsura/SHUEISHA Inc.

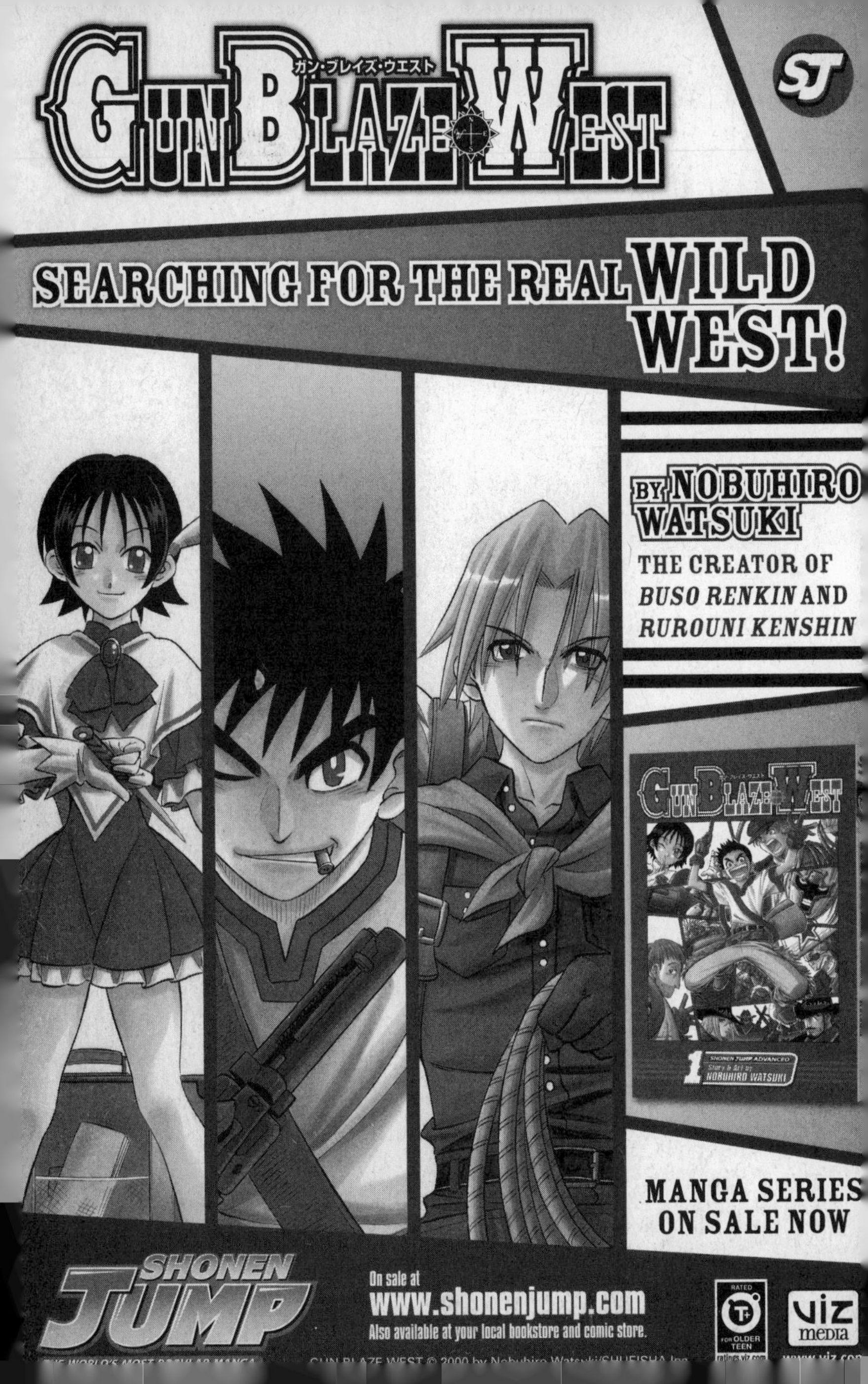
GUN BLAZE WEST
ガン・ブレイズ・ウエスト
SJ
SEARCHING FOR THE REAL WILD WEST!
BY NOBUHIRO WATSUKI
THE CREATOR OF *BUSO RENKIN* AND *RUROUNI KENSHIN*
GUN BLAZE WEST
1 SHONEN JUMP ADVANCED
NOBUHIRO WATSUKI
MANGA SERIES ON SALE NOW
SHONEN JUMP
On sale at
www.shonenjump.com
Also available at your local bookstore and comic store.
RATED T+ FOR OLDER TEEN
viz media
GUN BLAZE WEST © 2000 by Nobuhiro Watsuki/SHUEISHA Inc.